About the author

Sindre Bangstad is a Norwegian social anthropologist. He worked as an associate professor at
Oslo University College from 2008 to 2010, and
from 2010 to 2013 was a postdoctoral fellow at
the Department of Social Anthropology, University of Oslo. He is currently an affiliate researcher
at the Faculty of Theology, University of Oslo, and
is the author of the award-winning book *The Faces
of Secularism*.

ANDERS BREIVIK AND THE RISE OF ISLAMOPHOBIA

Sindre Bangstad

Zed Books
LONDON

Anders Breivik and the Rise of Islamophobia was first published in 2014 by Zed Books Ltd, 7 Cynthia Street, London N1 9JF, UK

www.zedbooks.co.uk

Copyright © Sindre Bangstad 2014

The right of Sindre Bangstad to be identified as the author of this work has been asserted by him in accordance with the Copyright, Designs and Patents Act, 1988

Set in Monotype Plantin and FFKievit by Ewan Smith, London NW5
Index: ed.emery@thefreeuniversity.net
Cover designed by Liam Chapple
Printed and bound by TJ International, Padstow, Cornwall

A catalogue record for this book is available from the British Library
Library of Congress Cataloging in Publication Data available

ISBN 978-1-78360-008-3 hb
ISBN 978-1-78360-007-6 pb

CONTENTS

IN MEMORIAM

Mona Abdinur (18), Oslo
Ismail Haji Ahmed (19), Hamar
Thomas Margido Antonsen (16), Oslo
Pamela Porntip Ardam (21), Oslo
Modupe Ellen Awoyemi (15), Drammen
Lena Maria Bergum (19), Namsos
Kevin Daae Berland (15), Askøy
Trond Berntsen (51), Øvre Eiker
Sverre Flåte Bjørkavåg (28), Sula
Torjus Jakobsen Blattmann (17), Kristiansand
Carina Borgund (18), Oslo
Johannes Buø (14), Mandal/ Longyearbyen
Monica Elisabeth Bøsei (45), Hole
Åsta Sofie Helland Dahl (16), Sortland
Sondre Furseth Dale (17), Haugesund
Monica Iselin Didriksen (18), Sund
Gizem Dogan (17), Trondheim
Andreas Edvardsen (18), Sarpsborg
Tore Eikeland (21), Osterøy
Bendik Rosnæs Ellingsen (18), Rygge
Hanne Marie Orvik Endresen (61), Oslo
Aleksander Aas Eriksen (16), Meråker
Andrine Bakkene Espeland (17), Fredrikstad
Hanne Anette Balch Fjalestad (43), Lunner
Silje Merete Fjellbu (17), Tinn
Hanne Kristine Fridtun (19), Stryn

Andreas Dalby Grønnesby (17), Hamar
Snorre Haller (30), Trondheim
Kai Hauge (32), Oslo
Rune Havdal (43), Øvre Eiker
Ingrid Berg Heggelund (18), Ås
Ida Marie Hill (34), Oslo
Karin Elena Holst (15), Mo i Rana
Anne Lise Holter (51), Våler
Eivind Hovden (15), Tokke
Guro Vartdal Håvoll (18), Ørsta
Rafal Mohamad Jamil Jamil (20), Egersund
Steinar Jessen (16), Alta
Maria Maagerø Johannesen (17), Nøtterøy
Ronja Søttar Johansen (17), Vefsn
Espen Jørgensen (17), Bodø
Sondre Kjøren (17), Orkdal
Margrethe Bøyum Kløven (16), Bærum
Syvert Knudsen (17), Lyngdal
Tove Åshill Knutsen (56), Oslo
Anders Kristiansen (18), Bardu
Jon Vegard Lervåg (32), Oslo
Elisabeth Tønnes Lie (16), Halden
Gunnar Linaker (23), Bardu
Tamta Liparteliani (23), Kutaisi, Georgia
Eva Kathinka Lütken (17), Sarpsborg
Hanne Ekroll Løvlie (30), Tyristrand
Even Flugstad Malmedal (18), Gjøvik
Tarald Kjuven Mjelde (18), Osterøy
Ruth Benedicte Vatndal Nilsen (15), Tønsberg

Emil Okkenhaug (15), Levanger
Diderik Aamodt Olsen (19),
 Nesodden
Hendrik André Pedersen (27),
 Porsanger
Rolf Cristopher Johansen Perreau
 (25), Trondheim
Karar Mustafa Qasim (19), Vestby
Bano Abobakar Rashid (18),
 Nesodden
Henrik Rasmussen (18), Hadsel
Ida Beathe Rogne (17), Østre Toten
Synne Røyneland (18), Oslo
Kjersti Berg Sand (26), Nord-Odal

Marianne Sandvik (16), Hundvåg
Fredrik Lund Schjetne (18), Eidsvoll
Lejla Selaci (17), Fredrikstad
Birgitte Smetbak (15), Nøtterøy
Isabel Victoria Green Sogn (17),
 Oslo
Silje Stamneshagen (18), Askøy
Victoria Stenberg (17), Nes
Tina Sukavara (18), Vadsø
Sharidyn Meegan Ngahiwi Svebakk-
 Bøhn (14), Drammen
Simon Sæbø (18), Salangen
Håvard Vederhus (21), Oslo
Håkon Ødegaard (17), Trondheim

ACKNOWLEDGEMENTS

This book has been long in the making. A great number of people in Norway were personally affected as relatives, friends or acquaintances of the seventy-seven unique human beings who lost their lives on 22 July 2011. There were no victims from my own family. Yet having for a long time had a concern with and interest in the state of Norwegian public discourses on Islam and Muslims, I realized soon after the horror of what had happened on 22 July 2011 had sunk in that I would have to write a book about it as a way of coming to terms with it both personally and professionally. What was originally conceived of as a 'memorial stone' to those who lost their lives at Government Headquarters and at Utøya gradually gestated into the book you now have in your hands.

There is a long list of people to whom I owe great thanks for their part in my intellectual and professional formation as a social anthropologist, and for their contributions to my thinking about the topic at hand, but space does not allow me to thank them all here. At Zed Books, I would like to thank Ken Barlow for taking the risk of publishing this book. Gavan Titley provided a welcome introduction to Zed. Sally Noonan in Canada and Richard Daly in Norway have contributed to improving the manuscript immeasurably along the way. My close family deserves my greatest thanks for having put up with an all too often distracted father and husband. I would like to acknowledge my debts to the following scholars, intellectuals and/ or friends in Norway and elsewhere: Cora Alexa Døving, Oddbjørn Leirvik, Kathinka Frøystad, Marius Linge, Mohammed Shoaib Sultan, Rune Berglund Steen, Kari Helene Partapouli, Mari Linløkken, Bengt Andersen, Olav Elgvin, Berit Thorbjørnsrud, Dag Herbjørnsrud, Kai E. Kverme, Julian Kramer, Bjørn Westlie, Christine M. Jacobsen, Jon Rogstad, Bjørn Bertelsen, Odin Lysaker, Sveinung Sandberg, Ervin Kohn, Anne Sender, Jonas Jakobsen, Lars Gule,

Knut Vikør, Thomas Hylland Eriksen, Anders Juvik Rupskås, Ammar Hamdan, Yngvil Mortensen, Ulrika Mårtensson, Lena Larsen, Lars Østby, Tore Rem, Arne Johan Vetlesen, Linda Alghazari, Mohammad Usman Rana, Stian Bromark, Maren Sæbø, Katrine Fangen, Hamzah Ahmed Rajpoot-Nordahl, Sarifa Moola-Nærnes, John Erik Fossum, Alf Jensen, Mette Kristin Stenberg, Bushra Ishaq, Mina Adampour, Michael Seltzer, Sigve Indregard, Iffit Qureshi, Göran Larsson, Mattias Gardell, Matthew Kott, Henrik Arnstad, Axel West Pedersen, Matti Bunzl, John R. Bowen, John L. and Jean Comaroff, Norman Stillman, Paul Silverstein, Gershom Gorenberg, Richard Ashby Wilson, Abdulkader I. Tayob, Aslam Farouk-Ali, Aslam Fataar, Waheeda Amien, Sa'diyya Shaikh, Ralph D. Grillo, Brian Klug, Liz Fekete, Maleiha Malik, Paul Gilroy, Prakash Shah, Faisal Devji, Peter Hervik, Susi Meret, Heiko Henkel, Samuli Schielke, Yolande Jansen, Michael Sells, Fernando Bravo López, Vidar Enebakk, Kaia Storvik and Joron Pihl. The usual caveats apply, and I alone bear the responsibility for any errors or inaccuracies.

PREFACE

To the extent that people associate anything with the small northern European country of Norway, terror would generally not be a term natural to associate with it. That would change on 22 July 2011, when a Norwegian right-wing extremist from the affluent western part of Oslo first set off a 950-kilo fertilizer bomb at Government Headquarters in the capital, then proceeded to the small island of Utøya, some sixty kilometres north of the city, where in the course of a one-hour shooting spree he would massacre scores of teenagers attending an annual youth camp organized by the youth league of the governing social democratic Labour Party. Seventy-seven Norwegians lost their lives on that fateful day, most of them innocent teenagers who had long and fruitful lives to look forward to. It soon became clear that the culprit, the then thirty-two-year-old Anders Behring Breivik, had perpetrated these horrific acts based on a conviction that Norway's social democrats were helping to turn the country into an Islamic dominion controlled by the 3.6 per cent of the country's population who are Muslims. To Behring Breivik and his fellow ideological travellers on the extreme right, it was social democrats who, as the main party in power, had facilitated this 'colonization' since the late 1960s, when the first mass immigration of Muslims to Norway took place. Behring Breivik's fantasies were – as would become clear through analysing the cut-and-paste tract that he uploaded on the internet hours before setting out on his killing spree, and through the testimony he provided to the Oslo Magistrate's Court during the ten-week trial in 2012 – largely not of his own making. Yet in the aftermath of the terror attacks of 22 July 2011, the analysis of Behring Breivik and his acts of terror in Norway has more often than not tended to focus on the terrorist's personality traits, rather than his ideological motivations. There is of course nothing new in this in the history of the public and intellectual rendering of acts of mass violence and terror from right-wing extremists. After the Second World War, and in the face of the documentation on the Holocaust or the Shoah, many erstwhile Nazi sympathizers in Germany and in other western European countries denied their own complicity by focusing on Hitler's alleged insanity, and they managed to convince themselves that if only they had known about *Der Führer*'s alleged insanity, they would never have supported or voted for the Nazis in the first place. Norway was occupied by the Nazis from 1940 to 1945. From that dark period, Norway bequeathed to the English language a new epithet for traitors: quisling. The epithet originated with Vidkun Quisling (1887–1945), who, in collaboration with the Nazi occupiers of Norway, pronounced himself prime minister on 9 April 1940, and led the collaborationist regime for five years, finally facing an execution squad at Akershus Fortress in 1945. Growing up as I did in the increasingly affluent Norway of the 1970s and 1980s, the hegemonic narrative about the country's history that I along with so many of my contemporaries was to learn was one in which heroic blond and mainly male Norwegians took to the woods and mountains in order to resist the German Nazis. But by the 1980s, the first cracks in the hegemonic narrative of Norway's role in the Second World War began to appear. We would eventually learn that the Norwegian police corps willingly assisted the Nazi occupiers in rounding up hundreds of Norwegian Jews for transport by the ship *Donau* to the extermination camps of eastern Europe; that the Norwegian state railway company NSB willingly let its trains be used for the transport of Norwegian Jews who had been interned by the Nazis to Oslo; that thousands of young Norwegian men volunteered for the Waffen SS's Nordic division Wiking for service on the killing fields of eastern Europe; that hundreds of young Norwegians volunteered as guards in prison camps in which they mistreated, tortured and abused Yugoslav and Soviet prisoners of war at will; and that Norwegian businessmen and conservative newspaper publishers made handsome profits through contracts with and ideological support for the Nazi occupiers. And we learnt that most Norwegians who lived through the Nazi occupation of Norway during the Second

World War did what many people tend to do during wars and oc-
cupations, namely survived by remaining aloof. And that Norway's
willing collaborators and executioners were in many cases left alone
by the Norwegian police, or given lenient sentences by Norwegian
courts after the war. Those of us who wanted to know, in other
words, knew very well that there were extremely dark undercurrents
running through modern Norwegian history, especially with regard
to how Norway and Norwegians have related to minorities of various
kinds. Nor were these extremely dark undercurrents exclusive to
the period 1940–45. For Norway is after all a nation-state which did
not allow Jews or Catholics entry into the country until 1854, and
which through most of its modern history pursued brutal assimilation policies towards the indigenous Saami population as well as
towards travelling Romas. The utopian fantasy of Norway as an
ethnically 'pure' and 'homogeneous' country is a recurrent theme
in Norwegian history, and by no means unique to the perpetrator of
the 22 July terror attacks. Anders Behring Breivik, who in his tract
2083: A European Declaration of Independence attempted to portray
himself as being opposed to both historical and contemporary
forms of Nazism, would in police interrogations after 22 July 2011
express admiration for Quisling, and in his trial endorse a long line
of Norwegian and European neo-Nazis.

'Those who fail to learn from history are doomed to repeat it'
goes the saying. There is no reason to think that Norwegians are
more prone to avoiding facing up to uncomfortable facts about
themselves or the society in which they live than any other people,
but the excessive focus on the personal mental idiosyncrasies of the
perpetrator of the 22/7 attacks in Norway has deflected any potential
for introspection among ordinary Norwegians about the direction
public discourse about Islam and Muslims, immigration and integration in Norway has taken in the past decade. Given this absence
of introspection, it is unsurprising that the public discourse about
Islam and Muslims, immigration and integration has changed little
since 22 July 2011.

The book you are about to read was conceived in the immediate
aftermath of the terror attacks of 22/7. It is written by a scholar

trained in social anthropology, and, it is hoped, reflects that particular scholarly training. It is written from the perspective of an anthropology which is engaged with and committed to human rights and the furthering of a multicultural (but alas not multiculturalist) society which is anchored in equal rights to dignity for all citizens regardless of personal faith or life stance. Academics looking for a contribution to terrorism studies – a field in which Norwegian scholars specializing in al-Qaeda and al-Qaeda-related terrorism have made an international mark in recent years – would perhaps be best advised to look elsewhere. And this is also due to the fact that the very orientation of terrorism studies in Norway meant that they – along with the Norwegian security services that they served in an advisory capacity from 2001 to 2011 – were more or less completely oblivious to any terror threat to Norwegian citizens other than that posed by al-Qaeda or its affiliates.

My aim with this book is twofold. It will shed light on the direction of Norwegian societal discourses regarding Islam and Muslims in recent decades. But inasmuch as the shifts of discourses are reflective of and relevant to similar shifts across most of western Europe, the book will also illuminate developments of interest to anyone concerned with Europe-wide debates on immigration, integration, Islamophobia and the rise of far-right political formations. Having settled in my country of origin with my family in 2007 after years of research and study abroad, it had soon become clear to me that the limits of what were considered acceptable ways of speaking about and to a minority making up about 3 per cent of the country's population at that time had shifted considerably since I left the country in 2003. By the winter of 2010/11, wild conspiratorial fantasies about an impending Muslim takeover of Norway and Europe articulated in and through the so-called 'Eurabia' genre were making headlines in mainstream Norwegian newspapers, with many Norwegian newspaper editors seeming to find this a perfectly sound state of affairs. This troubling development, it seemed to me, was not an artefact of history, but the result of a long and winding road towards the mainstreaming of far-right discourses in Norway, dating back to the 1980s, but greatly exacerbated by al-Qaeda's terror

attacks on the USA on 11 September 2001. It was a development
willed by specific political actors in Norway, who saw it in their
interest to generate a climate of fear centred upon the presence of
Muslims in Norway, and who found willing listeners in a context in
which tensions around immigration and integration became commonplace. This is not to suggest that all such fears are unfounded:
the threat from radical Islamist terror in Europe – including Norway
– has been real throughout the period in question. But it was also
a development abetted by the shifting conceptions of freedom of
expression and its limits among Norwegian liberal elites in the
media, in politics, in the legal field and in Norwegian academia
during the previous twenty years. These changing conceptions also
included the shift towards a view of the mediated public sphere as
an arena for confrontation rather than dialogue, caused by liberal
and mainstream Norwegian media editors struggling to maintain
public interest and corporate profits.

This book is, then, centrally concerned with analysing what in
scholarly literature is often referred to as 'hate speech', but which
is perhaps more accurately indexed as 'racist and/or discriminatory
speech'. And in this specific case, racist and/or discriminatory
speech targeting individuals who are – rightly or wrongly – identified as 'Muslim' – in the specific context of a late modern Norwegian
welfare state. Such speech – whether emanating from far-right
political milieus and expressed in the political speeches of populist
right-wing politicians or from the writings of authors in the 'Eurabia' genre – is, I will argue, a *necessary* if not *sufficient* explanatory
factor in the kind of terror that Norway faced on 22/7. The argument
in this book is not that Norway is a society that is exceptionally
racist, but rather that Norway should be seen as unexceptional
in this respect, and therefore as confronting the same challenges
regarding racism, intolerance and discrimination as other western
European societies in the modern era. That alone will be provocative, even intolerable, for Norwegians long accustomed to seeing
themselves – and being seen by others – as the embodiment of all
that is good and virtuous in the world. This book is an attempt to
describe the background to and the repercussions of such speech

not only in Norway, but also in the wider context of western Europe in recent times. It problematizes the contention that freedom of expression in its more liberal-absolutist inflections in and of itself can constitute a panacea for the challenges inherent in the persistence of intolerance and discrimination relating to minorities in Norway and Europe.

'This is the diverse Norway that we will stand up for. This is how we will honour those who are no longer with us.'
Jens Stoltenberg, prime minister of Norway (2000–01, 2005–13), Labour Youth Organization (AUF)'s Commemoration, Thorbjørnskaia near Utøya, 22 July 2013

For my daughters, still too young to know about the horror of it all; blessed to be born as children of a multicultural Norway which will eventually prevail over the prophets of intolerance and hate.

Prime Minister Jens Stoltenberg (Labor Party) greets AUF Chairman Eskil Pedersen among survivors and bereaved gathered at Sundvolden Hotel near Utøya on the day after the massacre which killed 69 AUF activists, mostly in their teens, on 22 July 2011. Minister of Justice Knut Storberget and security detail are in the background. This photo won the Norwegian Press Photo Awards for best photo in 2011 (photo: Tommy Ellingsen, Stavanger Aftenblad).

1 | HUMAN TERROR

And yet the great thing about being human is our ability to face adversity down by refusing to be defined by it, refusing to be no more than its agent or victim. (Chinua Achebe, *The Education of a British-Protected Child*, 2010, p. 23)

Terror unexpected: Oslo and Utøya, 22 July 2011

On 22 July 2011, in the midst of the school vacation, many Norwegians were enjoying summer holidays either at home or abroad. Those who remained in Oslo and its surroundings enjoyed the less crowded streets and picnic spots on the small islands in the Oslofjord, known mostly to locals. That day would see overcast weather in the morning, and pouring rain by the late afternoon. July 22 2011 would be the day that the small Scandinavian country of Norway[1] suffered its first ever large-scale terrorist attacks: a bomb placed in a parked van outside Government Headquarters in Oslo and a shooting spree on the small island of Utøya,[2] 60 kilometres north of Oslo, where the Labour Party Youth Organization (AUF) was holding its annual political camp. These attacks left a total of seventy-seven dead. Many more were maimed and scarred for life (Gjestvang 2012). At Government Headquarters the bomb blast at precisely 15.22.26 killed eight people, office workers and passers-by between the ages of twenty and sixty-one; nine others were severely injured, and another two hundred people received less severe injuries. In the shooting spree at Utøya, which lasted from shortly after the mass murderer's arrival at 17.15 to his arrest by a Delta (SWAT) team from Oslo Police at approximately 18.32, 69 people between the ages of 13 and 51 – most between 15 and 19 – of the 564 people on the island – were killed, 67 by shots to the head and two plunging to their deaths or drowning while trying to escape. Disguised as a police officer, the killer walked around the small island, calmly, systematically and without haste calling teenagers to him by pretending that, as a police officer, he had come to their rescue, and then shooting them in the head at point-blank range with either a Ruger shotgun or a Glock pistol. According to some witness testimonies from survivors, the terrorist appeared to be in an elated state, shooting while crying out 'Today you will die, Marxists!', and laughing loudly afterwards.

The twenty-storey Government Headquarters was left in ruins; its windows were completely shattered by the blast, as were those of neighbouring shops and buildings, some several hundred metres distant. The explosion could be heard several kilometres away.

Uppermost in most Norwegians' minds that afternoon, as soon as these events occurred, was a well-established scenario, one which Norwegians had been routinely fed by the Police Security Services (Politiets Sikkerhetstjeneste, PST), the terror experts at the Norwegian Defence Research Establishment (Forsvarets Forskningsinstitutt, FFI),[3] and the mainstream media: if Norway were struck by large-scale terrorist attacks of this kind, they would undoubtedly have been motivated or inspired by radical Islamism as a response to Norwegian military engagements in Afghanistan[4] or to the Norwegian involvement in the so-called cartoon crisis (2005/06).[5] And in its annual open threat assessment (the intelligence assessment made available to the media and the general public) the PST predicted in both 2010 and 2011 that it was mainly 'extreme Islamists' with global connections who posed a terror threat to Norway. Neither assessment indicated that groups considered by the PST to be on the extreme right represented a serious threat to Norwegian interests (PST 2010, 2011).[6] It was therefore not surprising that both national and international news media throughout the evening and long into the night of 22/7 featured 'terror experts' engaging in wild speculation about the identity of the perpetrators and the motives for the terror attacks, ascribing them to al-Qaeda or affiliated radical Islamist groups according to well-established media scripts (Nussbaum 2012: 49). Nor was it particularly surprising that most Norwegians – including many Norwegians of Muslim minority background – assumed that radical Islamists were behind the attacks.[7]

However, the initial media reports were wrong. The 22/7 attacks did not involve radical Islamists. The individual who surrendered to Norwegian police at Utøya late that same evening and who confessed to both attacks the following day was a white Norwegian from Skøyen in Oslo West with extreme right-wing views and an intense hatred of both social democrats and Muslims. He had wanted to be captured alive in order to be able to lead his ideological struggle by telling the world about his reasons for wanting to start a war in Europe (Lippestad 2013: 52).

A terrorist among us

Later that evening, the man who was to be charged with the terror attacks was named as Anders Behring Breivik. The thirty-two-year-old son of a short-lived relationship between the former senior Norwegian diplomat Jens David Breivik (1935–) and the auxiliary nurse Wenche Behring (1946–2013), Behring Breivik described himself as a 'conservative Christian'. However, as was amply illustrated by his deeds and in his tract, he was not in any respects a practising Christian. In his teenage years, he had nourished dreams of becoming a millionaire businessman, and he left high school before attaining his graduation diploma in pursuit of these dreams.

He was involved from 1997 to 2006 with the Norwegian populist right-wing Progressive Party (PP or FrP),[8] which since its emergence in 1973 as a small, obscure anti-taxation and anti-bureaucratic party, through the 1987 parliamentary elections and onwards, had become one of Norway's largest opposition parties. From 1987 the PP ran on the back of its anti-immigration and anti-Muslim discourse and policies. Postings on a web forum linked to the PP's youth organization, FpU, from 2002 to 2003 indicate that he was already then intensely preoccupied with the social democrats of the Labour Party and with an allegedly secretive 'Islamic invasion' of Europe, which would eventually lead to a 'civil war' in Europe (see Stormark 2012: 39, 49). FpU members with whom Behring Breivik was in contact at the time would allege to Norwegian media after 22/7 that he had expressed the view that Islam, rather than radical Islamism, motivated the 9/11 attacks on the USA (Østli and Andreassen 2011). According to Norwegian author Aage Borchgrevink, he convinced his mother to become a PP supporter (Borchgrevink 2012: 188). This claim is, however, contested by the Norwegian author Åsne Seierstad, who in her book about 22/7 claims that Wenche Behring Breivik throughout her adult life voted for the Progress Party (Seierstad 2013: 211).[9] She was often seen at the party's stand outside her local supermarket in her home district of Skøyen ahead of elections.[10] Having failed to get nominated to any significant position within the PP and its youth organization, FpU, Behring Breivik's formal involvement with the PP appears to have ended in disillusionment some time in 2006. That is not to suggest, however, that his support of the PP in any way abated: e-mails by Behring Breivik obtained by a Norwegian author and published in 2012 (Stormark 2012) suggest an intense preoccupation with the PP's electoral fortunes continuing well beyond 2006.

In the years that followed he was politically radicalized by endless hours on the internet. Yet right until late 2009 to early 2010, Behring Breivik was involved with an outfit called 'Friends of Document.no', which had close links with the more radical right-wing elements of the Progress Party centred upon its Oslo MP Christian Tybring-Gjedde. During this period Breivik contacted the PP's central administration with suggestions for how the party could win political power nationally (see ibid.: 244–5). So while Anders Behring Breivik's extreme acts may have much to do with his troubled personal background and mental problems in combination with radicalization through the 'echo chambers' of extreme right-wing milieus online (Eriksen 2011a), the argument I will advance in this book is simply that these 'echo chambers' were not of his own making. This book therefore also speaks to one of the fundamental challenges in late modern liberal and secular 'Western' democracies in the era of all-around identity politics and the 'culturalization of politics'. It is a fact that we, as modern liberal citizens, facilitated by the technological opportunities offered by an internet offering us 'parallel but separate universes', increasingly appear to live 'enclosed in our own bubbles' (Pariser 2011: 5). This situation is – as Cass Sunstein has reminded us (Sunstein 2009) – neither new nor original: there seems to be a basic human social psychological propensity for *biased assimilation* whereby people ignore contrary evidence (ibid.: 50–1), or even become more committed to their original point of view, and *motivated assimilation*, whereby people process information flows in a way that is distorted by their own emotions and their motivations (ibid.: 52).

Surveillance footage from the Government Headquarters on Grubbegata showed Behring Breivik making his escape from the scene of the blast – armed with a 9mm Glock 17 pistol and dressed in a fake police uniform purchased on the internet, complete with helmet and bulletproof vest. In spite of encounters with police in his teenage years, he had no criminal record, so he was able to obtain a weapon licence from the Norwegian police by registering as a member of an Oslo pistol club from 2005 to 2007 and again since the summer of 2010. His weapons had been legally purchased from registered Norwegian weapons dealers.

The 950-kilogram fertilizer bomb that would be used in the attack had been made by Behring Breivik at the farm – Vålstua – that he had rented from an elderly retired couple of farmers in rural Åsta in the municipality of Rena, some 165 kilometres north of Oslo, in April 2011. Two years earlier, in 2009, Behring Breivik had registered Breivik Geofarm with the Norwegian company register at Brønnøysund; the farm was officially a producer of ecological products such as fruits and root vegetables. In reality, the farm served as his cover for legally importing substantial amounts of fertilizer.

Behring Breivik, during subsequent police interrogations, never expressed any feelings of remorse for his actions. According to Behring Breivik's defence attorney, Geir Lippestad, right from the first of many police interrogations on 23 July, he echoed German SS chief Heinrich Himmler's statements about the massacre of European Jews on the Eastern Front in the course of the Second World War, when he described his actions as 'cruel, but necessary' (Kvilesjø 2011). Behring Breivik was reportedly able to recollect each and every murder in detail during the police interrogations (Brandvold 2012). Lippestad would later describe Behring Breivik's expression in the first police interrogation of the disappointment he had felt when he registered that the fertilizer bomb had failed to make any buildings in and around Government Headquarters fall to the ground, reasoning that only a limited number of people rather than the hundreds he had hoped for had been killed there. It was after this realization that he decided to execute his original plan B, namely the attack at Utøya (Lippestad 2013: 46). At court during the 22/7 trial, it was evident that Behring Breivik was at his most excited when describing the planning and execution of the attacks in all their dreadful details.

A taste of what was to come during the trial came in an open letter that Behring Breivik sent from his prison cell at Ila Prison to Norwegian media outlets in April 2012. Declaring white 'Boers' (Afrikaners) supportive of the racist and discriminatory apartheid regime in South Africa (1948–94) to be his 'anti-Communist brothers', as well as the first democratically elected South African president Nelson R. Mandela (1994–98) to be a 'terror leader' of 'the Marxist terror organization ANC', Behring Breivik signalled his support for apartheid by charging that the country's last white president under apartheid, Frederik W. de Klerk, had 'capitulated to the global Marxist lobby by negotiating the abolishment of apartheid' (Breivik 2012). During the 22/7 trial in Oslo Magistrate's Court Room 250, which ran for ten weeks from 16 May to 22 June 2012, and was concluded by the reading out of a ninety-page verdict by the presiding magistrate, Wenche Arntzen, on 24 August 2012, it became clearer than ever that Anders Behring Breivik adhered to an ideology which to all intents and purposes was fascist. For while in his cut-and-paste tract *2083: A European Declaration of Independence* he had attempted to distance himself from neo-Nazis and fascists, in his court appearance he endorsed a long line of Norwegian and European neo-Nazis who had been behind violence and terror since the 1980s; these ranged from the Norwegian neo-Nazi Erik Blücher to Jonny Olsen and on to the German neo-Nazi 'Zwickau cell', responsible for a string of murders against Turkish kebab shop owners in the 1990s and 2000s.

Marketing terror

Shortly before Breivik set out on his murdering spree, he uploaded on to the internet a 1,516-page document written under his English pen name Andrew Berwick and a YouTube video. In Chapter 3, I analyse the tract and how it links with neoconservative and/or Islamophobic discourses in Europe and the USA during the past decade (between 2001 and 2011).

By the evening of 23 July, Anders Behring Breivik had confessed to both the bombing at Government Headquarters and the massacre at Utøya. The same evening, authorities discovered both the online document and the YouTube video that introduced his grandiosely titled *2083: A European Declaration of Independence*. From this tract, it would become clear that Behring Breivik had been planning his attacks in meticulous detail for a number of years, and that in the event that he survived, he envisioned his trial as a public platform to spread his message. In fact, the tract contained a draft speech prepared for the trial, from which Behring Breivik would eventually read at his first court appearance.

Behring Breivik sent this tract to 1,003 e-mail contacts in Europe and in Israel, including far-right and populist right-wing politicians and activists whom Behring Breivik considered to be suitable 'Christian conservatives' and potential allies. Two hundred and fifty of the recipients are believed to be English (Taylor 2011a) – among them were many sympathizers with the English Defence League (EDL), whom Behring Breivik admired and had established contact with via Facebook. As late as March 2011 he used one of his internet aliases, Sigurd Jorsalfar, to post messages on a forum linked to the EDL. Here, he called upon right-wing activists in the UK to 'keep up the good work' and described them as a 'blessing to all of Europe' for working against a supposed 'Islamization' (Taylor 2011b). The only recipients in Norway named by the media at the time were the youngest member of parliament in Norway, Mette Hanekamhaug (1987–) of the PP and Jan Simonsen (1953–), a former MP for the same party (Rasch and Kristiansen 2011). In connection with the arrest and detention of the Norwegian neo-Nazi Varg Vikernes ('Louis Cachet') in the southwestern province of Corrèze in France in July 2013 on suspicion of plotting terrorism in France (BBC 2013), it would, however, become known that Vikernes too had been among the original recipients of the tract.[11] The number of recipients suggested that even if Behring Breivik knew that he was alone in the course of the actions he was to take in the following hours, he certainly did not conceive of himself as being alone in his ideas. That he had chosen Hanekamhaug and Simonsen as the recipients of his tract in Norway suggested a keen attention to Norwegian politics and the media: Hanekamhaug, who was elected to the Norwegian parliament (the Storting) in 2009, had been the front figure in the PP's 2010 campaign to get parliamentary support for a motion to ban the Islamic headscarf (the hijab) for underage Muslim girls in Norwegian schools (see Chapter 4). For his part, Simonsen had, as an MP for the PP from 1989 to 2001, been known for his virulently anti-immigration and anti-Islamic views; a long-standing and passionate defender of Israel (Vogt-Kielland 2002), he had proposed that George W. Bush and Tony Blair be nominated for the Nobel Peace Prize (awarded annually by the Oslo-based Nobel Peace Prize Committee) for invading Iraq in 2003 (Sønstelie 2003). And though the majority of far-right politicians and activists throughout Europe appear to have taken exception to Behring Breivik's action, a member of the French Front National (National Front), Jacques Coutela, in the immediate aftermath of 22/7, described him as 'an icon' and a 'main defender of the West' in the face of the 'Muslim invasion'. The Italian MP Mario Borghezio of the Lega Norte (Northern League) condemned his violence, but endorsed his ideas (see Nussbaum 2012: 6), as did Arne Tumyr of the far-right outfit Stop the Islamization of Norway (SIAN) in Norway. Kjersti Margrethe Adelheid Gilje, a hospital nurse of Christian background from the province of Rogaland who stood as a regional candidate for Demokratene (The Democrats)[12] in the Norwegian parliamentary elections of September 2013, in addition to being a member of SIAN and the Norwegian Defence League (NDL), exclaimed on her Facebook page during the 22/7 trial in late June 2012 that she 'fully support[ed] Behring Breivik's views' and proclaimed him a 'visionary' (Brandvold and Torvaldsen 2013). In newspaper interviews she characterized Islam as a 'diabolical ideology' which had to be 'totally extinguished from the face of the earth' (ibid.). In Russia, the young neo-Nazi leader Maksim Martsinkevitsj, a former leader of the neo-Nazi organization Format-18 (a direct reference to Adolf Hitler) and present leader of the neo-Nazi vigilante group Okkupaj-pedofilaj (Occupy the Paedophiles), who had in 2007 been imprisoned for three years for hate speech, referred to Breivik as a 'sacred man' who had done 'a good job', on a Russian talk show (cited in Enstad 2013). In the one and a half years that have passed since the 22/7 attacks (during the writing of this book), intelligence agencies from Slovakia to Poland and the USA have claimed to have averted terrorist attacks by perpetrators alleging inspiration from Behring Breivik. It is quite clear, then, that Norwegian right-wing bloggers and media columnists who in the course of the 22/7 trial declared that Behring Breivik 'represented no one' (see Stærk 2012 for the most prominent example) were involved in a deliberate distortion of the facts.

From his writings as well as from his testimony in the 22/7 trial, it is clear that Behring Breivik intended to use his tract to promote and market his ideas. In court, he would describe the acts of terror perpetrated on 22/7 as 'fireworks' for the digital launch of *2083* (cited in Hverven and Malling 2013: 59). In his tract, he cites the need to instigate a civil war in Europe in order to stop the 'Islamization of Europe' by European Muslims and to halt the enablers of said 'Islamization' in the form of 'cultural Marxists'. In an image in the tract, Behring Breivik wears a uniform with the emblem 'Marxist Hunter' on his left-hand shoulder. In the Norwegian context, social democrats figured prominently among those Behring Breivik thought of as members of this group. His terror targets were not random: AUF has the highest number of party youth activists with a minority background of any youth party organization in Norway (see Bromark 2012: 33), and a number of the victims were of minority background. One visiting international delegate from the former Soviet republic of Georgia was also among the dead.

Parts of the tract are cut-and-paste excerpts from the works of US and European neoconservative and/or Islamophobic authors from Robert Spencer to Bat Ye'or to Bruce Bawer, and from the Norwegian blogger Peder Are 'Fjordman' Nøstvold Jensen to Melanie Phillips; other parts are the diary of a man planning to terrorize his nation. Throughout the tract, which will be analysed in Chapter 3, Breivik positions himself as a self-styled saviour and redeemer of a white, Christian European civilization (Ruthven 2011).

Behring Breivik also had some specific targets among the crowd at Utøya, including former prime minister Gro Harlem Brundtland (1939–), whom Behring Breivik referred to not as '*landsmoderen*' (the mother of the nation) but as '*landsmorderen*' ('the murderer of the nation') in a post on the website Document.no;[13] the current minister of foreign affairs, Jonas Gahr Støre of the Labour Party (known and despised in anti-immigrant and Islamophobic circles for his principled defence of Norway as a multicultural society); and op-ed editor and political commentator Marte Michelet of the liberal daily newspaper *Dagbladet*, who had delivered a speech about racism and Islamophobia to the AUFers assembled at Utøya on 20 July. Gahr Støre's speech, which was covered extensively in the Norwegian media, was given on 21 July. AUF leader Eskil Pedersen was considered a 'B-target' by Behring Breivik. Michelet and Gahr Støre had long since left the island by the time of Behring Breivik's arrival. As for Brundtland, she left the island hours before Behring Breivik arrived. Pedersen was alerted to the situation by one of his political advisers moments after the shooting started, and was evacuated aboard the boat in which Behring Breivik had arrived.

Never again

In the aftermath of 22/7, Norwegian society saw large-scale, countrywide mobilizations of quiet and dignified protests against these atrocities, and a vocal defence of Norwegian democracy.[14] The Norwegian government declared 22 August a national day of mourning. In a ceremony in Oslo Spektrum, Oslo's largest concert hall, which was televised by both the national broadcasting corporation NRK and the private station TV2, the King of Norway, Harald VII, almost broke down in tears as he made his address: 'The tragedy has reminded us of the basics that connect us in our multicultural and diverse society.'

Crown Prince Haakon Magnus of Norway, who has a long record of support for anti-racist causes in Norway (Eriksen 2011a: 1), made a speech of unity, addressing viewers watching the ceremony right across Norway. He said, 'After July 22, we can never again permit ourselves to think that our attitudes and opinions are without significance.'

The red rose, a traditional symbol used by the Norwegian Labour Party, especially during election campaigns, became a national symbol; the demonstration in Oslo was dubbed the Rose Procession (*Rosetoget*). Public spaces in all of Norway's main cities were appropriated in symbolic and spontaneous acts of commemoration and grief. In Bergen's main square, the Blue Stone (*Den blå steinen*), a popular meeting place, was covered in flowers. The highest level of participation in collective commemorations was by sympathizers of the Socialist Left Party (SV); the lowest was found among sympathizers of the Progress Party (FrP). In the midst of the grief and despair, political dividing lines remained apparent: only 12 per cent of those polled and who agreed with the statement that 'there are enough immigrants and asylum seekers in the country' took part in collective commemorations, whereas 30 per cent of those polled who expressed disagreement with the statement reported having been part of these commemorations (ibid.). Researchers found that the terror attacks of 22/7 had led to modest increases in civic engagement, particularly among youth, increased interpersonal and institutional trust, and also led to a small increase in experienced fear in the population (Wollebæk et al. 2012).

In a gesture of political solidarity, out of respect for the victims, the survivors and the bereaved, all political parties represented in parliament decided to postpone the campaign for the September municipal elections until mid-August. The parties also called on their youth movements to cancel the traditionally important election campaign debates at high schools across the country. August saw a groundswell of public sympathy for the Labour Party and its youth organization AUF that led to a momentous increase in public support for the governing party in the opinion polls and thousands of new registered members for the Labour Party and the AUF. Senior officials and ministers from the Labour Party took part in a series of funerals across the country. In a suburb of the northern city of Trondheim, 5,000 people attended the funeral of Gizem Dogan (seventeen), a victim of the massacre at Utøya who was of Turkish parentage. The Turkish minister of foreign affairs, Ahmet Davutoglu, was present in an official delegation from Turkey. At Nesodden outside Oslo, Bano Abubakr Rashid (eighteen), a talented young woman of Kurdish parentage, who dreamed of becoming a professional politician, was laid to rest in a moving ceremony in which the last rites were read by a Norwegian Lutheran parish priest and an imam from the Islamic Council of Norway. In a humanist ceremony at Sundvolden Hotel near Utøya, where the survivors of the massacre on 22/7 had first been brought, the 'Mother of Utøya', Monica Bøsei, who had been among the first of Anders Behring Breivik's victims at Utøya, was commemorated. Prime Minister Jens Stoltenberg spoke in her honour.

On Friday, 12 August, the Norwegian government appointed a 22/7 Commission tasked with investigating the circumstances of the terror attacks, the responses of the police and emergency services, and the PST. Oslo lawyer Alexandra Bech Gjørv (forty-five) was named as head of the commission. Though the commission's report was due only in the summer of 2012, critical media attention would soon be brought to bear on both the PST and the police.

Prime Minister Jens Stoltenberg of the Labour Party urged Norwegians to respond with 'more democracy and more openness'[15] and with increased civil and political engagement and participation. Referring to another watershed event in Norwegian history, the German Nazi invasion of Norway on 9 April 1940, which was the start of five years of German Nazi occupation during the Second World War, Stoltenberg maintained that 'Our fathers and mothers had promised one another: Never again an April 9th – We say: Never again a July 22nd.'

However, the private citizen who initiated demonstrations via Facebook soon faced death threats. Reports emerged of harassment of Norwegian citizens believed to be Muslim on the streets of Oslo in the hours following the bomb blast at Government Headquarters: a young Muslim was called a 'quisling', the quintessential Norwegian term of abuse for 'traitors to the nation'[16] by an elderly Norwegian female; others of immigrant background were called 'terrorist bastards', 'sons of Bin Laden' and 'Muslim bombers' by passers-by (Murtnes 2011a) and immigrants reported being chased through the streets of Oslo. At Bislet, a young man of Indian and non-Muslim origins who had lived in Oslo for twenty years was chased through the streets by a crowd shouting at him to 'get the f— back to the place from which you came' (ibid.). A Muslim male dressed in white prayer robes was chased off Oslo's underground metro by other passengers (Stormark 2011: 88). At Grønland, a young Muslim woman who worked at a local shop was accused by a customer of being behind the attack (Murtnes 2011a). In a lot of Muslim families in the capital, young girls were asked by their parents not to venture outside for fear of repercussions.[17]

The Islamic community also reacted publicly. The Islamic Council of Norway (Islamsk Råd Norge or IRN) and its young secretary-general, Mehtab Afsar, who had strongly condemned the terror attacks, initiated a 'flower march' through the streets of the eastern parts of the capital, which was attended by the leaders of most of Oslo's religious congregations and many Norwegian politicians. Oslo's mayor, Stang, lauded Norwegian Muslims for their acts of solidarity in the aftermath of 22/7 and for having made it clear that they regarded the perpetrator as representing no one but himself. Stang also raised the question of whether this would have been the case if the perpetrator had in fact turned out to be a Muslim.

The secretary-general of the Islamic Council of Norway, Mehtab Afsar, told the *New York Times* shortly after the news of the bombings at Government Headquarters that 'This is our homeland; this is my homeland ... I condemn these attacks, and the Islamic Council of Norway condemns these attacks, whoever is behind them' (Mala and Goodman 2011).

The 22/7 Commission report

Internal evaluations of the National Directorate of Police (Politidirektoratet 2012) and the Police Security Services (PST 2012) in the aftermath of the terror attacks on 22 July 2011 amounted to little more than attempts at whitewashing Norwegian police authorities for a number of institutional and individual failures before and on the day of the attacks.

Ahead of the verdict and the sentencing in the 'July 22nd trial' at Oslo's Magistrate's Court on 24 August 2012, the 22/7 Commission published its 481-page report on the terror attacks. In the introduction to the report, the commission declared that the attack on Government Headquarters in Oslo on 22 July could have been prevented if security measures that had already been agreed upon had been brought into effect, and that a more rapid response by police authorities to the shootings on the island of Utøya would in fact have been possible (22/7 Commission 2012: 15). The report also concluded that with a better work methodology and a broader focus, the Police Security Services (PST) should have been able to trace the perpetrator before 22 July 2011 (ibid.). The commission's report was a damning indictment of a series of institutional as well as individual failures ahead of and during the events of 22/7. In sum, the report contended, '22/7 demonstrated serious failures in society's ability to obstruct and protect itself against threats' (ibid.: 450).

Norwegian police came in for particularly strong criticism. In the long litany of institutional and individual failures, the report listed the failure of the National Directorate of Police (Politidirektoratet) to put into effect, let alone consult, the plans it had developed for the eventuality of a terrorist attack (ibid.: 155);[18] the failure by the Oslo police, who had received tip-offs about the vehicle registration number of Behring Breivik's getaway car from a witness a mere ten minutes after the bomb blast at Government Headquarters, to communicate this to local and neighbouring police districts in time[19] (ibid.: 101); the fact that Kripos, or the National Criminal Police Central, sent out a national alarm only at 16.43 on 22 July, an alarm sent out via internal e-mail systems which failed to reach most police districts in Norway (ibid.: 150); the failure of the operational leader of Oslo police to mobilize the police helicopter when news of the shootings at Utøya first came in (ibid.: 289);[20] the failure of the elite police Delta Force to locate the port at Utøya, and to make use of the private boats that were already available and at their disposal (ibid.: 134–5).[21] The terrified and completely defenceless teenagers at Utøya used their mobile phones but were in many cases misinformed by extremely stressed police telephone operators, who failed to alert them to the fact that the terrorist they faced was, according to the available police information, dressed in a police uniform; who claimed that a police helicopter was on its way, and that there were police in the area long before that was actually the case (ibid.: 142). The Police Security Services (PST) was criticized by the commission for having left uninvestigated for no less than five months the available information from the international and UN-directed anti-terror operation Global Shield, in which Anders Behring Breivik was named among forty-one Norwegian individuals who had imported chemicals that could be used for fertilizer bombs (ibid.: 375, 378). The PST was furthermore criticized for having in effect been 'blind in the right eye' in the years before 22 July 2011 (ibid.: 385). The report noted that in its threat assessment of 2007 PST had already warned that Muslims in Norway could become targets of violent right-wing groups, yet that it had failed to prioritize this (ibid.). Asserting that the perpetrator Anders Behring Breivik had in fact long before his terror attacks made a series of 'extreme, hateful expressions hostile to Islam' (ibid.: 363), it also noted that PST had fallen seriously behind developments by failing to establish a unit in charge of the collection of digital information on internet radicalization (ibid.: 390). So preoccupied were the PST with the terror threat emanating from radical Islamists in Norway, in the years preceding the attacks, that even their operational information-gathering focused exclusively on sources within these radical Islamist circles, at least until the arrest and detention of Behring Breivik (ibid.: 232). It was only on the following day, Saturday, 23 July, that the PST started consulting sources in extreme right-wing political milieus. The government itself – and especially the bureaucrats and the political leadership at the Prime Minister's Office and the Department of Administration – came in for serious criticisms over their failure to close off public access to the street leading up to Government Headquarters, which the National Directorate of Police had recommended in 2004 (ibid.: 443). In light of the 22/7 Commission's extensive documentation of the failures of Norwegian intelligence and law enforcement agencies to track extreme right-wing activities ahead of 22/7, the political scientist Cas Mudde's claim to the effect that extreme and radical right-wing groups had 'received great (or even disproportionate) attention among European law-enforcement agencies' (Mudde 2011) seems little more than a sweeping generalization born out of academic ignorance. Though some tabloid media editors vociferously called for Norwegian Labour Party Prime Minister Jens Stoltenberg's resignation over the 22/7 Commission's damning report, the Norwegian parliamentary opposition stopped short of introducing a parliamentary motion of no-confidence (*mistillitsforslag*) in the prime minister and his tripartite government when the parliamentary committee for Oversight of the Constitution (*Kontroll- og konstitusjonskomiteen*) presented its preliminary report in February 2013.[22] It was perhaps less surprising that Norwegian terrorism experts, who had shown practically no interest whatsoever in the terrorist potential of extreme right-wingers in Norway before 22/7, and had for years briefed Norwegian intelligence agencies on terrorist threats (thus, arguably, leading the latter into focusing exclusively on terrorist threats emanating from radical Islamists in and outside Norway), would go to great lengths in order to exonerate the intelligence agencies as well as terrorism research institutes in Norway for any failures.[23] By declaring the case of Behring Breivik to be 'unique' and 'exceptional', various Norwegian terrorism experts adhered to the contemporary 'framing' of terrorism in terrorism research (see

Stampnitzky 2013), in which the centre of focus for understandable empirical reasons is and remains terror emanating from radical Islamist milieus, such terror being perceived as motivated almost exclusively by ideological factors (Lankford 2013). In this regard, radical Islamist terror is framed in a manner quite unlike that for various forms of extreme right-wing terrorism – which is framed as being expressive of individual psychopathologies. In the hegemonic narrative of the events of 22/7 'the links between Utøya and wider political reality' have to all extent and purposes been 'severed in yet another act of externalization' (Malm 2012: 198). The form of societal externalization that Norway has seen in the aftermath of 22/7 is by no means historically unprecedented. The narrative about Nazism and the Second World War that Germans told themselves until Germany started to come to terms with the atrocities its people had been part and parcel of in the 1960s was one focused on the individual psychopathologies of German Nazi leaders (see, *inter alia*, Pick 2012 on this).[24] This narrative provided an efficient means of avoiding any critical and general societal introspection about the horrors Nazism had inflicted on Europe in the name of Germany and its people. As we shall have occasion to see, the externalizing narrative framing the acts of terror perpetrated by Anders Behring Breivik on 22/7, which has become hegemonic in Norway in the aftermath, has been established by conscious efforts in Norway by authors, politicians and media editors and reporters alike. And so much so that Norwegian media editors two years later would excoriate anyone calling for introspection about what 22/7 may have said about the direction Norwegian society had taken in the years leading up to these terror attacks as exhibiting 'a totalitarian mode of thinking' (Sandvik 2013).

Islamophobic discourse and Islamophobia's mainstreaming

In Norway, the aftermath of 22/7 has been greeted by a plethora of publications in Norwegian concerning the personal background of Anders Behring Breivik;[25] various aspects of the terror attacks on 22/7;[26] and about the trial against Behring Breivik.[27] This book is not primarily about Anders Behring Breivik nor about the terror attacks he perpetrated on 22/7.

'Violence has the inherent tendency to create uncertainty about cause,' writes Donald L. Donham (Donham 2011: 8). And there are in any case so many unknowns in this case that a search for causal connections premised on mono-causal thinking would be futile. So let it be absolutely clear that accounts of 22/7 that reduce the terror that Norway experienced on that day to *either* psychology *or* ideology, rather than the co-imbrication of psychological and ideological factors, runs the risk of reductionism (see Gullestad 2012; Fangen 2012). Both psychiatric assessments of Anders Behring Breivik commissioned by the Oslo Magistrate's Court suggest that the perpetrator of the 22/7 terror attacks was and remains a severely mentally disturbed individual with personality traits which include extreme narcissism and an extreme lack of empathy for other human beings. Behring Breivik's legal counsel, Advocate Geir Lippestad, in a book on 22/7, discloses that even within Behring Breivik's legal defence team there were disagreements over the question of his sanity (Lippestad 2013). But the legal criterion for being declared criminally insane under Norwegian General Penal Code §44 is that a criminal perpetrator must be either psychotic or unconscious at the time of perpetrating a criminal act (see Rosenqvist 2012: 353 for this). Norway's tragedy on 22/7 'was not the work of a psychopath' (Nussbaum 2012: 48); nor are there any solid grounds to consider it the work of a 'paranoid schizophrenic', as Behring Breivik's first psychiatric assessors, Synne Sørheim and Torgeir Husby, in their almost complete ignorance about extreme right-wing discourse and tropes about Islam and Muslims in Norway, wanted Norwegians to believe. In its verdict from 24 August 2012, in which Anders Behring Breivik was declared sane and criminally liable and sentenced to twenty-one years' imprisonment, Oslo Magistrate's Court declared that the defendant's hostile views concerning Islam were linked to his extreme right-wing contacts on the internet, and that his critical views of immigration were shared by others (Oslo Magistrate's Court 2012). The court furthermore noted that central to anti-Islamist and extreme right-wing groups was the conspiratorial theory referred to as the 'Eurabia theory'. This book, then, is first and foremost about the ideology which inspired Behring Breivik's actions on 22/7, and about the fractures of contemporary Norwegian and European societies to which this ideology – or parts thereof – speaks.

Throughout this book, I will be using the term 'Islamophobia' in referring to 'indiscriminate negative attitudes and sentiments concerning Islam and Muslims' (Bleich 2011a: 1581). Now the term Islamophobia is a highly contested term both in and outside of academia in Norway, as in the rest of Europe. The contemporary contestation of the term has to do with the fact that it is not a neutral term (see Bowen 2005: 524) and that it has a dual function as both a *denunciatory* and an *analytical* term (see Bangstad 2012a). Zúquete argues that there is a lack of clarity regarding its meaning and to what it exactly refers (Zúquete 2008: 328), and Bowen laments that the term has come to be used in an 'overly broad way' and is 'highly polemical' (Bowen 2005: 524). Zúquete (2008) consequently calls for a 'restrained usage' of the term by social scientists. My using the term is first and foremost a pragmatic choice. Though the term itself may certainly not be ideal, inasmuch as it risks conflating negative attitudes towards Islam and Muslims, may seem to pathologize such attitudes, and may of course be misused and instrumentalized by Muslim actors who want to denounce any negative attitude towards Islam or Muslims as 'phobic',[28] it is by now a term which has 'come of age' (Klug 2012), and which furthermore seems better suited than the available alternatives.[29] A parallel with the (in the Western world) far more accepted term anti-Semitism may be in order at this point. There can be little doubt that some criticism of the state of Israel in our time is motivated by anti-Semitism, yet one realizes that the term may be misused and instrumentalized whenever it is suggested that all criticism of Israeli settlement expansion in the occupied Palestinian territories in breach of international law, and criticism of the slow drift of mainstream Israeli politics towards the extreme right in recent years, is characterized as being anti-Semitic in nature and motivation.

Mattias Gardell has defined Islamophobia as 'socially reproduced prejudices and aversions against Islam and Muslims, and actions and practices which attack, exclude and discriminate against people on account of these people either being, or being presumed to be Muslim, and to be associated with Islam' (Gardell 2011: 17). The fundament of Islamophobia is in other words a form of essentialist thinking about difference which is also found in various forms of racism. According to such essentialist thinking about difference, Muslims are believed to act and think in certain ways by virtue of their religious adherence. Through what has been described as an Orientalist practice of 'religio-centeredness' (Bayat 2007: 3) a Muslim is first and foremost regarded as a religious being. It follows from this that one may be the victim of Islamophobia regardless of whether one practises Islam or not. Gardell's definition of Islamophobia has the virtue of casting Islamophobia not only as a theory, but also as a practice (Gardell 2011: 15). For Gardell, Islamophobia forms part of a 'knowledge regime', as described by Michel Foucault. This implies that within the realms of this knowledge regime 'certain assertions, beliefs and arguments about Islam and Muslims are regarded as given truths through the logic of repetition itself and due to the fact that they are consonant with what we have always heard, and therefore know' (ibid.: 92). The first registered usage of the term Islamophobia stems from 1910, when it was used in publications by two French colonial administrators in West Africa by the name of Maurice Delafosse and Alain Queillien (López 2011: 562–3).

The first academic using the term in English, and in the sense in which it has become known in recent years, appears to have been Edward Said (1935–2003), who, in the essay 'Orientalism reconsidered' in 1985, argued that Islamophobia, understood as 'hostility towards Islam in the modern Christian West', had historically been 'nourished by the same sources as Anti-Semitism' (Said 2000: 353). Islamophobia as a generic term for fears of and hostility towards Islam and Muslims became mainstream only in the aftermath of the 1997 report by the British Runnymede Trust entitled *Islamophobia: A Challenge for Us All*. The Runnymede Trust report was instrumental in popularizing and legitimizing the term within the mainstream media as well as in academia (see Allen 2010: 194). Yet that report by and large left unanswered the question of how to define and delimit the term Islamophobia. 'The most important task therefore is to locate some way in which Islamophobia may be defined as clearly as possible, setting out what one means by Islamophobia, and equally importantly, what one does not' (ibid.: 120). Islamophobia is not only a contested term – it is nothing short of a resented term in qualifiably Islamophobic circles.

In these circles, both in Europe and the USA, various argumentative strategies have been launched in order to discredit the term, and to dissuade academics and the media from actually using it. Among these argumentative strategies, we find the creation of fictive and arbitrary historical genealogies for the term (such as the widespread notion that it was a neologism invented by the Muslim Brothers in Egypt – see Bawer 2012a for this claim – or by Iranian Islamists during the Iranian Revolution – see Storhaug 2010 – by Tariq Ramadan – see al-Kubaisi 2011 – or even by an alliance of Islamists and the ultra-left during the Rushdie affair); the argument that it pathologizes perfectly rational fears concerning Islam and Muslims, or that it delegitimizes legitimate critique of religious practices and faiths.

The simple answer to rejectionist discourses on Islamophobia is in my view not to discard the term, but to apply the term with discretion and care. So let me therefore be clear about the fact that it is for me not an expression of Islamophobia to harbour and articulate the thought that mainstream interpretations of Islam are often conservative and patriarchal with regard to proscribed gender relations, that mainstream interpretations of Islam are homophobic and that the religious interpretations of radical Islamists are abhorrent. Muslims who are intolerant of other faiths, homophobic and misogynistic, and who endorse violence and terror in pursuit of their politico-religious aims do in fact exist, and it would do violence to a sustainable concept of Islamophobia to qualify those who are critical towards them or their interpretations of Islam (whether Muslim or non-Muslim) as 'Islamophobic'. A case in point: Taimur Abdulwahhab al-Abdaly, a Swedish citizen of Iraqi background, set off a bomb, killing himself and injuring two passers-by on Drotningsgatan in central Stockholm on 11 December 2010, in the first terror attack attributable to radical Islamists in the Nordic countries. Thereafter, the Islamic Council of Norway mobilized for a demonstration against terror in the Norwegian capital of Oslo. On a bitterly cold day in Oslo, a dozen demonstrators turned up. The banner under which the secretary-general of the Islamic Council of Norway, Mehtab Afsar, addressed the small audience read 'Islam means Peace'. A mere 10 metres away from this demonstration, an even smaller group of far-right activists aligned with the Stop the Islamization of Norway (SIAN) had gathered with a slogan which asserted that 'Islam means War'.[30] The often heard and repeated argument by Islamophiles that 'Islam means peace' is in many respects – in the face of radical Islamists who *do* invoke Islamic foundational texts (however selectively; see Lincoln 2006; Lawrence 2005) in order to incite and legitimate terror and violence – just as essentialist as the argument of Islamophobes to the effect that 'Islam means war'. Islamophobes and radical Islamists are strikingly similar in their essentialist views on and interpretations of Islam, and the polarization that they seek to foster and nourish. Their discourses are a mutually reinforcing 'plague on both our houses'. Yet the fact that the overwhelming majority of Muslims in Norway and Europe are acting in good faith when they assert that 'Islam means peace', and are willing to assert that belief openly and publicly in the face of both radical Islamists and far-right activists who both assert that 'Islam means war', should, whatever analytical misgivings we may have about the essentialism of the assertion, provide some assurance.

But we need to 'take seriously the idea that Islam is best seen as a set of interpretive resources and practices' that individuals of Muslim background 'grapple with' and 'shape' (Bowen 2012b: 3). Like Bleich (2011a), I would not argue that those non-Muslim Norwegians and Europeans who are concerned by such phenomena as the presence of mosques, or of large concentrations of Muslims in certain urban neighbourhoods (especially so if they happen to live in the same neighbourhoods themselves), are *necessarily* 'Islamophobic'. Let me take a concrete case in point: when the Ahmadi Muslim Jama'at in Norway opened the doors of the largest purpose-built mosque in Norway, the Bait un-Nasr at Furuset in the north-eastern suburbs of Oslo in September 2011, it was amidst a heavy presence of armed police guards. Given that it was by members of a minority Muslim sect which is widely persecuted and discriminated against on the Indian subcontinent, and especially in Pakistan, where state authorities under pressure from Islamists declared Ahmadis to be 'non-Muslim' under the nominally socialist and secular prime minister Zulfikar Ali Bhutto in 1974 (Gualteri 2004: 135), the establishment of the mosque had been accompanied by opposition and threats from non-Muslim Norwegians as well as Sunni Muslims[31] from the time it was first referred to in the media in 1994. There was such opposition that the small Ahmadi congregation in Oslo, which according to its own estimates counted no more than 1,100 individuals in the Oslo region, and 1,500 nationally, had to postpone the opening owing to security concerns. A Labour Party MP of Muslim background whom I interviewed around this time told me that she had received hate mail referring to this particular mosque as a 'Muslim Brotherhood mosque'.[32] Ahead of the Progress Party's national convention in May 2011, Christian Tybring-Gjedde brought a newspaper reporter to the vicinity of the mosque in order to whip up sentiment against it. We shall meet Tybring-Gjedde on several occasions later in this book as one of the Progress Party's main traffickers in extreme right-wing rhetorical tropes about Islam and Muslims in recent years, and who delivered a speech for which he was reported to the police for possible breaches of the so-called Norwegian 'racism' paragraph, the Norwegian General Penal Code's §135(a). Here, he laughingly declared to the reporter in question that the mosque was an 'alien element' in the surroundings: 'symbolizing something which makes me concerned about the future of this country'. That 'something' was 'the Islamic expansion in Europe and Norway'. He charged that 'today's tax-financed cultural elite' was instrumental in bringing about this situation, since they allegedly competed in order to 'criticize our country'.

Tybring-Gjedde went on to argue that 'no [Norwegian] Muslims had raised their voices against Bin Laden' – demonstrating how little attention he had actually paid to a number of statements coming from Muslim religious leaders in Norway after 11 September 2001 – and that Muslims who did not represent 'gender equality, freedom of religion and freedom of expression and the other [Norwegian] values' had 'nothing to do here' (Mauno 2011). Yet the local concerns over the mosque from non-Muslim Norwegian residents at Furuset – as expressed to a scientist of religion at the same time – were far more temperate. These concerns centred upon the Bait un-Nasr's large and highly visible structure conveying the impression that Furuset was a 'Muslim' area, and that it might further a process in which the existing lack of common meeting places would now engender further segregation and intensify the living of disparate parallel lives among people living in the local neighbourhood.

What Tybring-Gjedde does in this case is to act as what Sunstein refers to as a 'polarization entrepreneur' (Sunstein 2009: 34), attempting to 'create communities of like-minded people' in the full awareness that these communities 'will not only harden positions but also move them to a more extreme point' (ibid.). In doing so, he basically uses Ahmadis, in spite of their being for good historical reasons some of the more ardent supporters of secularism among Muslims worldwide (see Gualteri 2004: 122), as a 'floating signifier' for a purported 'Islamic colonization' of Norway and Europe. In contradistinction to the views and sentiments expressed by the local residents interviewed, then, Tybring-Gjedde, true to his long historical record in this field, steps into the domain of Islamophobia.

The qualifier 'indiscriminate' in 'indiscriminate negative attitudes towards Islam and Muslims' (Bleich 2011a: 1587) is in fact what allows us to distinguish analytically between legitimate and phobic concerns relating to the presence of Islam and Muslims in a western European context. A mere dislike of increasing numbers of Muslims and Islamic infrastructures in one's neighbourhood is, in other words, not in itself qualifiably 'Islamophobic'; yet if you hold that Muslim citizens move into your neighbourhood as part of a long-term plan to 'colonize' or 'Islamize' your neighbourhood, your country or 'your' continent, and/ or that all Muslims are potentially violent, and that Muslim women reproduce so as to establish demographic dominance, then you have clearly veered into the realm of Islamophobic thought. Sociologist Ali Rattansi points out that Islamophobia is not necessarily racist, except when it takes what he refers to as 'hard' or 'strong' forms (Rattansi 2007: 108–9).

Those academics who are prone to a rationalistic bias, as well as a sizeable number of Muslims, have over the years suggested that the antidote to Islamophobia may be more balanced and nuanced information about the heterogeneity in contemporary interpretations of Islam and Islamic foundational texts, as well as about the heterogeneous nature of the lived lives of Muslims in various social and historical contexts. Hence, in the face of what she correctly diagnoses as an increasing intolerance towards Muslims in western Europe which challenges central tenets of classical liberal virtues advocated by European liberal thinkers, Nussbaum argues for a 'systematic cultivation of the "inner eyes"' or 'the imaginative capacity that makes it possible for us to see how the world looks from the point of view of a person different in religion and ethnicity' (Nussbaum 2012: 3).

Yet this ignores the fact that Islamophobic discourses emanating from extreme and/or populist right-wing milieus in Europe and the USA are not in the least interested in the finer details of Islamic interpretations and their heterogeneity, let alone in the complexities of what being a Muslim in a late modern liberal and secular context might conceivably mean.[33] For central to, and determinative in, the Islamophobic discourses are the ability to define what Muslims are (see Gardell 2011: 18) – or can be. What Goldberg refers to as 'the idea of the Muslim' (Goldberg 2006: 346) is therefore absolutely central to Islamophobic discourses, and the biases of the ways in which we filter and process information mean that reason and rationality – *pace* Nussbaum – may have relatively little to do with what gets established as dominant 'ideas of the Muslim' in particular social and historical contexts. It also ignores the radical democratization of freedom of expression in the era of the internet, which, as Lentin and Titley (2011: 27) argue, has made Muslims in particular 'prosaic objects of public debate, on which anyone can hold an opinion as to their essential compatibility, and the parameters of their permissible freedom' (ibid.). In effect, the academic who wades into mediated public debates on Islam and Muslims and attempts to put forward balanced and nuanced arguments under these circumstances is likely to be characterized by extreme and/or populist right-wingers alike as yet another 'apologist for Islam' or 'quisling' even,[34] who is part and parcel of the process of the purported 'Islamic colonization' of Europe.

One of my main research interests from the perspective of a social anthropologist involved in research on Muslim public intellectuals in Norway as well as on 'vernacular concepts of the secular' among youth of Muslim minority background in Norway has focused on the 'mainstreaming' of Islamophobia and Islamophobic discourse in Norway in recent years (Bangstad 2011).

I have written *Anders Breivik and the Rise of Islamophobia* to explore various facets of the public discourses concerning Islam and Muslims in Norway in the past decade in order to provide a background to the analysis of the ideology which appears to have motivated the déclassé mass murderer Breivik. For while Breivik is alone in the extremity of his actions, his ideology is far more widely shared, in Norway as in Europe and even the USA. This is not to suggest, however, that Anders Behring Breivik's ideological motivations must be seen as primary or even directly causative for, or of, the terror attacks on 22/7. John R. Bowen has insightfully argued that Behring Breivik had 'drenched himself in the writings of far-right, anti-Islam activists from the United States and Europe' and 'planned his killing spree as a way of saving Europe from Islam' and that while 'anti-Islam writings do not explain his actions' it is 'difficult to imagine those actions in the absence of such writings' (Bowen 2012a: 6). Acts of violence – like any other human acts – are 'embedded in an intricate matrix of causal relations' (Wilson 2011: 218), and when speech that incites violence is turned into actual acts of violence, it is to the recipient rather than the giver of the speech one must turn for explanations.[35] I suggest that the relationship between psychological motivations and ideology is a dialectical one, or in other words that Behring Breivik may have been a young man in search of an ideology which 'suited' his purposes. His ideology is therefore *necessary* – but alas not *sufficient* – in order to legitimize his actions (Gullestad 2012: 15). This means, however, that one cannot – as any number of Norwegian and European far-right politicians and activists have attempted to do in trying to distance themselves and their ideas from Behring Breivik in the aftermath of 22/7 – reduce ideology to something extraneous to these acts of political and human evil; the ideology must also be analysed (ibid.).

Norway and the rise of the far right

As was pointed out previously, Anders Behring Breivik had a background in the Norwegian Progress Party (the PP). It is perfectly clear in light of the available evidence in this case that he alone was responsible for the terror attacks of 22 July 2011. When members of all political parties represented in the Norwegian Parliament (the Storting) in the aftermath of Anders Behring Breivik's terror attacks stood shoulder to shoulder in declaring that these attacks were attacks on Norwegian democracy and on all those Norwegians who consider democratic principles to be fundamental and foundational values of Norwegian society, they were also united in their condemnation of the use of violence and terror as a means to further political ends. The PP's chairman, Siv Jensen, paid tribute to the young teenagers massacred at Utøya by declaring that 'today we are all AUF'ers'. The 'political family' of *far right* parties in western Europe, of which the PP is arguably part, as well as being one of the electorally most sucessful of such parties, by and large share negative and hostile views of Muslims and immigration. Be this as it may, for analytical purposes I find it important to distinguish between extreme right-wingers who endorse and espouse violence and non- and anti-democratic means, and populist right-wingers who are explicit and consistent in their support of democratic means and principles, and who reject violence (see Jupskås 2012: 55).

This distinction does not detract from the fact that the PP constituted part of Behring Breivik's ideological formation, and that rhetorical tropes concerning 'Eurabia' or the purported 'Islamic colonization' of Europe and Norway which appealed to Behring Breivik have also demonstrably had wide circulation and purchase in PP circles, especially after 11 September 2001. Many of these tropes are demonstrably of extreme right-wing provenance. At a rhetorical and discursive level, then, it becomes more difficult to distinguish between extreme and populist right-wing ideas.

There is an argument advanced by many mainstream right-wing politicians in Norway, as well as some intellectuals, to the effect that the PP has served the function of a 'safety valve' for Norwegians negative or hostile towards Muslims, channelling their sentiments and attitudes into a democratic process, and that the PP has thereby prevented the rise of extreme right-wing political formations in Norway. This is an argument I do not subscribe to. First of all, because it is an untestable hypothesis, and secondly, because there have been numerous instances in recent years in which central populist right-wing politicians have acted as mere 'voice amplifiers' and conduits for extreme right-wing ideas and views. This is a topic which will be further explored in Chapter 4 of this book.

Comfortable as it may have been for the Norwegian populist right (which does not exactly constitute a fan club for the present writer), it is not possible to disregard the ideological connections between the undemocratic and violent right forces on one hand, and the more democratic populist right on the other. To do so would be intellectually and academically dishonest, and simply would not suffice at an analytical level. Inasmuch as the public debate on the terror attacks in Norway and elsewhere (see Ruthven 2011) on 22 July 2011 has demonstrated the existence of serious political dividing lines with regard to the interpretation of the background to these attacks, this book will not find a particularly sympathetic audience among supporters of the PP. That is to be expected, and a price I am willing to pay as an author.

Norway is a country in which the PP (22.9 per cent of the votes nationally in the parliamentary elections of 2009, 16.3 per cent in the parliamentary elections of 2013) has adopted an ever more strident Islamophobic discourse in the past decade, to the extent that the party's leading MPs have spoken publicly about 'Islamization by stealth'; among other rhetorical pronouncements, they have compared the Islamic headscarf for women (the hijab) to the Ku Klux Klan hood. Political opposition parties of many stripes often engaged in irresponsible rhetoric, and since coming to power for the first time in the party's now forty-year history after the parliamentary elections of September 2013, PP ministers have been far more restrained than used to be the case in opposition in terms of political rhetoric concerning Muslims and other minorities in Norway. Islamophobic discourse has nevertheless not been restricted to the PP. Far from it. Established and mainstream Norwegian political parties, which long adhered to a *'cordon sanitaire'* policy with regard to both the discourse of and possible political alliances with the PP, have become concerned over the rising popularity of its anti-immigrant and anti-Muslim campaign. Paradoxically, and in particular from the late 1980s onwards, this concern led the right wing of the Norwegian Labour Party in Oslo to attempt to close the 'political space' the PP had established for itself among traditional Labour Party voters in the working class by appealing to similar popular and chauvinist 'native' sentiments. That attempt, in a manner reminiscent of the experience of the Labour Party in the UK when it tried to close down the 'political space' of far-right political formations in the British working class (see Trilling 2012), largely failed to dent the popularity of the PP. Instead, it arguably contributed to a situation in which the same far-right political formations' discourse on Islam, Muslims and immigration became ever more strident. Though it would be reductionist to argue that these political formations' discourse on Islam and Muslims is a causative factor in the emergence of radical Islamist forces in Norway, it is telling in the Norwegian context that these forces first started to coalesce in 2010, after years of polarized public discourse in Norway.

At a European level, Antonis Ellinas has demonstrated that established and mainstream political parties through appeals to nationalist sentiments among the electorate have in fact opened a political space for populist right-wing political parties (Ellinas 2011). Norway is in no way unique among western European countries in having experienced greater levels of popular scepticism concerning immigration in recent years (see Ceobanu and Escandell 2010 for western Europe, Aardal 2011 for Norway). What unites right-wing populists across western Europe is hostility to immigration (Ivarsflaten 2008). That hostility in Norway, as in large parts of western Europe, has in recent years largely come to be centred upon hostility towards Muslim immigrants. However, national representative survey data from Norway from recent years strongly suggest that negative attitudes and sentiments towards Muslims – which are more ubiquitous than negative attitudes and sentiments towards any other minority group in Norway, with the exception of the Roma (see HL Centre 2012) – are most commonly found among Norwegians with lower levels of education and income. It so happens that surveys reveal that individuals who express voter preferences for the Progress Party in Norway are also among those who have the most negative views of Muslims in Norway, and are also more likely than other respondents to have lower levels of education and income (see ibid.: 53).

Its popular purchase and legitimacy in one of the world's richest, most egalitarian and most peaceful countries has been linked to the ways in which the fear of Islam and Muslims has echoed 'missionary and universalizing impulses' in Norwegian society and politics relating to women's and gay rights, the welfare state, democracy and freedom of expression. Its popularization has also been linked to long

and concerted efforts by Islamophobic civil society activists working in close collaboration with populist right-wing/neoconservative
and Islamophobic activists in numerous other European countries,
from France to the Netherlands and Denmark, to mainstream these
discourses. Few systematic academic studies of the extent to which
such activism has succeeded in mainstreaming Islamophobic discourses have been undertaken in Europe and/or Scandinavia (but
see Hervik 2011 for one attempt). But for the USA, Bail (2012) has
demonstrated that organizations which deployed the media framing
of 'Muslims as enemies' in the wake of the 11 September terrorist
attacks by al-Qaeda on the USA in the years between 2004 and 2008
moved from the fringe to the mainstream of media coverage, and
were thus able to exercise considerable influence on mainstream
media, political and public discourse on Islam and Muslims. Similar
processes have arguably taken place in European and Scandinavian
societies in the same period.

Freedom of expression

This development has occurred at the same time as political,
media and intellectual elites in Norway have moved towards much
more absolutist – or more correctly what Eric Heinze (2006) refers
to as 'viewpoint absolutist' – conceptions of freedom of speech and
its limitations. Recent milestones on the road to such conceptions
in Norway have been Norway's involvement in the Rushdie affair in
1988–94; the government-appointed Freedom of Expression Commission from 1991 to 1996 and its aftermath; and the cartoon crisis in
Denmark and Norway from 2005 to 2006 (Klausen 2009). Central to
elite imaginaries (see Taylor 2004) as they relate to freedom of expression and its limitations in Norway is the contention that Norway's 3.6
per cent Muslim population embodies a potential threat to freedom
of expression as a central – in fact the most central – Norwegian
'value' according to national representative surveys from recent years
(see IMDI 2010, 2012). And this is the case, notwithstanding the fact
that Norwegians of immigrant background according to the available
polls are almost as likely as other Norwegians to support freedom
of expression.

In the legal field, the new hegemonic and much more absolutist conceptions of freedom of expression have been manifested in the fact that since 2007 Norwegian courts have very seldom convicted anyone for racist and discriminatory speech under the Norwegian penal code §135(a), and no one has been convicted in court for qualifiably Islamophobic speech; furthermore, there are few instances of racist and discriminatory speech that ever get reported to the police, and in a verdict criticized by both the United Nation's CERD (Committee on the Elimination of All Forms of Racial Discrimination) and the European Council's ECRI (European Council Against Racism and Intolerance), the Norwegian Supreme Court acquitted a Norwegian neo-Nazi leader charged with racist utterances in 2002. In Norway in recent years there has been a tendency for political, media and legal elites to argue that freedom of expression, *pace* international human rights standards, overrides other concerns and values. This, from a Europe-wide perspective, has made Norway something of an outlier with regard to practice in this field. It has also enabled far-right and populist right-wing activists to argue that they do not engage in racist or discriminatory speech directed against minorities, only that they practise a form of 'critique of religion' – something that is legitimate in light of freedom of expression and democratic legitimacy in a secular and liberal society. However, this is a strategy of rhetorical evasion made apparent by the academic literature on 'neo-racism' and/or 'cultural racism' from the late 1980s onwards (Gilroy 2002 [1987]; Balibar 1991), which was first applied to Norwegian empirical data by the late Norwegian social anthropologist Marianne Gullestad (Gullestad 2006).

The shift from biological to cultural markers of racism is one which in its early form emerges in the thought of the *Nouvelle Droite* (Alain Benoïst and others) in France in the 1970s (see Bar-On 2011), but becomes commonplace within European far-right milieus and political formations from 1984, the time of the electoral breakthrough of the French Front National. One should not be misled by the shift of signifiers, however: Phillips (2007: 56) argues that the fact that 'the discourse employs the language of culture rather than race does not ensure its innocence' (ibid.: 50). Though the 'rise of culture goes in parallel with the demise of race', it is, in the words of Lentin and Titley, 'not accompanied by a decrease in racism' (Lentin and Titley

2011: 76). The dominant conception of racism in Norway, which in terms of academic scholarship and interest in contemporary forms and articulations of racism constitutes a weak trend, is one which limits racism to differentialist thinking based on 'racial' or biological markers.

Fighting words, fighting deeds

With reference to the vast academic literature on the relation between 'fighting words' and 'fighting deeds' (see Klemperer 2006 and Vetlesen 2005 for two examples) I also want to problematize the sharp delineation between 'words' and 'acts', a distinction that has been made by mainstream Norwegian media editors and politicians since 22/7. For not only does this ignore the academic literature on perlocutionary speech acts (Austin 1962), but it is clear from much of this literature that Breivik's form of mass murder requires long and systematic ideological preparation whereby the perpetrator manages to dehumanize the victims through words.

Given the emergent literature on internet hate speech (Levmore and Nussbaum 2010), as well as the literature on how the structuring of internet search engines (Pariser 2011) may facilitate a filtering of views on politics and society, a filtering that reinforces extreme opinions (Sunstein 2009), rather than enabling pluralizing and democratizing opinions, I also want this book to contribute to the academic debate on how to combat racism, anti-Semitism and Islamophobia in our time (Bleich 2011a). These are analogous phenomena, inasmuch as they are all anchored in differentialist and essentialist social imaginaries.

The weight of words

In Chapter 2 of this book, I provide a historical background to mass immigration of Muslims to Norway since the 1960s, as well as a contextual analysis of their current predicament. *Anders Breivik and the Rise of Islamophobia* is centrally concerned with the question of what fears and anxieties coalesce in the discursive continuum of far-right political formations in Norway. In Chapter 3, I analyse Anders Behring Breivik's compendium entitled *2083: A European Declaration of Independence* in light of the anthropologist Arjun Appadurai's theories about 'fears of small numbers'. In Chapter 4, I analyse the extent to which Islamophobia has become part of the political mainstream through the populist right-wing Progress Party's trafficking in extreme right-wing discourses in Norway since 1987. In Chapter 5, I analyse the popular genre which most profoundly inspired Anders Behring Breivik, namely the 'Eurabia' genre, through some of its expressions in Norwegian and English popular literature and a Norwegian television documentary. In the final and concluding chapter, Chapter 6, I analyse how the shifting conceptions of freedom of expression and its limits in Norway in the past decades – in which Muslims are often cast as the main threats to its free exercise in and by liberal elites – have led to a greater level of acceptance for expressions of intolerance of minorities in Norway. I provide an analysis of the discursive terrain in which Norwegian social democrats in particular have become the targets of the 'hatred unbound' of Norwegian and European Islamophobes. I raise the question of whether Norway is a special case in this regard or whether it is affected by such discourses to the same extent and in similar manners as the rest of Europe. I offer examples of speech meant to promote hate. And I consider whether the right to express oneself freely outweighs the danger of allowing hatred to spread in Norway or elsewhere in Europe.

2 | MUSLIMS IN NORWAY

To be a Muslim in the modern world is both to be shaped by that world and to take part in its shaping. (Tripp 2009)

Historically, Norwegians have imagined their country as a homogeneous society in terms of ethnicity and forms of culture and/or religious expression. As the late Norwegian social anthropologist Marianne Gullestad often pointed out (Gullestad 2006), these Norwegian imaginaries of the nation did not necessarily correspond to actual historical realities since Norway had an indigenous Saami population, as well as travelling Roma communities, long before its post-Second World War immigration from so-called 'developing countries'. And Catholics and Jews have been present in Norway for centuries, even though the Norwegian Constitution of 1814, celebrated annually with children's flag parades right across the country on 17 May, Norway's National Day, had barred Jews from entry to Norway until 1851 and Jesuits until 1956. Members of these groups have been the targets of state assimilation policies and popular stigmatization at various periods of Norwegian history.

Large-scale immigration is in any event a relatively recent phenomenon in Norway. The country's historical status as comparatively poor, underdeveloped and peripheral meant that Norway was a migrant-exporting nation, at least before 1945: between 1810 and 1930, it is estimated that 800,000 Norwegians migrated to the USA (Khan 2009: 27). Affected by 'methodological nationalism', Norwegian historians have paid relatively little attention to the history of the Muslim presence in Norway, at least until very recently. The details of Muslim migration history to Norway were left for exploration by social anthropologists and sociologists (Korbøl 1972; Kramer 1978; Aase 1992; Brochmann and Kjelstadli 2008; Fangen 2008). In addition, popular accounts from reporters whose parents were part of the first wave of Muslim migration to Norway in the 1960s and 1970s have started to emerge in recent years (Mubashir 2007; Khan 2009). The very first Muslims to settle in Norway were probably Pakistani Ahmadi proselytizers (*muballigs*) arriving in the 1940s (Mubashir 2007). The Ahmadi sect, founded by Mirza Ghulam Ahmad (1835–1908) of Qadian in the present Indian parts of Punjab in the late nineteenth century, is considered heretical by mainstream Sunni Muslims in many parts of the world for holding that their founder was a (non-law-bearing) prophet, but have throughout their history been intensely preoccupied with *da'wa* (calling others to Islam; proselytization) in various parts of the world (see Gualteri 2004; Valentine 2008). Even though a few Norwegians were attracted to their message and converted to Ahmadi Islam, their role and impact were quite limited. According to Ahmadi sources, as of 2010 there were an estimated 1,500 Ahmadis living in Norway – about a thousand of whom were estimated to be resident in the capital, Oslo.[1] Most of these Ahmadis are of Pakistani descent, and arrived alongside Pakistani male migrant labourers in the 1960s and 1970s. The presence of Muslims in Norway emerged as a socially acknowledged reality only in the late 1960s, when the first Moroccan, Turkish and Pakistani labour migrants started to arrive (Brochmann and Kjelstadli 2008: 192–8). On the back of the discovery of significant Norwegian petroleum resources in the North Sea in 1967, these labour migrants, predominantly male and single, arrived in a Norway that was enjoying unprecedented economic growth and a rapid extension of the Norwegian welfare state (Halvorsen and Stjernø 2008). It was not as if Norway – a cold and inhospitable country in winter – was a preferred destination for many of these first migrants. As a case in point, in the spring of 1971, 600 Pakistanis arrived in Oslo as a direct result of the Danish decision to halt immigration to their country as of November 1970. In the course of one year, the number of Pakistanis in Norway had increased from 110 to 990 – making the Pakistani group the single largest group of 'non-Western' immigrants in Norway (Brochmann and Kjelstadli 2008: 197–8). Nor did Norway prove to be particularly welcoming to these immigrants. The spring of 1971 saw a media frenzy over the presence of Pakistanis in Norway, and reports that there was no appropriate housing and accommodation for them. At the historical height of their industrial bargaining might, LO, the central trade union organization, which is formally affiliated with the social democratic

Labour Party, expressed reservations about the potential of foreign migrant labourers to undermine organized labour in Norway (ibid.: 194). Most of the male immigrants who arrived from predominantly Muslim countries in that period belonged to an educated sector that either aspired to or was already established in the middle class of their countries of origin (e.g. Korbøl 1972): in Norway these immigrants had to settle for industrial and service work well below their educational qualifications. They often under-communicated their involvement in menial work when they communicated with relatives in their countries of origin, and in any event the comparatively high salaries of a booming industrial Norway were seen by many of them as making up for this shortcoming.[2] By the 1970s, however, there was a rapid industrial decline in Norway; this was set in motion by competition from emerging economies, high prices and production costs, as well as the outsourcing of production from Norway. It is therefore not coincidental that immigrants have become highly visible in the service sector; for instance, the taxi fleet in the capital, Oslo, is now completely dominated by males of immigrant or minority background. Public and media outrage ensued in 2007 when two Norwegian investigative reporters in a series of newspaper articles in *Aftenposten* documented that taxi-owners of Pakistani origin in Oslo, with the assistance of 'a white Norwegian' accountant, had for years defrauded Norwegian tax authorities of hundreds of millions of Norwegian kroner (Haakaas and Sæter 2010). The profits had been used to finance lavish properties and lifestyles in Pakistan. It would take Norwegian police years of work to get one of the main Norwegian-Pakistani kingpins, a taxi-owner by the name of Mohammed Aslam, arrested and extradited from Pakistan: he eventually appeared in Oslo Magistrate's Court for a new trial in early 2013. By 1975, cross-party political concern over immigration and the introduction of immigration quotas or cessations in many western European countries (most notably Denmark and Germany) led to the introduction of a ban on the immigration of foreign migrant labourers in 1975. Since then, and until Norway adapted the EU's Schengen rules[3] in 2002, immigration to Norway was predominantly linked to family reunification, and the entry of quota refugees from the UN, as well as refugees applying for asylum. Norway's participation in the Schengen Agreement has led to the emergence of significant in-migration of foreign labour migrants from formerly eastern European countries. So much so that the religious denomination which has seen the strongest growth in number of adherents in Norway in recent years is not Islam, but Catholicism, which, owing largely to the influx of Catholic eastern Europeans, had registered adherents outnumbering those of Islam in Norway by 2012 (Sletholm 2012a). In a Norwegian population totalling 4.8 million people in 2010, there were some 422,600 people of immigrant background, constituting 10.6 per cent of the population. In the course of the past decade, immigration to Norway has been at unprecedentedly high levels. These levels of immigration in the past decade are mainly linked to labour migration from formerly communist countries in eastern Europe – Norway, as an associate partner in the European Union's Schengen treaty of 1990, ratified it when it came into force in 2001 – and second, to family reunification. There has not been any pursuit of particularly liberal immigration policies by the Norwegian state. On the back of growing popular and cross-party scepticism about immigration from the mid-1980s onwards, various Norwegian governments, whether dominated by conservatives or social democrats, have pursued steadily more restrictive immigration policies since the 1990s. Norway in fact has 'one of Europe's tougher immigration policies' in the view of one observer (Saunders 2012: 11). According to nationally representative surveys, only 5 per cent of Norwegians surveyed in 2002 expressed the view that it should be easier for refugees and asylum seekers to be granted leave to stay in Norway (Blom 2012: 13). That percentage would remain stable until 2011 (ibid.).

This is a development also seen in a number of other western European states in the same period. In Norway as elsewhere this sentiment has been considerably nourished by the rise of popular right-wing parties, which have found demands for curbs on immigration to be important vote-catchers (Hagelund 2003; Jupskås 2012). This process has intensified to such an extent that many civil society observers now, in 2012, argue that Norwegian immigration policies and practices have become so restrictive that they are in breach of Norwegian human rights obligations (Steen 2012). The official statistics indicate that in the period between 1990 and 2011, a total of

524,957 people immigrated to Norway. Of these, 157,934 came as labour migrants, 196,283 for family reunification and 109,578 as refugees. Of the total number of immigrants to Norway between 1990 and 2011, 287,357 people were from countries classified as 'non-Western' for official purposes.[4] The population of immigrant background in Norway doubled in the ten years from 1999 to 2009 (SSB 2009). Even if all administrative districts (*kommuner*) in Norway now have residents of an immigrant background, immigrant settlement in Norway has during the past thirty years been a predominantly urban phenomenon. The rapidly expanding capital, Oslo, with its estimated 605,000 inhabitants in 2011 and projected population of 800,000 inhabitants by 2030, has by far the largest percentage of inhabitants of immigrant background in Norway. As of April 2011, 28.4 per cent of the city's population had an immigrant background, and it is estimated that one in five residents in Oslo were born in another country, and immigrated to Norway at some point (Politiet 2012: 5).[5] As of early 2011, an estimated 20 per cent of Oslo's population had a 'non-Western' immigrant background (Andersen 2012: 176). In the period between 2000 and 2010, the immigrant population was responsible for most of Oslo's population growth (ibid.: 184).

The burden of integrating new citizens of immigrant background has fallen disproportionally on the traditionally more deprived working-class districts of eastern central Oslo, as well as the working-class suburbs of north-eastern Oslo, originally developed in the 1960s and 1970s as part of social democratic social engineering in Norway. This has led to a situation of de facto residential and public segregation superimposed on the historical east–west divide along immigrant/ non-immigrant lines. In an eastern district of Oslo, which goes by the name of Alna, 42.5 per cent of the population had immigrant backgrounds in 2009, and at some of the public schools in the district, a process of 'white flight' (Vassenden 2007) has meant that there are few non-immigrant pupils left. However, it should be recalled that ethnic, cultural and/or religious homogeneity is in no way the result of these processes. Even if the potential consequences for integration of the fact that fewer and fewer residents have an 'ethnic' Norwegian background in these suburbs are not to be taken lightly, it is, in other words, not as if the increasingly immigrant-dominated north-eastern suburbs of Oslo are turning into Muslim-dominated 'enclaves'. The population of these parts of Oslo is highly heterogeneous (Eriksen and Høgmoen 2011). By 2008, individuals with a background in no fewer than 178 countries were represented in the eastern suburbs of Oslo (Eide and Eriksen 2012: 17). Though parts of the eastern suburbs are relatively deprived, the lack of dominance of any one particular ethnic group makes problematic the popular categorization of these parts of Oslo as a 'ghetto', let alone a 'Muslim ghetto' (see Andersen 2012: 179–80). In Oslo few politicians now seriously consider or propose measures that will limit any citizen's 'choice' of residential area in which to settle. That 'choice' is of course constrained by individuals' and families' financial resources. Survey data indicate that as the proportion of immigrants in urban areas of Norway with large concentrations of immigrants increases, the number of respondents with immigrant background wanting *fewer* immigrants in their residential neighbourhoods also increases (see Blom 2012: 28). The residential preferences of immigrants themselves are therefore not the main vectors in the residential segregation of immigrants in certain areas in urban Norway (ibid.: 9). For the foreseeable future, the constraints on the 'choices' available to immigrants with comparatively low income levels will mean a white Oslo west and an increasingly non-white Oslo east, and the maintenance, if not an increase in, levels of socio-economic inequality between east and west. It is also a myth that the eastern parts of Oslo with changing demographics have evidenced increased general levels of crime in recent years: at Furuset in Groruddalen in Oslo east the number of registered cases of crime fell from 1,200 to 400 per year from 2000 to 2010 (Eide and Eriksen 2012: 10). Nevertheless, it is a demonstrated fact that individuals of immigrant background are significantly overrepresented among those sentenced for a crime, as well as those imprisoned for crime, in comparison with individuals of 'ethnic' Norwegian background. Statistics from Statistics Norway from the period 2005 to 2008 suggest that 7.6 per cent of people of immigrant background in Norway had been sentenced for a crime, whereas the comparable level in the 'ethnic' Norwegian population was 5.0 per cent (Skanðhamar et al. 2011). Some immigrant groups were highly overrepresented among those sentenced in the period in question. These included individuals with a background from Iraq (17 per cent), Kosovo (16 per cent), Somalia (15 per cent), Afghanistan (14 per cent) and Iran (14 per cent) (ibid.). These are all Muslim-dominated countries of origin, even if socio-economic factors are the main predictor of committing and being sentenced for a crime in Norway.

Statistics on the number of Muslims in Norway are uncertain (see Sultan 2012 for an overview). This is due to the fact that while there are official figures for the number of people registered with Norwegian mosque associations, these figures do not include all people of Muslim background resident in the country at any given time. These unregistered individuals of Muslim background may or may not be practising Muslims. In estimating the number of Muslims in Norway, Statistics Norway, which does not collect data on individual religious identification for the purposes of its general population censuses, relies on estimates based on the religious profile in the immigrants' country of origin. According to these estimates, in 2009 Muslims constituted 3 per cent of Norway's population of 4.6 million (Jacobsen and Leirvik 2010: 387). That same year, 92,700 individuals, or almost 60 per cent of those with a Muslim background, were signed up as members of a Muslim organization (ibid.). Half of these were resident in the capital, Oslo, which meant that organized Muslims constituted between 6 and 7 per cent of Oslo's total population in 2009 (ibid.). By 2012, it was estimated that Muslims constituted 3.6 per cent of the Norwegian population of 5 million. The largest groups among Norwegian Muslims are, in numerical order, Pakistanis, Bosnians, Turks, Iranians, Moroccans, Somalis and Iraqis (Vogt 2008: 24).

Statistics on 'ethnic' Norwegian converts to Islam are generally unverifiable, but estimates suggest that more than a thousand Muslims in Norway may have such backgrounds at present (ibid.: 11). Mostly females, and often females married to Muslim men, this group accounts for no more than 1.5 per cent of the total Muslim population (Jacobsen and Leirvik 2010: 388).[6] In the 1980s, conversion to Islam among 'ethnic Norwegians' was so controversial that the first academic dissertation on these converts' experiences, written by a religious scholar affiliated with the University of Oslo, had to be classified in order to protect the anonymity and confidentiality of these converts.[7] 'Ethnic' Norwegian converts to Islam have played central roles in Islamic congregations and associations as organizers and spokespersons. This is, however, less the case at present than it was in the 1980s and 1990s. Among the most notable were the Sunni Muslim academic and activist Mrs Lena Larsen[8] and the Shia Muslim Trond Ali Linstad.[9] The first mosque in Norway was established by a group of Pakistani males in 1972 (Jacobsen 2009: 20). Two years later, the oldest existing mosque congregation in Norway was founded at Furuset in eastern Oslo (Vogt 2008: 38). Adopting the name the Islamic Cultural Centre (ICC), it is aligned with the Deobandi reformist trend, and has maintained close links with the Jama'at e-Islami in Pakistan (ibid.: 20). It remains one of the mosque congregations with the highest number of followers in Norway. Barelwis in Norway are represented in and through the largest mosque in Oslo, the Jama'at-e Ahl-e-Sunnat (ibid.). Internal conflicts within the Jama'at-e Ahl-e-Sunnat in the early to mid 1980s led to the establishment of the World Islamic Mission (WIM) in 1984 (ibid.: 68–9), combining followers of the Sufi Chistiyya and the Naqshbandiyya *turuq* (pl. of *tariqa*, Sufi brotherhood). The first purpose-built mosque in Norway was founded by the World Islamic Mission in Oslo in 1995 (Jacobsen 2009: 18).

There are now more than forty Muslim prayer locations in and around Oslo, three of which are purpose-built mosques (Jacobsen and Leirvik 2010: 390). Most mosques in Norway are to be found in flats, lofts and basements, warehouses and old factories (ibid.).[10] By 2009, there were 92,744 registered members of 126 Islamic religious congregations and associations in Norway. In a country in which 81 per cent of the population were registered as members of the Lutheran State Church (into which Norwegians are born, unless their parents state otherwise in their birth registration), 21.5 per cent of the 9 per cent of the population who were registered as members of other faiths or beliefs were Muslims in 2009. This meant that Islam was the largest religion outside the Lutheran State Church in Norway in 2009 (Schmidt 2010: 26, 29). In 2008, there were an estimated 163,000 immigrants and children of immigrant descent from predominantly Muslim countries living in Norway (Daugstad et al. 2008). There has been relatively little academic research on levels of religiosity, observance and practice among individuals of Muslim background in Norway. First, there is of course the problem of defining what is implied by the very terms 'practice' and 'observance' in Islam. A strict Muslim may hold the idea that this requires fulfilling all the tenets of the faith, such as performing the five daily prayers and the communal prayer (*jum'ua*) on Fridays, whereas a laxer Muslim may be convinced that a weekly communal prayer on Fridays would suffice. Secondly, levels of observable practice do not necessarily correlate with actual levels of practice. For example, it has been noted that female Muslims in Norway – while often being held to be more 'religious' than their male counterparts – to a lesser extent than Muslim males regularly attend Islamic prayers and rituals at mosques. This is – as pointed out by Vogt (2008: 17–18, fn. 13) a function of the fact that mosque accommodation for female Muslims is a relatively recent phenomenon in Norway, and of the fact that family patterns among many (but certainly not all) Norwegian Muslims mean that females are the primary care-givers for children, and may therefore be prevented from attending mosque regularly. Thirdly, membership of established Islamic religious congregations and associations is not in and of itself a reliable predictor of levels of religious practice and observance – given that there may be reasons other than strictly religious ones for such membership in the first place. For instance, survey data from Norway from 2006 suggest that nine out of ten immigrants from Somalia in Norway declare their religion to be 'very important' ('*svært viktig*') to them. Yet immigrant males of Somali background attend mosque to a lesser extent than immigrant males of Pakistani background in Norway (Blom and Henriksen 2008: 68). We do, however, have some data concerning self-reported importance attached to religiosity among Muslims in Norway. These are suggestive of a complex pattern in which levels of devotion vary significantly in and between different ethnicities. A researcher on youth in Oslo in 1996 found that 40 per cent of surveyed youth with a Muslim background declared 'religion' to be 'very important to them in their daily lives, with 85.5 per cent reporting belief in a God' (Øia 1998). In 2006, 27 per cent of respondents with a Muslim background in a poll reported that they attended 'religious ceremonies with others' on a monthly or more frequent basis, whereas 31 per cent of respondents with a Muslim background stated that they never attended such ceremonies (see Jacobsen and Leirvik 2010: 387). In 2006, 40 per cent of those surveyed with an immigrant background from Iran reported that religion was 'not important' (*ikke viktig*). Among immigrants with a background from Bosnia-Herzegovina, 25 per cent declared religion to be without importance to them. Norwegian-Iranian and Norwegian-Bosnian survey respondents also report dramatically lower levels of mosque attendance than other ethnic groups with a Muslim background in Norway (ibid.: 389). At the other extreme, 90 per cent of Somali immigrants surveyed reported that religion was very important to them, as did 65 per cent of Pakistani immigrants surveyed (Blom and Henriksen 2008: 67). In a recent survey-based study of religiosity among immigrants to Norway, Elgvin and Tronstad (2013) found that individual immigrants' level of religiosity appears to undergo insignificant changes with context, thus suggesting that immigrants who are non-religious as well as those who are religious at the outset remain so after settling in Norway.

Patterns of self-reported religious devotion among descendants of Muslim immigrants in Norway suggest that there may be lower actual levels of religiosity among descendants than among their parents who were first-generation immigrants (Løwe 2008: 67–9). But some caveats are in order at this point. Self-reported religiosity may be one of the better instruments for measuring religious devotion available from a quantitative methodological point of view, but it is not a reliable indicator. Correspondence with researchers at Statistics Norway – the state bureau of statistics, which, with the exception of Øia (1998), undertook the surveys referred to herein – has established that these questions were deemed too sensitive and problematic to include in surveys of the immigrant population in Norway. Furthermore, the data emerged as a result of household surveys conducted by trained interviewers from Statistics Norway. From the questionnaires it was not possible to ascertain where the interviews took place – but normally this would be in the confines of an individual's home. Nor was it possible to ascertain whether other household members had in fact been present during the interviews.[11] We happen to know from research on self-reported religiosity in other societal contexts that when an interviewee assumes that there is an expectation on the part of the researcher that personal religious devotion will be confirmed, and societal pressure to do so in the immediate environment, this may generate 'interview effects', leading to a tendency to exaggerate and over-report personal religiosity (Bruce 2004: 205). Such interview effects are certainly likely to have affected the outcome with regard to Norwegian-Somali survey respondents, as Somalis in Norway live in more crowded and deprived conditions than any other immigrant group.[12] Furthermore, it can also be safely assumed that the length of residence in Norway affects outcomes in this survey. Having arrived in Norway mainly after the breakdown of the Somali state in 1991 (Fangen 2008: 35), Somalis have had less time to accommodate themselves to Norway than most other groups. Basing his conclusions on recent quantitative data from the European Social Surveys (ESS), Connor (2010) has suggested that a hostile reception environment is a predictor of increased levels of religiosity among Muslim immigrants in Europe. Given that Somali immigrants in Norway have been declared the most 'troublesome' group among immigrants by the mainstream media and public officials alike for at least a decade now (Fangen 2008: 21), if Connor is correct, one would have reasons to expect significantly higher levels of religiosity among Somali Muslims than among other Muslims.

Even though the data available do not enable us to draw definite conclusions about the level of religious devotion among Muslims in Norway, they do provide valid reasons to suggest that levels of religiosity and practice among Muslim citizens are significantly higher, both among 'first-generation' Muslim immigrants to Norway and their descendants, than among non-Muslim Norwegians (Tronstad 2008a: 70). This is in line with findings from ESS surveys elsewhere in western Europe (Connor 2010), suggestive of a pattern in which Muslims are consistently more religious than non-Muslim populations. On the least religious and arguably most secular continent in the world (Berger et al. 2008), comparative social surveys (Norris and Inglehart 2004) provide solid support for the contention that Norway's population is among the least religious of populations around the world (Zuckerman 2008). Furthermore, during the past twenty years Norwegian social surveys have suggested that Norwegians in general are if anything becoming *less* religious. The notion that the increasing visibility of religion in Europe and the amount of media and political attention paid to it equates with an increase in religious practice is above all an 'optical illusion' (Roy 2010: 3, 5). From 1991 to 2008 the percentage of surveyed Norwegians who declared themselves to have 'no faith' increased from 10 to 18 per cent, and the percentage who declared themselves to 'believe without doubt' decreased from 20 to 15 per cent (Botvar 2010: 15). This presents us with a picture in which both 'belief' and 'unbelief' represent existential 'outliers' for most Norwegians, who are if anything most likely to be religiously indifferent.

By virtue of occupying a 'doxic' and 'naturalized' (Bourdieu 1978) position in Norwegian society, this religious indifference 'receives little attention and even less analysis' (Butler 2010: 209). Central to the 'Othering' of Norwegians of Muslim background in Norwegian social imaginaries[13] is the presumption of Muslim religiosity. Whereas 'the problem of Muslims' often seems to be cast as one relating directly to their religiosity in the eyes of many non-Muslim Norwegians, the 'problem of Norwegians' in the eyes of many practising Muslims in Norway often seems to be cast as one relating directly to their secularity.[14] And all the more so in a time in which the option of ideological 'unbelief' has become increasingly asserted in Norwegian public spheres. It is quite clear, however, that the number of Muslims formally affiliated with such religious congregations and associations in Norway has increased significantly in recent decades. From 1990 to 2010, the number of Norwegian Muslims registered with Islamic congregations and associations in Norway more than quadrupled (Schmidt 2010: 28).

There have certainly been media examples in recent years of over-reporting of registered mosque attendances in various mosques in Oslo in order to attract more municipal funding for mosque struc-tures – but academic accounts suggest that there may be significantly higher numbers of practising Muslims in Norway than officially registered as members of mosque congregations and associations (ibid.: 30). The first Muslim umbrella organization in Norway was the Muslim Defence Committee (Muslimsk Forsvarsråd), established in order to coordinate Norwegian Muslim protests against the publication of Salman Rushdie's novel *The Satanic Verses* in Norway in 1989 (Jacobsen 2009: 21). Consisting mainly of Pakistani mosque congregations, this committee was rather short-lived (ibid.: 33, fn. 14). A further spur for this process of formalization and organizational mobilization was the establishment of the Islamic Council of Norway [Islamsk Råd Norge, IRN] as an umbrella organization in 1993. A request by the Lutheran State Church in Norway in 1992 for the establishment of a contact group between Lutheran Christians and Muslims may have played some part in the establishment of the Islamic Council of Norway (Jacobsen and Leirvik 2010: 389).

Initially an umbrella organization organizing only Sunni Muslim congregations in Norway, it has in recent years included some Shia congregations. It is estimated that approximately 80 per cent of Norwegian Muslims are Sunnis, whereas approximately 20 per cent are Shias (Vogt 2008: 10). The Islamic Council in Norway rapidly established itself as a main interlocutor for Norwegian authorities at various levels, and as a partner in interreligious dialogue and ecumenical work for the Norwegian Lutheran State Church. This was not uncontroversial within Muslim circles: Norwegian Muslim adherents of the global Deobandi proselytizing movement the Tabligh Jama'at (TJ), present in Norway since the early 1970s, and in control of several mosques in Oslo, never formed part of the Islamic Council of Norway owing to this ecumenical emphasis. Young Muslim activists of a Salafist orientation affiliated with the student association IslamNet[15] have been among the voices most critical of the Islamic Council's centrist and pragmatist approach to relations with the state and with non-Muslim religious organizations. The Islamic Council of Norway played a pivotal role in defusing the tensions over a Norwegian Christian evangelical newspaper's reprinting of the so-called 'Muhammad cartoons' in 2005 and 2006, and through its engagement in interreligious dialogue has committed itself to public proclamations affirming the right to convert from Islam, and to condemnations of anti-Semitism and gender-based violence.[16] The 1990s also saw the emergence of Muslim student associations such as the Muslim Students' Society (Muslimsk Studentsamfunn, MSS), established at the University of Oslo in 1995, and the Muslim Youth of Norway (Norsk Muslimsk Ungdom, NMU), established in 1996

(Jacobsen 2011: 53). It is from the rank of cadres of this association, as well as other student associations, that some of the most active young Norwegian Muslim public intellectuals have emerged. Jacobsen (ibid., esp. 53–103) demonstrates in her ground-breaking study of young Muslim student activists in Norway that many of the Muslim individuals involved in these organizations wanted above all the possibility of providing an organizational and discursive platform for transcending the sectarian rifts of their parental generation in the name of Islamic 'unity'. They felt they had to distance themselves from the established Islamic authorities of their parental generation, authorities seen by younger Muslims to have a limited knowledge and command of the societal context of contemporary Norway by virtue of their lack of education and language skills. 'The insistence on the need for change and on the NMU and MSS as "untraditional" and "unconventional" positions the Islamic identities and practices of the "young Muslims" as modern and liberal in contrast to the assumed "traditionalism" and "conservatism" of "the parental generation",' writes Jacobsen (ibid.: 82). This included being 'modern' and 'liberal' in regard to practices of gender segregation – the NMU and the MSS in fact were 'among the first to challenge gender segregation as a principle for the organization of religious activities' (ibid.: 89). These organizations provided young Muslim females in particular with 'an opportunity to participate in a variety of late evening activities and to travel abroad without their parents' (ibid.: 90) – thus arguably enhancing female Muslim autonomy. Neither organization required female members to cover their hair with the Islamic headscarf (the hijab) (ibid.: 92). These organizations also represented a sharp contrast with the mainly male leadership in existing mosques and organizations (such as the Islamic Council of Norway, IRN) in that 'both the MSS and the NMU have had an essentially equal gender representation in their working committees' (ibid.).

Jacobsen's material on these organizations stems from the turn of the century; by contrast, when I conducted my interviews some ten years later, female leaders of the MSS would qualify it as an organizational problem that there were so few males in the leadership of their organizations.[17] That may be reflective of male Muslims having opted out, but also of a situation in which there are more female Muslim students around to recruit from, by virtue of women's relative numerical dominance among university students of Muslim background in Norway. It is clear from Jacobsen's study, though, that the envisioned Islamic 'unity' ultimately failed to materialize. The fact that many of the Norwegian Muslim public intellectuals referred to in my study have a background in these organizations should, however, not be taken to mean that there is an underlying unity of purpose and aim in what they do and say in the Norwegian mediated public spheres. There have been significant developments in terms of the discourse as well as the thinking among individuals involved in these organizations over the years, as there have been in mainstream Islamic organizations in Norway over the same period. The MSS, for example, in its current phase is arguably representative of what one may refer to as an 'Islamic contextualism',[18] which endorses central elements of the Norwegian societal context, such as human rights, gender equality, the welfare state and democracy.

Muslims in Norway have long been fractured along ethnic, national, generational and ideological lines. As Jacobsen (2009: 20) remarks, the main trend in the institutionalization of Islam in Norway until the 1990s was the establishment of mosques and affiliations along 'national, linguistic and doctrinal lines'. Divisions pertaining to national and ethnic origin remain salient. However, the establishment of umbrella organizations such as the Islamic Council of Norway in the 1990s, institutional pressure from a Norwegian state which was in search of Muslim organizational interlocutors, as well as a public which increasingly tended to regard 'Muslim' as a cross-cutting and overriding category, acted as a catalyst for extensive Muslim cooperation and coordination across historical lines of division.

A further impetus for such a development was provided by 'second-generation' Muslim descendants in Norway, who through their student and youth associations since the 1990s have been concerned with bridging such lines of division, and have increasingly gained influence within mosque congregations and as Muslim representatives to the general public. An ideological affiliation with what has been termed 'post-Ikhwani' or 'Salafi reformist' ideas of Islamic revivalism and a quest to find 'Islamic authenticity' through the avoidance of Islamic jurisprudence (*fiqh*) aligned with the traditions of particular schools of law in Islam (*madhahib*) among these Muslim youth in Norway may be seen as a precondition for this bridging (see Jacobsen 2005 for this). The World Islamic Mission (WIM), the Islamic Cultural Centre (ICC), Rabita and the Idara Minhaj ul-Quran[19] since the 1990s have seen the emergence of young Muslims born and raised in Norway claiming space in Norwegian mediated public spheres.

What is a Muslim? Norwegian Muslims between categorization and self-identification

At the age of sixteen, in 1986, Norwegian-Pakistani Khalid Hussein published the first novel by a 'non-Western' immigrant to Norway. Entitled *Pakkis* (*Paki*), the novel was a semi-autobiographical account of the life of a fifteen-year-old Norwegian-Pakistani boy growing up in Oslo. Hussein, who arrived without his parents from Pakistan at the age of five, had grown up in Sagene in eastern Oslo. In the early 1980s, the primary school which Hussein attended, Sagene skole, was targeted by Norwegian right-wing extremists on the basis that the school had a high proportion of pupils with a minority background.[20] Minority children's attendance in the children's flag parades during the annual Norwegian National Day celebrations on 17 May proved particularly problematic for these extremists. Ahead of the 17 May celebrations in 1983, the school received bomb threats and demands that the school keep the celebrations '*raserene*' (racially clean). The student council at the school, where approximately 80 out of 300 pupils had minority backgrounds (mainly Pakistani and Moroccan), also received neo-Nazi propaganda pamphlets in the mail. The teachers at the school responded to these threats by demanding that local police in Oslo provide police protection in order to ensure that all the school's pupils – regardless of ethnic and national origin – could celebrate the National Day. The police in Oslo declined to provide such protection, however. The teachers then responded by cancelling the 17 May celebrations and informed the parents and the public about the reasons for doing so. The central school administration in the municipality of Oslo requested that the teachers at the school remain silent about the racist threats the school had received, and that they proceed with the celebrations as planned despite the lack of police protection.

The teachers at the school decided, however, to break the public silence about what had happened, and to mobilize against the racist threats. The following year, the school was still receiving threats ahead of 17 May. As a young boy, Khalid Hussein, who went on to become a film-maker, had been among the pupils at Sagene marching in the children's parade through the streets of Oslo and to the Royal Palace in a direct challenge to the Norwegian right-wing extremists. By 1999, Norwegian-Pakistani Labour Party politician Rubina Rana (1956–2003) had become the first citizen of 'non-Western' immigrant background in Norway's history to lead the 17th of May Committee in Oslo, but even she faced death threats for marching in front of the children's parade dressed in Norwegian traditional costume (the *bunad*).

Hussein's book was noteworthy for its title too. For by using the term *Pakkis*, Hussein, in an act of appropriation similar to the appropriation of abusive racial epithets ('nigger', et cetera) in Afro-American culture, could be seen as attempting to wrest the term from the racist Norwegians of his childhood. For our purposes, Hussein's act of appropriation is also interesting for another reason. For whereas immigrants from Muslim countries throughout the 1970s and 1980s were publicly referred to by reference to their national origin, by the 1990s this was to change dramatically. No Norwegian academic has as yet undertaken a study of precisely how and when these discursive shifts took place, but by the late 1990s it was certainly the case that the erstwhile 'Pakistanis', 'Turks' or 'Moroccans' had definitely become 'Muslims' in and through Norwegian public discourses. Similar discursive shifts occurred throughout western Europe in the same period (see Allevi 2005: 7). This proved a momentous change. From then onwards, Muslim 'exceptionalism' in Norway would no longer be produced and reproduced with reference to ethno-nationalistic terms, but with reference to the supposed 'religio-centrism' of Muslims (Bayat 2007: 3).

In referring to this 'religio-centrism' in the analysis of the Muslim Middle East and the 'Muslim world', Bayat points to the influence of the 'continuing prevalence of Orientalist thought in the West', to 'the persistence of authoritarian rule by local [Muslim] regimes', and to 'the regional emergence and expansion of socially conservative and undemocratic Islamist movements' (ibid.). So while Bayat's term may be useful, it cannot provide a satisfactory explanation of the discursive shifts which occurred in relation to Muslims in Norway. In Norway, the salience of the term 'Muslim' as a category of public discourse and as a category of self-identification since the 1990s can be linked to (1) its increasing use as a term of categorization by non-Muslim Norwegians, especially in the media, in the public sphere and by state actors; (2) its increasing use by Muslim Norwegians themselves as a term of self-identification in the course of organizational formalization and mobilization (or 'Muslim identity politics'); and (3) the influence of 'neo-Orientalist' paradigms of thought and analysis (Lewis 1990 and Huntington 1996, and the industry of popular books derived from this paradigm) when it comes to the relationship between Islam and Muslims.

The very salience of the term 'Muslim' in its monist and determinative readings in Norwegian and European public discourses since the 1990s (Adamson 2011) presents the researcher with some conundrums. For if it is the case that one needs to *un*think some core popular assumptions about the nature of the relationship between Islam and Muslims in order to explore the spaces in between religiosity and secularity among Muslims in liberal and secular contexts such as Norway (Bangstad 2009), then the very use of the term 'Muslim' might be seen as a bit of a double-edged sword. For does it not serve to reinforce and reproduce the very assumptions about the nature of the relationship between Islam and Muslims which are in need of being *un*thought, and in doing so assist both the identity politics of nativist Islamophobes and Muslim identity politics? There is, I would argue, no easy solution to this ontological problem. But for pragmatic reasons having to do with the pervasiveness of the very term, and readability of the text, this monograph will be using the term 'Muslim' throughout. My usage of this term, however, comes with the caveat that the term is a sociological denominator, which does not endorse any particular, let alone deterministic, interpretation of what being a Muslim might or might not entail.

Muslims and everyday discrimination

Even though the integration of immigrants in the labour market in Norway, according to figures from the Organisation for Economic

Co-operation and Development (OECD), is among the best in western Europe (OECD 2012), rates of unemployment among people of immigrant background in Norway are currently 3.5 per cent higher than those of people of 'ethnic' Norwegian background. According to labour market statistics from Statistics Norway, however, 7.0 per cent of immigrants with residence rights in Norway were unemployed as of August 2012, compared with a rate of 2.0 per cent unemployment in the 'ethnic' Norwegian population. The variance between OECD and Statistic Norway's figures is down to different modes of measuring unemployment rates, as well as the fact that OECD's figures relate to an earlier year than those of Statistics Norway. Immigrant men were more likely to be employed than immigrant females (5.9 per cent as against 7.5 per cent unemployment; comparable rates among 'ethnic' Norwegians were 1.0 per cent among men and 2.1 per cent among women). The same statistics also suggested that immigrant unemployment had decreased by 1 per cent from 2011 to 2012 (SSB 2012). Yet these figures also obscure relatively wide discrepancies in rates of unemployment between people of different origins: the highest levels of unemployment were found among immigrants from Africa (14.3 per cent) and Asia (8.7 per cent), and the lowest among immigrants from eastern Europe (7.0 per cent) and/or EU states (6.0 per cent) (ibid.). It cannot plausibly be argued that the discrepancy between rates of unemployment for people of immigrant and 'ethnic' Norwegian background is down exclusively to labour market discrimination. For it is also a fact that Norway has an increasingly skills-based economy, and that levels of education among people of immigrant background in Norway vary significantly. Labour market research has demonstrated that a higher proportion of people of immigrant background than 'ethnic' Norwegians have academic qualifications at a doctoral level. Yet it is also the case that people of immigrant background are overrepresented among those with little or no formal educational qualifications in Norway (Steinkeller 2012).

Survey data from Norway during the past ten years have indicated a relatively consistent pattern whereby immigrants of Muslim background are disproportionately affected by discrimination in the labour and housing markets, and by discrimination in the public sphere in general. A survey conducted by Statistics Norway in 2005/06 found that Norwegian-Somalis (who, as we have seen, are among the most recent immigrants to Norway, and the most religious among immigrants of Muslim background) reported more discrimination with regard to employment and housing than any other group of 'non-Western' immigrants. Men were more affected by such discrimination than females in all groups surveyed (Tronstad 2008b: 128–36). Research on labour market discrimination from 2012 demonstrates that applicants with a Norwegian-Pakistani-sounding name are 25 per cent less likely to get called in for interviews by Norwegian employers when their qualifications and work experience is the same as that of 'ethnic' Norwegian applicants (Midtbøen and Rogstad 2012). Since females of 'non-Western' immigrant background are both less likely to apply for work and to be working, and many females of 'first-generation' immigrant background are at a particular disadvantage in terms of relevant education, skills and experience, the gender difference with regard to experiences of discrimination may also have to do with such females being less active in various public arenas in Norway than their male counterparts. There are also indications that state welfare policies in the form of the extensive cash for childcare benefits for stay-at-home parents first introduced by the centre-right coalition government of Kjell Magne Bondevik (1997–2000) in 1998 may adversely impact on the labour market participation of immigrant women in Norway. Interestingly, in many respects, the participation in the public arenas by the descendants of 'non-Western' immigrants from Muslim countries now coming of age in Norway appears to reverse this gendered structuring. There is solid data indicating that young females in this group both outperform their male peers at all levels of education, and are much more likely to take the higher levels of education required to succeed in a knowledge-based advanced economy such as Norway's. An indicator of this is that the board of the Muslim Student Society (MSS) at the University of Oslo now overwhelmingly consists of female Muslim students. We may in fact be witnessing what scholars in other contexts have been referring to as a 'quiet revolution' (Ahmed 2011) by virtue of which young Norwegian Muslim women are empowered through education and labour market participation to a much greater extent than their mothers in the 'first generation' ever were. This 'quiet revolution', however, stands in an ambivalent relationship with white Norwegian secular and state feminism, inasmuch as many of these young Muslim women do not necessarily want to abandon their Islamic faith in the process, and look askance at secular Norwegian feminists, who more often than not consider this a precondition for female empowerment. The impact of these developments over time is, however, somewhat unpredictable. The strong tradition of state feminism in Norway (Hernes 1987) has been an important contributory factor to a political and societal climate in which the legal regulation of various facets of gendered traditions within various religions, but Islam in particular, has become legitimate and widespread in recent decades.[21] When a state such as Norway appropriates the role of what Gayatri Chakravorty Spivak memorably referred to as 'saving brown women from brown men' (Spivak 1993: 93), which the Norwegian state has very much been inclined to do since the 1990s, it can lead to internal debate and reform, but also to reactive and defensive forms of identity politics (Jacobsen 2009: 26). It may also be that the Norwegian state, through its governance of Islam and of Muslims[22] at various levels, has succeeded admirably in 'saving brown women', but at the cost of marginalizing 'brown men'.

As far as the Norwegian intelligence services' approach to Muslims is concerned, in a report from April 2013, the EOS Commission – a parliament-appointed oversight body for the intelligence services – documented that the Norwegian Police Security Services (PST) had over the course of ten years, in contravention of their instructions, surveilled two unidentified Muslim groups in Norway and individuals linked to these groups on the exclusive basis of the surveilled individuals' Islamic faith.[23] The illegal surveillance had continued for years in spite of the fact that no indication of potential or actual plotting of violence had been detected. Apart from a few critical comments in the media from Norwegian politicians of Muslim background (see Gitmark and Løkeland-Stai 2013), the report was met with silence from politicians and media editors alike.

Narratives of victimhood: the rise of Salafism in Norway

The 'cartoon crisis' in Norway from 2005 to 2006 and the so-called 'war on terror' from 2001 to 2008, in combination with experiences of other examples of social, political and economic marginalization and stigmatization among Norway's Muslim minority, seem to have generated a strong sense of victimization among certain sections of urban Muslim youth. As a result, the pragmatic, compromise- and dialogue-oriented approaches of the centrist and mainstream Islamic Council of Norway would be challenged by the emergence and rising popularity of Salafism among Norwegian Muslim youth. The very term 'Salafism' has its etymological origins in the Arabic transliterated term for the first four generations of the successors of the Prophet Muhammad, namely *al-salaf al-salih* or the 'pious or righteous ancestors'. The term is in itself of modern lineage: it was, according to Wiktorowicz (2006: 19), never used in the time of the Prophet and His Companions, and its usage has therefore resulted in often virulent contestation among Salafis themselves. Part of the academic challenge of writing about Salafism is its fragmentation and heterogeneity (see Haykel 2009: 45–6; Meijer 2009: 3).

As a descriptor for reformist interpretations in Islam which sought to anchor contemporary faith and practice among Muslims by advocating that Muslims return to the Islamic foundational sources, the term was introduced in academic literature by the distinguished French Orientalist Louis Massignon (Lauzière 2010). Massignon used the term in reference to Rashid Rida''s (1865–1935) and Muhammed 'Abduh's (1849–1905) 'modernist school of thought' (*madrasa fikriyya*). But contemporary Salafis do not necessarily trace their intellectual lineage back to Rida' and 'Abduh, who are instead often excoriated by contemporary Salafis as 'deviant rationalists' (Wiktorowicz 2006: 212) for their opposition to Ibn Taymiyya, and to other Islamic scholars' anti-rationalistic and literalist interpretations of the Islamic foundational texts. Lauzière (2010) argues that 'today, *salafiyya* is first and foremost a label that Sunni purists use to designate their approach to Islam'. The term is usually understood to refer to a rigorist creed and religious methodology that share a 'family resemblance ... to Wahhabism or are intimately linked to the religious establishment of Saudi Arabia' (ibid.: 370). Salafis consider the Qur'an and the *ahadith* (the Prophetic traditions) to be 'the only legitimate sources of religious conduct and reasoning' and generally represent a 'more literalist and more puritan approach to Islamic doctrine and practice'

(Hegghammer 2009: 249). Al-Rasheed (2007: 3) notes that the Saudi Wahhabi Salafiyya 'does not have much in common with' what she refers to as the 'modernist Salafiyya' (or, in other words, the Salafi tradition after 'Abduh and Rida') since the former emerged in central Arabia prior to the modern encounter with the 'West', whereas the latter emerged as a result of this encounter, and as an articulation of a Muslim quest for advancement.

Salafis have globally, after the Saudi state started bankrolling Islamic movements favourably disposed towards the various ultra-conservative Saudi interpretations of Islam as a means of countering the influence of secular-oriented Arab nationalists in the aftermath of the petroleum crisis of 1973, received much support from Saudi Arabia (see Al-Rasheed 2002 for this). El Fadl (2005), for his part, regards the co-imbrication of modernist Salafi and Wahhabi from the 1970s onwards as a corrupting and radicalizing factor in and for modernist Salafism. This is not to suggest, however, that Saudi Arabia's sponsorship of Salafism at a global level is either a necessary or a sufficient explanation for its global presence (see Haykel 2009: 37 for this point). One may distinguish between puritan Salafis and radical Salafi-jihadis. Though they share much of the same approach to creed and religious methodology, and the aim of an Islamic state or an Islamic caliphate, puritan Salafis, unlike radical Salafi-jihadists, do not endorse the use of violence and terror in pursuit of their worldly aims.

What Salafis furthermore share, regardless of their views on terror and violence, is also a strong sense of representing a 'true, authentic' Islam, as set against the supposed 'unbelief' of non-Muslims as well as non-Salafi Muslims; a strong rejection of Sufi faith and practices as well as of Shia Islam (see Haykel 2009: 41); ultra-conservative views of gender relations (see Al-Rasheed 2013 for this in the context of Saudi Arabia); and a general opposition to *taqlid* or the 'imitation' of any particular *madhab* (Haykel 2009: 42). Hegghammer (2009: 249) notes that the term 'Salafi' as a self-descriptor used by 'conservative Sunni Muslims and Islamist groups of different shades and orientations is often better understood as a bid for legitimacy than an indication of a specific political programme'. The self-appellation 'Salafi' is 'simply a synonym for "authentic"' (ibid.). While Hegghammer claims that the term is popular among Islamist actors in that it connotes doctrinal purity (ibid.), it is not necessarily the case that Salafi Muslims everywhere describe themselves as such publicly. For inasmuch as Salafism is seen by Salafis themselves as representing the only 'authentic' and 'true' Islam, for many Salafis it may in fact make more sense describing themselves simply as Muslims, and their creed (*aqida*) simply as that of 'Islam'. This has certainly been the case in Norway, where identifiably Salafist groupings which started to emerge from 2008 onwards hardly ever refer to themselves as such, at least publicly.

A case in point is the first puritan-activist Salafi group in Norway, namely IslamNet, who, though they subscribe to Salafi ideas and practices, rarely ever use the term to describe themselves publicly. What I have said so far is not to suggest that Salafism in its contemporary incarnations is anything like a static and unchanging orientation: events in the Arab world after the fall of the secular autocracy in Egypt under Hosni Mubarak (1981–2011) suggest that Salafis may, if it suits their purposes, come to endorse participation in democratic structures and procedures, at least partially, as a step towards the realization of their ultimate aims. Though Salafism must – like any other Islamic orientation – be studied in and through its local articulations, it is quite clear that the emergence and adaptation of so-called 'new media' by Salafis across the world have enabled and facilitated a Salafi discourse that is much more global and transnational than it was even in the 1990s (see Lacroix 2011). Roy (2010) also suggests that the current popularity of Salafism among Muslims in Europe must be seen as a modern product of secularization and the delinking of 'religion' and 'culture' generated in and through this process of secularization.

IslamNet: puritan-activist Salafis[24]

In early 2009, a media scandal erupted when the private television broadcaster TV2 disclosed that a Muslim student association by the name of IslamNet at what was then called Oslo University College (Høgskolen i Oslo, HiO or OUC) had reinvited a Norwegian-Pakistani imam, Zulqarnain Madani, to lecture at a function hosted by them.[25] Madani, of the Tabligh Jama'at-controlled Aisha Masjid in Oslo, was of Pakistani origin, and had his degree in Islamic studies from the University of Medina in Saudi Arabia. In September 2008, the previous year, Madani had lectured to IslamNet-affiliated Muslim students at the university college, and TV2 had obtained video footage of that lecture. TV2 now broadcast excerpts from this video, both online and on its daily news show. In the video, Madani could be seen lecturing to IslamNet about the terror attacks on the USA on 11 September 2001.

In his lecture, Madani made allegations about the identity of the perpetrators of the 11 September terror attacks which were clearly anti-Semitic and conspiratorial. Amid public and political outrage over the fact that a Norwegian liberal and secular educational institution would permit such public expressions of anti-Semitism from a Muslim religious authority addressing students, the then rector of OUC, Sissel Østberg, while taking clear exception to Madani's remarks, sought to defend what she regarded as IslamNet's 'freedom of expression'. Østberg, an associate professor at OUC before she became rector, and having a background on the left in Norway, had herself a background in ethnographic research on the everyday lives of young Muslim Norwegians of Norwegian-Pakistani background (see Østberg 2003). The then minister of higher education, Tora Aasland from the Socialist Left Party, when questioned about the incident in parliament by an MP from the Progress Party, took a similar line to that of Østberg.

The leadership of IslamNet withdrew the 2009 invitation to Madani. The reason for withdrawing the invitation (as cited by the leadership of IslamNet) was nothing to do with the external pressure generated by the media scandal, but rather with a conflict relating to Madani's insistence on propagating interpretations of *fiqh* exclusively from the Hanafi school of law (*madhab*). In the media, IslamNet's leader, a young engineering student at OUC of Norwegian-Pakistani background from Rasta in Akershus outside of Oslo, named Fahad Ullah Qureshi, made matters even worse by feigning a neutral position with regard to Madani's anti-Semitic views, while suggesting that people who were interested in learning more about the 11 September attacks on the USA should consult the 'documentary' *Loose Change*, a series of films written and directed by Dylan Avery and released between 2005 to 2009, which advanced conspiracy theories about the attacks and suggested that elements within the US government were responsible for them.

A female student at OUC, of Norwegian-Pakistani background and who also worked as a freelance reporter for the private broadcaster TV2, disclosed that she had been exposed to threatening and abusive behaviour by Qureshi when trying to cover one of IslamNet's meetings. I was at the time an associate professor at Oslo University College. In the aftermath of the first media scandal relating to IslamNet's activities on campus, I attempted to find out more about the organization and its activities. With that in mind, I contacted staff members at the Engineering Faculty, the faculty from which the organization's leadership appeared to have emerged. In conversations with me, female non-Muslim members of staff disclosed that they had in the course of the past year experienced a series of attempts at converting them to Islam through rather aggressive proselytizing from IslamNet members. Some female staff members had been annoyed by young male Muslim students aligned with IslamNet who came forward during supervision and tried to convert their supervisors. Their main professional and educational concern related to the fact that many of their students with an immigrant background (and Oslo University College, with an estimated 18 per cent of students having an immigrant background, had more such students than any other higher education institution in Oslo at the time) performed relatively poorly in exams. They believed that this had a lot to do with a lack of adequate language skills in Norwegian.

In order to remedy this situation, they had been granted funding from the central administration at OUC for an Urdu-speaking teaching assistant. Yet as it turned out, this teaching assistant, herself a successful graduate from the Engineering Department of Norwegian-Pakistani background, was boycotted, and apparently even harassed, by some of the young Muslim male students. What the staff at the department had been oblivious to was that the teaching assistant they had employed was in fact an Ahmadi, and that the boycott and harassment of her on the part of the male Muslim students aligned with IslamNet stemmed from the fact that they – in line with both mainstream Sunni views in Pakistan as well as Salafi views – considered her a non-Muslim.

IslamNet provided an instructive example of how a proverbial secular and liberal road to hell may be paved with good intentions: my enquiries about IslamNet and its activities at OUC also led to the discovery that the campus prayer rooms that had been made available to students, regardless of religious faith, as part of the university college's policy of accommodating an ethnically and religiously diverse student population, had in fact been completely monopolized by Muslim students aligned with IslamNet. In breach of the expectations of the university college administration, IslamNet had on its own initiative started segregating the small prayer rooms, insisting that it was religiously inappropriate for female Muslim students to pray alongside male Muslim students, making a great deal of fuss when discovering that the prayer niches (*mihrabs*) in one of the campus prayer rooms were not placed in the direction of Mecca after all, and insisting on segregating all its afternoon functions on campus according to gender.

IslamNet, which in the course of the following years would emerge as one of the most popular and most controversial groups among Muslim youth in Norway, was formally established in October 2008. Strongly preoccupied with *da'wa* or the 'calling of Muslims to Islam', its central leadership around Fahad Qureshi had a background in the circles of the global and most successful modern proselytizing movement in Islam, namely the Tabligh Jama'at (TJ), an ultra-conservative Deobandi movement established in response to Hindu proselytization in Mewat in British colonial India in the 1920s.[26] Qureshi had grown up at Rasta near Lørenskog outside of Oslo, with a father who was a long-standing member of the TJ, and who had nourished his son's technological interest and savvy by producing wedding videos in Muslim communities in and around Oslo. In 2009, Qureshi invited Abdurraheem Green (born 1964 in Dar es Salaam, Tanzania, as Anthony Green), a well-known British convert to Islam and Salafi proselytizer or *dai'i* (for details on Green, see Hamid 2009), to address IslamNet in Oslo. Green, together with another British convert to Islam, Yusuf Chambers, also runs the consultancy Green and Chambers Consulting. In London, Green appears to have handpicked Qureshi among other candidates to lead Salafi *da'wa* attempts in Norway. Green and Chambers form part of a global Salafi proselytizing network centred upon the controversial Indian Muslim TV evangelist Zakir Naik and his Islamic Research Foundation (IRF) in Mumbai, India. Naik is also a central figure on the Islamic satellite TV channel Peace TV, which forms part of his media empire.

In 2010 Naik was barred from visiting the UK by British authorities on the grounds of 'unacceptable behaviour' (BBC 2010). The 'unacceptable behaviour' in question appears to relate to a number of controversial statements about the provenance of the 11 September terror attacks in 2001. In the words of Brekke (2012), Naik 'operates a media empire, English language schools' and 'his television preaching is watched by millions of Muslims across the world' (ibid.: 97). Naik is the proverbial lay preacher, having been educated as a medical doctor, and having no formal religious authority (ibid.). 'Speaking in English, he addresses the growing number of Muslims who are able to relate to a globalized idea of what Islam should be' (ibid.). Nevertheless, Naik is a controversial figure in his native India, in liberal circles, owing to his attacks on other religions, and among Indian Muslim *ulama* (religious scholars) for blatantly ignoring established religious authorities, and insisting on the right of ordinary Muslims to interpret the Qur'an for themselves (ibid.).

Both Green and Chambers have been regular guests and lecturers at IslamNet events (known as biannual 'Peace Conferences') in Oslo and its surroundings ever since. After the first media scandal involving IslamNet in early 2009, there followed a long period of intense media scrutiny of the association and its activities. Both the liberal and tabloid daily newspapers *VG* and *Dagbladet* in their coverage opted to characterize IslamNet as 'extremist' (Johnsen 2010; Meland 2010), thereby suggesting that the association endorsed violence and terror. The Muslim liberal lawyer, politician and Fritt Ord's Freedom of Expression Award-winner Abid Raja of the Social Liberal Party Venstre, in statements to the media, as well as in a 2010 book (Raja 2010), argued that IslamNet had links to radical Salafi-jihadists (of whom more later), without substantiating these claims. As for Qureshi himself, he alleged that IslamNet was willingly cooperating with the Police Security Services (PST). This led him to be denounced as an 'infidel' (*kafir*) by some of the Salafi-jihadists in the small radical Islamist group which would later be known as the 'Prophet's

Ummah'. By 2010, the ongoing critical media attention on IslamNet and its activities and presence at OUC's campus had led the central administration at OUC, which had by then arranged meetings with Qureshi and his leadership to which they failed to turn up, to decide that the OUC's facilities would no longer be made available free of charge for use by IslamNet. The reason cited to the media by the rector, Østberg, was that the college was in principle opposed to IslamNet's practice of gender segregation. This seemed to be more of a pretext than the actual reason, inasmuch as the association had always practised gender segregation at its public events at the college, and the OUC's central administration had been aware of this fact from the very beginning. By the following year, IslamNet events were being held at the OUC again: IslamNet now paid 'lip-service' to the OUC's requirements regarding non-segregation of events by arguing that its members voluntarily chose segregated seating at events, and by allowing others to sit wherever they preferred. The new rector, Kari Toverud Jensen, declared that by permitting IslamNet to hold lectures and events at OUC, the OUC demonstrated its commitment to 'dialogue', even though IslamNet's own conception of what 'dialogue' with the many non-Muslims and Muslims on and off campus was very obviously limited to the promotion of Salafi *da'wa*.[27]

From the very outset, IslamNet's approach to *da'wa* has been inspired by conservative Christian TV evangelization in the USA and globally. Yet it comes with a particular twist derived from a long history of 'Islamic apologetics' in which IslamNet positions itself. It does so by emphasizing that it is involved in 'defending' or 'explaining' Islam. While its core leadership is male and has an immigrant background from the Indian subcontinent (Pakistan and Bangladesh in particular), most followers of IslamNet are, as it happens, Norwegian-Somalis, who overtook Norwegian-Pakistanis as the single most stigmatized and discriminated Muslim group in Norway. This occurred owing to the rapid settlement of thousands of Somalis fleeing the civil war in the 1990s, which engulfed Somalia after the fall of the dictator Mohammed Siad Barre in 1991. The 'narrative of victimization' by the Norwegian media, politicians and other elites was presented to this group by IslamNet's leadership. This narrative holds great appeal to its members and supporters. IslamNet's website is easily the most professional of Islamic websites in Norway, and IslamNet has also proved very adept at using various social media such as Facebook (FB), various discussion forums and online videos in order to mobilize its followers.

At present, IslamNet has an estimated 12,000 followers on FB, and 2,000 paid-up members. This should of course not be read as implying that it has more than two thousand active followers, as many of them may be FB followers for different reasons. From the point of view of its Islamic orientation, IslamNet has developed from a more eclectic approach to Islamic sources and authorities in its initial phases to a fully fledged endorsement of puritan Salafism in the most recent years. This means that the Islamic scholarly authorities, to whose Islamic edicts or *fatawa* IslamNet followers are often referred on their website, are increasingly scholars from the Saudi Salafi canon. In new regulations for board members made available on their website some time in late 2012, IslamNet makes it clear that it demands absolute and unquestioning loyalty to the teachings of the ultra-conservative late Saudi *ulama* Abdul Aziz bin Baz (1910–99) and Muhammad Nasiruddin al-Albani (1914–99) from its present and future board members. IslamNet rather absurdly and without any substantiating references alleges that these are scholars whose opinions are 'accepted' by a majority of Muslims around the world.[28] The claim, if true, would mean that a majority of Muslims around the world 'accept' the legal ruling that females should not be permitted to drive cars, and that the sun orbits around the earth, as these were both legal edicts issued by the obscurantist Bin Baz in his lifetime.

IslamNet has not exactly been popular with established and mainstream Islamic organizations and congregations in Norway. Having gained public attention as an uncompromising figure who dared say what he meant about anything from gender equality to the death penalty and thereby provided a living embodiment of all that ordinary liberal and secular Norwegians despised and feared in ultra-conservative interpretations of Islam, Fahad Qureshi and IslamNet deliberately sought out confrontations with, for example, the Islamic Council of Norway. In the winter of 2012, IslamNet published a recording of a furious conversation between Qureshi and

Senaid Koblica, the Norwegian-Bosnian leader of the Islamic Council of Norway (ICN), on their website. The conversation was taped and published without Koblica's knowledge or consent. The aim was clearly to delegitimize the ICN and Koblica in the eyes of a wider Muslim public in Norway, by making his broken Norwegian look bad, and by suggesting that Koblica and ICN failed to 'stand up' for 'Muslim' rights.[29] However, for many young Norwegian Muslims who had initially taken an interest in IslamNet's novel and media-savvy approach to *da'wa* – an eclectic mixture of popular-cultural and Islamic references (see Linge 2013a: 47) – this open challenge and derogatory attitude to established Muslim religious authorities in Norway proved a last straw. Since then, IslamNet's popularity among Muslim youth in Norway appears to have been waning.

The Prophet's Ummah: angry brown men

The first radical Islamist among Muslims in Norway to become publicly known was Najmuddin Faraj Ahmad (1956–) or 'Mullah Krekar'. Born in Suleymaniya in the Kurdish-dominated regions of northern Iraq, Krekar first came to Norway as a refugee in 1991. Krekar, an Islamic scholar by education, had a background as a radical Islamist activist in the so-called Islamic Movement in Kurdistan or IMK. Krekar's aim was to establish an Islamic state in the Kurdish region of Iraq, as a step towards the establishment of an Islamic caliphate. This put him at odds with mainstream Kurdish nationalists who, in the course of the 1980s and 1990s, fought a permanent war against the brutal authoritarian and secular regime of Saddam Hussein. In Norway, Krekar's wife and four children were granted full refugee status and rights to permanent residence, but by contrast he was granted only leave to stay on humanitarian grounds. Unknown to Norwegian authorities at the time, Krekar had, throughout the 1990s, continued to travel back to the Kurdish region of Iraq. By September 2001, a faction of the IMK established the Jund al-Islam, which would later become Ansar al-Islam. As a long-standing activist of the IMK, Krekar became the *amir* or leader of Ansar al-Islam. Ansar al-Islam declared itself an associate of al-Qaeda, a fact which in the course of the so-called 'war on terror' brought Ansar al-Islam international attention. Owing to local opposition among Kurds in northern Iraq, Ansar al-Islam's attempt to establish an Islamic state and to enforce its rigorous interpretations of the shari'a never seem to have amounted to much, though Human Rights Watch Report's on the movement suggested that it had pursued a reign of terror against villagers around Biyara and Tawela in northern Iraq.

In Norway, Krekar's leave to stay was revoked in 2002 as a direct result of the media disclosures about the long period of deception and double-dealing in his relations with Norwegian authorities. By 2003, Ansar al-Islam would play a central role in the spurious argument put forward by US Secretary of State Colin Powell before the UN Security Council in New York in order to legitimize the impending US invasion of Iraq (Brekke 2012: 1). Ansar al-Islam, in the view of US authorities, was the sinister nexus between Saddam Hussein's regime and al-Qaeda. Powell 'described a situation where Ansar al-Islam, headed by Mullah Krekar, was harboring al-Qaida fighters from Afghanistan and at the same time collaborating with Saddam Hussein' (ibid.). In 2003, the Norwegian centre-right government issued Krekar with an extradition order. By then he was wanted by Iraq's Kurdish authorities. The order could not be fulfilled, however, since both international human rights conventions and Norwegian law prevented Norwegian authorities from extraditing individuals who would risk capital punishment in the countries to which they were extradited, something neither Iraqi Kurdish or national authorities in the aftermath of the US invasion of Iraq seemed willing to guarantee he would be exempt from.

In 2003, national as well as international media reports suggested that an attempt by the CIA to kidnap Krekar on the streets of Oslo had been called off at the last minute; in the following nine years Krekar hardly ever left his apartment at Tøyen in eastern Oslo for fear of being kidnapped by the CIA. From his small apartment, Krekar continued to issue online *fatawa* or religious edicts to a small group of followers in Norway and in Iraq, and to give interviews to international media (for a useful overview of the Krekar case until 2005, see Brekke 2005). In these interviews and statements online, he would laud Osama Bin Laden, al-Qaeda and Abu Musab al-Zarqawi, the leader of 'al-Qaeda in Mesopotamia', and issue various threats against and condemnations of Kurdish nationalists in Norway as well as in Iraq. In 2006, the UN placed Krekar on its Terror List. Krekar, who had taken Norwegian authorities to court over the government's decision to extradite him, lost his legal battle when in 2007 the Norwegian Supreme Court declared him a danger to national security. Mainstream Norwegian Muslims, long exasperated with Krekar's many attention-seeking statements in various media, and the impact they had on non-Muslim Norwegians' perceptions of Muslims, sought in various ways to make him leave the country. In one of the more inventive attempts, in 2006 the Norwegian-Pakistani businessman Tawaser 'Tommy' Sharif, through Norwegian media, offered Krekar a lump sum of Norwegian kroner (NOK) 500,000 – if he would only leave.

In 2010, a series of gunshots were fired at Krekar's apartment in Oslo, lightly wounding one of his sons. In the aftermath of the shootings, which have so far not been resolved by police investigations, Norwegian media discovered Facebook pages with thousands of followers in which barely veiled incitements to violence against Krekar had been posted, along with precise directions to his apartment. In an interview in Arabic with Arab news media in Oslo in 2011 (he had by that time declared himself unwilling to be interviewed by Norwegian media), Krekar issued open death threats against prominent Norwegian politicians who had been involved in the decision to extradite him in 2003. On a radical Islamist webpage, he also issued warrants for the killing of two named Norwegian residents of Kurdish origin, who had publicly burnt sections of the Qur'an in symbolic remembrance of the thousands of Kurdish victims of Saddam Hussein's regime's use of mustard gas in the vicinity of Halabja in northern Iraq during the *Anfal* Campaign in 1988. In April 2012, Krekar was sentenced in the Oslo Magistrate's Court to five years' imprisonment for his threats against Norwegian politicians as well as the threats against Norwegian Kurds.

Among those attending Krekar's trial at Oslo Magistrate's Court was a small group of radical Islamists of Salafi-jihadist orientation. This small group, calling itself 'The Prophet's Ummah', had, according to both the Police Security Services (PST) and Norwegian terror experts, started to coalesce in 2010. It had initially referred to itself as 'The Volunteers' (*'De Frivillige'*) on various social media in Norway. The much more Islamic-sounding name 'The Prophet's Ummah' –

which also entailed a verbal bid for Islamic legitimacy – had first started to appear in 2012. In 2010, a Norwegian-Pakistani from Oslo east by the name of Arfan Qadeer Bhatti (1977–), who had a long criminal record involving assaults with knives and shootings, was a prominent member of the Young Guns gang in Oslo, and was widely suspected of having fired shots at the Jewish synagogue in Oslo in 2006, emerged as the leader of the Prophet's Ummah. In the late 1990s, prior to one of his eight criminal convictions, Bhatti had already been diagnosed as having a dissociative personality disorder. He was among a small group of Muslims who, via Facebook, managed to mobilize 3,000 demonstrators, mainly young and Muslim, at Oslo's University Square in central Oslo on 12 February 2009. The demonstrators were protesting against the fact that the liberal tabloid *Dagbladet* had on 3 February published on its front page a cartoon depicting the Prophet Muhammad as a pig. Paradoxically, the cartoon, originally drawn by a female Israeli settler with extremist views in Hebron in the occupied Palestinian West Bank, had been brought to *Dagbladet*'s attention by Bhatti himself. Bhatti alleged that he had found the cartoon on a Facebook page linked to the Police Security Services (PST). On 3 February, hundreds of Muslim newspaper agents in Oslo refused to carry *Dagbladet* on their newspaper stands, and the following weekend hundreds of Muslim taxi-owners in and around Oslo left their taxis parked in a peaceful protest.

Having learned in advance that Bhatti was one of the central organizers of the demonstration, the Islamic Council of Norway issued a press statement in which they warned Norwegian Muslims against taking part in the demonstration. The demonstration at Oslo University Square proceeded peacefully, but one of the invited speakers, Mohyeldeen Mohammed (1986–), a troubled Norwegian-Iraqi Muslim from the small town of Larvik, used the occasion to warn against a 'September 11 on Norwegian soil' if Norwegian liberal media continued apace with such provocations. Mohammed, who at the time was a student of introductory Arabic at the University of Medina in Saudi Arabia (from which he would later be expelled for 'political activity'), would in the aftermath also become known for declaring to a Norwegian newspaper reporter that he supported capital punishment for homosexual practice. From the very outset, the Salafi-jihadist groupuscule around Bhatti was closely monitored by the PST. In February 2013, a twenty-four-year-old Norwegian convert to Islam by the name of Per Yousef Bartho Assidiq (Assidiq 2013) disclosed on his personal blog that he had been recruited as an informer for PST at the age of nineteen in 2009. The PST had approached him at his place of work in the small town of Larvik, on the basis of his known Facebook contacts with Mohyeldeen Mohammed, a childhood friend. Assidiq, who struggled with both Asperger's and ADHD, and received copious amounts of hate mail and threats from Norwegian right-wing extremists after converting to Islam in early 2009, described his discomfort at being pressured to act as an informant for the PST for two years. The PST's pressure on him ceased only when his mother, in a fit of rage, contacted the PST directly in order to complain.

By February 2012, the group around Bhatti and Mohammed tried to mobilize support for a demonstration against the Norwegian military presence in Afghanistan, but amid warnings from the ICN, a mere thirty demonstrators turned up for the demonstration in front of the Norwegian parliament in Oslo. Some associates of this group were arrested by Norwegian police a few days in advance of the demonstration, after the discovery of a YouTube video containing footage of the Norwegian king, the prime minister and the minister of foreign affairs, replete with *nasheed* chants characteristic of Salafi-jihadist videos and death threats. When fury over the YouTube video *Innocence of Muslims*, produced by an American-Egyptian-Coptic former criminal and his associates among extreme right-wing US Islamophobes, led to demonstrations instigated by Salafis in the Middle East as well as other parts of the Muslim 'world' in September 2012, Bhatti and Mohammed's group mobilized for a demonstration outside the US embassy in central Oslo. This attracted an estimated eighty demonstrators, and lavish attention from the Norwegian media, which predictably found a group willing to chant slogans in support of Osama Bin Laden and al-Qaeda more interesting than the fact that a similar, but entirely peaceful, demonstration organized by the ICN, and supported by the Lutheran Bishop of Oslo, Ole Bjørn Kvarme, as well as the Conservative Party mayor of Oslo, Fabian Stang, attracted 6,000 Muslims.

Following this incident, intense media attention was brought to bear on the group, which was estimated by sources within the Norwegian Muslim communities to number fewer than a hundred followers, with a maximum of twenty to thirty individuals as hard-core members.[30] Rather unsurprisingly, it turned out that, like Bhatti, a number of the leading figures in the Prophet's Ummah had long and serious criminal records (Zaman 2012). Attraction to radical Islamism or Salafi-jihadism is more often than not framed by terrorism experts and laypersons alike as a function of ideology, and, as such, distinctive from attraction to right-wing extremism, which, as we have seen, is usually framed as a function of individual psychology. Yet even the most cursory study of the background of the core members of the Prophet's Ummah in Norway points to troubled personal backgrounds. Bhatti and Mohammed, along with an unknown yet small number of volunteer jihadists, had made their way to the border regions of Afghanistan, Pakistan and Syria by late 2012. In Syria, some Norwegian Muslims were reported to have aligned themselves with the Jabhat al-Nusra, a Salafi-jihadist group operating in and around Aleppo in northern Syria (Bakkefoss 2013), and designated as a terrorist group by US authorities in December 2012 (Al-Jazeera 2012). By November 2013, the Police Security Services (PST) in Norway estimated that a total of forty Muslims from Norway had travelled to Syria and aligned themselves with Salafi-jihadist factions there. Four of these were believed to have been killed in action (Svendsen et al. 2013). Political concern over the potential radicalization of young Norwegian Muslims reached fever pitch after it became known in October 2013 that two young Norwegian-Somali girls from Bærum outside Oslo, aged sixteen and nineteen, had travelled to Syria on their own (Brenna and Hopperstad 2013). Meanwhile, in Norway, a new spokesperson for the 'Prophet's Ummah' emerged in Ubaydullah Hussain, real name Arslan Maroof Hussain, a man in his late twenties who had until recently appeared a talented and well-integrated young Muslim from Oslo east. In October 2012, he was arrested, and charged with threats against two newspaper reporters in e-mail correspondence, as well as Facebook threats directed against Jews in Norway. The indictment was later extended to include serious fraud, as the Oslo police discovered that Hussain was in possession of funds completely out of proportion to his income. In December 2012, Norwegian media reported that Hussain and the Prophet's Ummah had established links with the rabble-rousing radical Islamist Anjem Choudary (NTB 2012c), formerly of Hizb ut-Tahrir, al-Mujahiroon, al-Ghurabaa, Islam4UK and Muslims Against Crusades. Choudary, who had visited Oslo and Norway to appear as witness for the defence of Mullah Krekar in the appeals court at Borgarting Lagmannsrett in the autumn of 2012, was seen posing with two young members of the group in pictures which Hussain had posted on his Facebook page. In October 2013, Arfan Bhatti, who had at that point been missing for ten months after travelling to Pakistan for jihad, was located at a prison in the Federally Administrated Tribal Areas (FATA) in north-western Pakistan by the Norwegian TV2 (Zaman 2013). He informed TV2's reporter that he had been sentenced to six years' imprisonment under the so-called Frontier Crimes Regulation (FCR) Section 40,[31] but did not want any contact with or assistance from Norwegian authorities, as this would in his view amount to accepting assistance from 'infidels' (*kuffar*). However menacing the message of the 'Prophet's Ummah' seemed to Norwegians, however, it seemed clear that Hussain and those of the group's sympathizers who remained in Norway were more interested in the media attention they could get than in planning actual acts of terror and violence on Norwegian soil. They were proverbial 'polarization entrepreneurs' and 'hobby jihadists', basking in the popular outrage their statements, broadcast at amplified volumes by the Norwegian media, generated. But if there is anything the case of Anders Behring Breivik and the 22/7 terror attacks underlined, it was the strategic necessity for any would-be terrorist to keep below the radar of the police intelligence agencies.

A centre which cannot hold?

'Things fall apart; the centre cannot hold; / Mere anarchy is loosed upon the world,' wrote the Irish poet William Butler Yeats. It is premature to write a modern history of Islam in Norway. Now, at the time of writing, it would seem that the pragmatism and dialogue-oriented approach of mainstream Norwegian Muslims, institutionalized since the 1990s in and through the centrist umbrella organization the

Islamic Council of Norway, is seriously challenged by the emergence of Salafi groupings attracting a sizeable number of Norwegian Muslim youth (and the puritan Salafis are certainly more attractive than the Salafi-jihadists). A number of today's young Muslims seem far angrier and more oriented towards conflict than their elders ever were. There is no denying that the current identity politics of some Norwegian Muslim youth gives grounds for concern, and that there seems to be a greater level of internal polarization according to generational and doctrinal lines among Norwegian Muslims. Yet this is in part an optical illusion generated by the lavish attention Norwegian liberal media are paying – in a time of decreasing sales and revenues – to young and marginalized Muslims in Norway who are interested in and are willing to play the role of the Muslim which non-Muslim Norwegians have valid reasons to fear. It is no coincidence that young Muslim males feature most prominently in the landscape of this new Muslim identity politics. In the media silences about what goes on in Norwegian Muslims' everyday lives that are hidden behind the media headlines, young Norwegian Muslims continue their onward silent march towards educational and professional attainment, a greater public presence and a greater level of mutual tolerance and respect in an increasingly multicultural Norwegian society.

3 | THE FEAR OF SMALL NUMBERS: ON READING A TERRORIST TRACT

Black milk of daybreak we drink you at night. (Paul Celan,
Death Fugue, 1952)

A declaration of independence

Anders Behring Breivik's grandiosely titled *2083: A European Declaration of Independence*, the 1,516-page tract that he uploaded on the internet and sent to some 1,003 European and other 'cultural conservatives' in the hours before committing the atrocities of 22 July 2011, is in all respects a strange document. It is structured like a hypertext, which allows for 'extensive cross-referencing between related sections of texts and associated graphic material' (see ODE 2003). This is both an ideological tract and a detailed instruction manual for potential future solo terrorists. Much of it is a pastiche: it is composed of excerpts from academic articles, blog essays and Wikipedia entries that Behring Breivik appears to have found during his lengthy sessions on the internet; it is also partly composed of Behring Breivik's own words. He appears to have taken two years to write it. The very length of the document and the limited time devoted to its production suggest that it may indeed be an expression of the author's state of hypergraphia, or an 'overwhelming urge to write'.[1]

Not all excerpts in the tract are properly attributed, and it would be beyond the scope of this study to ascertain precisely which of the many words are actually Behring Breivik's own. He uploaded this document on to the internet under the pen name 'Andrew Berwick', supposedly writing from 'London'. London has a wider symbolic function for Behring Breivik in the tract, in that it was here that he alleges that a new secretive network of Knights Templar, who will eventually push back the Islamic 'conquest' and 'colonization' of Europe, was founded in 2002. The document, written in UK English,[2] certainly contains a number of grammatical infelicities and misspellings that are most obvious in the sections apparently written by Behring Breivik himself. Yet despite these imperfections, his writing suggests a competence in English which is above average for Norwegians with high-school qualifications. When Behring Breivik wants to be emphatic about a particular point in the tract, much like young adolescents, he tends to use capital letters: 'WE DO NOT WANT AND WILL NOT TOLERATE ISLAM IN EUROPE!' This we find in Section Three of the tract. Similar use of capital letters is to be found in the thousands of e-mails that Behring Breivik wrote in the years leading up to 22/7 (see Stormark 2012). The third and final section of the document, 'A declaration of pre-emptive war', bears the heaviest imprint of Behring Breivik's own personality and imaginings. It is also the most disturbed, delusional and incoherent part of the tract. 'Pre-emptive war' is, of course, meant to imply that the acts of terror executed on 22/7 were part of a legitimate 'self-defence' of the 'European indigenous people' whom he envisions he is representing and defending. He appears to have borrowed the term from the neoconservative lexicon of the Bush administration ahead of the 2003 US military invasion of Iraq. Section Three includes a personal log (MF 3.154), an 'interview' with a 'Justiciar Knight Commander of the Pauperes Comilitones Christi Templique Solomonici (PCCTS), Knights Templar' (MF 3.153), photo material of Behring Breivik which forms part of his marketing package, and extensive and unflattering comments on his friends and family. Section Three is interestingly introduced by a 'legal disclaimer' asserting that it is a work of 'fiction', the 'description' and 'methods' of which the 'author' or 'distributor' does not accept or condone. It seems likely that this legal disclaimer was included as a safety precaution in the event of the tract being discovered by the Norwegian Police Security Services (PST) or other intelligence units in Norway prior to 22/7. For in that case, it would be an open question whether its author would be liable for criminal prosecution. The chilling effects that the tract generates stem not only from the post hoc knowledge of Behring Breivik's actually having turned his 'fighting words' into 'fighting actions', but also from the sheer calculated nature and meticulous planning of the acts of terror outlined in it. The bombing of Government Headquarters in Oslo on 22/7 was part of a diversionary tactic which predictably led the 'enemy forces' to concentrate in one location, while Behring Breivik continued on to his next target. Utøya was likely to have been selected owing to its being 'soft' and 'unprotected'. Behring Breivik claimed that there were other terrorist cells in the process of being activated when arrested at Utøya. These claims were a deliberate attempt to mislead the police, an attempt he had outlined in his tract.[3] The document even contains a prepared speech to the court to be used in the event that Behring Breivik should survive. He did in fact cite directly from this speech in his first court appearance.

2083: A European Declaration of Independence was more or less completely ignored by the first psychiatrists tasked with assessing Behring Breivik's state of mind, namely Torgeir Husby and Synne Sørheim. In the heated public debate which ensued in Norway after the release of their report and its conclusion, one could easily be led to the assumption that Behring Breivik was either simply mad or a political terrorist motivated by ideological hatreds. But on closer scrutiny, the distinction may not be as clear cut as many would like to think. For paranoia 'is the most intellectual of the mental disorders, the one most likely to be associated with complex political ideologies' (Robins and Post 1997: 9). And 'the political paranoid has not fully departed the world of reality' but 'rather, he clings too single-mindedly to a part of it, exaggerating to a pathological degree' (ibid.: 19).

Behring Breivik's tract may be full of personal fabrications, statistical manipulation and partly unattributed uses of other people's texts, yet the underlying ideological logic expressed in it is clear and terrifying enough. In short, it describes an ongoing 'Islamization of Europe', which forms part of a constant 1,400-year war between Christendom and Islam, the political and social elites of Europe (the 'cultural Marxists' and the 'multicultural/ist alliance') which have entered into a 'devil's pact' with the enemy leading to the impending establishment of a Eurabia dominated and governed by Muslims. Like Bat Ye'or (see especially Ye'or 2011) Behring Breivik sometimes appears to believe that the de facto Islamization of Europe and Norway has already taken place. For example, in a post on Document. no on 3 December 2009, he refers to himself as a 'first-generation dhimmi'. 'Dhimmi' is Ye'or and other Eurabia authors' term of choice for a person supposedly living under Islamic rule, or 'dhimmitude', in contemporary Europe. The term 'dhimmitude' is a neologism which combines the transliterated Arabic term for non-Muslim under Muslim rule, i.e. 'dhimmi', with the French suffix for 'being in a state of', i.e. *'tude'*. Denoting not only a material condition, but also a psychological state, the term 'dhimmitude' has been ascribed to the Lebanese Maronite Phalangist leader and warlord Bashir Gemayel (1947–82) (Griffith 1998: 620).[4] According to the tract, for 'Christian conservatives' who want to defend European culture and values, all democratic means have now been 'exhausted' and violence against the very same elites who enabled Muslims to establish 'bridgeheads' for the impending 'Islamization' of Europe on European soil is the only available option left if Europeans are to survive the 'existential threat' to Europe and Europeans posed by Islam and embodied by the presence of Muslims resident in Europe.

Behring Breivik considered the terror attacks as a way to 'market' his tract. The paradox of this is of course that a tract of this length does not appear to serve marketing purposes very well. Behring Breivik's marketing package included a YouTube video introducing the tract and a series of photos of himself posing in various outfits. Behring Breivik envisions himself as a chivalric knight of the 'Knights Templar' or PCCTS (see MF 3.11), a secretive outfit supposedly dating back to the Crusades and allegedly re-established at a secret session attended by twelve Europeans in London in April 2002 (see MF 3.12).[5]

Behring Breivik sees 'shock attacks' such as 22/7 as a way to create 'important military and ideological reference points' and to break through 'the strict censorship regime of the cultural Marxists/multiculturalists' imposed 'through the media'. Such terror attacks are, in Behring Breivik's own imaginings, instruments for 'educating' the 'European peoples' about 'the ongoing political, social and demographical [sic] development' (MF 3.16). Behring Breivik refers to 'phases 1 and 2' in the ongoing 'Western European civil war'. Phase 1 is said to have started with the NATO bombings of Serbia in 1999 and will last until 2070. It is no less than 'a primary objective' to distribute the tract in order to rally 'more Europeans for the cause' by 'creating awareness of specifically defined topics' (MF 3.16).

Øyvind Strømmen has suggested, on the basis of Behring Breivik's own postings on an internet forum linked to the PP's Youth Organization FpU (Fremskrittspartiets Ungdom) from 2002 to 2003, that the centrality of the NATO bombing of Serbia in 1999 is a post-hoc rationalization aimed at adapting Behring Breivik's personal history to the ideological narrative of the tract (Strømmen 2011a: 68). However, it has been established that he visited West Africa as early as 2002. In the tract, he alleges that he travelled to Liberia's capital, Monrovia, to meet a Serbian war criminal (described as 'a Serbian crusader and war hero who had killed many Muslims in battle'; MF: 3.153). Norwegian police have identified the Serbian war criminal that Behring Breivik claims to have met as Milorad Ulemek (1965–) (Johansen and Foss 2012). Ulemek is a former soldier in the French Foreign Legion who in the course of the Balkan wars in the 1990s volunteered for the war criminal Arkan's (Žejlko Ražnatović, 1952–2000) Serb Volunteer Guard (aka 'Arkan's Tigers') and later became a commander in a Special Operations Unit (JSO) of the Serb Army. In 2007 a Serbian court sentenced Ulemek to forty years' imprisonment for having masterminded the assassination of Serbia's pro-Western prime minister, Zoran Djindić (1952–2003), in Belgrade in 2003 (ibid.), and for having participated in the assassination of former Serbian prime minister Ivan Stambolić in 2000 and attempted assassinations of Serbian opposition politician Vuk Drascović (1946–) in 1999 and 2000.[6]

Serbia during the Balkan wars of the 1990s is, in Behring Breivik's tract, a crucial symbol of a purported heroic and visionary 'resistance' to the alleged 'Islamization' of Europe. So much so that in a European world remade by a 'cultural conservative elite' coming to power, the Serbs would be offered financial compensation for the NATO bombing of Serbia in 1999.[7] So even if questions relating to Serbia and Serbian ultra-nationalism appeared to elicit little interest from Behring Breivik's side in court, what has become known of Anders Behring Breivik's many postings on various websites in the years preceding the terrorist attacks on 22/7 does suggest a consistent interest in Serbia and Serbian ultra-nationalist narratives.

Propaganda by deed

The most basic element of any act of terror is communication. The concept of 'propaganda by deed' was introduced in 1876 by the

Italian Federation of the Anarchist International (Townsend 2002: 55), which declared terrorism to be 'the most efficient means of propaganda and the one most capable of breaking through to the deepest social strata' (ibid.). However, acts of terror in and of themselves do not necessarily communicate, and there is nothing new in terrorists publishing material outlining their causes – especially in the age of the largely uncensored internet.

'Spectacular operations ... are the only way to be heard' (MF: 3.153). What is striking in Behring Breivik's case is precisely the extent to which his act of terror is subsumed under the desire to propagate the message of his tract. In one of several breaches of his own safety precautions in spring 2011, he sent out a version of his tract, under the name 'Andrew Berwick', to a serious and well-established Norwegian academic publisher, offering this firm the publication rights.[8] Behring Breivik also referred extensively to the tract he was writing in a series of posts in 2009 on the Islamophobic website Document.no.

In Section 3.60 of his tract, which provides instructions to possible future 'resistance fighters', Behring Breivik likens 'Justiciar knights' or 'resistance fighters' to 'marketers' or 'sales representatives'. There is a clear imprint of Behring Breivik's own past as a low-ranking telephone salesman, work he was quite good at, according to his former colleagues who later recalled his salesmanship back in the late 1990s. 'It is important', he writes, 'that all resistance fighters learn the basics of sales and marketing. Failing to understand basic primary concepts of sales and marketing will significantly limit the impact and efficiency of the message we wish to send' (MF 3.60).

Behring Breivik's main influences

'Anders Behring Breivik has his own ideology, which none of us really understands,' asserted the ousted chief of the Police Security Services (PST), Janne Kristiansen,[9] in the parliamentary hearings in November 2012 with regard to the 22/7 Commission's report (Engset and Sandvik 2012). In Norway after 22/7, Kristiansen can hardly be said to be alone in putting forward this assertion. A long line of people from academics to court psychiatrists to politicians have similarly denied that Behring Breivik espoused and acted upon an ideology. Two basic questions which have to be addressed in this context, then, are what the term 'ideology' can be said to refer to, and to what extent Behring Breivik, based on his writings and public statements, can be seen as having an ideology.

'Ideologies ... map the political and social world for us,' writes political scientist Michael Freeden (Freeden 2003: 2). 'Through our diverse ideologies, we provide competing interpretations of what the facts might mean. Every interpretation, each ideology, is one such instance of imposing a pattern – some form of structure or organization – on how we read (and misread) political facts, events, occurrences, actions, and how we see images and hear voices' (ibid.: 3). Ideology as a form of political map-making is also a central theme for a number of other academic authors on the topic (see Mannheim 1936; Eagleton 1991; Hawkes 2003; Žižek 1994). We often tend to assume that an ideology is an entity with a capital 'I', or, in other words, that the term must refer to some sort of grand and coherent narrative about how the world should work, underpinned by much and elaborate theorizing of a more or less rational sort. For that is what the usage of the term has led us to expect in connection with ideological '-isms' such as liberalism, socialism, Marxism, Nazism or Islamism. Yet much of what we readily accept as ideologies with a capital 'I' is not necessarily coherent and all-encompassing, let alone exclusively rational: Nazism certainly mobilized structures of affect, rather than rationality, sensology rather than ideology in relation to European 'strangers within our gates', and with horrific consequences; Islamism's mobilizing of affect in relation to the 'Western' often falls short of the rational. In light of Freeden's definition of the term ideology, it makes perfectly good sense to describe Behring Breivik as having and espousing an ideology. By arguing and maintaining that Behring Breivik's actions on 22/7 were ideologically inspired, however, I do not mean to suggest that his actions can be explained in and through ideological factors alone. Mono-causal explanations of this complex phenomenon are best avoided. Whether one wishes to understand acts of terror in particular, or also the existing support for ideologies of hatred in general, one must consider them as the concert of a number of different factors that have functioned together (see Fangen 2012: 178). Anders Behring

Breivik's *2083* is a cut-and-paste, hybrid document, and one that borrows heavily at that, but nevertheless it constitutes an ideology that clearly and identifiably locates itself on the extreme right wing of the ideological spectrum. Unlike the right-wing ideologues whose writings he is inspired by, Behring Breivik views himself first and foremost as a 'man of action'. In his tract, he writes disparagingly of individuals whose response to the 'existential threat' from Islam and Muslims in Europe is to 'establish another right-wing blog'. In court during the 22/7 trial, Behring Breivik, who could name only one author whose work he had actually read, namely Ayn Rand[10] (see Enebakk 2012: 80), described himself as a 'mere salesman for thoughts that others have made' (cited in ibid.: 81).

For all its factual misrepresentations, historical distortions and contradictions, this tract does reflect Behring Breivik's wish to appear ideologically coherent.[11] In the aftermath of 22/7 he claimed that his ideology was fully formed when he was twenty-one. But this is difficult to reconcile with the fact that the 'Eurabia' authors he appears to be most inspired by did not publish their work on 'Eurabia' until after 2004.

There are those who, in the aftermath of 22/7, rushed to the dubious conclusion that Behring Breivik was detached from mainstream sources of information (see Ash 2011). There can be little doubt that part of the radicalization process undergone by Behring Breivik in the years leading to 22/7 was his seeking alternative sources of information – 'counterpublics'[12] structured by Islamophobia – on the internet. Yet a thorough investigation demonstrates that many of Behring Breivik's sources were in fact quite mainstream and hardly unusual (Brown 2011a). His tract links to Wikipedia articles some 134 times and to mainstream media some 108 times, compared to, for example, 104 links to European nationalist sources (ibid.).

So who are the authors who feature most prominently in Behring Breivik's imaginaries? As it turns out, they are all authors who promote 'Eurabia' theories. The term 'Eurabia' itself is used no fewer than 171 times in his tract *2083* (Van Vuuren 2013). From 7 September 2009 to 25 March 2011, Anders Behring Breivik actively posted comments on Document.no under his own name.[13] These posts provide further data on his sources of ideological inspiration and world view: on 3 December 2009, he names Bat Ye'or, Robert Spencer and 'Fjordman' as his main sources of inspiration (Brown 2011b).

In a post on Document.no dated 14 September 2009, in which he underlines the need for a 'pan-European platform' to generate a 'cultural conservative consolidation', he refers to a 'pan-European/US milieu' including Robert Spencer, 'Fjordman', Atlas (Pamela Geller of the right-wing blog *Atlas Shrugs*) as the current 'epicentre of political analysis'. These are, to Behring Breivik's mind, authors of what he refers to as 'the Vienna School', an apparent intertextual play on the centrality of the Ottoman defeat at the 'Gates of Vienna' in 1683, an association familiar to followers of the blog site of the same name (Strømmen 2011b: 22). A post by Behring Breivik on Document.no dated 2 December 2009 suggests that he conceives of this 'school' as a 'cultural conservative' alternative and challenger to the 'Frankfurt school' in modern critical theory, which is seen as composed of 'cultural Marxists'. Another post on the same website some days later, on 6 December 2009, indicates that Behring Breivik conceives of the Norwegian Progress Party (PP) as adhering to '"the Vienna school"'. He is, as I will show in Chapters 4 and 5, correct in assuming that PP politicians have read and used 'Eurabia' authors extensively in recent years, though it is not known whether these include his own favourite 'Eurabia' authors, and few PP politicians are likely to recognize his term for this group of like-minded counter-jihadists. His tract links to Spencer's *Jihad Watch* some 116 times, Edward Le May's *Gates of Vienna* blog (where 'Fjordman' was particularly active) some 86 times, and 'Fjordman' 114 times (Brown 2011a).

'Fjordman's writings are absolutely central to Behring Breivik: No fewer than 45 of "Fjordman's" blog essays are included in Behring Breivik's tract' (Borchgrevink 2012: 168). The very title of the tract is borrowed from an essay by 'Fjordman' that was published at *Gates of Vienna* in 2007 (Strømmen 2011b: 22). Behring Breivik's favourite quote ('The tree of liberty must be refreshed from time to time with the blood of patriots and tyrants'), repeated in mantra-like fashion in Section Three of *2083*, comes from Thomas Jefferson, but Behring Breivik appears to have found it in a blog essay by 'Fjordman' published at *Gates of Vienna* in 2008 (Enebakk 2012: 84). According to Behring Breivik's Document.no post on 2 December 2009, he first discovered 'Fjordman's' essays in 2008. Behring Breivik's enthusiasm is quite unrestrained. In December 2009, he recommended 'Fjordman's' blog essay 'Defeating Eurabia' as 'the perfect Christmas gift for family and friends' at Document.no. Behring Breivik also expressed his enthusiasm for 'Fjordman' and his blog writings by sending him a number of e-mails from 2009 to 2010 and by asking in late 2009 to meet him in person (Hopperstad et al. 2011). But according to 'Fjordman's' own account, he turned down a meeting with Behring Breivik 'not because he [Behring Breivik] was referring to violence [in his e-mails], but because he appeared to me as being a bore – like a salesman of vacuum cleaners' (ibid.). 'Fjordman's' own central influence is undoubtedly Bat Ye'or (see Chapter 5), with whom he appears to have been in close contact throughout his years as an extreme right-wing Islamophobic blogger.

'Fjordman's' identity revealed

Prior to 22/7, few Norwegians would have heard about the blogger 'Fjordman'.[14] However, his work was known to a number of Norwegian 'Eurabia' enthusiasts. One of his essays had been included in an appendix in *Selvmordsparadigmet* (*The Suicide Paradigm*), a biological racist monograph by right-winger Ole Jørgen Anfindsen, and lesbian secular feminist Hege Storhaug and her state-supported organization Human Rights Service (HRS) had referred extensively to his essays.[15] In the netherworld of European counter-jihad websites, 'Fjordman' has been a star for a number of years; it was here that the future mass murderer Anders Behring Breivik must certainly have first encountered his writings.

In the weeks following 22/7, Norwegian and international news reporters and editors searched frantically to uncover the real identity of 'Fjordman'. On the advice of his lawyers, who must have known about the leaks from the Oslo police headquarters, leaks that were to characterize the 22/7 investigations from the very outset, 'Fjordman' revealed his identity in an exclusive interview with the tabloid *VG* on 5 August 2011. In the tabloid's eagerness to get the scoop, its reporters gave Peder Are 'Fjordman' Nøstvold Jensen a virtually uncontested forum in which to present his extreme right-wing views on Islam, Muslims and immigration. The then thirty-six-year-old

Nøstvold Jensen, a care worker at a daycare centre in an Oslo suburb, proved to be the proverbial dour Norwegian Everyman, replete with blue jeans, white T-shirt and a shoulder bag. Nøstvold Jensen, born and raised in Ålesund on the Norwegian west coast (Sætre 2013a), had been an undergraduate student of Arabic at the University of Bergen and at the American University in Cairo, Egypt. A two-page article in his home-town newspaper *Sunmørsposten* in 2000 shows a young and bespectacled student eagerly anticipating his departure for Cairo. In Norway, such a family and educational background do not typically predispose one to adopt and to propagate extreme right-wing views. And as a matter of fact, his family appears to have had sympathies for the Social Left Party (Sosialistisk Venstreparti, SV), and as a young man Nøstvold Jensen was for a short period active in this party's youth branch, the Socialist Youth (Sosialistisk Ungdom, SU) (Enebakk 2012: 49).

According to Nøstvold Jensen's own account in *VG* and that of his extreme right-wing friends in Denmark, it was in Cairo that he experienced his 'radical epiphany'. According to these friends, the twenty-six-year-old Peder Are Nøstvold Jensen witnessed Egyptians 'celebrating' the terror attacks on the Twin Towers in New York and the Pentagon in Washington, DC, on 11 September 2001. His neighbours, according to Nøstvold Jensen, celebrated the attacks by having cakes (Vikås et al. 2011b). As with many urban legends in circulation among extreme right-wing adherents of the 'Eurabia' genre, it is impossible to verify this narrative.[16] Nøstvold Jensen would later backtrack on this account, and claim that 9/11 was a mere chain in a personal process which took years to develop, but that it had certainly escalated as a result of his experience in Cairo on that day (Sætre 2013a: 100). From 2002 to 2003, Nøstvold Jensen worked for the Temporary International Presence in Hebron (TIPH), a Scandinavian-led monitoring mission in the Israeli-occupied city of Hebron on the West Bank, established in the wake of Baruch Goldstein (1956–94), an Israeli-American extreme right-winger and settler from the Israeli settlement of Kiriyat Arba on the outskirts of Hebron, having massacred twenty-nine Palestinian worshippers and wounded another 125 at the Mosque of Abraham in Hebron in 1994. None of his colleagues at TIPH had recollections of him engaging in 'extreme rhetoric' (Brox 2011). During Nøstvold Jensen's TIPH service, two TIPH observers – one Turk and a Swiss – were gunned down by armed Palestinian men in the village of Halloul near Hebron (Enebakk 2012: 51). The gunmen were, according to media reports at the time, from the Fatah-aligned al-Aqsa Brigade.

In 2004, Nøstvold Jensen obtained a master's degree from the Centre for Technology, Innovation and Culture (TIK), the Faculty of Social Sciences, University of Oslo. His sixty-page dissertation *Blogging Iran: A Case Study of Iranian English Language Weblogs* (Jensen 2004) is an entirely unremarkable and mediocre desk study of English-language weblogs written by Iranians in Iran and in exile during the years of Iran's reformist president Mohammad Khatami (1997–2005). The academic appointed to supervise Nøstvold Jensen's thesis at TIK reported that the student never showed up for any of his supervision meetings, and submitted his thesis without his supervisor's knowledge or assistance (Slaatta 2012: 65).

By 2003 Nøstvold Jensen had started posting internet comments under the pseudonym 'Norwegian kafir' ('*Norsk kafir*') on international blogs (Enebakk 2012: 55). Then, in 2005, after some of his op-eds and letters to the editors were rejected by Norwegian mainstream newspapers, Nøstvold Jensen started blogging as 'Fjordman'. By September 2006, 'Fjordman' had advanced to the status of an 'expert' alongside other self-proclaimed luminaries such as Hege Storhaug, Bat Ye'or, Lars Hedegaard and Bruce Bawer. These experts interacted on an internet forum about the 'death of multiculturalism' on *FrontPage Magazine*. *FrontPage Magazine* was established by the neoconservative ideologue David Horowitz. 'Fjordman' made a name for himself in far-right Islamophobic circles: after 22/7, both Robert Spencer of *Jihad Watch* in the USA (Thorenfeldt and Meland 2011) and Alan Lake, a financier for the English Defence League (EDL) in the UK (Krokfjord and Meldalen 2012), would assert that they had met 'Fjordman' on numerous occasions. From the account of Bruce Bawer, who had been in regular social and e-mail correspondence with 'Fjordman' in the years preceding 22/7, 'Fjordman' had been personally introduced to Robert Spencer and Bat Ye'or (Gisèle Littmann) by Bawer at a right-wing conference in commemoration of the slain Dutch populist right-winger Pim Fortuyn in The Hague in 2006 (see Bawer 2012a).

In spite of 'Fjordman's' belated claims that he found Anders Behring Breivik much too 'boring' to meet, 'Fjordman' was sufficiently interested in Behring Breivik to have spent time engaging in a series of exchanges with him on Document.no. Documentation of these exchanges has led observers to remark that he appeared by far the more radical of the two. 'Fjordman', initially convinced that the terror attacks of 22/7 were the work of radical Islamists, followed the events closely through the media that afternoon and evening. As news of the bombing at Government Headquarters came in, 'Fjordman' gleefully 'reminded' his readers at *Gates of Vienna* that the Norwegian government was 'the most suicidal and cowardly of all European governments' and that Prime Minister Jens Stoltenberg of the Labour Party 'knelt down before Islam'. As news of the attack at Utøya followed, 'Fjordman' described the AUFers as 'a group of anti-Israeli pro-Palestinian young socialists'.

In the aftermath of 22/7, leading Norwegian terrorism researchers expressed the view that 'the leading counter-jihad writers [of the genre that inspired Behring Breivik] have virtually never advocated violence' (see Hegghammer 2011). Yet anyone familiar with the blog essays of 'Fjordman' would know that he had a long record of advocating violence, deportations and the pursuit of ethnic cleansing against Muslims in Norway and Europe.[17]

In *Native Revolt: A European Declaration of Independence*, published at Brusselsjournal.com on 16 March 2007, 'Fjordman' threatened that unless the EU was dismantled, unless multiculturalism was rejected and Muslim immigration stopped, 'appropriate measures' to 'protect our own security and ensure our national survival' would have to be taken. It would not be fully inappropriate to interpret the term 'appropriate measures' here as indicating that 'he is willing to go further' than non-violent means (Strømmen 2007: 23; see also Strømmen 2011b: 57).

In the blog essay 'Preparing for Ragnarök'[18] posted on *Gates of Vienna* on 2 May 2011, 'Fjordman' further asserted that 'we need to make sure, though, that those who have championed the poisonous ideas of multiculturalism and mass immigration of alien tribes *disappear with it*' (cited in Vepsen.org 2011, my emphasis). And in an often repeated statement, 'Fjordman' wrote that 'Islam and all those who practice it must be totally and physically removed from the Western world' (cited in Meland and Melgård 2011). In 'Fjordman's' 2008 blog essay 'Will Holland survive the 21st century?', he 'advises' 'Westerners in general' to 'arm themselves immediately … with guns and the skills to use them' (cited in Enebakk 2012: 71). When a faction of the counter-jihad movement temporarily broke off relations with the violent English Defence League (EDL) in 2011, 'Fjordman' stood by his support of the EDL (see Sætre 2013a: 251). The Norwegian journalist and popular author Øyvind Strømmen was quick in the aftermath of 22/7 to characterize 'Fjordman' as a 'fascist' thinker (as cited in Torgersen 2011). Though there are certainly elements in 'Fjordman's' thinking which lend themselves to his characterization as a fascist (such as the calls for revolutionary forms of nationalist violence aimed at moulding 'the people' into new nationalistic units led by new elites with 'heroic' values), other elements stand at odds with classical forms of fascism, and rather suggest that we are here dealing with a new and hybrid form of extreme right-wing ideology.

Although 'Fjordman' was called in for questioning by the Oslo police in connection with their investigations into 22/7 and the actions of Behring Breivik, he has to date not been charged with any criminal offence. Peder Are Nøstvold Jensen has spent much time and energy from his abode outside of Norway in distancing himself from his ideological fellow traveller Anders Behring Breivik's actions on 22/7. The means for doing so has been to characterize Behring Breivik as a 'violent psychopath' or 'madman' in interviews, blog essays and letters to the editors at various Norwegian mainstream newspapers, and to allege that he himself had never stood for anything but 'anti-terrorism' or 'non-violence' in his writings (see Enebakk 2012: 46 for this). 'Fjordman' was called as witness for the defence in the 22/7 trial, but in the end refused to testify. In conversation with his first psychiatric assessors, Behring Breivik is reported to have said that 'Fjordman writes a lot between the lines, but everyone understands it' (Brenna et al. 2011b). In police interrogations, Anders Behring Breivik's own mother is said to have asserted that 'Fjordman was number one for Anders' (Vikås et al. 2012). In light of the available evidence from Behring Breivik's own tract *2083* and 'Fjordman's' blog entries on various counter-jihadist websites in the years from

2005 to 2011, the conclusion that Behring Breivik was greatly inspired by 'Fjordman's' world views as well as his repeated incitement to violence in a purported defence of a 'European culture and heritage' is in fact unavoidable (see also Enebakk 2012: 48 for this).

In spite of its hybrid, cut-and-paste character, the ideology articulated in Behring Brevik's tract *2083* is fascist in character. Notwithstanding Behring Breivik's own repeated and seemingly obsessional disavowals of fascism in the tract, which one should of course not necessarily take at face value,[19] it remains a fact that fascism is a notoriously imprecise and unreliable analytical term and is frequently used as an 'all-purpose term of abuse' (Passmore 2002: 11). Interestingly enough, Behring Breivik uses it as an all-purpose term of abuse himself when referring to 'left-wing fascists' and when referring to Islam as a 'fascist ideology'. Nevertheless, among elements of the ideology expressed in Behring Breivik's tract that would qualify as fascist is the belief in and a romanticizing of a revolutionary 'cleansing' violence; the appeal to so-called tradition, especially with regard to ascribed gender roles; an anti-intellectualist contempt for existing 'elites' and a Manichaean world view. Yet if fascism is 'a form of ultra-nationalist ideology and practice', Behring Breivik's pan-European or 'macro-nationalist' ideas (see MF: 3.84) and his distancing himself from a totalitarian one-party state model are points that stand at odds with the usual qualification 'fascist'.

The very use of the term fascist may, however, obscure some of what is distinctive and new in the hybrid, cut-and-paste ideology expressed in the tract.[20] Behring Breivik abhors US-style laissez-faire capitalism just as much as he abhors Marxism and Islamism. He purports to support a secular state – even though the official religion of such a state would be Christianity (MF: 3.81). At times he appears as an avatar of environmentalism who could almost be left-wing. The tract even has ideas on 'cultural conservative ways' of dealing with overconsumption, pollution and overpopulation. 'We live in a time of excessive consumerism, where the acquisition of wealth and prestige is the driving force in our lives,' he laments in a tone reminiscent of a Norwegian Zen Buddhist (MF: 3.73).

Uncomfortable as it may be, without examining the tract in which Anders Behring Breivik outlines his motivations, one cannot understand the nature of the peculiar world he had inhabited during the months and years that led up to 22/7 – let alone the horror of his actions on that day. It is necessary to examine this tract to try to understand his attempts to legitimize these terrorist acts as he addresses his imaginary audience. Legitimization, in the words of discourse theorist Antonio Reyes, 'refers to the process by which speakers accredit or license a type of social behavior ... The process of legitimization is enacted by argumentation, that is, by providing arguments that explain our social actions, ideas, thoughts and declarations. In addition, the act of legitimizing or justifying is related to a goal, which, in most cases, seeks our interlocutors' support and approval' (Reyes 2011: 782). What becomes apparent through an attentive reading of Anders Behring Breivik's tract is that his thoughts and ideas do not suddenly appear out of thin air. They are more often than not his adoption of someone else's thoughts and ideas. For example, Behring Breivik borrows extensively from authors of a neoconservative[21] and/or counter-jihadist[22] orientation in an attempt to create 'a hybrid of various right wing [sic] concepts' which to his mind would have 'the potential to gain the support of ... 35% of Europeans' (MF: 3.153). Although the tract appears to be an ideological melange of seemingly unconnected and often contradictory ideas and thoughts, it does reflect a profoundly instrumentalist and neoliberal idea of politics. This is a conception of politics viewed as war in a post-ideological era. This is, after all, a context in which the field of ordinary politics is increasingly presented in financial modelling, where politics is seen as focusing on maximizing mass appeal through various 'marketing strategies'.

The properties of language

Anders Behring Breivik's writings indicate an acute awareness that language is intimately connected to power. Words are weapons (Poole 2006) and exercising control over them is crucial to 'cleansing' Europe of Islam and Muslims. And so, Behring Breivik wages a virtual war on the ordinary meaning of words, terms and concepts. He does so as a way to rationalize the horrendous acts of terror he laid out in meticulous detail; moreover, he does so in an attempt to appear to have a purchase on reality and legitimacy despite his monstrous views and actions. For in his mind, the power of the European social, political, intellectual and media elites is such that the common sense of 'ordinary Europeans' (which he grandiosely imagines himself to represent) is constantly and repeatedly being lost in the 'psychological warfare' of the European 'multiculturalist alliances/cultural Marxists'.

Political correctness

'Political correctness is a mandatory lie in European societies,' Behring Breivik writes (MF: 3.8). The term was popularized by cultural conservatives in the United States in the course of the so-called culture wars of the late 1980s and early 1990s as a way of attacking 'liberal elites' for their defence of gay rights, abortion rights and equal civil rights for individuals of ethnic minorities. As Richard Bernstein noted in 1990, 'the term "politically correct", with its suggestion of Stalinist orthodoxy, is spoken more with irony and disapproval than with reverence' (Bernstein 1990).

To underline the importance of the term for Behring Breivik, the tract contains excerpts from an essay by US cultural conservative pundit William Sturgiss Lind (1947–). Lind's essay is entitled 'The origins of political correctness'. First published in 2000, it has become a key reference for cultural conservatives and it has been posted in English on a number of conservative websites. Lind is a former director of the Center for Cultural Conservatism, and columnist for the *Marine Corps Gazette* and *The American Conservative*. The Center for Cultural Conservatism is linked to the Free Congress Foundation (FCF); the FCF was funded with seed money from ultra-conservative Paul Weyrich in 1974. In his essay, Lind asserts that 'political correctness is cultural Marxism' (Lind 2000). For Lind, the origins of 'political correctness' are unequivocally to be found in 'cultural Marxism', which Lind regards as an attempt to translate the classical economic Marxism of Karl Marx and Friedrich Engels into cultural terms. In line with the 'culturalization of politics',[23] a process to which he both adheres and contributes, Lind clearly sees 'culture' as the central domain of political, intellectual and social contestation in our era. 'Political correctness' as conceived of by Lind and other 'cultural conservatives' implies that there is a potentially treacherous political and academic elite dominating Western societies. He maintains that this elite actively silences (through censorship and demands for self-censorship) the wishes and aspirations of the *vox populi*, whether these be on immigration issues, gay rights, gender relations or the rights of ethnic minorities. The 'we, the people' of cultural conservatives is not necessarily explicitly colour-coded in its discourse, but it does not take much guessing to understand that it claims to be speaking on behalf of WASPs (White Anglo-Saxon Protestants) who are seen as facing a barrage of threats to the status quo that arise from the multiculturalist, feminist, anti-racist and gay and lesbian rights movements. In the Norwegian context, usage of this term has for a long time transcended left–right divides, which means that relatively few of those who frequently use the term in a disparaging sense seem to be aware of its most recent historical origins among US conservatives in the course of the 'culture wars'.

Cultural Marxists

Anders Behring Breivik's definition of 'cultural Marxism' in his tract is, to put it mildly, quite wide ranging. He defines the content of 'cultural Marxist/multiculturalist Alliance 100' (MA100) as the '100 political parties who indirectly or directly support the Islamization of Europe through their support for European multiculturalism' (MF 3.43). The 'multiculturalist establishment' of western Europe today is 'a direct result of Soviet's [sic] WW2 and cold war victory'. The real reason the Soviets can be considered 'victorious' has in fact nothing to do with communism itself: 'Multiculturalism', here defined as 'internationalist Marxism', 'prevailed and was gradually institutionalized in Western European countries through it being spearheaded by the UK, French and German left-wing establishment'.

But the crucial criterion for categorizing a party or movement as 'cultural Marxist' is not at all whether those so characterized espouse some form of Marxist thought or other. In fact, most political parties included in the category quite simply have had nothing whatsoever to do with Marxism, either today or in the past. Instead, according to Behring Breivik's own logic, the crucial criterion for inclusion is whether or not a party is said to espouse 'multiculturalism'. There are no attempts made to define the term 'multiculturalism' in *2083* (see also Hverven 2012: 40). For Behring Breivik, as for so many others in Norway and elsewhere in Europe, 'multiculturalism' is basically a floating signifier. 'The beauty of multiculturalism, for its opponents, is that it can mean whatever you want it to mean as long as you don't like it' (Lentin and Titley 2011: ix). Furthermore, Lentin and Titley argue that 'rejecting multiculturalism has become the proxy for the rejection of lived multiculture' (ibid.: 17). Now, if through the eyes of its main proponents among liberal theorists, multiculturalism referred to a normative political theory about multicultural societies (see Parekh 2000 for one such formulation), then according to all available evidence, and in spite of the conceits of Norwegian populist right-wing academics and politicians (see Toje 2012, for example) who in recent years have argued the opposite, Norway has never been a state, nor had a single government that pursued identifiably multiculturalist policies.[24] In his portmanteau category of the 'Multiculturalist Alliance' of 'Cultural Marxists/suicidal humanists/capitalist globalists' in Norway, Behring Breivik has included *every* political party in Norway with popular support in national (parliamentary) elections greater than 3 per cent[25] – except for one: the PP, of which he was once an active member. Proclivities towards 'cultural Marxism' are also highly gendered: under the chillingly titled 'Killing women in the field of battle', he states summarily that 'approximately 60–70% of all cultural Marxists or suicidal humanist[s] are female' (MF: 3.46). Any 'resistance fighter' will simply have to learn how to kill women, 'even attractive ones'.

The opposition faced by Behring Breivik and other 'cultural conservative resistance fighters' who may think of responding to his call to arms is in all respects monumental; therefore, 'the 3-phase process of destroying and replacing the current cultural Marxist/multiculturalist regimes of Western Europe will not be easy or painless' because they control the media, the political apparatus and the academic institutions of Europe. But these regimes need to be fought for the simple reason that they 'are still committing genocide against the indigenous peoples of Europe by exposing them to more than 25 million Muslims' (MF 3.23). This category of prisoners of conscience may not be known to Amnesty International or Human Rights Watch, but the very same regimes are responsible for the incarceration of 'more than 150,000 [cultural conservative] brothers and sisters for opposing their policies' (MF 3.23).

The 'heroic' visionary

As Bruce Hoffman noted in *Inside Terrorism* (Hoffman 2006), 'the terrorist is fundamentally an *altruist*: he believes that he is serving a "good" cause designed to achieve a greater good for a wider constituency – whether real or imagined – that the terrorist and his organization purports to represent' (ibid.: 37). Part of the narcissistic delusions of grandeur articulated in Behring Breivik's tract relate to his conceptualization of himself as a unique hero designed to wake Europeans from their current slumber over the threats posed by Islam and the presence of Muslims in Europe. Behring Breivik casts himself as a visionary who is able to see into the dark future, learn lessons therefrom, and act accordingly. Thus he asserts in a personal diary (in Section Three of the tract) that 'regardless of the … cultural Marxist propaganda, I will know that I am perhaps the biggest champion of cultural conservatism Europe has ever witnessed since 1950'. For there are only a few select Europeans like Behring Breivik himself who are able to see through 'their governments' indoctrination campaigns' and break the shackles of their identification with their polities when it is 'attacked or criticized' (MF: 3.153). 'People in general will oppose us … because they do not know what we know; their governments have made sure of that.' And what is it that is hidden from the view of all citizens except the enlightened and initiated few (who are familiar with, for example, Bat Ye'or's work on 'Eurabia')? What is hidden is the conspiracy aimed at 'Islamizing' Europe, the conspiracy that the EU and its 'multiculturalist/cultural Marxist' elites are involved with.

The battle for legitimacy in which Behring Breivik engages in his tract is also a battle over the definition of the enemy. In a highly revealing passage, he offers the following advice concerning the definitional battle of terms:

> Don't let the multiculturalist define what racism is or isn't. Keeping an African against his will in the basement is racism. Loving your extended family/your ethnic group and fighting for ethnic

and/or indigenous rights does not make you a racist, quite the opposite in fact. It makes you a civil rights activist. Creating a pro-indigenous and/or pro-ethnic movement does not make it a 'white supremacy' ['white supremacist'] movement, but rather an indigenous rights movement or even a civil rights movement. Anyone who calls you a racist due to these reasons proves very clearly that HE [sic] is the real racist, as he obviously ONLY [sic] attacks European rights [sic] movement. He is therefore an anti-European racist supporting the anti-European hate ideology known as multiculturalism. The cultural Marxists/multiculturalists have gone to great lengths to change the very definition of the word racist ... Loving your ethnic group and fighting for the interests of your tribe is NOT [sic] and will never be racist. Nevertheless, the cultural Marxist system would have everyone think otherwise.

The attentive reader of this section will already have noted that part of the rhetorical armoury for disavowing claims of racism here consists in reinscribing what the author clearly sees as an existential struggle for the preservation of one's 'ethnic group' – defined in basically biological and racial terms consonant with racialist modes of thinking – through the insertion of terms with positive historical connotations. The racism of our time is in Simon Weaver's terms a 'liquid racism' (Weaver 2010) or a racism which refuses to be named and contested as such, and Behring Breivik is on this point a child of our times. So the existential struggle becomes part of a struggle for 'indigenous rights', as if 'white' native Europeans represented a 'tribe' in the Amazon forest on the verge of its very extinction, or a struggle for 'civil rights', as if Behring Breivik were a latter-day Martin Luther King Jr marching through Selma, Alabama, during the civil rights struggle in 1965. The model of one's own ethnic group as an extended family and ideally expressed in the ethnically homogenous nation is of course one known to all scholars of modern nationalism from Benedict Anderson (Anderson 1983) to Ernest Gellner (1983). Though it can hardly be said that Behring Breivik's representation of his own family in the tract presents the family model as being anything like a unit of affection.[26] Still, the emotional effect the writer intended to generate among readers through his repeated invocations of the 'ethnic group' as an 'extended family' is supposedly affectionate.

Behring Breivik in the 'narrative of entitlement' (Vetlesen 2011) that is *2083* presents himself as a Christ-like redeemer of Europe, a Nietzschean *übermensch* who has been accorded the powers of decision over the life and death of thousands, if not millions, of Europeans. He has awarded himself this role in the cultural-conservative Europe that will rise as a phoenix from the ashes that will be the cleansing consequence of a continent-wide civil war, a war he intends to instigate. It is on this point in the tract that Anders Behring Breivik is at his most delusional and where his thoughts are most reminiscent of the apocalyptic and millenarian undercurrents in medieval European Christianity (see Cohn 1957; Gray 2007).

Multiculturalism

If we are to believe Anders Behring Breivik, multiculturalism is 'as evil and racist as Nazism and as brutal as Stalinism'. For Behring Breivik and 'Fjordman', 'multiculturalism' is basically a floating signifier that can mean anything (Lentin and Titley 2011: ix) – and which also acts as a rhetorical proxy: 'Blaming multiculturalism ties the package together: it discredits a foreign element – Islam – and it identifies the fifth column that let it in, those past proponents of multiculturalism' (Bowen 2011). The existence of differences between various multicultural regimes is inconsequential to the imaginaries of extreme right-wingers. On this point, academic experts on multiculturalism and multiculturalist policies may protest that Norway happens to be a country which cannot be said ever to have pursued multiculturalist policies (Banting and Kymlicka 2006).[27] But for Behring Breivik, Norway is 'the most suicidal country' in Europe when it comes to this matter. In his detailed description of statements he prepared for his own court appearance and those of 'other patriotic resistance fighters', Behring Breivik writes that 'The current multiculturalist regimes of Western Europe are not at all democratic, *this country* [i.e. Norway] *is not democratic*. They haven't been democratic since the 1950s. *This country* [i.e. Norway] *is a multiculturalist dictatorship run by tyrants*' (MF 3.70, my emphases). Behring Breivik, 'Fjordman' and Bawer are absolutely convinced that multiculturalism forms part of the hegemonic understandings of liberal elites in Norway. This is their belief even though multiculturalism is a normative political theory that extremely few Norwegian politicians or intellectuals, either on the left or the right, can be said to have endorsed in recent years. The mantra of multiculturalism as 'an anti-European hate ideology', which recurs throughout the tract, is certainly not Behring Breivik's own invention. It recurs often, as a leitmotif, in the blog essays of 'Fjordman'.

The question of racism

Throughout his tract, Behring Breivik vehemently denies that what he represents is a form of racism. He asserts that he is 'a laid back type' who is 'quite tolerant on most issues' and is 'not in fact a racist and never has been'. To buttress these claims, he informs the reader that his godmother was a political refugee from Chile and that he had friends in his childhood and youth of Chilean, Pakistani, Eritrean and Somali background. The underlying assumption here is that one cannot hold racist ideas if one has friends of a 'non-Western' ethnic or national background. Furthermore, he asserts that 'we, the PCCTS, Knights Templar, are not a racist organization' (MF: 3.84). Paradoxically, this comes in a section in which Behring Breivik takes exception to 'the multiculturalist glorification of race-mixing and interracial relations', since these 'do not correspond to … the wishes of the large majority of Europeans' and warns that 'within approximately 100–150 years, or within 4–5 generations … the Germanic/Nordic race in several countries will be diluted or annihilated to such an extent that there will be no one left with Nordic physical characteristics: blond hair, blue eyes, high forehead, sturdy cheekbones'. 'Race-mixing', according to Behring Breivik, is not only disastrous for this reason, but also owing to the 'fact' that 'it leads to suicidal children with severe mental problems' (MF: 3.84). Behring Breivik's obsession with 'racial mixing' gives the game away. Similar concerns were central to both the racist ideologies of Nazism and apartheid.[28]

Behring Breivik's tract even offers advice to the incipient cultural conservative 'resistance fighter' about how to avoid accusations of racism. They should simply avoid 'race'. This is in fact a rhetorical strategy used for years by extreme right-wing Islamophobes in Norway from the Norwegian Defence League (NDL) to Stop the Islamization of Norway (SIAN) – who claim on their websites to be against all forms of xenophobia and racism. But on the very same pages of the tract that Behring Breivik outlines strategies for avoiding accusations of racism, he contradicts himself, for he writes extensively about 'the Nordic race' and the 'need to preserve it' by avoiding 'racial mixing'. In police interrogations after his arrest, Behring Breivik reportedly praised Vidkun Quisling, the Norwegian Nazi prime minister who held office during the German Nazi occupation of Norway from 1940 to 1945, for having had 'sound, Christian cultural ideals' (Krokfjord et al. 2012).[29] Behring Breivik shares with 'Fjordman' his obsession with rhetorical denials of racism. In a 'Fjordman' citation that Behring Breivik uses to introduce Section Three of his tract, 'Fjordman' asserts that 'we will not accept any accusations of racism'. Similar denials of racism have a precursor in the French New Right (*La Nouvelle Droite*) of the 1970s: its thinkers, such as Alain de Benoist, 'translated xenophobia and intolerance into a liberal-democratic language' (Passmore 2002: 92) through arguing that it was engaged only in a political struggle to preserve the national majority's 'equal rights' in the face of alleged ongoing attempts to dismantle these by minorities and their supporters (ibid.: 93). In the contorted logic of this discourse, proponents of multiculturalism are seen as 'the real racists' (ibid.: 119).

The tactical shift of the grounds for racist-exclusionary politics away from 'race' and over to 'culture' and/or 'religion' has been well documented by international scholars of racism for some time. It is by no means limited to the extreme right. In 1995, anthropologist Verena Stolcke noted that '... the political right in Europe has in the past decade developed a political rhetoric of exclusion in which Third World immigrants ... are construed as posing a threat to the national unity of the "host" countries because they are culturally different. This rhetoric of exclusion has generally been identified as a new form of racism' (Stolcke 1995: 1). Stolcke argues furthermore that 'even though the term "race" may therefore be absent from this rhetoric, it is racism nonetheless, a "racism without race"' (ibid.: 4). Cultural theorist Paul Gilroy notes that 'for every courageous soul prepared to recognize that racism does exist in Britain, or to suggest that it is an entrenched problem worthy of sustained political consideration and moral reflection, there are likely to be at least two indignant voices raised in opposition' (Gilroy 2002 [1987]: xxxvi).

In 2006, Norwegian social anthropologist Marianne Gullestad argued that 'because of Norway's innocent self-image, the recent European research on racism has not been seriously discussed in Norwegian academic life. Norwegian scholars have been relatively uninterested in racism. When racism is on the scholarly agenda, it is usually given the narrow scientific definition' (Gullestad 2006: 227). By the term 'the narrow scientific definition', Gullestad had in mind the restriction of the term racism to the advocating of exclusionary practices and policies on the basis of biological markers of difference. Gullestad here makes a crucially important point: it is precisely through the retention of these narrow definitions and the lack of interest in international debates on new forms of racism that influential Norwegian academics have collaborated with the widespread 'denial of racism'[30] in Norwegian society pre-22/7.[31] Such denials have featured prominently in public debates on Islam and Muslims in Norway in recent years and have created a situation in which racism is discursively limited to the racism of biological markers and identified with extreme fringe groups, and the everyday experiences of racism suffered by minorities in Norway are played down.[32]

The construction of Islam and of Muslims

'Minorities do not come pre-formed,' writes cultural anthropologist Arjun Appadurai in *Fear of Small Numbers* (Appadurai 2006: 42). Part of the so-called intellectual work in which Anders Behring Breivik engages in his tract consists of defining the 'enemy' (Lyon 2012: 112). He maps his own conceptual world by ascribing fixity to various identities that in their hybridity and fracture threaten to undermine the nation understood *primarily* as an ethnos. Primarily, for it is Muslims whom Behring Breivik wants to purge from Europe: Sikhs, Hindus, Jews and Buddhists are in principle welcome in the ranks of the 'cultural conservatives' as long as they accept subordinate roles as defined and dictated by Christians. For after the coming to power of 'cultural conservatives', Behring Breivik declares that 'Christendom [sic] will be the only official religion in European countries' (MF: 3.81). He has learned the lessons of the new Huntingtonian identity politics. Thus, wherever national purity, fixity and homogeneity have been lost, they must be restored. Most important in this respect is the fixity ascribed to Islam and to Muslims. Any scholar of Islam would of course know that the very question 'what is a Muslim?' is difficult to answer (e.g. Bilgrami 1992), but that does not stop Behring Breivik from providing the answer for and to himself.

Appadurai (2006: 11) argues, 'The elimination of difference itself ... is the hallmark of today's large-scale *predatory narcissisms.*' Appadurai defines 'as predatory those identities whose social construction and mobilization require the extinction of other, proximate social categories, defined as threats to the very existence of some group, defined as we' (ibid.: 51).

Behring Breivik's stated aim is the ethnic cleansing of Muslims from Norway and Europe. In the aftermath of 22/7, the Norwegian terrorism researcher Thomas Hegghammer (2011) argued that Behring Breivik 'wants to expel, not kill Muslims in Europe'. Yet Behring Breivik in fact stipulates very specific conditions for not having to kill Muslims. Under 'security measures' to be implemented by a 'cultural conservative tribunal' appointed after the European 'cultural conservatives' come to power (MF: 3.1), Behring Breivik asserts that 'all Muslims are to be immediately deported to their country of origin' and that 'anyone who violently resists deportation will be executed'. Under the section 'assimilation policy', which is presented as an 'offer' to Muslims in Europe which 'will expire on Jan 1, 2020' (MF: 3.10), Behring Breivik outlines his demands: to remain in Europe, Muslims will have to convert to Christianity, change their names to a 'Christian' and/or 'European' name; accept prohibition of the use of 'Farsi, Urdu, Arabic, Somali'; accept 'the demolition of all mosques and Islamic centres'; the eradication of 'all traces of Islamic culture in Europe'; the prohibition of all 'attempts to celebrate Islamic holidays', including Ramadan and 'Id; accept a compulsory limit of two children for any 'ex-Muslim couples'; accept the prohibition of 'all correspondence with Muslims abroad' as well as 'travel to Muslim countries' or countries in which more than 20 per cent of the population is Muslim. A person who espouses such ideas does not merely want to 'expel Muslims' from Europe; he wants to ethnically cleanse them from Europe.

In the world of Behring Breivik, Islam is not a faith at all, but rather a political ideology in search of world dominance. As such, Islam has been in an ongoing 'civilizational war' with Christendom and with Europe for 1,400 years (MF: 3.13). This view was advanced in Bernhard Lewis's address to the American Enterprise Institute (AEI) in Washington, DC, entitled *Europe and Islam*, in 2007 (Lewis 2007: 4). Lewis argues that modern Muslim immigration to Europe is basically a means of colonization and of turning Europe Islamic. Lewis – citing the religious imaginaries of radical Islamists – refers to Muslim immigration combined with radical Islamist terror in Europe as a 'third wave of attacks against Europe' (ibid.: 8), and in a 2004 interview with German newspaper *Die Zeit*, Lewis predicted that Europe would be 'Islamized' by the end of the twenty-first century (Carr 2006: 5). Behring Breivik, as we have noted elsewhere, is convinced that this process will have been completed by 2083, unless current developments are stopped in their tracks by means of violent actions leading to the eruption of European civil war and the eventual purging of both Muslims from Europe and the 'multiculturalist' 'category A and B' traitors who are accused of guaranteeing the presence of Muslims here.

Central to Behring Breivik's vision of a Muslim-dominated Europe is Lebanon, a country that 'was a Christian territory once with 80% Christians in 19911 [sic]. Now, in today's Lebanon, there are less than 25% Christians left' (MF: 3.153). One notes here the emphasis on demography: numbers mean dominance. It might come as news to the many Lebanese citizens who believe that all Lebanese were losers during the civil war between 1975 and 1991, but now they are told 'the Muslims [of Lebanon] won the war,[33] and Europe just let it happen' (MF: ibid.). As a result – and this may come as even more of a surprise to the Lebanese – 'the remaining Christians [of Lebanon] live under harsh dhimmitude, and everyone in their right mind is attempting to flee the country' (ibid.). Consequently, '... armed resistance is the only option we have left to save Europe from the same fate as Lebanon' (ibid.). 'Islam', for Behring Breivik, is a 'political ideology of hate' in search of the enslavement (or dhimmitude, in the words adopted from the 'Eurabia' author Bat Ye'or; see Chapter 5) and genocide of 'indigenous Europeans'. Like Lewis, Behring Breivik is convinced that Europe is undergoing a monumental civilizational decline, and is concerned that 'multiculturalism' and 'political correctness' have turned Europeans into ambivalent, weak and effeminate beings who, unlike Muslims, are uncertain about their identities and no longer know what they want (Lewis 2007: 14–15). To repair what is now a fractured European world, Europeans must unite under the banner of 'cultural conservatism' to withstand the existential threat from Islam. Although Behring Breivik's version of imagined 'cultural conservatism' makes space for atheists and agnostics, as long as these persons identify with a Christian legacy and heritage, his cultural imaginary also entails a 'returning to Rome' and a pre-Reformation Catholicism. By purging Christianity of the elements of liberal post-Reformation Christian theology found today in both Protestantism and Catholicism, Europeans will also be purged of the civilizational weaknesses that these kinds of theology impose. For the modern Church is to Behring Breivik's mind 'using pacifist, fanatically egalitarian and gender-inclusive language' (MF: 3. 81) and what is needed is something more muscular: 'Christian leaders who are willing to call for defensive Crusades' (ibid.) and to support 'a Crusader Pope' in Rome (ibid.).

In their work on political paranoia, Robins and Post argue that 'the image of the enemy that the paranoid creates is often a projection of his own feelings, a mirror image of himself' (Robins and Post 1997: 93). And so, for Behring Breivik, the fear of 'Islam' is often mixed with a subtle admiration for the ideological and religious zeal and strength of what he considers to be the convictions of radical Islamists who engage in terror. Behring Breivik is, in this sense, a mirror image of those he declares as his enemies. For he too yearns for a world of political, ideological and ethnic purity, of absolute certainties, and of male patriarchal dominance.

Behring Breivik claims that al-Qaeda represents 'true Islam' (MF: 3.155). This will strike most readers as bizarre, but the claim is far more common than many think. Ayaan Hirsi Ali is among the neo-conservative authors who claim to have found 'the key' to the 9/11 attacks in the pages of the Qur'an (Ali 2010: xiv). And for Behring Breivik, al-Qaeda 'follow[s] the teachings of the Qur'an and as such have [sic] more than 100 million sympathizers and supporters' (MF: ibid.). Once more, the obsession with numbers. But estimates of the number of supporters of al-Qaeda globally have never remotely approached such figures. The most extensive global poll on this issue, a Gallup Poll conducted among Muslims in thirty-five countries between 2001 and 2007 (Esposito and Mogahed 2007: xi), found that 7 per cent of those polled held that the 9/11 terror attacks on the United States were 'completely justified' (ibid.: 69). But only 13 per cent of these 'radical Muslims' held that attacks on civilians were 'completely justified' (ibid.: 70).

Al-Qaeda's unacknowledged but 'most important' achievement is to have made Islamist groups hitherto declared anathema by the Western powers seem 'moderate'. In this respect, Behring Breivik, who sees the struggle against the purported 'Islamization' of Europe as both ideological and military, wants to emulate al-Qaeda's strategy. According to one of his defence lawyers, Behring Breivik has asserted in conversations with them that he wanted to express extreme opinions in order to move the threshold of what is considered extreme, and at the same time to make what has been considered 'radical' appear as 'moderate' (NTB 2012b). In so doing, he engages in a strategy of deception similar to the one in which he believes al-Qaeda is engaged. In Behring Breivik's mind, the very nature of Muslims is that whatever they do and wherever they do it, whether they happen to be Shias or Sunnis, they are practising *taqiyya* or 'dissimulation'. *Taqiyya*, which was originally a concept in Shia Islam,[34] has become a key term for 'Eurabia' authors such as Bat Ye'or. To them its very existence in Islam implies that Muslims, whatever their orientation or beliefs, are never to be trusted. For in reality, al-Qaeda, according to Behring Breivik's tract, 'work in tandem with the so-called moderate Muslim organizations'. Though they may use different means and methods, 'they all have the same goal'. That goal is 'conquering everything non-Muslim'. Behring Breivik's vision on this point is strikingly similar to that of, for example, evangelical Christian polemical author Mark Gabriel (see Chapter 4).

The figure of 'the Muslim' in Behring Breivik's fantasies is static and unchangeable, overdetermined by the person's allegiance to Islam and unaffected by local contexts and particularities. We are, in other words, dealing with the proverbial *Homo islamicus* described in critiques of Orientalism (see Lockman 2007). According to this point of view, whether a Muslim living in Europe is first, second or third generation, he or she is still never to be trusted. A Muslim is a Muslim is a Muslim. It hardly needs stating that this claim does not accord with available research on the lives of Muslims in Europe (Maliepaard et al. 2010; Jacobsen 2011; Connor 2010). This research suggests that 'to be a Muslim in the modern world is both to be shaped by this world and to take part in its shaping' (Tripp 2009), and that levels of religious practice, lifestyles and orientation vary significantly with generation, ethnic background, level of education and so forth.[35] In the cultural-conservative Europe envisioned by Behring Breivik, Islam will be banned because it is, by definition, a 'fascist, violent, discriminating and genocidal political ideology' (MF: 3.3) or a 'genocidal anti-kafr [sic] hate ideology' (MF: 3.4). Not only that, but 'the Qur'an and the Hadith [sic]' will be 'banned altogether' (MF: 3.10). The discerning reader of these passages will recall that Dutch right-wing politician Geert Wilders, a self-declared champion of free speech, has repeatedly called for the Qur'an to be banned on the purported grounds that it is similar to Adolf Hitler's *Mein Kampf* (Dickey 2012).

In the view of Behring Breivik, Muslims are a much more powerful force in the world than they might seem from the state of contemporary Muslim societies. Behring Breivik does not so much oppose the presence of Muslims in the world (which, after all, is a given) as he does their presence in Europe. 'We do not necessarily oppose the creation of a caliphate led by devout Muslims in the Middle East' (MF: 3.53). For 'an Islamic Caliphate is a useful enemy to all Europeans as it will ensure European unity under Christian cultural conservative leadership' (ibid.).[36]

As we will see in Chapter 5, a central tenet of the 'Eurabia' literature, which appears to have profoundly inspired Behring Breivik's own thinking, is that the European Union (EU) has worked in tandem with Muslim states since the early 1970s to 'Islamize Europe' and to turn it into 'Eurabia'. But not only that: according to Behring Breivik, the United Nations in New York is in fact 'Marxist-Islamic' or 'Muslim-dominated' (MF: 3.3). Norway is 'at the forefront in the propagation of "self-annihilation" policies such as dialogue and appeasement toward Islam'. The Nobel Peace Prize awarded each December in Oslo is in fact a 'tool of Islamic appeasement efforts' (MF 3.153). Muslims have, by virtue of their steadily increasing power in Europe, been able to perpetrate the 'first degree murder' of no fewer than '44,800 indigenous Europeans' between 1960 and 2010. Furthermore, Muslims have been responsible for the 'rape of approximately 1.1 million European women' in the same period.

True to the logic of much literature in the 'Eurabia' genre, numbers matter, but the provenance of fabricated statistics does not matter at all. For his first claim, Behring Breivik does not provide any sources whatsoever. For the second, he purports to have extrapolated the figures from 'Swedish statistics on rape'. Behring Breivik has a discernible 'fear of small numbers' (Appadurai 2006). For whereas 'native Europeans' suffer from what he refers to as a 'birth deficit' (i.e. a demographic decline), Muslims in Europe and elsewhere, in spite of reports of rapidly declining fertility rates (Pew Reports 2011), have the numbers:

> 2009 – Western Europe is being invaded again, this time through demographic warfare (mass Muslim immigration in combination with high Muslim birthrates). The forces of Islam are flooding the gates once more ... Aided and abetted by the cultural Marxist/ multiculturalist elites of Western Europe. (MF 3.13)

Time is running out:

> We have only 20–70 years before we are demographically over-whelmed by the hordes of Islam. Demography is king, and unless we manage to deport all Muslims from European soil within the next 20–70 years, Europe will be lost. (MF: 3.82)

Numbers, statistics and percentages have an almost talismanic property throughout Behring Breivik's tract. For example, when he enumerates 'category A and B traitors' in states across Europe, he writes that there are exactly '4,848' such 'traitors' in Norway (MF: 3.44). How Behring Breivik has come to this very specific number we do not know. But in his obsession with numbers, he is in certain respects definitely a child of his time. Since the early 1990s, 'measuring the Muslim' has become a virtual obsession for western European states, leading to a tendency to both ascribe particular configurations of identity among those so classified by 'native' Europeans and to define oneself through these very configurations of identities among Muslims themselves (Spielhaus 2012).

Behring Breivik's numbers are almost without exception grossly inflated and exaggerated – as they must be if one is sincerely to believe, as Behring Breivik and many of his fellow adherents of the 'Eurabia' genre do, in the prospect of a Muslim-dominated Norway and Europe in the near future.[37] Inflated numbers are thus needed when one realizes that Muslims constituted a mere 3.6 per cent of the population in Norway as of 2011 and 6.0 per cent of the population in Europe. For example, Behring Breivik states that there are some '1 million Muslim immigrants' arriving in Europe every year, that in Norway some 300,000 to 400,000 of 'the newly arrived immigrants' are Muslim (MF: 1.353), and that more than '85 per cent of the colonizers [that is, the immigrants] are Muslims' (ibid.).

Behring Breivik attaches his most romantic vision to Norway's 1950s when 'we were more or less a pure Nordic country' (ibid.). 'Now', however, Norwegians experience '30,000–50,000 non-Nordics pouring in annually' (ibid.). This, of course, has precious little to do with actual numbers: the most recent estimate provided by Statistics Norway (SSB) is that there were some 185,000 individuals of Muslim background living in Norway (Østby 2011). Approximately half of these were signed-up members of mosque congregations in Norway (Jacobsen and Leirvik 2010: 387).

'Suspiciousness is the most evident presenting characteristic, the sine qua non, of the paranoid. To the paranoid, things are not what they seem to be. He does not permit himself to be distracted by apparently innocent facts, but claims to see through them,' write Robins and Post in their study of the politically paranoid, entitled *Political Paranoia: The Psychopolitics of Hatred* (Robins and Post 1997: 8). 'With keen attention, the paranoid interprets away (often with great ingenuity) facts that do not fit with his delusions and seeks clues and "real meanings" in every event and comment. The search is rigidly intentional. In the paranoid's worldview, events do not simply occur, they are deliberately caused by someone. For the paranoid, coincidence does not exist. Everything happens by design' (ibid.).

As noted previously, to both Behring Breivik in his tract and 'Fjordman' in his many blog essays, all suburban riots in underprivileged areas of European metropolises are 'Muslim riots' and, as such, are part of an underlying logic whereby Muslim youth advance the cause of the 'Islamization of Europe' through violent means. This hardly squares with any of the findings of academic research into these riots (see Cesari 2005; Fassin 2006; Muchielli 2009). But Behring Breivik has not read any of this research, and will in any case not be bothered by any opposing empirical evidence. For the 'fact' that these riots are 'Muslim riots' is, according to the logic of Behring Breivik's tract, deliberately suppressed by the European news media; after all, 'more than 95 per cent of today's journalists, editors [and] publishers are pro-Eurabians (supporters of multiculturalism)' (MF: 3.3) and there is 'no such thing as a free press in Europe' (MF: 3.6).

As we have seen, Behring Breivik regards the news media in Norway and Europe as central to the so-called 'multiculturalist/cultural Marxist alliance', so it should not be surprising to learn that he contemplated attacking the large mainstream media houses in Norway, including the Norwegian Broadcasting Corporation NRK, as well as the mass-circulation newspapers *VG* and *Aftenposten* (Andersen 2012).

Urban legends of the kind found in much 'Eurabia' literature are also part of the construction of those who constitute 'Muslims' in Behring Breivik's tract. Anders Behring Breivik relies on the anecdotal 'evidence' of his 'personal experiences' in trying to authenticate his peculiar world view.

Writing about his background in the third section of the tract, Behring Breivik alleges that two of his fellow pupils, females respectively of Turkish and Pakistani background ('Elif' and 'Modazzer'), suddenly disappeared during school holidays, never to return. While it is certainly the case that Muslim schoolgirls have been abducted to their parents' country of origin to be married off or have been disciplined in Norway,[38] we know from media investigations into Behring Breivik's schoolmates that a Muslim girl of Pakistani background named in his tract as having disappeared from school to be married off is in fact married and has resided in Oslo throughout her life. But in the case of Muslims, Behring Breivik thinks everything that happens in their lives is due to their being Muslim. Thus, we also learn from the tract that Pakistani Muslim male youths who allegedly rob Behring Breivik's friends in the streets of Oslo do so to extract the religious taxes (*jizya*) demanded of the 'subordinate non-Muslim population' in 'Eurabia's' putative new 'caliphate' – the so-called dhimmis, to use the terminology of Bat Ye'or and other 'Eurabists'.

Such bogus interpretations and narratives are standard in much of 'Eurabia' literature. According to Behring Breivik's tract, his alleged childhood friend of Pakistani Muslim background, who is named and fully identified in the tract, is known to have taken part in 'gang rapes' of a white 'ethnic' Norwegian girl in a park in Oslo. This is allegedly part of a ritual demonstration of 'male Muslim dominance' vis-à-vis 'ethnic Norwegian boys', so emasculated that they fail to protect the white 'ethnic' Norwegian girls whom the Muslim boys have learned to regard as 'whores' (MF: 3.153). Muslims are not only an existential threat for Behring Breivik; Muslim males are also a sexual threat. There are strong echoes here of the sexual frustrations and deprivations of a young white Norwegian male whose sexual career does not appear to have been very successful. Yet we should not necessarily take this at face value either: leaks from the police interrogations in the 22/7 case suggest that Behring Breivik in the years leading up to 22/7 had a series of homosexual encounters (see Borchgrevink 2012: 191; also Knausgård 2012). The veracity of anecdotal stories such as those of Bawer and Behring Breivik is, of course, difficult to ascertain, but there are solid reasons for assuming that these are urban legends. Behring Breivik uses them to create a personal mythos around himself and to lend credence and legitimacy to his actions.

A pro-Zionist anti-Semite

[Behring] Breivik is 'vehemently hostile to Nazism', argues the prominent historian on fascism, Roger Griffin, in a recent book (Griffin 2012: 209). That assertion appears to have been written some time before Anders Behring Breivik in Oslo Magistrate's Court during the 22/7 trial during the late spring and summer of 2012 endorsed and identified with a long line of neo-Nazis in Norway and elsewhere in western Europe. Yet it also reflects a very superficial reading of *2083* on Griffin's part. For even the most cursory reading of Behring Breivik's tract reveals that his stated support for Israel has very little to do with its character as a modern homeland for Jews, but rather reflects his hatred of Muslims, and that his disavowal of historical Nazi ideology and policies, as well as contemporary neo-Nazis, is purely strategic and instrumentalist. He conceives of Israel as a front-line state and potential ally in the struggle against the 'Islamizing' of Europe. He purports to have a profound distaste for Hitler (MF: 3.153), yet declares '60 per cent of the NSDAP's[39] policies' are 'great classical conservative policies' (ibid.). In police interrogations, Behring Breivik has described as his allies the German neo-Nazi ring behind a series of murders of German Turks since the 1990s. Behring Breivik is, in fact, not only an Islamophobe, but an anti-Semite as well, and as such, a living contemporary embodiment of the structural resemblances between anti-Semitism and Islamophobia (see Bunzl 2007).

As philosopher Slavoj Žižek has noted, the paradox we face in Behring Breivik's thoughts is that of the very recent creation of a European 'pro-Zionist anti-Semite' (Žižek 2011).

Why social democrats, and not Muslims?

So why, then, if Behring Breivik's ultimate aim was to cleanse Europe of Muslims and all traces of their historical and modern presence in Europe, did he not attack specifically Muslim targets? His tract does not provide any clear answer. We know from police interrogation leaks that Behring Breivik toyed with the idea of massive attacks on identifiable Muslim targets in downtown Oslo as early as 2001 (Kristiansen et al. 2012), and in the tract he takes the reader through potential terror targets. His list of 'primary targets' in 'phase 1' includes 'major Muslim targets' such as gatherings for *id-ul-fitr* (celebrations at the end of Ramadan), which are attended by more than two thousand Muslims (MF: 3.41). Here, he envisages that attacking Muslim women in particular will incense Muslims – their male relatives would then 'swear blood vengeance and join Jihadist networks' – and would lead to a radicalization of Muslims and a spiral of attacks and counter-attacks between Muslims and non-Muslim

Europeans. Now, there can be no doubt that Behring Breivik's overriding aim was to ethnically cleanse Norway and Europe of Muslims by instigating a continent-wide civil war. Yet one of his posts on the far-right and Islamophobic website Document.no, dated 31 October 2009, suggests that a strategic calculation was at work. For here, Behring Breivik advised his fellow travellers to 'focus on the actual evil – multiculturalism – and not on the result of this evil. If there is a leaking water pipe, one has to focus on stopping the leakage first, not on collecting the water!' (cited by Hverven 2012: 35). In this metaphorical rendering, Norwegian social democrats *qua* purported 'multiculturalists' represent the leaking pipe, whereas Muslims and their presence in Norway are merely a result of that leakage.

Now, to return from the metaphorical leakage to the previous source of information: the police interrogation leaks do seem to provide us with some clues. Breivik explained that he abandoned all plans to attack specifically Muslim targets for strategic and conceptual reasons. Such attacks, he assumed, would give Muslims in Norway 'massive sympathy' from the population. Furthermore, he explained that he did not want to attack Muslims for being 'traitors' because he does not consider them Norwegians. His racist logic is apparent: even in their presence, Anders Behring Breivik is not prepared to recognize Muslims as worthy of being acknowledged as fellow citizens and human beings.

4 | CONVERGENCES

And incidentally, won't you tell me what I really am? (Franz
Kafka, Letter to Felice Bauer, 1916)

The aftermath

At the heart of the Oslo and Utøya terror attacks on 22 July 2011
was a paradox: how could one of the most peaceful, least crime-
ridden, most prosperous and least socially unequal countries in the
world have generated such acts of terrorism? The attacks profoundly
shocked most Norwegians and generated a fair amount of soul-
searching. Quite apart from the discovery that the perpetrator was
not a 'radical Islamist' but 'one of us' – a white 'ethnic' Norwegian
– there was the realization that *it could happen here.*

National and international media searched for suitable words and
reintroduced the notion that Norway had 'lost its innocence' (Åmås
2011a). To what extent was this really the case? The answer would,
of course, depend on exactly who was asked. One could perhaps
have asked the Norwegian Jewish Holocaust survivors who were
rounded up for deportation by ship to the concentration camps of
eastern Europe by Norwegian state police in 1942–43. Or one could,
for example, have asked the bereaved adoptive family of young Arve
Beheim Karlsen (seventeen), a child born in India who in 1999 was
chased by a group of local racists into the Sogndal river at Naustdal
in western Norway; the mother of Benjamin 'Labarang' Hermansen
(fifteen), a boy of Norwegian-Ghanaian parentage, knifed to death by
neo-Nazis from the skinhead group Boot Boys at Holmlia in Oslo east
in 2001; or the widow and orphans of Norwegian-Somalian Mahmed
Jamal Shirwac (forty-six), murdered in his own car in Trondheim
in 2008 by sixteen shots fired by a Norwegian who was declared
psychotic, but who had for a long time followed right-wing extremist
websites and had set out from his flat planning to kill Muslims or
burn down mosques.

A central concern for many Norwegian media editors post-22/7 was underlining the distinction between *words* and *actions* (Åmås 2011b). This was in effect a rhetorical move designed to counter any notion that the political and intellectual climate of Norway in the years leading up to 22/7 may have affected the ideas of Anders Behring Breivik concerning the alleged existential threat to Norway and Europe embodied by the presence of Muslims here, and the alleged 'need' to ethnically cleanse Europe of this presence. A further impetus to the societal externalization of 22/7 was provided by a plethora of books by prominent Norwegian authors which in the ensuing years have provided the media and the public at large with never-ending commentary on the troubled private life of Anders Behring Breivik, his mother and sister (see Borchgrevink 2012; Seierstad 2013; Christensen 2013 for the most prominent examples of this genre), and which by and large reduced 22/7 to a question of the perpetrator's individual psychopathology. An antidote would, however, be provided by Anders Behring Breivik's defence attorney, Geir Lippestad, who, unlike any of these authors, had frequent contact with the mass murderer in the year from his arrest in July 2011 to his conviction in August 2012. Anders Behring Breivik, Lippestad would later write in his published account of the case (Lippestad 2013: 112), may have 'indeed experienced a mother in crisis, but not more of a crisis than many other children in Norway experience. His childhood alone can not account for his subsequent development.' Police investigations have not yielded any evidence that Behring Breivik had accomplices in planning or executing the attacks. Yet it is quite clear both from his tract and his statements to the court that he did not conceive of himself as an ideological 'lone wolf' (Spaijj 2010). If that was the case, it would be hard to explain why he sent his cut-and-paste tract to 1,003 contacts that he deemed suitably 'cultural conservative' Christians on the populist and far right in countries across Europe, in the USA, Canada and Israel.

As Ruthven has pointed out (2011), in the narrative framing[1] of the 22/7 terror attacks it is possible to discern a divide between the left and the right in the political spectrum, a divide broadly applicable to the Norwegian context. In the narrative framing of the political right, the terror attacks on 22/7 have little, if anything, to do with the direction of Norwegian society in the preceding years;

the ideological motivations behind these attacks are seen as almost irrelevant, and the perpetrator is cast as a lone madman. In the narrative framing of the political left, the ideology of these attacks is of paramount importance and the perpetrator is cast as an expression of Islamophobic ideologies in Norwegian society in the years preceding 22/7. To the extent that these narrative frames are posited in contradistinction to one another, they may of course both miss something: it is entirely possible to be a lone madman, yet act out ideological fantasies of purity and existential danger which are, in fact, far more mainstream, more widely shared in society.

Behring Breivik spent considerable time on the internet, so much so that one could well see his radicalization as a classic case of 'internet radicalization' mirroring that of a number of young European Muslims who turned to radical Islamism in the aftermath of 9/11. And Behring Breivik was not a passive bystander or lurker. Norwegian police investigations revealed that he used some thirty aliases on the internet and twenty e-mail addresses and that he posted on more than forty sites (Sandli 2011), including those of mainstream Norwegian newspapers, such as *Aftenposten* and the tabloid *VG*. When he was using his real name, his posts were generally more polite in language and content than when he wrote under aliases. He regularly posted comments under his own name or his Facebook pseudonym 'Sigurd Jorsalfar'[2] on sites ranging from the right-wing (i.e. Hegnar Online)[3] to the Islamophobic (i.e. Document.no)[4] to neo-Nazi ones (i.e. Stormfront and nordisk.no). He was particularly active on Document.no in 2009, to the extent that he contacted its editor, Hans Rustad, to commend him for his efforts and suggest a formal cooperation with a view to establishing a magazine together.

In the aftermath of 22/7, anyone who had ever had any contact with Behring Breivik or shared any of his Islamophobic ideology spent much time and energy distancing themselves from the mass murderer. This included politicians from the Norwegian populist right-wing Progress Party (PP) and the editor of Document.no, Hans Rustad. Behring Breivik had been a member of the Progress Party Youth (FpU) from 1997 to 2007 (22/7 Commission 2012: 342), and a member of the Progress Party from 1999 to 2004. Though Behring Breivik failed to get nominated for any position in PP circles, and his interest in democratic party politics seems to have abated as early as in 2003 (Stormark 2012: 26), he contacted the PP's national office in late 2009 (ibid.: 245). On the evening of 10 December 2009, the day when US president Barack Obama received the Nobel Peace Prize at City Hall in the Norwegian capital of Oslo, Behring Breivik was one of an estimated twenty people attending a meeting of 'Friends of Document.no' at Oslo's University Street (ibid.: 243–4). Perhaps the most prominent member of this funding and coordinating body was the PP member of parliament Christian Tybring-Gjedde from Oslo, who in the years preceding 22/7 had stood out as one of the main traffickers in extreme right-wing rhetorical tropes concerning Islam and Muslims among central PP politicians in Norway. While the editor of Document.no, Hans Rustad, had taken exception to the clear incitement to violence against Muslims in Norway and in western Europe emanating from Anders Behring Breivik's main ideological inspiration, Peder Are Nøstvold Jensen, aka 'Fjordman' (see Enebakk 2012 for this), Rustad had in fact played around with 'fighting words' directed at Muslims on the blog he edited. In a blog entry titled 'Sex as weapon' (*'Sex som våpen'*) from December 2009, Rustad argued that 'Muslim males rape Western women ... as part of a war' (cited in Borchgrevink 2012: 178). In the aftermath of 22/7, reviews which openly endorsed 'Fjordman's' incitements to violence would appear on Document.no (see Winkel Holm 2012).

In the aftermath of 22/7, and in the face of a resurgent PP poised to form part of a future right-wing coalition government headed by the Conservative Party (Høyre) after the Norwegian parliamentary elections in September 2013, few analysts have dared to analyse the ways in which the populist right-wing discourse on Islam, Muslims and immigration in Norway in the past decade has at times intersected with extreme right-wing discourses on the same topics (but see Malkenes 2012 and Døving 2012 for two notable exceptions). This is not to argue that there is no distinction between extreme and populist right-wing discourses on Islam, Muslims and immigration in Norway or anywhere else. A principal distinction has to do with extreme right-wingers' open endorsement of violence and non-democratic means, and populist right-wingers' explicit rejection of violence and non-democratic means (Jupskås 2011). Yet, as Warburton notes, 'the point at which a strongly voiced opinion shades into incitement to harm is rarely obvious' (Warburton 2009: 31).

This chapter will demonstrate that central PP politicians in Norway have for the past twenty-five years cast Muslims in Norway – currently estimated to represent 3.6 per cent of the total population – as an 'existential threat'. From an analytical point of view, therefore, extreme and populist right-wing discourses on Islam and Muslims form part of a continuum, rather than political discourses in complete isolation from one another. To undertake such an analysis is obviously to invite some trouble in the present political and social context in Norway, in which the PP has toned down its anti-Muslim and anti-immigration rhetoric with a view to being viewed as a serious future government partner for the Conservative Party, but in which the attitudes concerning Muslims and other minorities in Norway among its electoral constituency remain largely unchanged (see HL Centre 2012: 53). Some analysts (see interview with Øyvind Strømmen in Lepperød 2011) have advanced the hypothesis that the PP's rhetoric on Islam and Muslims in the past decade has, by voicing popular concerns, acted as a brake on the popularity of extreme right-wing political formations in Norway. These analysts argue that these views are thus channelled into the democratic political arena and thereby neutered. As has been raised in Chapter 1, the problem is that such a hypothesis is empirically virtually untestable *ex post facto*, and that it ignores the extent to which populist right-wing formations may also act as 'voice amplifiers' for extreme right-wing discourses, and thereby contribute to the normalization and legitimization of racist and/or discriminatory speech (see also Avelin 2012). Let me also point out that to explore the intersections between extreme and populist right-wing discourses on Islam, Muslims and immigration in the past decade or so is not to suggest that Islamophobia in Norway and Europe at present is a phenomenon whose popularity is in any way exclusive to the populist political right (see Allen 2010).

Opinion polls conducted after 22/7 indicate that as a result of 22/7, Norwegians had become more positive about Norway as a multicultural society. A groundswell of popular sympathy for the Labour Party and its youth wing was expressed in high levels of support in the polls before the September 2011 municipal elections and in the thousands of new registered members of AUF. Yet among populist right-wing and Islamophobic civil society activists there was little evidence of self-reflection or a will to change.

Nor were there many words of contrition from those members of the Norwegian Progress Party (PP) who had adopted an increasingly vitriolic political discourse on Islam and Muslims in the years leading up to the events of 22/7. This appears to have remained the case, even though immediately after 22/7 the PP leadership appeared to have instructed the party organization to tone down its rhetoric on these issues. A number of low-level politicians were disciplined, suspended or expelled from the party for hate speech exhibited on their Facebook pages and directed against Norwegian social democratic leaders. Internet hate speech against non-Western immigrants, however, appeared still to be *comme il faut* in PP circles after 22/7.[5]

In an interview with the national broadcaster NRK on 24 July, PP party chairwoman Siv Jensen described it as 'horrendous' (*'avskyelig'*) to link Behring Breivik and his rhetoric to the PP, and thereby positioned the PP as a victim of 22/7 (Malkenes 2012: 76). In an op-ed in the *Wall Street Journal* on 3 August, Jensen charged that 'some media and commentators, mainly on the left, are trying to use the atrocities of one man to smear and slander the Progress Party in our nation's time of grief' (Jensen 2011). In a statement he was later forced to retract and publicly apologize for, the Progress Party's MP Per Sandberg (during Question Period in the Norwegian parliament on 23 November 2011) accused the Norwegian Labour Party of having 'played the role of the victim after 22/7' (Skarvøy et al. 2011). For his part, Christian Tybring-Gjedde declared in hindsight, in mid-August 2011, that a controversial op-ed that he had written about a year earlier, in which he had charged the Labour Party with 'wanting to tear the country apart' and 'stabbing our culture in the back' by allowing 'mass immigration' and conducting 'multicultural experiments', remained 'politically rock solid' (Tybring-Gjedde 2011). By January 2012, Tybring-Gjedde, who had gone on sick leave owing to death threats, would appear in the self-designated role of a 'dissident' martyr for freedom of expression, having in his own mind 'stood up against a heavy superficial enforced consensus' characteristic of Norwegian society (Tybring-Gjedde 2012). In mid-August 2011, Siv

Jensen declared that while she personally regretted some of the terms she had used in immigration and integration debates in recent years, she would not abandon the controversial term 'Islamization by stealth', which she herself had introduced in Norwegian political discourse in 2009 (Haukali 2011). In a December 2011 op-ed in *Aftenposten*, the PP's former spokesperson on immigration and integration, Per Willy Amundsen, declared himself to be on the side of 'science, the Enlightenment, progress, Western civilization and secularization', and thereby implied that his and the PP's political opponents were somehow 'against' such values, and resuscitated the term 'Islamization by stealth' ('*snikislamisering*') in party circles (Amundsen 2011).

Based on a concept introduced by linguist Ruth Wordak in the analysis of populist and extreme right-wing rhetoric, Malkenes suggests that the approach of the PP after 22/7 has been one of 'calculated ambiguity' whereby central party members communicate different messages to different political audiences (Malkenes 2012: 75). To the offended, the party offers what may seem like apologies, but these are apologies that are not likely to be interpreted as such by those sympathetic to right-wing extremism. The choice of words may be different, but the substance has remained unchanged (ibid.: 83).

The Progress Party and the mainstreaming of Islamophobic discourse in Norway

Politically and socially, Norway is not an island on its own in contemporary western Europe. Radical right and populist right-wing parties in western Europe are estimated by political scientists to have increased their proportion of electoral support six times since the mid-1980s (see Jupskås 2012: 223). What these parties have in common is a political platform that is and for a long time has been anti-immigration and anti-Muslim in nature (ibid.: 200). These parties feed on popular resentments of immigration and of immigrants, the numbers of whom have increased throughout western Europe since the 1980s (ibid.: 119). The Norwegian social anthropologist Fredrik Barth noted in his introduction to the seminal volume *Ethnic Groups and Boundaries* (Barth 1969) that ethnic mobilization was often the result of the actions of ethnic entrepreneurs. With reference to the work of Cass Sunstein, I will suggest, however, that instead we refer to politicians and activists engaged in the promotion, legitimization and amplification of anti-immigrant and/or anti-Muslim attitudes and sentiments in contemporary Norway and in western Europe as 'polarization entrepreneurs'. According to Sunstein (2009), 'polarization entrepreneurs' 'attempt to create communities of like-minded people, and they are aware that these communities will not only harden positions but also move them to a more extreme point' (ibid.: 34). 'Polarization entrepreneurs', in Sunstein's view, engage in planned acts designed to promote polarization at some level or other.

Political scientist José Pedro Zúquete has noted that 'the increasing importance of the issue of "Islam" [in European politics] has led to a *de facto* mainstreaming of opinions and policies previously deemed too "extreme" and relegated to the periphery of the political spectrum by centrist parties' (Zúquete 2008: 332). Furthermore, 'the extreme right has co-opted issues that a large number of mainstream politicians, on both the mainstream Right and Left, find it hard to disagree with, if not fully support. This development has rendered the distinction between what is "mainstream" and what should be categorized as "extreme" difficult and, at times, hopelessly muddled' (ibid.). Belgian political scientist and expert on radical right parties in Europe Cas Mudde likewise notes that 'Islamophobia is certainly not an exclusive feature of the populist radical right, but reaches deep into the political mainstream of most Western countries' (Mudde 2007: 84) and that, since the 1980s, 'Muslims have been targeted most consistently and vehemently in the propaganda of populist radical right parties' (ibid.: 70).

In light of the part played by the Norwegian PP in instigating and legitimizing Islamophobic and anti-immigration discourses and policies in Norway for decades, it is hardly surprising that Behring Breivik was attracted to this party in his late teenage years. The precursor to the PP, Anders Lange's Party (ALP),[6] was established in 1973 by political maverick Anders Lange (1904–74) on a classical populist anti-taxation and anti-bureaucratic political platform. Inspired by the successes of the Danish Progress Party under Mogens Glistrup, ALP was renamed the Progress Party (PP) in 1977. In 1987 it first discovered the electoral appeal of anti-immigration and particularly anti-Muslim rhetoric. This is not to suggest that the original ALP was innocent of racist and discriminatory ideas: 'Anyone supportive of black majority rule in South Africa is a traitor to the white race,' wrote Lange in his newspaper *Hundeavisen* (*The Dog Paper*) in 1963 (Bjurwald 2011: 199), three years after the Sharpeville massacre in which apartheid police forces massacred sixty-nine peaceful demonstrators in the township of Sharpeville on South Africa's Witwatersrand (Lodge 2011). Sharpeville, more than any other incident, brought international attention to the racist nature of the apartheid regime in South Africa (1948–90). Tacit support of the apartheid regime would represent a long and continuous line in PP politics. In the 1980s, PP chairman Carl I. Hagen warned against majority rule of 'Hottentots and Bushmen' in South Africa in the party's internal newspaper, and the party's MP Fridtjof Frank Gundersen wrote letters to the editors in Norwegian mainstream newspapers expressing the party's opposition to the international sanctions against the apartheid regime and warning about an impending 'one-party state and dictatorship' and threats to 'white security' should a black majority be allowed to govern a democratic South Africa (Solhjell 2011). The PP was the only party in the Norwegian parliament which voted against Norway's imposing of sanctions against the apartheid regime when parliament finally voted on the issue after years of civil society mobilization with that aim in 1987.

Among the ALP members elected to the Norwegian parliament in 1973, when the party obtained 5 per cent (107,784) of the votes, was a highly decorated Norwegian Second World War resistance fighter, prominent lawyer Erik Gjems-Onstad (1922–2011). He was later expelled from the party for recommending that voters choose the Conservative Party in 1976. But in the ALP of 1973, he was second only to Anders Lange himself. Gjems-Onstad strongly supported the apartheid regime in South Africa as well as Ian Smith's racist regime in Rhodesia; he visited these countries on a number of occasions and provided their intelligence services with information on Norwegian politicians and intellectuals (Lunde 1979). He later became a central figure in the Norwegian Popular Movement against Immigration (Folkebevegelsen mot innvandring, FMI), established in Haugesund in 1987.

Under Arne Myrdal (1935–2007), FMI featured a number of

Norwegian Nazi sympathizers, nourished contacts with neo-Nazis in Norway and Sweden, and was involved in attacks on immigrants and asylum centres, particularly in its stronghold around Arendal in southern Norway in the late 1980s and early 1990s. Dr Eschel M. Rhoodie,[7] who worked as a secretary in the South African Information Department under C. P. Mulder in the 1970s, alleged in the book *The Real Information Scandal* (1983) that the apartheid government channelled funds to the ALP to support their 1973 electoral campaign. In the UK the *Guardian* reported in 1979 that the apartheid regime had channelled the significant amount of 180,000 Norwegian kroner to the ALP ahead of its electoral campaign in 1973 (Sæbø 2013). The PP has always strenuously denied these allegations. The party's historical archives, which document the party's history dating back to its founding as the ALP, are deposited at the National Archives in Oslo. Yet the PP has refused public access to the archival records relating to this episode to this day (Blindheim 2013). Yet there is no doubt whatsoever that Rhoodie and other central bureaucrats in the apartheid regime saw the Norwegian ALP as a supporter of apartheid and that central politicians in the ALP in its early years supported the regime (Jorde 2008).

It was under Anders Lange's successor Carl I. Hagen (1944–), who had broken away from the party to form the short-lived Reform Party in 1974, that the ALP transformed itself into a populist party with mass appeal in Norway. By 1978, Hagen had been elected chairman of the party renamed the Progress Party (PP), a position he would continue to hold until 2006. Though issues relating to immigration and integration have been central to the party's electoral appeal, the PP is not a 'single-issue party' (Mudde 1999). Part of its electoral appeal in the past two decades has related to its adoption of a political rhetoric of passionate support for the welfare state (Rydgren 2007: 245) coupled with anti-elitism. This was bound to appeal to an electoral constituency that has more people living on social welfare (Gjerstad 2011) and with lower levels of education than any other party's (Aardal et al. 2007: 13). The traditional working-class and blue-collar electorate is in Norway – as elsewhere in western Europe – to a large extent responsible for the successes of right-wing populist parties (Pelinka 2013: 10). In Norway, the party's successes in recent decades must also be seen in the context of the ongoing crises of democratic legitimacy[8] affecting mainstream and historically dominant political party formations – and not the least the social democratic Labour Party. Before the 1997 parliamentary elections, the PP declared itself a caretaker of the working class that was opposed to a social democratic Labour Party that had allegedly deserted the welfare state (Fekete 2009: 3). Among unskilled workers in Norway, the PP had by the time of the parliamentary elections of 2005 surpassed the Labour Party in terms of electoral support (Bjørklund 1999: 17). In the parliamentary elections of 2009, 36 per cent of the voters classified as workers voted for the PP; 33 per cent of voters classified as workers voted for the Labour Party (Berglund et al. 2011: 28); 24 per cent of PP voters and 17 per cent of LP voters were classified as workers (ibid.: 30, 35). The shift towards support for the PP among historical Labour Party-controlled political constituencies in Norway must also be understood with reference to a process seen throughout Scandinavia in recent decades, and well summarized in what the legendary slain social democrat prime minister of Sweden, Olof Palme (1927–86), once referred to as the discontent of rising expectations (*de stigande förväntningarnas missnöje*) (Berggren 2010: 282): as expectations of what the welfare state could and should deliver increased exponentially throughout the post-Second World War period among all strata of society, populist right-wing parties that promised more lavish use of public funds than any other political formations were well positioned to benefit in terms of popular and electoral support.

The very term 'populism' is contested in academic literature. D'Eramo (2013: 8) rightly notes that political formations claiming to represent 'the people' and described as 'populist' until at least the middle of the twentieth century would have worn the epithet as a badge of honour. D'Eramo hypothesizes that the term becomes a term of opprobrium used by mainstream parties against its political opponents at the same time as the category 'the people' loses its centrality in political struggles in the Western world. D'Eramo argues that these processes are linked to the rise of a neoliberal technocratic hegemony and the fall of class-based politics. Yet in the case of Norway and the Progress Party, D'Eramo's analysis is not necessarily applicable. For until very recently, the PP's political discourse made extremely frequent references to 'the people', whose interests it invoked and claimed to represent in its political slogans, and its chairwoman, Mrs Siv Jensen, is on record as having declared as late as 2007 that she was 'proud to be leading a populist party' (as cited in Lode 2013). It was only upon coming to power for the first time as the junior partner in a coalition government with the Conservative Party, Høyre, in 2013, and learning that international media not only described it as a populist right-wing party but in its coverage of the Norwegian parliamentary elections of September that year explicitly linked the PP with its one-time member Anders Behring Breivik, that the PP discovered that it had a problem with being described as a populist right-wing party. Rushing to the defence of the PP, the new Conservative Party prime minister Erna Solberg demanded an apology from a socialist left MP and minister of foreign aid in the previous government, who had dared to describe it as a right-wing populist party on social media. 'I am proud to be leading a party concerned with listening to the people. That has nothing to do with right-wing populism,' the future finance minister, Siv Jensen, now declared to the media, while the PP's advisers scrambled available resources in order to put the message across to international news media that the party would henceforth like to be seen as part of a liberal party family in western Europe, and denied having had any links whatsoever with the Swedish Democrats (SD) or the Danish People's Party (DPP), much to the consternation of the latter. There was, however, little support to be found for Mrs Solberg and Jensen among Norwegian political scientists who had dedicated their academic careers to studying the PP, and who overwhelmingly contended that it was correct to describe the party as a populist right-wing party.

In the words of the political scientist David Art, the Progress Party 'has attracted the same type of voters that in the past voted for Social Democrats' (Art 2011: 160). Yet even if the PP presents itself to the Norwegian electorate as an anti-elitist and anti-technocratic party, and has voters that are generally less educated than voters for other parties, its political staff and candidates in recent years reveal a different story. Art (ibid.: 164) found that all its eighteen full-time political advisers in 2006 were in possession of university degrees.

The party has in recent years received substantial funding from some of the wealthiest Norwegian businessmen and investors.[9] It is an open question what nascent divisions between a highly educated technocratic elite and its core constituency of less educated members and sympathizers will mean for the party's political future – especially after the former won the scramble for ministerial positions after its coming to power after the parliamentary elections of September 2013. With a median age of 49.5 years, the PP also had the oldest voters of any party in 2009 (Berglund et al. 2011: 26). In line with a general trend whereby male voters are attracted to parties on the right and female voters to parties on the left, the PP in 2009 had the support of 26 per cent of male and 20 per cent of female voters (ibid.). In terms of regional support, in that year the PP was strongest on the Norwegian west coast and in the Oslofjord region (ibid.). The PP's electoral appeal has also related to its positioning as a party that is 'tough on crime', and its claim to being a party of and for secular feminists has been central under the leadership of Carl I. Hagen's political successor Siv Jensen (1969–) since 2006. Anthropologist Lila Abu-Lughod has argued that 'the lines between progressives and right-wingers have blurred in [a] shared concern for Muslim women' (Abu-Lughod 2013: 7). And the PP's secular feminism, which emerged only in the aftermath of the significant successes of Norwegian state feminism in the 1970s and 1980s (which the PP had by and large been opposed to), came in a particular package, namely one which had a particular emphasis on patriarchal and/or misogynistic attitudes among Norway's minorities, and among Muslims in particular. The PP's new-found feminist concerns were more often than not about the proverbial 'white women saving brown women from brown men' (Spivak 1993: 93), a theme which had wide traction beyond its own electoral constituencies. The PP thereby successfully externalized the problem of discrimination and oppression against women in Norway. Political scientists have argued that adopting the defence of women's rights as a central issue for populist right-wing political formations was pioneered by such parties in Scandinavia and the Netherlands (Akkerman and Hagelund 2007).

By the mid-1980s, Norwegian right-wing extremists considered Islam and Muslims as the main new threat. Pamphlets circulated by

Bastian Heide in the name of the extreme right-wing party Nasjonalt Folkeparti (National Popular Party) – pamphlets for which Heide was sentenced for racism by a Norwegian court in 1985 – described immigrants from Third World countries as people 'breeding like rats' and 'polluting our culture' (Strømmen 2012: 6). Declaring a 'Norway for Norwegians', Heide was particularly exercised by Norwegian politicians permitting Muslims to build mosques in Norway (ibid.). A 1986 National Popular Party pamphlet declared that Norwegian politicians had 'submitted to foreign gods' by letting 'thousands of Muslims who now demand the right to practise their religion' into the country (Vepsen.org 2012: 11). It was a nineteen-year-old member of the National Popular Party who was behind the first Norwegian terror attacks against Muslims. The bomb attack on the Nor Mosque belonging to Norwegian Muslims of the minority Ahmadiyya sect in Oslo west on 14 June 1985, left no one dead. But that was only because members of the congregation who would usually assemble in the cellar of the mosque on the night in question had by chance congregated in a private home instead (Strømmen 2011b: 34–5).

A transfer from Jews to Muslims as the perceived main existential threat against Norway occurred among Norwegian right-wing extremists during the mid to late 1980s, a time in which Norway received an increasing number of refugees and asylum claimants from Muslim countries. In *My Father's War* (*Min Fars Krig*), the award-winning Norwegian author Bjørn Westlie describes how his late father, who had served as a Norwegian volunteer for the Waffen SS Nordic division Wiking on the killing fields of Ukraine during the Second World War, and a number of his fellow travellers among Norwegian Nazis, by the 1980s had simply replaced Jews with Muslims as the new 'enemy within' (Westlie 2008). Muslims, viewed as a new existential threat, were absolutely central to the programme of the far more popular and influential Folkebevegelsen mot innvandring (FMI or Popular Movement Against Immigration), established in Haugesund on the west coast of Norway in 1987 (Strømmen 2011b: 34): Its leader, the former Labour Party local politician Arne Myrdal, declared that he was part of a 'resistance movement' which was 'fighting against the Muslim invasion of our country, and against the national traitors who assist them' (cited in ibid.: 34, my translation).

Extreme ideas, Aristotle Kallis has argued, 'begin their life cycle as politically and socially marginal and radical counterpropositions to established "mainstream cognition"' (Kallis 2013: 55). The emergent extreme right-wing rhetoric about Islam and Muslims in Norway in the mid and late 1980s provided a reservoir into which PP leaders would occasionally dip. During an election rally in the rural town of Rørvik in the county of North Trøndelag on 7 September 1987, ahead of that year's parliamentary elections, the charismatic and popular party chairman (uncontested from 1978 to 2006) Carl I. Hagen (1944–) read out a letter he allegedly received from a Norwegian Muslim citizen by the name of Muhammad Mustafa. Hagen was widely credited with having fashioned the party he inherited into one of Norway's most popular. In the letter dated 8 July 1987, Mustafa was cited as having written that Hagen 'was fighting in vain' against Muslims, since 'Islam will conquer Norway too' and that 'one day, mosques will be as common in Norway as churches are today' and the 'heathen cross in the flag would be gone'. And the reason for this was that 'we' Muslims 'give birth to more children than you' and that 'many right-believing Muslim men in fertile age' come to Norway each year. If this political rhetoric now sounds like an early version of the 'Eurabia' hypothesis (see Chapter 5), it is simply due to the fact that this is exactly what it is.

Norwegian mainstream newspapers soon revealed that the letter was a forgery, and a man named Muhammad Mustafa from Oslo demanded financial compensation of 500,000 Norwegian kroner from Hagen for having defamed him publicly. Mustafa, a Muslim who sustained himself and his family as a pizza baker (Strømmen 2011b), had received a number of racist phone calls as a result of Hagen's claims. The matter was eventually settled out of court, after Hagen agreed to compensate Mustafa.

However, many voters appeared to be undaunted by this scandal, and in the 1987 parliamentary elections the PP received its best result to date: 12.1 per cent of the national vote. The background to the PP's success in channelling anti-immigrant sentiment lay in a significant rise in the number of people applying for asylum in Norway from 1986 to 1987, after Denmark had implemented new restrictions on asylum seekers in 1986 (Jupskås 2009). A pattern had been set, and the PP's anti-immigration and anti-Muslim rhetoric has become a staple of its political platform. A number of academic studies of the party's growing popularity and influence in Norway in the 1990s (see Aardal 1999; Hagelund 2003; Jupskås 2009) concluded that the PP's programmatic scepticism towards immigration and immigrants was central to it. While there is no doubt that the party was consistent in its support for and defence of democratic means of affecting Norwegian mainstream politics, certain party members and parliamentarians would continue to borrow ideas and rhetoric from Norway's extreme right and, after 9/11, to read and reference 'Eurabia' authors in their political discourse. The strategic reasoning of a party positioning itself as the voice of 'the common man' – white, with low levels of education and likely to feel disempowered – by pandering to as well as sharpening this imaginary citizen's hardening views on immigration and Muslims is not difficult to detect. In a national and representative survey on views of the welfare state, the sociologist Axel West Pedersen found that 16 per cent of respondents who identified themselves as voting for the PP placed themselves on the 'extreme right' of the political spectrum. At the time, that would amount to an estimated 60,000 voters.[10] The survey in question does not tell us whether these 16 per cent of the PP's voters would include acceptance of violent and non-democratic political means in their definition of what it meant to have extreme right sympathies. But it does tell us that PP strategists have been correct in assuming that there is a political constituency of extreme right-wing sympathizers among Norwegians that could and would be mobilized in support of the party by invoking extreme right-wing ideas and sentiments. The often anecdotally based and/or fabricated evidence that this rhetoric invoked was geared to appeal to this electoral segment, could be switched 'on' and 'off' at will, and did not carry much of a responsibility for a party in seemingly perennial opposition. The 'Mustafa' letter provides one case in point. Another is provided by an allegation in the 2013 autobiography of the PP's former vice-chairman and spokesperson on immigration Per Sandberg (Sandberg 2013) in which Sandberg refers to a small municipality on the west coast of Norway as having been forced to construct a new primary school when a man of Somali origin had – upon the advice of a named state bureaucrat – allegedly tricked Norwegian immigration authorities into granting him family reunification with three wives and their twenty-two children. A local newspaper which did some basic research into the story was in November 2013 able to document that the story was entirely bogus (Hattestein 2013). When confronted with this, Sandberg, one of the PP populists who was left out of the PP's first cabinet after the Norwegian parliamentary elections of September 2013, responded with a shrug, asserting that 'it could have happened' (Kristiansen 2013).

In 1995, Norwegian newspapers revealed that the PP MP and spokesperson on immigration issues Øystein Hedstrøm took part in a secret meeting at Godlia Cinema in Oslo. The meeting was also attended by the openly racist Hvit Valgallianse (White Electoral Alliance),[11] the Popular Movement Against Immigration and other extreme-right organizations. During this meeting, Hedstrøm called for a united front against immigration (Strømmen 2011b: 161). These disclosures did nothing to dent electoral support for the PP. Norwegian political scientists later concluded that opposition to immigration was the main vector in the gains made by the PP in the 1995 municipal elections (Bjørklund 1999). Party chairman Carl I. Hagen removed Hedstrøm from his post as party spokesperson on immigration, but later congratulated *Dagbladet*, which first reported the Godlia meeting, for the electoral result (Strømmen 2011b: 162). In the 1995 election campaign, issues relating to immigration were central: 47 per cent of those polled who cast their votes for the PP said that immigration was the main reason for their choice of party (Hagelund 2003: 48).

In an attempt to expand the PP's base of support since 1990, particularly after 2001, the party started chasing conservative and evangelical Christian voters who had traditionally had a preference for the Christian democratic party Kristelig Folkeparti (KrF): the Christian People's Party (CPP). From 1985 to 2005, the PP's level of support among organized religious people in Norway increased from 1.6 per cent to 15.2 per cent; the support for the CPP among this category decreased from 54 per cent to 24 per cent (Raknes 2012: 145). The PP expressed unreserved support for the state of Israel, made highly critical claims concerning Islam and Muslims, and emphasized questions relating to values and morals (Jupskås 2009: 56–7). In a speech to the Christian evangelical congregation *Levende Ord* (Living Word) in Bergen (Norway's second-largest city, on its west coast) in 2004, Carl I. Hagen argued that 'small [Muslim] children are used as suicide bombers [by Muslims] in order to Islamize the world'. 'We Christians', Hagen continued, 'are very concerned with children. "Let the small children come unto me, said Jesus." I cannot understand that [the Prophet] Muhammad could have said the same [here, there is a roar of laughter from the audience]. In case he had said anything reminiscent, it would have been "let the small children come to me, so that I can exploit them in my struggle to Islamize the world"' (Alstadsæter 2004).[12] In the same speech, Hagen also compared Muslims to Nazis by asserting that 'Muslims have, like Adolf Hitler, made it clear a long time ago that their long-term aim is to Islamize the world' (Tjønn et al. 2004).[13] A staple of far-right political rhetoric on Islam and Europe in recent decades, the analogy between Muslims and Nazis would later be made by a number of far-right European politicians from Geert Wilders in the Netherlands to Marine Le Pen in France (Betz 2013: 76).

Methodologically, just as when he introduced the so-called Mustafa letter in 1987, Hagen's speech traded in Islamophobic tropes concerning an impending Islamization of Europe and Norway. We know from Hagen's own recommended reading offered to a newspaper reporter later that year that he was inspired by the blood-curdling book *Islam and Terrorism* by Mark A. Gabriel, an Egyptian-born convert from Islam turned Christian evangelical polemical author (Gabriel 2002;[14] Leirvik 2006: 152).

Originally published by the evangelical Christian publisher Charisma House in Florida (a self-designated publisher of books for 'spirit-filled Christians who are passionate about God'), *Islam and Terrorism* was published in a Norwegian translation by the evangelical Christian publisher Prokla-Media in 2002. By 2004, the book had sold so well that it had a second printing. Prokla-Media has close links with the evangelical Christian proselytizing movement called 'Youth with a Mission in Norway'. Copies of *Islam and Terrorism* were sent to a number of Norwegian MPs as part of the publisher's marketing campaign.[15] In the publisher's introduction, the readers are told that the author is a 'man who has grown up with Islam, who knew the Qur'an by heart from childhood, who has been an imam in the Egyptian city of Giza and a professor of Islamic history in Cairo' (Gabriel 2002: 5, cited from the Norwegian edition).

Yet even if the publisher's introduction admits that Gabriel describes Islam as a 'religion of hatred' he argues against 'hate and all forms of discrimination against Muslims' (ibid.: 6). Mark Gabriel's narrative about Islam and terrorism is anchored in a personal coming-of-age story that traces the authentic Muslim's turning from the 'darkness of Islam' to the 'light of evangelical Christianity'. His message is quite simple: al-Qaeda's terrorist attacks on 9/11 were not an aberration in Islamic history, but were its logical consequence. For 'hatred is inherent to Islam' (ibid.: 25); Islam's history can 'only be characterized as a river of blood' (ibid.), and Islam's final goal is 'Islamic rule throughout the world' (ibid.: 63, 107). 'Islamists' are described by Gabriel as 'those who practise violence and acts of terror', practise 'the authentic Islam such as the Qur'an prescribes' (ibid.: 66). Note the collapse of any distinctions between Islam and Islamism and between moderate Islamists who oppose the use of violence and radical Islamists who endorse it; this rhetorical collapse is also ubiquitous in so-called 'Eurabia' literature (see Chapter 5). Gabriel informs his readers that Islamists think that war includes 'deceit' and therefore holds that 'lies are an important part of the war led by Islam' (ibid.: 117). There are 'three stages' to the colonization of non-Western lands by Muslims 'according to the Qur'an': when Muslims are in a minority, and weak, they adhere to the law of the land, but work untiringly to increase their numbers. In the second stage, they prepare for the third stage, the 'jihad' or 'holy war' against infidel non-Muslims (ibid.: 111–13). On this conception, Muslim immigration to Europe or the United States is nothing less than part of a grand deceitful scheme for 'Islamizing' the West. And mosques are 'centres for war planning' (ibid.: 124) and, as such, inherently dangerous in non-Muslim lands.

We know too little about PP leader Carl I. Hagen's readings to ascertain whether he believed Mark Gabriel's claims, but if he did, it becomes easier to understand why he and his party, as well as PP supporters (including Hege Storhaug and Bruce Bawer at the

Human Rights Service – HRS – in Oslo[16]), in the past decade have repeatedly called for curbs on 'non-Western' immigration directed particularly at Muslims.

In May 2005, the PP's then spokesperson on immigration, MP Per Sandberg, informed the Norwegian media that the PP's parliamentary caucus had received 'information' from 'sources in the Pakistani milieu in Oslo' about a secretive extremist Muslim network in Oslo with '30,000 members of Pakistani origin' who had sworn an 'oath of loyalty' to it (Mosveen et al. 2005). The network was said to be 'fundamentalist, anti-democratic and potentially violent'. Its members were alleged to have been scouting for reasonably priced properties around Oslo, with the intention of building mosques and facilities used for 'training in violence'. Sandberg also duly informed the media that he was meeting the Police Security Services (PST) to report on the information he had obtained from his sources. Coincidentally, Hege Storhaug's HRS, whose own closeness to the PP was by then well known,[17] had also obtained the same 'information' and forwarded it to the PST. The PST made no statement about the matter to the Norwegian media.

The bogus nature of the 'information' the PP and HRS had been 'kind enough' to share with the Norwegian public through the most popular (and most widely read among PP voters) *VG* would be demonstrable through the fact that there were, as of 2004, only 26,286 individuals of Pakistani origin in the whole of Norway (Østby 2008: 18). Sandberg and Storhaug's claims about the 'information' they had received implied not only that there were far more people of Pakistani origin living in Norway than was recorded in official statistics, but also that each and every one of these people was part of the very same 'extreme network'. A newspaper reporter worth his or her salt might perhaps have bothered to ask the fundamental question why supposedly confidential information about alleged terror preparations on Norwegian soil was shared with the tabloid media at the same time that it was shared with the PST if one wanted to prevent such preparations taking place. It is noteworthy, however, that the *VG* reporters who covered this story appear not to have asked any critical questions about Sandberg and Storhaug's 'information', nor about their sources. It was politics as usual in the mutually beneficial polarization loop between Norwegian tabloid media and the populist right wing, whereby the former increase their sales, and the latter their level of popular support.

Islamization by stealth

In a speech to the PP's party congress in February 2009 before the parliamentary election in September, party leader Siv Jensen warned against the 'Islamization by stealth' ('*snikislamisering*') of Norwegian society. 'The reality is that we are at the point of allowing an Islamization by stealth of this society [i.e. Norway], and we have to put a stop to it,' she asserted. 'We cannot allow particular groups to decide the direction of societal development in Norway.' Jensen concluded, 'We [i.e. the PP] will not allow special demands [*særkrav*] from particular groups.' It was all too clear that the particular groups that Jensen had in mind were the Muslims – who at the time were estimated to make up 3 per cent of Norway's population. When asked to provide cases of this ongoing 'Islamization by stealth', the party provided a list that included demands to wear the hijab as part of a police uniform; to provide halal food (animals slaughtered for food according to Islamic ritual) for Muslim inmates in Norwegian prisons; and to allow schools to practise gender segregation (as some Oslo schools allegedly did).

However, not only the PP claims ownership of the term 'Islamization by stealth'. The right-wing extremist and Islamophobic organization Stans Islamiseringen av Norge (Stop the Islamization of Norway) (which alleges that it has 10,000 followers on Facebook and has links with similar organizations in Europe and the United States) claimed that it was in fact the first to introduce the concept, long before Jensen's speech. According to author Øyvind Strømmen, it is a rhetorical concept strikingly similar to one found among the counter-jihadists and 'Eurabia' fantasists who inspired Anders Behring Breivik, and it had been used on *VG*'s web debate platform as early as 2003 (Strømmen 2011b: 191). Prominent US Islamophobic author Robert Spencer's[18] 2008 book on 'stealth jihad' seems to have popularized the term in 'counter-jihadist' circles on the web (Spencer 2008).[19] Spencer's concept of what this entails is much like Jensen's: a quiet subversion of 'our values' by Muslims using non-violent and democratic means to further their alleged agenda of 'Islamizing' Western societies.

While the importance of immigration issues has certainly varied for the PP's electorate over time, immigration has been the one issue over which it has claimed the most 'political proprietorship' (see Hagelund 2003); it is also the area in which the party's rhetoric and policies have had the most influence over other mainstream parties in Norway. The influence of the PP on immigration issues is indicated by an opinion survey a mere month after 22/7. In a representative sample of the Norwegian population, 956 Norwegians were asked which party was 'best placed to solve the challenges concerning immigration': 21.9 per cent stated the PP, second only to the Labour Party (28.1 per cent) (Karlsen 2011). On no other issue would the PP obtain similar levels of stated support for their policies. On the basis of the party's result in the municipal elections of September 2011 (11.4 per cent nationally), one may surmise that the party's appeal to voters on immigration issues reaches beyond its core electoral constituency, a fact well known in other parties, not least the governing Labour Party.

The PP's rhetoric on immigration, Islam and Muslims, which increasingly conflated the three in the decade after 11 September 2001, came packaged with the charges that 'the politically correct elite' (represented most prominently by the dominant social democratic party, the Labour Party) was misleading the Norwegian public about the long- and short-term consequences of immigration, particularly of Muslim immigration. As political scientist Cas Mudde has noted of populist radical-right parties in contemporary Europe, 'the key internal enemy of all populist radical right parties is "the elite," a broad and indeterminate amalgam of political, economic, and cultural actors'.[20] This elite, often described as a technocratic elite unconcerned with the plight of ordinary white men and women, 'is criticized in both nativist and populist terms', i.e. as 'traitors to the nation and as corruptors of the people' (Mudde 2007: 65).

The PP's critique of parties in power over immigration and integration came couched in a political rhetoric whereby the PP presented itself as the only political party in Norway opposing særkrav (special demands) from religious minorities. In fact, as indicated by the party's proposals in the parliamentary debate on a new immigration law (*Utlendingsloven*) in 2008, it was perfectly willing to undermine the universality of secular law and Norway's international human rights obligations by proposing particular 'Muslim refugee quotas' (the PP singled out Somalis, Pakistanis and Afghans). The argument, as presented by the then party spokesperson on immigration Per Willy Amundsen, was that Muslims were harder to integrate than other minorities and that regardless of their reason for applying for refugee status in Norway, their numbers had to be limited.[21]

The rhetoric intensifies: 2010 to 2011

The Islamophobic rhetoric from PP MPs intensified in 2010 and 2011. In May 2011, Christian Tybring-Gjedde, a PP MP from Oslo and then chairman of the Oslo PP, addressed the party congress at a hotel near the Gardermoen International Airport outside Oslo. Tybring-Gjedde had by then developed a long record of anti-immigration and Islamophobic statements and he worked closely with Hege Storhaug's Human Rights Service (HRS)[22] and Document.no.[23] In March 2010, Tybring-Gjedde had argued in an interview that 'to dress one's children in hijab is as bad as dressing them up in a Ku Klux Klan hood' (Dagbladet 2010). 'The hijab is not an innocent piece of cloth,' Tybring-Gjedde charged, and 'Norway must now take a forceful position with regard to the Islamization which is occurring right in front of our eyes' (ibid.). In 'Dream from Disneyland' (*Drøm fra Disneyland*), an op-ed article co-authored with Kent Andersen, his close party ally and a board member of the Oslo PP, and published by *Aftenposten* in August 2010, Tybring-Gjedde accused the governing Norwegian Labour Party (LP/AP) of 'wanting to tear the country apart' by allowing 'thousands of immigrants' with their 'un-culture' into the country every year. 'What is wrong with Norwegian culture, since the Labour Party wants to replace it with multiculture?' Tybring-Gjedde and Andersen had written, concluding: '[A multiculture] which represents structured rootlessness, and will tear our country apart' (Tybring-Gjedde and Andersen 2010). Positioning themselves as the vox populi of those who 'love Norway' – as against the governing Labour Party – Tybring-Gjedde and Andersen charged that the Labour Party was 'stabbing our own culture in the back' by conducting a 'multicultural experiment' (ibid.). The rhetoric of Tybring-Gjedde and Andersen at this point is, as pointed out by Malkenes (2012: 53), eerily reminiscent of the conspiratorial myths about left-wing 'internationalism' and the notion of 'the Communist' as a traitor to the nation (Seymour 2011) that were central to historical right-wing extremism in Europe (see Fløgstad 2012), including that found among 1930s Nazis in Norway. Not only that, but in its construing of the role of the Norwegian Labour Party as 'traitors to the nation' who conduct 'multicultural experiments' on an unwitting and/or unwilling population, it comes perilously close to the world view promoted in Anders Behring Breivik's tract. At the time of its publication, well-known Norwegian right-wing extremists certainly recognized its tone and tenor as being identical to their own, and expressed their unconditional support through the Norwegian media (Skevik and Johansen 2010).

In January 2011 Kent Andersen wrote in his personal blog that there were 'striking similarities between the three great ideologies of humankind: Nazism, Communism and Islam'. Islam is deliberately construed here as a political ideology rather than a religion; this is central to much of the Islamophobic and 'Eurabia' literature of recent years.[24] The analogy between Islam and Nazism or communism, used by Islamophobic right-wing European politicians from Geert Wilders of the Dutch Freedom Party (Partij van de Frijheit, PVV) to Marine Le Pen of the French National Front (Front Nationale, FN), also suggests that Islam will have to be fought by non-Muslim Europeans in ways similar to those used to fight Nazism and communism. And this 'fighting' would seem not to exclude violence. Andersen also raised the question of whether 'moderate Muslims' actually exist: 'as if there was something like "moderate Nazis."'

This rhetorical trope also owes a debt to Islamophobic and 'Eurabia' literature, in which a central tenet is that to the extent that Muslims publicly profess abhorrence of violence and terrorism, they are being disingenuous about the 'real Islam' (i.e. the Islam of violence and terrorism) and practising 'dissimulation' or *taqiyya*.[25] The charge of double-speak directed against structurally weak minorities in Europe is not new – it was central to classical anti-Semitic discourse and featured prominently in Hitler's *Mein Kampf* (see Malkenes 2012: 32). This is significant for Islamophobes as it raises the prospect that there are no people of Muslim background who are to be trusted under any circumstances, since, to their minds, the practice of *taqiyya* gives licence to dissimulate regarding the absence of Islamic faith. Thus, to those who view the world in this manner, there are no such things as 'good' and 'bad' Muslims (Mamdani 2004), and so the division between those two categories of Muslims, central to the so-called 'war on terror', is by and large considered a fiction. Andersen had in earlier posts referred to the Labour Party as *kulturquislinger* (cultural quislings or traitors to Norwegian culture) and was unapologetic when contacted in February 2011 by a Norwegian newspaper.

Christian Tybring-Gjedde refused to take exception to Andersen's statements about Islam; PP chairman Siv Jensen refused to comment; and the PP spokesperson on immigration and integration, Per Willy Amundsen,[26] characterized Andersen's statements as 'interesting' and 'completely unproblematic' (Therkelsen 2011). Tybring-Gjedde's failure to take exception to Andersen's statements was hardly surprising, inasmuch as Tybring-Gjedde in an invited lecture to 'Friends of Document.no', which came about on the initiative of Hans Rustad as a direct result of Tybring-Gjedde and Andersen's infamous August 2010 op-ed 'Dream from Disneyland', presented 'statistics' on the number of Muslims in a future Europe drawn from 'Eurabia' literature and declared the situation in Norway and Europe to be 'worse than in the 1930s' (Torgersen et al. 2011). Tybring-Gjedde's address to the PP party congress in May 2011 took this one step further:

> In Groruddalen[27] blonde girls are harassed and color their hair dark, children are threatened for having Salami sausages in their lunch bags, boys with immigrant background threaten Norwegian[28] boys with beatings if they do not get more time on the football field, ... cars are torched, and the windows of school buildings broken. This is not something that the mono-cultural Member of Parliament Tybring-Gjedde has conjured up. It is a part of the reality in multicultural Groruddalen in Oslo. (Johnsrud 2011)

Tybring-Gjedde went on to characterize immigrant boys as *hissigere* than Norwegian boys. *Hissig* connotes anger and resentment and a lack of self-control and self-restraint that potentially leads to violence.

He had Muslim residents of Groruddalen particularly in mind, which was also evident from the assertion later in his speech that 'Islam cannot stand values of freedom, and the power of Islam [in Norway] increases day by day. Therefore, immigration from Muslim countries must be substantially reduced.'

Returning to his charge of the social democratic and governing Labour Party having turned Norway into a 'multicultural Disneyland', Tybring-Gjedde concluded by listing a series of political demands from both the Labour Party and the Conservative Party (Høyre): that new immigrants in Norway were to be faced with demands of 'unconditional love [ubetinget kjærlighet] for Norway and *our* [my emphasis] Christian cultural heritage'.[29] Tybring-Gjedde's rhetoric illustrates a point made by British political scientist Matthew Goodwin in a recent Chatham House report on so-called populist extremist parties (PEPs) in Europe (Goodwin 2011). Goodwin notes that anti-immigration stances and anti-Muslim sentiments are main drivers of support for these parties throughout western Europe. Feelings of being threatened by immigrants and Muslims experienced by these parties' supporters (who are overwhelmingly male and working-class), Goodwin argues, '... do not simply stem from economic grievances ... they appear to stem from a belief that immigrants, minority groups and rising cultural diversity are threatening the national culture, community and way of life' (ibid.: 11).

Norway is perhaps a particularly salient case in point in this regard, for it has weathered the storms of the ongoing global financial crisis, particularly acute in the United States and Europe, better than most other countries. Norway has comparatively low levels of unemployment and socio-economic inequality, and feelings of an economic threat from immigrants can hardly explain why Norway, in the ten years leading up to 22/7, has had one of the strongest and most popular populist right-wing parties in Europe.

The 'culturalist turn' in the Norwegian debate on immigration and integration came as early as the 1990s, was spearheaded by the PP and politicians and intellectuals aligned to the right wing of the Labour Party, and formed part of a 'culturalization of politics' which developed in tandem with rising levels of socio-economic inequality and a liberalization of the Norwegian economy. As political scientist

Wendy Brown points out, this 'culturalization of politics' 'reduces non-liberal life to "culture" at the same time as it divests liberal democratic institutions of any association with culture' (Brown 2006: 23). Supposedly neutral and universalistic liberalism is, in political philosopher Charles Taylor's words, '[itself] the reflection of particular cultures' (Taylor 1994 [1992]: 44). The 'culturalization of politics' meant that 'non-white' Norwegians of immigrant background in general, and Muslims of immigrant background in particular, came to be seen as having 'cultures' that were (more or less) incompatible with non-historicized, universalistic and non-negotiable Norwegian 'values'. Liberal values such as freedom of expression, human rights, women's and gay rights were 'nationalized' (see Laegaard 2007) to such an extent that only Caucasian Norwegians related by blood were seen as being capable of fully embodying these liberal values in an 'authentic manner'. This was for all practical purposes not a civic but a remodulated ethnic nationalism.

As these 'core' and non-negotiable Norwegian 'values' expanded to include gay rights, a greater societal acceptance of such rights and legislation advancing the right to civil same-sex partnership and eventually marriage in the 1990s and 2000s,[30] the Muslim male also became an alleged threat against gays and lesbians in Norway (see Bangstad 2011). Scholars have argued that much of the contemporary gay rights discourse in Norway serves to demarcate the 'liberal' from the 'illiberal', a tolerant 'we' from an intolerant 'them' – with the dividing line understood as mapping a non-Muslim/Muslim line of demarcation (Gressgård and Jacobsen 2008).

The role of other parties

Up to this point, my focus on far-right (from extreme to populist right-wing) political formations and their discourse on Islam and Muslims, and the trafficking between them, may seem to suggest that I hold the view that the use of Islamophobic rhetorical tropes in Norway has been limited to the far right. It would be simplistic in the extreme, however, to argue that Islamophobia and similar forms of neo-racism have not affected other parties of the centre and left of Norwegian politics in the past decades. After all, these parties compete with the PP for votes in an open electoral market in which there is every indication that popular sentiments concerning immigration and immigrants have become more negative in recent decades. In a study of the changing tone and tenor of the statements on immigration and integration from the Progress Party, the Conservative Party and the Labour Party in the period from 1985 to 2009, Simonnes (2013) has found incontrovertible evidence of steadily more negative statements on these issues from the latter two parties, a tendency coinciding with the electoral rise of the PP in the same period. This is strongly suggestive of a situation in which the latter two parties have tried to 'shore up' popular support by gradually changing their tune on immigration and integration.

However, the Norwegian Progress Party has been able to set the political agenda on immigration and integration in Norway to an extent it has not been able to do with other issues in the political debate (see Hagelund 2003). It is also a fact that its sympathizers display more negative attitudes and sentiments concerning Muslims and other minority groups in Norway than do sympathizers or supporters of any other party in Norway (HL Centre 2012: 53). Both Gullestad (2006) and Hagelund (2003) have argued that the Norwegian political discourse on immigration and integration has served to demonize the PP and thereby, to a certain extent, deflect attention from forms of xenophobia, neo-racism and Islamophobia among voters and representatives of other political parties. Let us consider some examples of the political range of Islamophobia in Norway in the past decade.

The first book in the 'Eurabia' genre from a Norwegian publishing house was Oriana Fallaci's *The Rage and the Pride*, brought out in a Norwegian translation in 2003 by the respectable Gyldendal publishing house. But the first published book in the genre by a Norwegian author was *Letter to Lady Liberty: Europe in Danger* (*Amerikabrevet: Europa i fare*), from the print-on-demand publisher Koloritt in 2007 and funded by the prestigious Fritt Ord Foundation in Norway. Its author, Hallgrim Berg (1945–), a prominent Norwegian politician and member of parliament from 1977 to 2001 from the Conservative Party (Høyre), was passionate about 'standing by the United States and Israel' regardless of these states' actual policies.[31] Berg advocated the view that Europe was in fact in a civilizational war with 'radical Islam' and at the point of being overrun by Muslims owing to demographic factors. *Letter to Lady Liberty* cited Oriana Fallaci and Bat Ye'or and even referred approvingly to 'Fjordman'. It received a lot of media attention, and sold tens of thousands of copies. While clearly uncomfortable with a respected party member's venture into the darker recesses of Islamophobic literature, Berg's Conservative Party refused to censor or criticize him publicly. To say that Berg was completely unapologetic about his promotion of Eurabia literature after 22/7 would be an understatement. In *Klassekampen* in November 2011 Berg described Bat Ye'or's *Eurabia – the Euro–Arab Axis* (2005a) as 'a sharp book of history, with clear analysis, documentation and assertions and predictions of what lies in store for Europe'. As for 'Fjordman's' synopsis of the book, the *Eurabia Code* (copied in Behring Breivik's tract), Berg asserted that 'it has [useful] perspectives for the curious and interested reader' (Berg 2011; see also Olsen and Bisgaard 2011).

Early in 2011, the chairman of the Socialist Left Party (SV) in the suburb of Nordstrand in Oslo, Morten Schau, was forced to resign his party membership owing to his parallel involvement in the organization Stop the Islamization of Norway (SIAN). SV was then a junior partner in the Norwegian centre-left tripartite government. After his resignation, Schau told his local newspaper that he 'wanted to fight against the Islamization of society'. When asked what he meant by this, Schau pointed to 'small girls dressed in hijab, religious symbols worn by public servants and gender segregation'. Schau said, 'I didn't think SIAN would be seen so negatively [by my own party]' (Sundsbø 2011). Norway's minister of oil and energy, Ola Borten Moe, in early 2011 recruited a publishing editor at Aschehoug, Halvor Fosli, as his personal adviser. Fosli, who had never held a position, let alone party membership, in the Norwegian Centre Party (Senterpartiet), was recruited by Borten Moe on the basis of writings of an Islamophobic nature posted on Fosli's personal Facebook page. In 2010, Borten Moe described Norwegian citizens living in inter-cousin marriages (most prevalent among Norwegian-Pakistanis, hence among Muslims) as engaging in 'incest' and declared Norwegian and European superiority in civilization by asserting that 'we don't have much to learn from the Arab world'.

Karita Bekkemellem, formerly minister for children and families for the Labour Party (2000–07) and the leader of the Labour Party's Women's Organization (1998–2007), during a Norwegian TV show in 2009, compared the use of the Islamic headscarf (the hijab) with 'female genital mutilation'. As a cabinet minister, Bekkemellem had close contacts with Hege Storhaug of HRS, to the extent that in her autobiography, *My Red Heart* (*Mitt røde hjerte*), published in 2008, she described Storhaug as one of her personal heroes.

These examples are arguably anecdotal evidence, and there is no doubt that when it comes to promoting and legitimizing Islamophobic expressions in the Norwegian mediated public spheres in recent decades, the PP has by far the worst record in Norwegian politics. Yet these examples do suggest that the naturalization of Islamophobic statements, expressions and modes of thought has by no means been limited to the PP.

The role of the media

In 2007, Swedish sociologist and expert on radical right-wing movements in Europe Jens Rydgren argued that there had been 'no systematic study of the role of the mass media in the rise of new radical right-wing parties' in Europe (Rydgren 2007: 255). Yet he suggested that 'important changes in the mass media over time … may play a role in the electoral fortunes of new radical right-wing parties' (ibid.). By 'important changes in the mass media', Rydgren pointed to the shift in a number of Scandinavian countries, including Norway, from a limited number of public service TV channels in the early 1980s to a wide variety of commercial TV channels in the 1990s. In Norway, there was a concurrent shift from party-aligned newspapers to independent and often tabloid newspapers that significantly increased the demands for commercial viability and faster production on newspaper editors and reporters. If anything, these concerns became even more prominent with the introduction of round-the-clock internet editions of Norwegian newspapers in the early 2000s. This commercialization of Norwegian (and Scandinavian) media led to more 'opportunities for visibility of emerging new political contenders in the media' (ibid.).

The relationship between the media and right-wing populists in the PP in Norway is ambivalent and ambiguous: open support for the Progress Party in the mainstream Norwegian news media is difficult to find, and the antagonism of PP party leaders towards the media led the then party chairman Carl I. Hagen to famously dub the national broadcaster NRK '*Arbeidernes Rikskringkasting*' or ARK, in a rhetorical play on the NRK's alleged links with and biases towards the Norwegian Labour Party (Arbeiderpartiet, AP). Academic studies of the coverage of the 2005 parliamentary election campaign, however, suggested that the private national broadcaster TV2 framed the election as centrally focused on immigration policies and, by tacitly linking immigration to crime, contributed to the PP's electoral success (Mjelde 2007: 101). Studies of the voting preferences of Norwegian media reporters also generally indicate low levels of support for the PP (see Respons 2012). But as regards scepticism towards Islam and Muslims, the PP could count on support far beyond its core constituencies, and also in the media. Moreover, its professed support for absolutist conceptions of freedom of expression in recent decades meant a coalescing of views between liberal media editors and PP politicians as regards the alleged threat against these freedoms emanating from Muslims (see Bangstad forthcoming).

Academic studies of the coverage of Islam and Christianity in the Norwegian media have concluded that 'overall, Christianity is covered positively, and Islam fairly negatively' (Storvoll 2007: 2). In the case of Denmark, social anthropologist Peter Hervik (2011) demonstrated how various Danish media such as *Ekstra-bladet* and *Jylland-Posten* from the late 1990s had played an instrumental role in the rise of electoral support for and influence of the populist right-wing and strongly Islamophobic Danish Peoples' Party (Dansk Folkeparti, DPP).

In Norway too, a shift towards more absolutist conceptions of freedom of expression occurred during the 1990s and 2000s. This shift had strong support among liberal and mainstream media editors, who, as a result of the Rushdie affair and its repercussions in Norway, as well as the cartoon crisis in 2005/06, identified Muslims as the main threats against these new conceptions of freedom of expression. These developments would, in sum, open the field for ever more virulent articulations of Islamophobia in mainstream media platforms from 2001 to 2011.

In the aftermath of 22/7, Oxford historian and *Guardian* columnist

Timothy Garton Ash argued that if mass murderer Anders Behring Breivik had only read some mainstream newspapers, his world views would have been 'punctured by fact, reason and common sense' (Ash 2011). As far as unwarranted conclusions go, this would be hard to beat. The fact is, Behring Breivik seems to have been quite a voracious consumer of Norwegian newspapers; his participation on internet debates at *VG Nett* and *Hegnar Online* and his meticulous accounts in his tract of hours spent reading newspapers, listening to the radio and watching news broadcasts on television attest to that. Furthermore, in light of the available evidence, it is a depoliticizing and decontextualizing myth that he could not have found 'fighting words' echoing his own in the Norwegian mainstream media from 2001 to 2011; they were there in the form of mainstream newspaper editors' endorsement of 'Eurabia' literature, generous reviews of the same literature in these newspapers, and op-ed editors permitting Islamophobic expressions in their sections.

In a series of articles in April 2004, timed to coincide with the publication of a Norwegian translation of Fallaci's Islamophobic polemical rant *The Force of Reason* (*Fornuftens styrke*) by Gyldendal in 2004, *Aftenposten*'s correspondent in Italy, Kristin Flood, endorsed and promoted the work of this prominent 'Eurabia' author. Owing to the ongoing attempts to put Fallaci on trial for racist and discriminatory statements in several European countries at the time, Flood knew that Fallaci had in her book both referred to European Muslims as 'breeding rats' and declared that Europe was at war with Muslims. Yet in Flood's newspaper articles on Fallaci, there is not a single noteworthy reservation concerning Fallaci's 'Eurabian' fantasies; in fact, Flood refers to Fallaci as having a 'razor-sharp pen' in a regurgitation of the blurb on the back of the Norwegian edition of Fallaci's 2003 book (Flood 2004a, b). But this was not all. In October 2005, the *Morgenbladet*, which has a largely academic readership, published a review of Bat Ye'or's *Eurabia: The Euro-Arab Axis*; the review was by their regular reviewer Tord Østberg, a medical doctor from Oslo. The review was a laudatory endorsement.

The book's most significant contribution is the author's thoroughly documented presentations of the will of European states to invest in the cultural and ideological work regarded as necessary in order to ease immigration from Muslim to Christian cultures. Since this project appears to have been hidden from European publics, it seems reasonable to suggest that the actors themselves have regarded it as pretty controversial. Ye'or's disclosure therefore appears as an adequate enrichment of the immigration debate. (Østberg 2003)

Aftenposten's former op-ed and cultural editor Knut Olav Åmås (1967–), perhaps the most politically and intellectually influential Norwegian op-ed editor in light of *Aftenposten's* wide readership and circulation,[32] has in editorial columns twice recommended the 'Eurabia' books of the US-born but Norwegian-based author Bruce Bawer and endorsed the work of the popular Somali-born atheist Ayaan Hirsi Ali (Åmås 2006, 2010), who, in an echo of 'Eurabia' tropes, refers to Muslims in Europe as 'a potential fifth column' (Ali 2010: 139). In the aftermath of the 22/7 terror attacks, Åmås would be confronted with his prior endorsement of the writings of Bawer, yet declared that those who confronted him with this were 'ultra-leftists' and that he had not endorsed the parts of Bawer's book in which he expressed his 'Eurabia' views (Murtnes 2011b). This was a half-truth, inasmuch as none of Åmås's editorial endorsements of Bawer's 'Eurabia' books had carried any reservations about their content, and inasmuch as it was in no way only Norwegian 'ultra-leftists' who had criticized Åmås for these endorsements in the aftermath of 22/7.

In 2009, two reporters working for *Dagbladet* wrote an item published on the newspaper's website (Thorenfeldt and Meland 2009). 'If the Muslims become the majority' was based on a hypothetical question the reporters had posed to those referred to as 'public debaters' (*'samfunnsdebattanter'*). It was illustrated by a graphic of the flag of 'Norabia' in which the Islamic half-moon had replaced the cross on the Norwegian flag. The website's visitors could vote on whether they agreed with Hege Storhaug of Human Rights Service (HRS) that the shari'a would be imposed in the event of a Muslim majority in Norway, or with lecturer Nazneen Khan-Østrem of Oslo University College that this was unlikely. Two years later, some 100,000 readers had voted online: 77 per cent sided with Storhaug and a mere 23 per cent with Khan-Østrem. In what is perhaps the clearest example of Norwegian media providing legitimacy to one of the most central tropes of the Islamophobic 'Eurabia' genre, namely the notion of excessive Muslim fertility and non-Muslim demographic decline, only a short link was provided to an earlier news item pointing to the fact that researchers at Statistics Norway (Statistisk Sentralbyrå, SSB) had come to the conclusion that only 11 per cent of the Norwegian population at the uppermost estimate would be Muslim by 2060 (Meland 2009; see Brunborg and Texmon 2010).[33]

In a similar media exercise in legitimizing Islamophobia, the national broadcaster NRK in October 2011 published the results of an opinion poll commissioned from the data-gatherer and pollster Norstat, in which a national and representative sample of 1,000 Norwegians had been asked whether they thought 'there were too many Muslims in Norway' and whether 'Islam was a threat against Norwegian culture' (Liestøl and Wernersen 2011): 25 per cent of the sample responded affirmatively on the first question, 24 per cent on the second. However, as was evident from the *NRK Dagsrevyen* report on 27 October, Norwegians' estimates concerning how many Muslims there actually are in Norway vary enormously with location and level of education. Among the interviewees who appeared on the NRK broadcast there was a carpenter based in rural Norway who suggested that there were about one million Muslims out of a total population of 5 million in Norway. Such control questions were never asked in the survey, suggesting that its results had more to do with highly flawed research methodology than with xeno- or Islamophobia.

On 2 April 2011, two reporters employed by NRK, Mina Gabel Lunde and Tormod Strand, were found guilty of violating the Code of Media Ethics by the Norwegian Press Ombudsman, the PFU (Pressens Faglige Utvalg) (PFU 2011). The PFU is a self-regulatory body of the Norwegian media, in which formal complaints against specific media coverage are assessed by a team of experienced and senior Norwegian media editors. In a feature report broadcast by *NRK Lørdagsrevyen* on Saturday, 6 November 2010, Strand's voice-over introduced the feature ominously:

> Islam has come to stay in Norway. New mosques are being built.
> Saudi Arabia and Iran compete for the hearts and minds of Euro-

pean Muslims – a very conservative [and] extreme variety of Islam. It is known that Saudi Arabia offers petroleum funds in order to build mosques in Norway. Tonight, NRK is able to report that Iran sends imams to Norway. The aim is to prepare Norwegian Muslims for action, says a source to NRK.

The story focused on a specific Shia mosque in Tveita, a north-eastern suburb of Oslo. The Imam Ali Mosque maintained links to the Iranian embassy in Oslo and the Shia Ahl-ul-Bayt Foundation, an arm of the Iranian Islamist regime that works to advance Shia and Iranian interests across the world. The sources for the allegations against the mosque were three anonymous individuals of Muslim background living in Norway. In all likelihood, they were exiled Iranians and, as such, individuals with their own political agendas to advance, which were quite obvious from the story. The individuals were introduced as 'insiders' who feared for their lives to such an extent that they had to remain anonymous, and as such they proved to be dramatic, authentic and credible sources for the news feature. There was no mention of the politics of exiled Iranians in Norway; given the background of most Norwegian-Iranians as refugees from the Islamist regime in Iran after 1979, this would imply that it is in the perfectly understandable interests of many of the most politically active among them to do everything within their means to demonize the Iranian regime and its representatives in Norway.[34]

> The imams are sent here in order to spread the attitudes of Iran. Their religious role is a figleaf for spreading a hostile message against the West. Through their preaching, they prepare their listeners ideologically, so that they will in the future be willing to perpetrate terrorist acts, if the orders for that are given.

The claim was, in ever so few words, that Iran was preparing Shia Muslims in Norway for terrorist attacks in Norway. In light of the still-strong suspicions that Iran was involved in the attempted assassination of Salman Rushdie's Norwegian publisher, William Nygaard, in 1994 in Norway, it would be difficult to argue that Iran has a proven track record of non-aggression against Norwegian interests. Yet the serious claim advanced by Tormod Strand and Mina

Gabel Lunde was never substantiated by any non-interested parties and they were convicted of violation of the Code of Media Ethics for not having allowed the imam and the mosque in question to respond to the allegations.

It would be simplistic to argue that the extreme right-wing discourses on Islam and Muslims in Norway have been given a public platform in and through the media owing to any profound ideological sympathies for these discourses among newspaper reporters and editors in Norway. It has more to do with shifting conceptions of freedom of expression and its limits among Norwegian media elites, the conviction on the part of many Norwegian liberals after 9/11 and the cartoon crisis of 2005 and 2006 that liberal values are at great risk from Islamists, and the ability of a refashioned extreme right-wing discourse to appear as if it represents only an endorsement and a defence of liberal values.[35] In the first place, Norway has never had anything similar to *Fox News*, the *Wall Street Journal*, the *New York Post*, the *Daily Mail* or the *Daily Telegraph*, and it has few, if any, newspapers or TV stations that are discernibly and exclusively right-wing. Secondly, the newspaper that has provided the most space for Islamophobic and/or racist right-wing voices in Norway in recent years is historically radically left-wing: *Klassekampen* (for details, see Zaheer et al. 2011). Originating in the 1970s as a propaganda outlet for the Maoist-Leninist AKP-ml (Arbeidernes Kommunistparti-marxist-leninistene or the Worker's Communist Party–Marxist-Leninist) it has, under its current editor Bjørgulv Braanen, developed into a mainstream centre-left newspaper geared to appeal to highly educated Norwegians. *Klassekampen* does, of course, argue that this is part of its commitment to freedom of expression and is aimed at exposing the Islamophobic right wing, but part of its coverage of these actors has in fact consisted of providing them with unrestricted access to the newspaper to advance their views and their fabrications.

The point of this is not so much to demonstrate that there has been a consistent line of Islamophobia in the Norwegian media for the past ten years: such a claim is simply not borne out by the empirical data. One finds that throughout this period there have been countervailing and opposing voices. The point is to argue that there is a *knowledge regime* in a Foucauldian sense at work here[36] and that, within this regime, certain ways of speaking and writing about Muslims in Norway, ways that often veer into the Islamophobic, have become almost naturalized and therefore legitimate in and through the media in the course of the period in question.

5 | DUSKLANDS: THE EURABIA GENRE

For him, humanity was divided between the rogues and the honest: there was nothing in between. (Anton Chekhov, *Ward no. 6*, 1894)

Introducing 'Eurabia'

Central to Anders Behring Breivik's tract *2083: A Declaration of European Independence* is the so-called 'Eurabia' genre. Anders Behring Breivik's fellow ideological travellers are to be found among the adherents and the promoters of this genre. The 'Eurabia' genre is profoundly conspiratorial and apocalyptic. At the centre of the genre stands what the anthropologist Arjun Appadurai has described as a 'fear of small numbers' (Appadurai 2006). 'The fear of small numbers' in this context relates to a discernible fear among members of white majorities in Norway and the rest of Europe of gradually becoming a minority. Such fears, in Appadurai's vision, have increased as a result of neoliberal globalization and global identity politics, giving rise to a view of ethnic and/or religious 'others' as being overdetermined by one particular aspect of their identities. According to the 'Eurabia' genre, Norway and the rest of Europe are in the process of being taken over by Muslims bent on establishing 'Islamic rule' and imposing 'shari'a'. In this chapter, I draw on Appadurai's insightful analysis in order to explore the main tenets of the genre, its main proponents internationally, and the most well-known contributions to the genre in Norway during the past ten years. As we shall have occasion to see, Norway and Scandinavia have in fact provided significant loci for the production and dissemination of contributions to the 'Eurabia' genre.

One afternoon in February 2011, I received a puzzling phone call at my office in the Department of Social Anthropology at the University of Oslo. The caller, a woman in her sixties, introduced herself as a teacher who had for many years taught the Norwegian language to minority youth in Oslo. She spoke in a calm and gentle manner. The background to her call, she informed me, was that I had referred to the 'Eurabia' genre in a short letter to the editor of the Norwegian *Aftenposten* some days earlier. She wanted to know whether I knew this genre well, since I was at the time one of very few Norwegian academics she had seen refer to it in print. 'Not really,' I said, 'but enough to know what the main ideas of the genre are.'

It turned out that this woman was an avid, utterly convinced and committed reader of 'Eurabia' books. These are books that basically advance the idea that there are ongoing plots aiming to Islamize Europe and turn the whole continent into part of a global and restored Islamic caliphate. In its strong version, promoted by the doyenne of 'Eurabia' literature, Bat Ye'or (Gisèle Littman), the 'Eurabia' thesis holds that there is a formal cooperation between Muslim states in the Middle East and the EU and that this cooperation is hidden from the European general public. The hypothesis is that this is aimed at establishing 'Eurabia' and has been operating since the petroleum crisis of 1973.[1] Central to the purported establishment of a European 'Eurabia' is demography. For 'Eurabia' supposedly proceeds by virtue of means such as Muslim mass immigration and comparatively high fertility patterns on the part of female Muslims living in Europe. Strømmen and Indregard (2012: 23) advance a literalist reading of the 'Eurabia' genre, whereby only popular literature and films which explicitly use the term in the post-2001 context can be said to constitute contributions to the genre. Yet to my mind this fails to acknowledge the simple fact that the rhetorical tropes central to the 'Eurabia' genre and thesis had by the time it was popularized by the late Italian feminist author and polemicist Oriana Fallaci in her *The Force of Reason* (*La Forza della Ragione*), first published in Italian in 2004, long been in circulation in extreme and populist right-wing milieus in western Europe and the USA. A case in point is the fabricated 'Mustafa letter' introduced in the parliamentary election campaign in Norway in 1987 by the then Progress Party chairman Carl I. Hagen (see Chapter 4). The assertions made in this letter contain all the central elements of the 'Eurabia' genre.

Bat Ye'or, née Gisèle Oreibi, the daughter of an Italian-French Jewish couple, was born in the upper-class area of Zamalek in Cairo, Egypt, in 1933. The Oreibis were forced to leave Egypt in the aftermath of the 1956 Suez War and they arrived as stateless refugees in London in 1957. Oreibi attended University College London (UCL). In 1959 she married the historian David G. Littman (1933–2012), whose surname she adopted, and she became a British citizen. In 1960 she moved to Lausanne, Switzerland, with her husband.

The canard that Gisèle Littman is a qualified 'historian' or a 'scholar of Islam' is central to her *faux*-academic promoters, from Robert Spencer via Bruce Bawer to Irshad Manji;[2] in fact, although she attended undergraduate courses at both University College London and the University of Geneva in Switzerland, she never graduated with a degree from either of these institutions (see Duin 2002). She is, in other words, 'not an academic and has never taught at any university' (Schwartz 2006). However, this has not prevented her from being called as an expert witness in hearings of the Senate Foreign Relations Committee and the Congressional Human Rights Caucus in the USA in 1997 and 2002, nor from being invited to lecture at Georgetown, Brown, Yale and Brandeis universities in the USA in 2002. She also appeared at an academic conference at the Hebrew University in Jerusalem in 2006.[3] Littman writes and publishes primarily in French, and a number of her books and articles are translated by her late husband. David G. Littman rather unsurprisingly shared his wife's interpretations of 'Eurabia' and 'dhimmitude'.[4] He represented various NGOs at the UN Commission on Human Rights in Geneva.[5] In the USA, Gisèle Littman's work has for a long time been published by Farleigh Dickenson University Press, while in Israel her work is published in Hebrew translations by Schocken Publishing House. Though a 1980 French publication of hers on the 'dhimmis of Islam' was referenced by the Orientalist historian and later neoconservative ideologue Bernard Lewis in a footnote to his monograph on *The Jews of Islam* (see Lewis 1984: 194), Littman's work by and large existed in a state of pseudo-academic obscurity before 11 September 2001. It is also noteworthy that Bernard Lewis would later take clear exception to the dim view of Jewish historical existence in pre-modern Muslim lands promoted by Ye'or, and to her term 'dhimmitude' (Lewis 2006).

It would be an understatement to assert that the work of Gisèle Littman/Bat Ye'or is regarded as failing to meet basic standards of academic research among most qualified historians of Islam and the

Middle East.[6] Yet the pseudo-scientific appearance of Littman's work, replete with academic paraphernalia such as extensive footnotes and references, is central to its ability to convince readers (see Linton 2012: 121). The work of Gisèle Littman/Bat Ye'or is cited approvingly and at length by writers – from Harvard historian Niall Ferguson (Ferguson 2004)[7] to Bruce Bawer (Bawer 2006) and Robert Spencer (2008) to Anders Behring Breivik's favourite Islamophobic and extreme right-wing ideologue Peder Are 'Fjordman' Nøstvold Jensen.

Ye'or's influence on 'Fjordman' is profound.[8] Ye'or makes her first appearence as a reference in a text by 'Fjordman' entitled 'Islam and the open society', published by the tabloid *VG* in 2003 (Jensen 2003). 'Fjordman's' own writings engage in a stylistic mimicry of Ye'or's in that the conspiratorial fantasies and fabrications that mark the work of both authors come packaged in a pseudo-academic prose, replete with extensive citations and references to documents and secondary literature (see Slaatta 2012: 61 for this point). Bat Ye'or's *Eurabia: The Euro-Arab Axis* (2005a) is, if anything, the standard work of the genre. Yet according to Van Vuuren (2013), the term 'Eurabia' makes its first appearance in a French publication by Ye'or in 2002 (Ye'or 2002).

Ye'or's 2005 book purportedly describes 'Europe's evolution from a Judeo-Christian civilization'[9] into a post-Judaeo-Christian civilization that is 'subservient to the ideology of *jihad* and the Islamic powers that propagate it' (Ye'or 2005a: 9). This shift, contends Ye'or, 'came as a result of the oil crisis of 1973 when the European Economic Community (EEC)[10] at the initiative of France and the Arab League, established the Euro-Arab Dialogue (EAD). Since then, the EAD has been in the vanguard of engineering a convergence between Europe and the Islamic states of North Africa and the Middle East' (ibid.: 10). Eurabia is, according to Bat Ye'or, ultimately directed against Israel and the USA and reflects 'increasing Islamic penetration of Europe and its growing influence on European policy' (ibid.).

For Ye'or, 'Euro-Arab culture is permeating, even overwhelming, all levels of West European society' (ibid.: 11). The EU's 'Eurabians' are allegedly key to this development, for 'faceless networks of a huge administration uniting the EU and OIC (Organization of the Islamic Conference)'[11] have managed to create 'a Kafkaesque world functioning as a totalitarian anonymous system' that maintains 'political correctness and censorship' (Ye'or 2011: 20). By 2011, in *Europe, Global-ization and the Coming Universal Caliphate* (ibid.) Ye'or writes as if the final Islamization of Europe is already nearing its completion.[12]

A key concept for Bat Ye'or is dhimmitude. Though derived from the Arabic term for historically protected, though ultimately subordinate non-Muslim peoples – dhimmi – the term is in fact a neologism. For Ye'or, the term refers to '[the] obligatory submission [of non-Muslim peoples] by war or surrender to Islamic domination' (Ye'or 2005a: 148). 'The study of dhimmitude, then, is the study of the progressive Islamization of Christian civilizations' (ibid.: 149). The term appears to make its first apparence in English, in the transla-tion of Ye'or's 1996 book *The Decline of Eastern Christianity under Islam: From Jihad to Dhimmitude* (Ye'or 1996), which had five years previously appeared in French. In a review of this book in *Middle East Policy* in 1997, academic scholar Robert Brenton Betts noted that the title of Ye'or's book was misleading, since it was 'in equal, if not greater measure' about Judaism rather than about Eastern Christianity (Betts 1997: 200). This is not entirely coincidental, for Ye'or is centrally interested in advancing the ahistorical notion of a 'common [historical] condition of Jews and Christians [under Islam]' (Ye'or 2005a: 156) in order to generate support for Jewish–Christian alliances in support of Israel in the present.

Dhimmitude in Ye'or's conception refers to 'the whole web of disabling political, historical, sociological and cultural circumstances that enmesh a Christian or Jewish population that has been brought under Islamic hegemony' (Griffith 1998: 620). Dhimmitude, as applied to contemporary Western societies, also in Ye'or's conception refers to a state of mind. 'The civilization of dhimmitude does not develop all at once', but 'is a long process that involves many elements and a specific mental conditioning' (Ye'or 1995, cited in Spencer 2005: 31). One can therefore even be living in a state of dhimmitude without ever realizing it. Hence, owing to 'the psychological impact of intel-lectual terrorism', the entire West, Ye'or proclaimed as early as 1996, has 'entered into a phase of dhimmitude without realizing it' (Ye'or 1996: 219). This, ultimately, leads to 'self-destruction' (Ye'or 1995, cited in Spencer 2005: 31).

Few people among Bat Ye'or's readers and admirers seem to be

aware of the political and intellectual origins of the term dhimmitude. Irshad Manji thinks that Ye'or '*coined* the word dhimmitude
to describe Islam's ideology of wholesale discrimination against Jews
and Christians' (Manji 2004: 61, my emphasis). Robert Spencer argues
that Ye'or has 'pioneered the study of dhimmitude as a distinct
phenomenon' (Spencer 2005: 31). Yet the neologism dhimmitude,
according to one source, appears to have been invented by the slain
Lebanese Maronite warlord and Phalangist (Kata'eb) militia leader
Bashir Gemayel (1947–82) (Griffith 1998: 620). In a speech at Dayr
al-Salib (The Monastery of the Cross) in the Maronite Christian
heartlands of Mount Lebanon on 14 September 1982, Gemayel was
later reported[13] to have declared that Lebanon's Maronite Christians,
whom he claimed to represent both as a political and a militia leader,
'refused to live in dhimmitude'. It was the last speech Gemayel ever
made, for later that day he would be killed in a bomb attack along
with twenty-five others at the Kata'eb headquarters in West Beirut.
While the Kata'eb immediately assumed that Palestinian militias
were responsible, and avenged themselves by massacring thousands
of Palestinian civilian refugees in the camps of Sabra and Shatila in
Beirut in full view of an Israeli army commanded by General Ariel
Sharon in the days that followed, the perpetrator of the attack was
in reality a Maronite Christian aligned with the pro-Syrian Syrian
Socialist National Party (SSNP) by the name of Habib Shartouni
(1958–). He was arrested and confessed to the murder in the course
of the following days, asserting publicly that Gemayel, by collaborating with the Israeli army, had 'sold Lebanon out to Israel', and he
would spend eight years in prison in Lebanon without charges or
trial before escaping to Syria during a Syrian military campaign in
Lebanon in 1990. In an interview with a US-based online counter-
jihadist publication from 2011, Gisèle Littman claimed that she, rather
than Gemayel, had in fact coined the term in 1982, and that it had
become known to Gemayel the same year through 'mutual friends'
(Gordon 2011). In any case, this claim provides yet another indication
of Bat Ye'or's long-standing links with extremists, for the historical
record leaves no doubt that under Gemayel's command, the Kata'eb
engaged in a series of atrocities against civilians in Lebanon in its
purported defence of a Christian-dominated Lebanon. What we do

know for certain is that Ye'or first used the term dhimmitude in her publications one year after Gemayel's assassination, in an article in French published in the obscure Italian journal *La Rassegna Mensile di Israel* (Ye'or 1983).

For Bat Ye'or, as for 'Eurabia' authors in general, Lebanon is central, as a purported harbinger of Europe's future of dhimmitude, unless Muslim immigration and demographic increase is stopped in its tracks. For in Bat Ye'or's rendering, the Lebanese civil war from 1975 to 1990, in which Israel invaded its northern neighbour to prop up its Maronite Christian proxies and to expel the Palestine Liberation Organization (PLO) from its Lebanese bases in June 1982, only to be bogged down in a sectarian spiral of violence that led to its withdrawal to a security zone in South Lebanon in May 1983, meant nothing short of a 'destruction of Lebanese Christianity' (Ye'or 1996: 218). As we have seen in Chapter 3, this distorted view of Lebanon also appears in Anders Behring Breivik's tract.

It is not only Lebanon which has exercised Bat Ye'or's mind over the years, however: in the midst of the Balkan wars in the 1990s, Ye'or gave a speech in Chicago at the invitation of an outfit called the Lord Byron Foundation for Balkan Studies. This foundation had been established by the one-time political adviser to Margaret Thatcher Alfred Sherman (1919–2009), and Sjrda (Serge) Trifković, a close associate and political adviser to the Serbian ultra-nationalists Radovan Karadzic and Biljana Plavsić, and it promoted ultra-nationalist Serb agendas. Sherman was convinced that by recognizing independent Bosnia, Western powers had allowed a 'European Islamistan' to be established.[14] Ye'or had by this time started to be read by Serbian ultra-nationalists. As early as 1994, she had declared in an interview with *Midstream*, a Jewish monthly journal in the USA, that Bosnia was a 'spearhead' for the 'Islamization of Europe' (Sells 2003: 362, 382). Ye'or's speech in Chicago in 1995 was titled 'Myths and politics: the tolerant pluralistic Islamic society: origin of a myth' and is reproduced in its entirety in Anders Behring Breivik's tract. Here, Bat Ye'or claimed that the UN's decision to recognize a 'Muslim state in the former Yugoslavia' was 'a compensation offered to the Islamic world for the devastating 1991 Gulf War' which would bring 'sufferings, miseries and trials in its wake'.[15]

'A decent conspiracy theory is made up of hard facts; the invention lies in drawing the connections,' wrote Thomas Jones apropos Bat Ye'or's 'Eurabia' book in 2005 (Jones 2005). 'It would be a stretch of the historical record' to suggest that the EAD 'amounted to European subservience to a monolithic Islamic "cause"', writes Jonathan Laurence (2012: 47). But this is precisely what Bat Ye'or implies that it does. In its forceful version, the 'Eurabia' thesis amounts to a classical *conspiracy theory* (Keeley 1999) in which a highly tendentious selection of historical data and facts are marshalled in support of the notion that Europe and its cultures and values are slowly being undermined by the presence of Muslims in its midst.

Conspiracy theories are – as Sunstein (2009) points out – linked to the human propensity for *biased assimilation* of information, or the fact that we as human beings often ignore powerful contrary evidence (ibid.: 50). According to Sunstein, conspiracy theories may, but need not necessarily, reflect individual pathology (ibid.: 108); yet affective factors and antecedent beliefs, and not merely information, are central to their successes (ibid.: 110, 112).[16] Though there is nothing historically new about conspiracy theories (think, for example, of the Salem witch-hunt, or the Protocols of the Elders of Zion), the internet facilitates the circulation and legitimization of conspiracy theories at a historically unprecedented level, as it enables users to choose to hear 'more and louder versions of their own views, thus reducing the benefits that come from exposure to competing views' (ibid.: 80). Or, in other words, to construct one's own 'echo chambers' of like-minded people.

The main villains of the 'Eurabia' conspiracy theory, which is strongly pro-Israeli and politically right-wing, are rather unsurprisingly 'the left': after the collapse of communism in 1989, 'Third Worldists, neo-Communists, and Islamists' are considered to have created 'a powerful jihadist coalition against Western democracies and their allies'. The power possessed by this clandestine alliance is vast: according to Ye'or, European universities are 'controlled by the Palestinians' – see Ye'or's interview with Schwartz (2006) for this. This coalition is so 'deeply rooted in the Euro-Arab political alliance' (Ye'or 2005a: 12) that the 'International Left' are, in the words of 'Eurabia' author Bruce Bawer, 'the new quislings' (Bawer

2012a). Central to any conspiracy theory is the notion that the truth is being hidden from the common man and woman by a powerful elite and that only a privileged few are sufficiently knowledgeable and clear-eyed to see the coming storm. Ye'or clearly sees herself as one of this latter group 'While Europeans live within Eurabia's constraints, few are really conscious of them on a daily basis, beyond a somewhat confused awareness. Eurabians are the agents and key enforcers of this all-encompassing new Eurabian policy and culture' (Ye'or 2005a: 12). If Europeans must be awoken from their slumber by authors in the 'Eurabia' genre, there are worse ways of doing so than using disturbing titles that indicate the need to be 'eternally vigilant' and 'sleepless' in one's defence of 'freedom'. As pointed out by Carr (2006), central to the popular credibility of the tendentious claims of the 'Eurabia' genre is the contention of its authors that whatever the context, Muslims – regardless of their backgrounds, levels of religious belief and practice, or political views – are essentially one and the same: instruments of a 1,400-year-old Islamic struggle to establish Islamic control over Europe. Individual Muslims may or may not be aware of this 'fact'. In line with the arguments of the Orientalist historian Bernard Lewis in his post-9/11 tract *What Went Wrong? Western Impact and Middle Eastern Response* (Lewis 2002), it is axiomatic in this genre that Muslims hate 'us' and have been hating us for a very long time, and not for anything 'we' might have done, but on account of what 'we' are (see Lyon 2012).[17]

The letter to Lady Liberty

The first book in the 'Eurabia' genre written by a Norwegian was *Letter to Lady Liberty: Europe in Danger* (*Amerikabrevet: Europa i fare*) by Hallgrim Berg (1945–), published in 2007 (Berg 2007). When Berg launched the follow-up to the *Letter to Lady Liberty* in 2013 with *Demokrati eller islamisme: Europa under islam?* (*Democracy or Islamism: Europe under Islam?*) (Berg 2013), published by the Christian evangelical publisher Hermon Forlag, one of the panellists invited to comment on the book was the young and rising star of the Conservative Party (Høyre) in Norway, the MP Torbjørn Røe Isaksen (1978–),[18] who, after the Norwegian parliamentary elections in September 2013, would become the new minister for research and education. While he took exception to Berg's promotion of the 'Eurabia' thesis, Røe Isaksen's very presence at the launch suggests that Berg's ideas in Conservative Party circles are considered to have a level of popular support among the mainstream right-wing electorate which necessitates party engagement with them. It is difficult to conceive of Røe Isaksen's presence at this launch as signifying anything but a tacit political acceptance of 'Eurabia' ideas as having a legitimate place in Norwegian political discourse.

Berg's book is designed as a series of letters sent to 'Lady Liberty', who is, of course, the United States, represented by the Statue of Liberty in New York harbour at Ellis Island. In the context of the US war on terror, the book hails the United States as the 'foremost symbol of freedom in the world', holding out the torch of 'freedom and enlightenment' (Berg 2007: 7). It is to the United States with its 'power and will to stand up against totalitarian ideas' that Europeans must now turn if European civilization is to survive the onslaught of 'Islamic expansionism' (ibid.: 26, 27). Berg also admires the United States for its close relationship with Israel in the context of the turbulent Middle East.[19]

On its very first page, we learn that contemporary Europe '... is exposed to a Muslim invasion and a galloping Islamization' (ibid.). Democratic Europe is '... at the verge of developing into a new Arabia, a *Eurabia*' (ibid.: 8). 'Step by step', European tolerance for the intolerant ones 'who want to destroy democracy and replace it by sharia laws' leads us into 'cultural and national suicide' (ibid.: 9). There is a decay in liberal democracy that may lead to the very 'dissolution of Western civilization such as we have known it up until now' (ibid.). Berg is, in his own opinion, a man of modest capabilities; in an address to the European Council in Strasbourg in 1991, he had warned against 'some of the aspects referred to by Bat Ye'or' (ibid.: 23). But at that time, he had 'no inkling of the documentation that this woman has provided concerning what happens in and from Brussels' (ibid.). For EU bureaucrats '... constantly promote an "EU ideology" called multiculturalism' (ibid.). It might be news to the same EU bureaucrats, but under the rubric of multiculturalism, furthermore, all 'ethnic, cultural and religious particularities' are to be endorsed as 'equally important and valid'; 'anyone wanting to preserve democracy at the level of the nation-state is to be portrayed as suffering from xenophobia'; and 'one may refer to all those wanting to limit immigration from the third world as "racists"' (ibid.).[20] For Berg, as for most of the other popular authors in the 'Eurabia' genre, time is fast running out for a Europe faced with an existential threat from Muslims: 'Spain is already at the point of being lost' to the 'Islamic invasion' (ibid.: 32). Next in line is a 'wavering France', which 'no longer knows what to do' (ibid.: 33) and 'may easily have a Muslim majority in twenty-five years' (ibid.). Berg ominously predicts that by 2050, 'at the very latest', France will officially be known as 'Arance or Frarabia' (sic) (ibid.).

Note here the centrality of fabricated demographics, which is a characteristic of the genre (see Pilbeam 2011; Larsson 2012). By virtue of this logic, which we also find expressed in Anders Behring Breivik's tract, France is in the 'weakest' position of all European countries because it has a higher percentage of inhabitants of Muslim background than any other European country. But one should not rest assured that Norway, with its 3.6 per cent inhabitants of Muslim background, is safe from 'Islamic expansionism'. For regardless of the projections of the demographers at Statistics Norway (SSB), who render such a scenario statistically impossible, there are of course other people who have 'with clear logic claimed that Norway ... may have a Muslim majority as early as around 2040 or 2050' (Berg 2007: 52).[21] As is the case with the 'Eurabia' genre in general, there is a certain circularity to the arguments being advanced, inasmuch as authors and intellectuals who happen to share the writer's world view are cited approvingly over and over again as authoritative sources confirming highly tendentious data and statistics.

To Berg, as to 'Fjordman' and Behring Breivik, al-Qaeda represents Islam: the 9/11 terror attacks on the United States, according to Berg, 'led to cheers and applause in the Muslim ghettos surrounding Amsterdam, Brussels, Cologne, Paris, Stockholm and Torino', as well as 'cries of jubilation and joy in multicultural classrooms in Oslo, the city of the Peace Prize' (ibid.: 37). True to the extremely low standards of validation of anecdotal and empirical claims in the 'Eurabia' genre, Berg provides no sources for these claims.[22] Like US neoconservative commentator Norman Podhoretz, Berg conceives of himself as engaged in a 'fourth world war': a war between 'democracy' and 'Islamic forces' (ibid.: 148).

Berg also shares a central tenet of extreme right-wing Islamo-phobic discourse, found in the work of 'Fjordman' and Behring Breivik, in which 'the Left' in Western countries is conspiring with the 'totalitarian Islamic right' to undermine liberal democracy (ibid.: 81). Media reporters, editors and academics are involved in this conspiracy: 'Four out of five active journalists and editors are to be found way out on the ideological left' (ibid.) and 'the apparatuses of power and the media are shot through with cultural relativism' (ibid.: 151).

Connecting the US–Euro dots: Bruce Bawer

The 'Eurabia' genre is, if anything, a transnational genre, in which certain interpretative frames and rhetorical tropes circulate in ever recurring modes without ever being tested against data that lead to other conclusions. Because Bruce Bawer has lived in Norway since 1999 and has the background, contacts in transnational Islamophobic networks and rhetorical eloquence required to address both US and European audiences in a wide range of print and electronic formats, he has been central in the attempt to mainstream the 'Eurabia' literature. Still, Bawer provides his readers with a new twist to his 'Eurabia' literature. For when he settled with his male Norwegian partner, Tor André, in Oslo west in 1999, it was with a background as a gay Republican literary critic. Bawer's gay identity is key to his thinking, as it is a key to his understanding of Islam and Muslims as an 'existential threat' to Europe. In this, he is reflective of a significant shift on the extreme and populist right wing in western Europe in the past decade, in which political movements, only recently overtly homophobic, have in many countries come to endorse liberal values and the rights of gays and lesbians as an intrinsic part of their Islamophobic agendas (see Butler 2009 and Puar 2007). The central figure in this transition was the late Dutch politician Pim Fortuyn, a flamboyant homosexual who was assassinated by Dutch animal rights activist Volker van der Graaf (thirty-two) in 2002, and for whom Bawer expresses a great deal of admiration in his 'Eurabia' books.

Bawer is throughout his books staunchly pro-Israel and a

passionate defender of the 'war on terror' under George W. Bush (2000–08). Yet even though his books rage against the 'liberal elites' of multicultural USA and Europe, his gay identity makes him an ambivalent partner for extreme right-wingers. One of those who perceived this was Anders Behring Breivik, who in comments posted on Document.no noted that in light of the need for a broad 'cultural conservative' consolidation, 'Bawer may not be the right person for the work of bridge building'. For Bawer, in Behring Breivik's conception, was a liberal anti-jihadist, and not a cultural conservative. 'I suspect', wrote Behring Breivik, 'that Bawer is too paranoid (in regard to his gay orientation).' Furthermore, 'it appears that he fears that "cultural conservatives" may constitute a threat to gays in the future'.

Soon after settling in with his partner, Bawer appears to have established contact with the lesbian secular feminist Hege Storhaug.[23] In Bawer's books and columns, Storhaug, whose long record of heavily biased and tendentious statements about Muslims in Norway has made her into a source the Norwegian media treat with a great deal of caution, appears as an authoritative source on Islam and Muslims in Norway. Among other right-wing actors in Norway with whom Bawer established contacts were Hans Rustad of Document.no and Walid al-Kubaisi. In Denmark, he established close links with Lars Hedegaard and Helle Merete Brix, who also have close links with Hege Storhaug and Rita Karlsen of HRS.

As director of the Danish Trykkefrihetsselskapet (The Free Speech Society), the one-time member of the populist right-wing Danish People's Party (DPP) Lars Hedegaard in 2009 established an outfit by the name of the International Free Press Society in Copenhagen, Denmark. The Danish precursor had been established in 2005 in response to the cartoon crisis (Lehman 2011: 33).

Hedegaard, a former editor-in-chief of the newspaper *Information* and columnist for *Berlingske Tidende* and *Weekendavisen* in Denmark, had since 2003 emerged as a central nodal point for the dissemination of Islamophobia throughout Scandinavia. Hedegaard and Brix maintained close links to US neoconservative Daniel Pipes of Campus Watch and consulted extensively with Pipes during the cartoon crisis (ibid.). The list of advisers to the International Free Press Society is a virtual 'who's who' of European and US anti-Muslim right-wing activists and 'Eurabia' authors, from Bat Ye'or to Mark Steyn, Robert Spencer and Geert Wilders.[24]

In Norway, Hege Storhaug and Rita Karlsen of the HRS made no bones about the fact that they considered the political rhetoric on Islam, integration and Muslims in Denmark which marked the years in power of Anders Fogh Rasmussen (2001–08) as providing an ideal for Norway. The Liberal Party's Fogh Rasmussen, who came to power on a platform promising much more restrictive immigration policies and who introduced a series of measures aimed at restricting Muslim immigration to Denmark in particular, governed with the support of the populist right-wing Danish People's Party (DPP). Denmark under Fogh Rasmussen was also a role model referred to by allies of Hege Storhaug in the Norwegian Progress Party.

After 22/7 the Swedish anti-racist magazine *Expo* named Hedegaard as one of the ten most influential individuals in Europe and the United States among those spreading anti-Muslim hatred (ibid.). For Norwegian anti-Muslim activists, Hedegaard's networks have certainly been important. As cases in point, the HRS website regularly reprints opinion pieces and news items written by Helle Merete Brix, and Hans Rustad's Document.no regularly features opinion pieces by Katrine Winkel Holm. Winkel Holm is the daughter of the former MP for the DPP Søren Krarup,[25] a vice-chairman for Lars Hedegaard's Free Press Society and editor of the e-zine Sappho.dk. In February 2012, Document.no published a book review by Winkel Holm in which she lauded both 'Fjordman' and Bruce Bawer (Holm 2012). In a case that caused consternation among his friends and supporters in Norway, from Hege Storhaug at HRS to Hans Rustad at Document. no, Hedegaard was convicted by a Danish court for criminal offences in May 2011 under §266B of the Danish Penal Code for racist hate speech directed at Muslims (Søndberg and Abdolhosseini 2011). The case related to a video posted on Sappho.dk in 2009 in which Hedegaard asserted that Muslims who commit rape do so because it is their 'right in Islam' (ibid.). Hedegaard appealed against the verdict to the Danish Supreme Court and was acquitted in April 2012 on the technical grounds that his racist and discriminatory statements had been recorded without his knowledge and consent (Malacinski 2012). In an as yet unsolved assassination attempt, Hedegaard was shot at by an armed intruder at his home in Copenhagen in February 2013 (see Bangstad 2013: 9).

It has become common for Norwegian media editors and reporters to refer to Lars Hedegaard as a person who merely engages in 'criticism of Islam'. Yet this in actual fact amounts to taking Hedegaard and other Scandinavian right-wing Islamophobes who endorse and support his views at face value when they insist that 'reason' and the 'facts' are on their side, and that they only engage in legitimate critique of Islam and Muslims, rather than Islamophobia.[26] For during a conference in Toronto in 2010, Hedegaard has been reported by Danish media as declaring that 'we are at war with Islam ... a total war [which will last] until one of the parties win or surrender'. Furthermore, as a result of the situation Hedegaard perceives European societies to find themselves in, he advocated 'the right to arm ourselves' and declared that 'politicians who act against us [in doing so] shall be removed from office by force' (Netavisen P77 2010).

In a series of books following 11 September 2001, Bruce Bawer argued that Europe and the United States had similar interests in the 'war on terror' – if only the European political, media and academic elites would realize it. Both *While Europe Slept: How Radical Islam is Destroying the West from Within* (nominated for the National Book Critics Circle Award[27]) in 2006 and *Surrender: Appeasing Islam, Sacrificing Freedom* in 2009 were published by Doubleday in New York. Bawer focused his attention on Islam and Muslims because of 9/11, which was 'utterly transforming – and clarifying' (Bawer 2009: 77). Or maybe not: in *Surrender*, he asserts that 'my own wake-up call about all this came in 2000' (ibid.: 35) when he supposedly discovered that 'all you had to do to travel from a modern post-Enlightenment democracy to a strict patriarchy out of seventh-century Arabia was to walk a few blocks' (ibid.) in the cities of western Europe. Like many other 'Eurabia' authors, Bawer casts wide the net of 'radical Islamists' on the path to undermine Western freedoms and civilization. For 'Islam' rather than 'Islamism' is Bawer's concern. 'Islam ... doesn't flavor – it transforms, subdues, conquers,' Bawer boldly asserts in *While Europe Slept* (Bawer 2006: 28). Young European Muslims are 'alien intruders' in Bawer's conception, and they do not change according to circumstances and the societies in which they live:

Polls show[28] that young European Muslims today – even those born in Europe – identify more with their ancestral homelands than with the countries whose passports they carry. No surprise there. After all, their families have never really left the Islamic world – they brought it with them. Their neighborhoods ... are embryonic colonies that will continue to grow as a result of immigration and reproduction. (Ibid.: 32).

Bawer confidently asserts that the main threat is demographic and he does so without any empirical data whatsoever. He engages in fear-mongering, asserting that 'within a couple of generations, many [European] countries will have Muslim majorities' (ibid.: 33). The reality is grim (ibid.), for 'in some urban areas of Europe, all order has broken down' (ibid.: 39) by virtue of the presence of Muslims. European children are regularly 'dumped in Koran schools' (ibid.: 58), and 'some estimates[29] suggest that 90 per cent of European Muslim wives are physically abused' (ibid.: 59). Many of western Europe's 'large immigrant communities' are in fact 'led by fundamentalist Muslims' looking forward 'to the establishment in Europe of a caliphate governed according to sharia law' (ibid.: 3).

In Bawer's view, young European Muslims to a large extent support radical Islamism: 'On 9/11 [2001], young Muslims across Europe had applauded al-Qaeda in the streets; when Madrid was struck [in 2002], there were more festivities; after the murder of [Theo] van Gogh [in 2005], still more' (ibid.: 200). It matters little that, with the exception of limited numbers affiliated with radical Islamists, few if any Europeans registered such 'celebrations', 'applauses' and 'festivities' 'across Europe' on the part of European Muslim youth on these occasions; what matters is that Bawer tells his readers that this is so.[30]

Muslims are never to be trusted: even some 'successfully assimilated' Western Muslims have 'alien mindsets' (Bawer 2009: 40). It is male Muslim youth in particular who represent a threat to 'order', 'freedom' and 'civilization', and they do so by virtue of embodying 'Islam': for the 'marauding [Muslim] kids "embody" their parents' values', have been 'raised to be belligerent' and 'taught that God [has] given them authority over women, and made them superior to infidels'. 'They see Western society as the enemy, European men as wimps, European women as sluts' (ibid.: 38).

While Europe Slept weaves a narrative of a 'defeatist' Europe with European governments' 'passivity in the face of al-Qaeda's terrorism, Saddam's [Hussein] tyranny, and the rise of Islamism within their borders' (Bawer 2006: 150). Throughout the book, Bawer chastises ordinary Europeans for being insufficiently supportive of George W. Bush's 'war on terror' (ibid.: 82), the European media for never reporting on US soldiers 'doing good' in Iraq (ibid.: 85), and 'the Western European multicultural elite' for being 'almost without exception, allied with the Islamic right' (ibid.: 212). In the contorted logic of Bawer's world, the Spanish voters who ousted the conservative government of José María Aznar after the terror attacks on Madrid in 2000 had sent the message that 'the terrorists had won' and had voted in 'the terrorist's candidate' in expressing their support for the social democratic candidate José Luís Rodriguez Zapatero (ibid.: 157, 158).

The future will be a 'Europe ruled by sharia law' (ibid.: 229). In *Surrender*, Bawer extends the argument, so that it is no longer only Europe, but the entire West which is 'on the road to sharia' (Bawer 2009: 64). And should readers have any doubt as to what that entails, Bawer knows what that means: '... converts from Islam to other religions would be executed', 'thieves would have their arms amputated', 'adulterous women would be stoned to death' and 'so would gay people' (ibid.: 25).

It matters little here that few but the most hardline Islamic states in the world (Iran, Saudi Arabia) actually practise such interpretations of the shari'a, let alone that all survey data suggest that few European Muslims favour such interpretations. Norway, Bawer's home since 1999, is particularly ineffective when it comes to 'dealing with' immigrants in general and Muslim immigrants in particular: for in Norway, 'political correctness ... reigned supreme' (ibid.: 35); Bawer and his gay partner are faced with a 'wiry youth ... raving at us in a Middle Eastern language, his eyes ablaze with rage' when walking the streets of Oslo (ibid.: 37);[31] 'Oslo cops' 'back off from dealing with immigrants' (ibid.: 40–1); and establishment politicians are 'vigorous in their misrepresentation and ridicule of America', since they are social democrats marked by 'nostalgia for the good old days of Soviet

Communism' (ibid.: 115, 118).[32] Not that Norwegian or European social democrats have historically been known for their sympathies for Soviet communism, of course, but in the eyes of many Americans unfamiliar with Norway or Scandinavia, it would naturally be hard to tell the difference between a social democrat and a Marxist.

The mainstream media are often cast as the unwitting allies of multiculturalists and Islamists in counter-jihadist literature. They also appear as such in Bruce Bawer's 2006 and 2009 'Eurabia' books. In *Surrender*, Bawer asserts that 'on the road to shari'a' 'the media is in the driver's seat', 'helping the jihadists' (Bawer 2009: 64–5). And the prime example of this, not only for Bawer but also for 'Fjord-man' and Behring Breivik, was the suburban rioting in France in 2005. These riots, we are informed, were 'in large parts assertions of Muslim authority over Muslim neighborhoods, and thus jihadist in character' (ibid.: 65). But the media 'covered up' or 'drastically de-emphasized' 'the rioters' Muslim identity' (ibid.). The liberal media in the United States and the UK are particularly bad in this regard: the *New York Times* and the BBC play the part of 'Dhimmitude Central' with regard to Islam – in other words, are willing allies in the struggle to 'Islamize' the West (ibid.: 89).

But all is not lost: all over Europe there is nascent European populist right-wing activity. Denmark in particular inspires hope in Bruce Bawer; things had changed there with the parliamentary elections of 2001 (ibid.: 181). In Denmark, Queen Margrethe is part of the 'liberal resistance' (ibid.: 205) while Prime Minister Anders Fogh Rasmussen is portrayed as one of 'a few individuals who refuse to accept Islamization[33] without a struggle' (ibid.: 132). In 'downtown Copenhagen', Bawer meets other 'heroic resisters': Lars Hedegaard and Helle Merete Brix (ibid.: 185). Hedegaard tells Bawer that there is an ongoing 'Islamicization' of the Nordic countries, and that Denmark is being 'surrendered to Muslims' (ibid.: 186). Hedegaard is in a dystopic mode, and argues to Bawer that 'native Europeans, after enough daily doses of anti-Semitic and pro-Muslim propaganda, might reach a point at which they'd actually accept Muslims' right to execute Jews' (ibid.: 187). One might suspect that Hedegaard and Bawer, as autodidacts on Islam, trade in essentialistic notions, imply-ing that Islam 'commands' Muslims to 'execute Jews' for no reason other than their being Jews. Hedegaard, like 'Fjordman' and Behring Breivik, sees clouds of war emerging on the horizon as a result of the presence of Muslims in Europe: its future 'will be war ... like Lebanon' (ibid.: 188–9). Europe is, according to Bawer, facing its 'Weimar Moment' (ibid.: 193), with European Muslims cast in the role of the German Nazis who brought the liberal German Weimar Republic to heel in 1933.

Across the straits from Copenhagen, in multicultural Sweden, however, Bawer finds that things are 'going to hell in a handbasket' with 'the number of ghettos rising at a dizzying speed' and 'a murder rate twice that of the United States' (ibid.: 205). Sweden certainly has its share of challenges, but its murder rate of 1.21 per 100,000 did in fact compare extremely favourably with most states in the USA in 2005. However, there are heroic 'resisters' there too: the Swedish Democratic Party (the Swedish Democrats, Sverigedemokraterna), which, coincidentally, and unacknowledged by Bawer, has strong roots in the Swedish neo-Nazi movement (see Strømmen 2007: 102–13), is 'the one party that acknowledged the problems and wanted to put them on the national agenda' (Bawer 2009). In Norway, it is the Progress Party, with which Bawer's close ally Hege Storhaug has strong links, which represents 'the silent majority' of '... ordinary citizens tired of being governed by elites who for decades had mocked their national pride, taxed them heavily to support an inefficient welfare state, and endangered their national security through reckless integration policies' (ibid.: 222). And in the Netherlands, Bawer casts the late Pim Fortuyn (Bawer 2006: 165) and Geert Wilders (Bawer 2009: 22) in the role of 'heroic resisters'.

In the aftermath of 22/7, Bruce Bawer's rhetoric concerning the political, media and academic elites of his adopted country would become ever more strident and libellous. 'Inside the world of the Oslo murderer', an op-ed by Bawer published in the *Wall Street Journal* on 25 June 2011 (Bawer 2011), offered few words of comfort to the many Norwegians bereaved and in mourning, let alone to the survivors. For the 'real victims' of 22/7, according to Bawer, were none other than Bawer and his fellow 'critics of Islam'. For their case had 'been seriously damaged by Anders Behring Breivik', a 'murderous madman' who had now become 'the poster boy' for 'criticism of Islam'.

Bawer nevertheless took the opportunity to express a faint hope that 'Norwegian leaders would respond to this act of violence by taking a more responsible approach to the challenges they face in connection with Islam'.

Note the paradoxes: the same Bawer who had argued that Spanish voters had 'succumbed to terrorism' after the Madrid bombings in 2002 was in 2006 calling for Norwegian political leaders to avail themselves of the opportunity to be pressured into a specific course of action with regard to Islam and Muslims by extreme right-wing terror. The very same Bawer had in his 2006 book taken Dutch newspaper reporters to task for attempting to cast the left-wing assassin of Pim Fortuyn in 2002, Volker van der Graaf, as a 'lone madman' (Bawer 2006: 169), which was of course exactly what Bawer was attempting to do with Behring Breivik.

Bawer warns that those Norwegians in mourning for the worst massacre and acts of terror in their country's history should not allow themselves to forget the threat that Islam poses in their country, as in 'the rest of Europe'. Bawer noted that Behring Breivik 'considered the Labor Party, Norway's dominant party since World War II, responsible for policies that are leading to the Islamization of Europe – and thus guilty of treason'. But he conveniently forgot to mention that this was more or less the view he himself had advocated in the years preceding 22/7. This became clear in his new book, *The New Quislings: How the International Left Used the Oslo Massacre to Silence Debate about Islam* (Bawer 2012a). But what happened at Utøya in the days and hours leading up to Anders Behring Breivik's atrocities on 22/7? According to Bawer, Utøya was the scene of 'Israel-bashing' and the urging of Labour Party youth to 'support groups that are internationally recognized as terrorists – and therefore, to embrace the idea that the cold-blooded murder of innocent men, women and children is a legitimate means of achieving an ideological end' (ibid.). Like Behring Breivik, he saw this being instigated by the leaders of the Norwegian Labour Party. This was the degree to which Bawer's ideological position allowed him to sympathize with the murdered teenagers at Utøya and their bereaved families. In effect, Bawer slurred consistent social democratic opposition to Israeli settlement expansion, the slow but steadily progressing rightward shift of mainstream Israeli politics (Remnick 2013) and copious human rights abuses in the occupied Palestinian territories since the 1990s as being somehow anti-Semitic in intent.

With reference to Vidkun Quisling, Bawer also appropriated a standard rhetorical device of extreme right-wing discourse on Norwegian social democratic elites.[34] He now, in a momentous distortion of historical logic whereby the extreme right becomes centrist left in Norway, designated the social democratic leadership as 'Quislings'. In the aftermath of 22/7, these 'Quislings' had, according to Bawer, attempted to 'silence debate about Islam'. Not that anyone living in Norway in the months after 22/7 and who had been reading Norwegian mainstream newspapers regularly had registered that the 'debate about Islam' had disappeared, let alone been 'silenced'. Norwegians, of course, know very well that usage of this term against political opponents implies an incitement to violence against those so named: Quisling was one of only eleven Norwegian Nazi collaborators who were executed for treason after the Second World War. Use of this term in this context also implies that those so designated are collaborating with 'latter-day Nazis' in the form of Norwegian and European Muslims. The rhetorical designation of contemporary Muslims as wearing the mantle of Nazis is of course also part of the standard repertoire of populist right-wing Islamophobes from the PP's Kent Andersen (Chapter 4) to 'Fjordman' and farther on to Anders Behring Breivik.

However, more disturbing to Norwegian readers of Bawer's 2012 book was the fact that he lifted two fabricated assertions straight off the pages of Behring Breivik's tract. Bawer approvingly cites Behring Breivik's bogus claim that the radical leftist-anarchist group Blitz comprises the 'storm troops' of the Labour Party and his unsubstantiated claims that 'over the years, innumerable Norwegian teenagers have been killed by Muslims'. Some might also take issue with Bawer's repeated characterization of Bat Ye'or's *Eurabia* from 2005 as 'a sober work of solid documentation', with the bogus claim that the term 'Islamophobia' was coined by the Muslim Brotherhood and his admittance that he had close social contacts with 'Fjordman'.[35] Bawer's use of the term 'quisling' led even his erstwhile admirers in the Norwegian Progress Party to publicly distance themselves from him. The PP's former spokesperson on immigration and integration issues, MP Per Willy Amundsen, acknowledged that he knew Bawer's writings well from previous years and sympathized with Bawer's critique of Norwegian elites, but said that the linking of these elites with Quisling was 'tendentious and a-historic' (Brandvold and Simenstad 2012). Amundsen also said that he felt confident of having the support of PP voters in taking exception to such linkages (ibid.).

Introducing 'Eurabia' to Norwegian television viewers

The notion of a 'Eurabia' conspiracy bears a striking structural resemblance to the Tsarist anti-Semitic forgery *The Protocols of the Elders of Zion*. The late Edward Said (1935–2003) did not live to see the popularization and mainstreaming of the 'Eurabia' genre, but in the article that introduced the concept of Islamophobia to an English-speaking academic audience in 1985, he pointed out the common roots of anti-Semitism and Islamophobia (Said 2000 [1985]: 353).

Books written for a popular market have their limitations in terms of reach, given also the fact that adherents of extreme right and populist right-wing parties and movements in western Europe are often minimally educated, male and not necessarily avid readers of books in English. Television, then, provides a much more powerful medium for 'Eurabia' propagandists. In this section, I will analyse what is arguably the most central contribution to the domestication and mainstreaming of the 'Eurabia' genre in Norway in recent years: a documentary partly financed and fully screened by the second-largest television broadcaster in Norway in late 2010.

On Monday, 29 November 2010, the private Norwegian TV channel TV2 screened the documentary *Frihet, Likhet og Det Muslimske Brorskap* (*Freedom, Equality and the Muslim Brothers*) by the Iraqi-born émigré author and film-maker Walid al-Kubaisi (1958–). The film argues that there is a plot directed by Islamist Ikhwan al-Muslimin (The Muslim Brothers) in Cairo, Egypt, to establish an Islamic caliphate in Europe and Norway, through the use of 'baby trolleys, the hijab, democracy and freedom of expression'. YouTube clips from al-Kubaisi's film would soon make their appearance in translated versions on various counter-jihadist websites, and al-Kubaisi would be cited approvingly twice in Anders Behring Breivik's tract *2083*. It was therefore unsurprising that when a television crew from al-Jazeera Arabic in Doha, Qatar, in the aftermath of Behring Breivik's terror attacks interviewed SIAN leader Arne Tumyr for a documentary on right-wing extremism and Islamophobia in Scandinavia, Tumyr named al-Kubaisi as the only Muslim in Norway he would approve of.[36]

In keeping with the point of view of Joan Scott (2007: 9), I argue that 'the situation of Muslim immigrants in Europe can be fully grasped only if the local[ized] context is taken into account'. Nevertheless, I also contend that Norwegian public debates on Islam and on Muslims must be seen in the context of a general right-wing shift in European politics since 2001, in the sense that the rhetorical tropes central to anti-Muslim and anti-Islamic discourses in Norway draw a great deal of inspiration from similar debates in other European countries, such as the United Kingdom, Germany, the Netherlands and France. Similar to their counterparts in other European countries, the anti-Muslim and anti-Islamic discourses in Norway are the crystallization of gradual processes of dissolution of traditional left–right divides in politics and society.[37] By virtue of a claim to 'cultural authenticity' so-called secular Muslims like Walid al-Kubaisi are in this terrain able to carve out spaces as prominent authenticators of Islamophobic and right-wing discourses (see also Ahmed 2011; Dabashi 2011; Mahmood 2011 for this).

Truth, lies and a documentary

Walid al-Kubaisi was born in Baghdad in Iraq in 1958, graduated with a bachelor's degree in electronic engineering from the University of Baghdad and then worked as a reporter. By 1981, fearing being called up in the war against Iran (1980–88), he had decided to leave Iraq. According to his own accounts (al-Kubaisi 2009), he spent some time travelling in the Middle East. In 1986 he was granted protection on humanitarian grounds in Norway. Public recognition as a writer in Norway came through the publication of *Min Tro, din Myte* (*My Faith, Your Myth*) (al-Kubaisi 1996). In this book, al-Kubaisi characterized media exposures of meetings between an MP of the Progress Party and right-wing extremists as 'unfair' (ibid.: 214), and alleged that 'racism in Europe increases proportionally with the progress of Islamism'.[38] The 1990s saw a significant shift in the tenor and content of Norwegian debates on immigration and integration as the Labour Party drifted towards the right in response to the increasing popularity of the PP and its hardline message on these issues.

This was particularly the case in Labour Party ranks in Oslo. Al-Kubaisi had started reading Samuel Huntington on the 'clash of civilizations'. In 2009, al-Kubaisi declared to *Morgenbladet* that Huntington 'was the true prophet of our time' and, furthermore, 'Islamization constitutes an act of war', and also that 'the fortresses of Europe are threatened from within by the daily *clash of civilizations*' (Morgenbladet 2009).

By 2006, through a network of strong supporters in Norwegian academia and in literary circles, al-Kubaisi had managed to obtain a state scholarship (*statsstipendiat*), which guaranteed him a basic income for the rest of his life, courtesy of the then Ministry of Culture and Education in Norway. The state scholarship was secured through a letter of support penned by Professor of Philosophy Gunnar Skirbekk (1937–) from the University of Bergen, and signed by thirty-four senior Norwegian academics, authors and intellectuals.[39] In the letter, Professor Skirbekk described his long-standing personal friend al-Kubaisi as a 'moderate Muslim' – in spite of the fact that al-Kubaisi was at the time an openly declared atheist.

Al-Kubaisi had by then for some years already started consorting with far-right and Islamophobic activists in Norway. In 2004, he accepted an invitation to present a lecture at the recently established Forum mot Islamisering (Forum Against Islamization, FOMI). FOMI was a precursor to the organization Stans Islamiseringen av Norge (Stop the Islamization of Norway, SIAN). Among the central members of FOMI was Arne Tumyr, an early member of the Norwegian Humanist Association and a newspaperman, presently chair of SIAN; the lawyer and resistance hero from the Second World War Erik Gjems-Onstad, who in Norway had a record of passionate support for apartheid South Africa and Ian Smith's racist regime in Rhodesia (see Chapter 4); and the chair, Jarle Synnevåg, a senior researcher at the Norwegian Defence Research Establishment (FFI), who in 2002 was fined for having breached the Norwegian racism paragraph § 135 (a) of the General Penal Code, and forced to resign from the FFI owing to a series of racist web posts directed against Muslims after 9/11. FOMI also included Arne Borgir, the former Norwegian Waffen-SS soldier in the German Nazi SS division Wiking, sentenced to imprisonment for treason after the Second World War, who was present when thousands of Ukrainian Jews were rounded up and killed by the SS near Lviv in 1942/43. Until his death in 2003 Borgir was a prominent Norwegian Holocaust denier (Strømmen 2007: 110). In a newspaper column in 2004 in the leftist daily *Klassekampen*, published under the classic 1980s racist slogan *Norge for nordmenn* (Norway for Norwegians), al-Kubaisi declared that he could see nothing wrong in consorting with FOMI members (al-Kubaisi 2004). Al-Kubaisi showered Arne Borgir with plaudits for declaring that 'Norway was for Norwegians'.[40] That slogan, as most Norwegian readers over a certain age would know very well, was the main slogan of extreme right-wingers in Norway in the 1980s and 1990s.

The documentary

Walid al-Kubaisi's documentary starts ominously, with a shot of the film-maker in his self-styled role as a bohemian Parisian intellectual, pompously proclaiming to the viewer that Europe's historical sins in the form of colonialism, racism, the Holocaust and so forth have hereby been forgiven.[41] Invoking the traditions of the European Enlightenment, and rhetorically positing himself as its heroic defender against a European Muslim 'fifth column' wanting to submit Europe to Islamism and the introduction of shari'a 'law', al-Kubaisi provides an interesting instantiation of '... conservatives defending a superior Western culture who claim the Enlightenment as their source of inspiration' (Todorov 2009: 122). Like popular Somali-born author Ayaan Hirsi Ali, al-Kubaisi is eminently useful for the populist right wing's anti-Muslim discourses precisely by virtue of his personal claim to cultural 'authenticity'. As the documentary's producer, Per Christian Magnus, expresses it: 'Through his adolescence in Iraq, Walid al-Kubaisi is among the Norwegians who know this [Islamist] ideology well. He has followed the debate in Arab media for a number of years, has himself attended an imam school, and has contacts in Iraq, Syria, Egypt and Morocco' (Magnus 2010).[42]

According to the film, there had been a common orchestration to the riots in the *banlieues* of Paris, France, in 2005 (Fassin 2006) as well as Muslim protests (*l'affaire foulard*) against the banning of the wearing of 'conspicuous signs' of religious affiliation in public schools (the *Loï Stasi*, 2004) in France in 2003 (Scott 2007; Bowen 2007), and the worldwide protests against the publication of the 'Mohammed cartoons' in Denmark and Norway deemed offensive to many practising Muslims (Klausen 2009; Asad et al. 2009). This orchestration had been conducted by the Muslim Brothers as part of the same 'plot'. Academic researchers who have explored in detail the background to the French suburban riots that lasted from 27 October to 17 November 2005 (see Muchielli 2009; Cesari 2005; Vidino 2010 in particular) have found no evidence whatsoever of a specifically Muslim religious incitement, let alone an Islamist incitement, to these riots.

According to al-Kubaisi, the original script of the film had been entitled *Djevelens verksted* (*The Devil's Workshop*) (al-Kubaisi 2010a) and was designed to spread '*sunn frykt*' ('healthy fear') (Bisgaard 2010) about the '*snik-islamisering*' (Islamization by stealth) of Norwegian society (ibid.). This term, which was of extreme right-wing provenance, had, as we saw in Chapter 4, been introduced by the PP's chairwoman Siv Jensen in a speech to the party's congress in February 2009 and had since then become a staple of the populist right-wing vocabulary on Islam and Muslims in Norway. It was, however, according to the film-maker himself, 'an anti-racist movie' (Sandvik 2010), and had been inspired by the European fight against Nazism in the 1940s (Bisgaard 2010). 'I have made a film warning against the fascism of our time,'[43] said al-Kubaisi during the launch (ibid.).[44]

The documentary featured interviews with a number of Egyptian and Arab secularist intellectuals, as well as a Yemeni Islamist and the Egyptian Islamist leader Mohammad Mahdi Akef;[45] with satellite television footage provided by MEMRI,[46] the film was launched amid a flurry of newspaper op-eds by al-Kubaisi and interviews with al-Kubaisi in the Norwegian mainstream media. When the Cairo correspondent of *Klassekampen*, Amal Wahab, interviewed a number of the Egyptian intellectuals featured in the documentary, it became clear that all of those she had been able to contact felt misrepresented in the documentary (Wahab 2010). The documentary itself shows that none of these interviewees had been informed of the central thrust of the documentary, namely a Muslim Brotherhood conspiracy to establish 'Islamic rule' over Norway and Europe. To the extent that these secularist intellectuals' fears concerning the influence of the MB feature in the documentary, they relate exclusively to their fears for Egypt's future.

In a media campaign devised by neoconservative newspaper reporter Jon Hustad of the relatively small and marginal weekly newspaper *Dag og Tid*, al-Kubaisi managed to generate an enormous amount of white heat over a period of approximately two weeks by making certain deliberate provocations. Al-Kubaisi's provocations were directed against a generalized Norwegian 'left' that was accused of being either 'defeatist' or 'accommodating towards' Islamism (Spaans 2010) or, by implication, being 'Islamist sympathizers' (al-Kubaisi 2010b). Furthermore, his provocations targeted the mainstream Islamic Council of Norway (Islamsk Råd Norge) and Muslim public intellectuals of a documented secular orientation who were cast as 'errand boys for the Islamists' ('*løpegutter for islamistene*') (Sandvik 2010) or 'secret members of the Muslim Brothers in Norway' ('*hemmelige medlemmer av det Muslimske Brorskapet i Norge*').[47] The Norwegian three-party coalition government was taken to task by al-Kubaisi for allegedly engaging in 'dialogue with Islamists' through its regular contacts and consultations with the Islamic Council of Norway. Al-Kubaisi also alleged that he had 'proved' in the documentary that Tariq Ramadan was the 'European representative of the Muslim Brothers' ideology'. While there is no doubt that Ramadan is an exponent of the *wasatiyya* or 'centrist, moderate' trend within contemporary Islamism which the Muslim Brothers also adhere to, the documentary does not substantiate in any way the claim that Ramadan 'represents' the Muslim Brothers.[48] An interesting rhetorical shift on al-Kubaisi's part had also occurred: having publicly declared himself an apostate from Islam shortly after his arrival in southern Norway in 1987 and having publicly described himself as an 'atheist'[49] in 2008 and a 'humanist and a free-thinker' as late as in 2009 (see al-Kubaisi 2009), al-Kubaisi now declared in an interview with *Klassekampen* to launch his film that he was 'a practising Muslim' (Spaans 2010).

Prior to TV2 screening the documentary, there had been a public screening sponsored by Fritt Ord at Vika Cinema in central Oslo on Thursday, 25 November. The debate that followed was facilitated by al-Kubaisi's media strategist Jon Hustad. Here, the invited panellists from Norwegian Muslim organizations, such as the secretary-general of the Islamic Council of Norway, Mehtab Afsar (1973–), and Muslim public intellectual Mohammed Usman Rana, were actively prevented from exercising *their* freedom of speech by loud booing as well as shouts of 'Shut up!' (*'Hold kjeft!'*) from the well-dressed audience.

More surprising still, for those who knew little about al-Kubaisi's strong networks in the Norwegian media and academia, was the fact that there was considerable discursive support for the documentary by prominent Norwegian public intellectuals and academics.

Instrumentalizing white heat

Those who expected political repercussions from the white heat generated by the documentary did not have to wait for long. In an interview with the regional daily liberal newspaper *Bergens Tidende*, al-Kubaisi said that 'the hijab is the main symbol of the Muslim Brothers' and that 'the Islamists believe it is God's command that all women should wear the hijab' (Sandvik 2010). The day after TV2 screened the documentary, *Aftenposten* featured a prominently placed commentary by Mazyar Keshvari (1981–), who had been born to refugee parents from Iran and who was at the time councillor for the PP on Oslo's City Council. In 'The dangerous grip of the Islamists' (*Islamistenes farlige grep*) Keshvari cites al-Kubaisi's documentary *in extenso* and argues that 'the massive immigration to Norway and to Europe' and the 'fact'[50] that 'Muslim women have many children, and European women few' mean that 'we are now faced with the most important and determinative struggle over values' – 'a struggle between liberal humanistic values and totalitarian Islamist values' (Keshvari 2010). The Islamists' main 'characteristic' was, according to Keshvari, the hijab.

By the following week, it was clear that the PP would use al-Kubaisi's documentary as a platform for another attempt to push legislation through the Norwegian parliament (the Storting) prohibiting the use of the hijab and other forms of Islamic attire for women or children in Norway's schools. Few Muslims in Norway expressed any support for the proposed hijab ban. The fixation on the symbolic politics of Muslim female attire is not a new one for the PP. In the shifting terrain of late modern politics across western Europe, the veil or Islamic headscarf is 'implicated in a meta-discourse of nationalized liberalism versus Muslim illiberalism' (Lentin and Titley 2011: 94). And this nationalized liberalism is, as we noted in Chapter 4, one in which populist right-wing parties have increasingly been able to trade on the issue of women's rights within minority communities, instrumentalize women's rights and thereby broaden their appeal.

The PP's attempt to push through this legislation was fronted by its young, female and ethnic Norwegian parliamentarian Mette Hanekamhaug (1987–). The party's spokesperson on immigration and integration, the MP Per Willy Amundsen (1971–), who after 22/7 would be removed from his post, followed up with a newspaper op-ed (Amundsen 2010) in which he referred to al-Kubaisi's film and argued that the Islamists of al-Kubaisi's documentary wanted Norway to be 'more like Iran and Saudi Arabia' and that the film 'had warned that the *hijab*, the *niqab* and the *burka* were symbols for radical Islamists'. Echoing al-Kubaisi's declaration of the onset of a 'struggle against the Muslim brothers' (Hustad 2010), Amundsen issued instructions for 'the struggle for freedom' and ominously warned that unless 'we' 'take up the fight against the Islamists and their totalitarian ideology', 'freedom will be lost'. This was the same Per Willy Amundsen who would, during the spring of 2011, wonder aloud on his personal Facebook page whether a 'new crusade' against Muslims would be necessary.

The PP's parliamentary motion on the hijab

The PP's parliamentary motion on the hijab in public schools, built around arguments directly from Walid al-Kubaisi's documentary and public statements (see al-Kubaisi 2004 in particular), makes for interesting reading. The motion argued that 'the hijab symbolizes values that represent a radical rupture from the liberal values that Norway is founded upon [and that] the hijab is a serious impediment to successful integration'.

Furthermore, the text of the motion alleged that 'the Muslim Brothers were the first to take the hijab in use as a symbol'. It attributed the modern-day hijab to 'a variety of the attire worn by the female proselytizer Zainab al-Ghazali'.[51] This claim, which is not supported by any references, stemmed from an op-ed published by al-Kubaisi in *Aftenposten* in 2004 under the presumptuous title 'The true story of the scarf and the veil in Islam' (al-Kubaisi 2004). There was little factual evidence to support this contention on al-Kubaisi's part.[52]

Citing al-Kubaisi's 2004 op-ed in *Aftenposten*, in which al-Kubaisi had argued that 'the hijab is a political uniform of the militant Islamist movement', it argued for 'courageous measures' from the Norwegian state in banning the use of the hijab for children in Norwegian public schools. 'When children are forced to use the hijab, they are socialized into a gendered apartheid, into a kind of proselytizing which argues that women are of lesser value, and must cover themselves in order not to arouse uncontrollable male sexual desires.' Furthermore, 'to attribute blame to women for rape in this manner is in itself serious, but it is even worse when this mode of thought leads to what one today sees tendencies towards, in which small children are dressed in hijab in order not to arouse male desires'.

Having thus invoked misogyny, patriarchy, male rape and paedophilia as arguments against the hijab, the text ends with an alarmist, yet familiar universalistic trope about what Spivak (1993) once referred to as 'saving brown women from brown men': 'Women from Muslim countries cry out for help from the West. Norway cannot do much about women's oppression in Muslim countries, but Norway can and should be a beacon for gender equality, regardless of faith and nationality. Norway should proceed to set a good example by outlawing the use of hijab in children's schools.' The Norwegian parliament was not convinced: in April 2011, the PP's parliamentary motion to ban the use of the hijab on children in Norwegian public schools was turned down. Only MPs from the PP voted in favour of the motion.

Conclusion

This chapter has explored Anders Behring Breivik's ideological fellow travellers among proponents of the 'Eurabia' genre in Norway and internationally. In the aftermath of 22/7, these all without fail took exception to Behring Breivik's violent course of actions. Yet it is undeniable that Behring Breivik was profoundly inspired by the genre, and the systematic hatred and fear of Muslims that the genre is designed to generate. It is fair to say that the genre and its proponents in Norway – Berg, Bawer and al-Kubaisi – have since been somewhat discredited in the Norwegian context. Yet this chapter has revealed that one need go back only to the winter of 2010/11 in order to find a public situation in Norway in which the mainstream media focused massive attention on and provided legitimacy for the rhetorical tropes that are central to the 'Eurabia' genre, and in which populist right-wingers aligned with the Progress Party tried to capitalize on the white heat generated by contributions to the genre in order to further their anti-Muslim and anti-immigration agenda. It would therefore be naive to think that such a situation may not once more return.

6 | THE WEIGHT OF WORDS

The treatment of aliens, foreigners, and others in our midst is a crucial test case for the moral conscience as well as political reflexivity of liberal democracies. (Seyla Benhabib, *The Rights of Others. Aliens, Residents and Citizens* 2002)

Under what conditions does freedom of speech become freedom to hate? (Judith Butler, 'Response to Asad and Mahmood', in *Is Critique Secular?* 2009)

Words and acts

This book has provided detailed explorations into the thought of the Norwegian mass-murdering right-wing extremist Anders Behring Breivik and his fellow ideological travellers. We have explored both Behring Breivik's own tract, *2083*, the writings of his main ideological inspiration, Peder Are 'Fjordman' Nøstvold Jensen, and the 'Eurabia' genre, which inspired them both. We have also explored the mainstreaming of ideas, arguments and rhetorical tropes of extreme right-wing provenance in and through Norwegian political discourse on Islam, Muslims and immigration in Norway in recent decades. In order to understand the latter process, we must however also explore what has arguably been a *sine qua non* for the mainstreaming of Islamophobia in Norwegian society and politics, namely the shifting conceptions of freedom of expression and its limits among liberal media, intellectual and legal elites in the same period. In an essay on the Rushdie affair, the social anthropologist Talal Asad notes that modern secular cultures have their own 'sacred geography' (Asad 1993: 10). In late-modern Norway, it appears that nothing is more sacred than freedom of expression or speech. In a representative sample taken from an opinion survey from 2010, 96.1 per cent of the Norwegians polled agreed that freedom of expression characterized Norwegian society to a 'very high' or 'high' degree (IMDI 2010: 27) and freedom of expression was ranked far higher than any other characteristic of Norwegian society, such as, for example, socio-economic or gender equality. In a similar survey, 90 per cent of Norwegians with an immigrant background said that they viewed freedom of expression as a 'central value' in Norway. These surveys cannot tell us the extent to which Norwegians regarded the centrality of this value as a desirable state of affairs. But they do seem to indicate that freedom of expression has become a central *doxa* in Norway, or, in Bourdieu's words, part of that 'which goes without saying' (Bourdieu 1978).

Central Norwegian media editors pre-22/7 declared with pride that they were *freedom of expression fundamentalists* (*ytringsfrihetsfundamentalister*) (for such a use of the term, see Åmås 2007) and were able to construe a discursive situation in which those who argue in line with international human rights conventions that freedom of expression is but one of many human rights and as such has to be balanced with other rights were more often than not cast as opponents of freedom of speech and as potentially anti-democratic and illiberal. With reference to both the Rushdie affair (1988–94) and the cartoon crisis (2005/06), those in Norway who argue that there are definite limits to freedom of expression under international human rights conventions and treaties have been accused of being in league with those who are trying to exempt 'religions', particularly Islam, from a 'critique of religion' with reference to either blasphemy laws or the so-called 'defamation of religions'.[1] This is a 'slippery slope' argument, most famously advanced by the late legal philosopher Ronald Dworkin (1931–2013), in which 'a purpose to protect human beings' turns into a ban on criticizing 'any belief'.

The existing legal protections against racist and/or discriminatory speech are ultimately aimed at protecting individuals, not groups (Waldron 2012: 56). Norway, like most other Western countries, upholds such restrictions on freedom of expression. While these restrictions comprise legal protections, they offer no protection whatsoever against 'insult', 'blasphemy' or the dubious concept of 'defamation of religions'.[2] This is something that is often confused, even among academics who specialize in this field. It is not, and cannot be, the duty of a liberal and democratic state to protect individuals or groups against feelings of 'offense' (ibid.: 15), which, after all, can arise from the flimsiest of pretexts. This distinction is in fact well established in Norwegian law as well as in the practice of the Norwegian Supreme

Court. The blasphemy provisions of the Norwegian Penal Code, §142, which make it a criminal act to 'by word or deed publicly insult or show contempt for any creed whose practice in the realm [of Norway] is permitted', while still formally on the statute books, have not been used since the 1930s, when the atheist poet Arnulf Øverland was prosecuted for referring to Christianity as the 'tenth plague of the country' (*'den tiende landeplage'*) in a highly publicized lecture. It is, for all practical purposes, a legal dead letter (see Høstmælingen 2005: 1008). In terms of the so-called 'racism' paragraph §135(a)[3] of the Norwegian General Penal Code, the Norwegian Supreme Court has long maintained a distinction between 'defamatory' speech against 'religion' and racist and discriminatory speech against individuals. In the case against Vivi Krogh in 1981,[4] the court found Krogh guilty of breaches against §135(a) for having distributed thousands of leaflets with racist and discriminatory statements against Pakistani (Muslim) immigrants to Norway. However, the Supreme Court noted in its verdict that it considered the leaflet's statements concerning Islam and Norwegian immigration policy – regardless of their offensiveness – as speech protected under the freedom of expression clause of the Norwegian Constitution (i.e. §100).

The late Ronald Dworkin (1931–2013), who may be seen as a strong and passionate defender of US First Amendment interpretations of freedom of speech in their more absolutist formulations, contends that since free expression is a necessary condition of political legitimacy in any democratic society, we risk unduly interfering with political legitimacy and undermining liberal democracy if free expression is curtailed.[5] In his view, the right to 'shock, mock and ridicule' is to be upheld more or less without regard to the consequences. So much so, that in Dworkin's case he also defended a policy of free speech absolutism[6] in the midst of the attempted genocide in Bosnia (see Holmes 2012), which had been preceded by years of racist and discriminatory speech inciting Serbs to violence against Bosnian Muslims (see Cigar 2003).

At a *New York Review of Books*/Fritt Ord conference on 'Challenges to multiculturalism' at Literature House in Oslo, approximately one year after 22/7, Dworkin asserted that the incidence of hate crimes in the USA had fallen in recent decades, and that it had also done so in countries in Europe with no legislation against 'hate speech'[7] or countries in which such legislation was not applied.[8] The implication for Dworkin was that the best remedy against hate crimes is for any state to abandon legal protections against 'hate speech'. There are a number of problems with such assertions. First, in most countries, we do not have anything like a reliable historical statistical baseline for diachronic comparisons of hate crimes. In the USA, it was not until the passing of the 1990 Hate Crime Statistics Act that Congress managed to mandate federal collection of local data on such crimes (see Bleich 2011a: 116). In Norway, police authorities have registered and published data on such crimes only since late 2006, after gay rights groups brought public attention to the phenomenon of hate crimes (Bruknapp 2009). Since published police records on incidences of hate crimes in the Norwegian capital of Oslo began in 2007, there have been more hate crimes targeting individuals on the basis of their ethnicity and/or religion than hate crimes targeting individuals on the basis of their non-heterosexual orientation, yet in Norwegian mainstream media, it is the latter which receive by far the most attention (see Bangstad 2011). In 2010 the Oslo police in its last report on hate crimes in the Norwegian capital openly admitted that owing to lack of knowledge about the existence of this reporting category of crime, it is likely that a number of such crimes are not registered by police as hate crimes, and furthermore that such crimes may therefore be under-reported.[9] Secondly, a problem with using statistics on the incidence of hate crimes as a basis for comparisons within, as well as between, nation-state jurisdictions is, of course, the variation and inconsistency not only in that which is categorized as a 'hate crime', but also police registration of hate crimes. Moreover, the propensity for victimized individuals to report hate crimes varies a great deal between and within different national contexts, rendering cross-country comparisons virtually impossible. Of the twenty-seven member states of the European Union, only Finland, Great Britain and Sweden collect and publish in any systematic fashion data on levels of hate crimes motivated by racism (Jupskås 2012: 221). Furthermore, owing to the unreliability of reporting and inconsistency of available statistics in the USA on this issue, it cannot in fact be established with any degree of certainty that hate crimes have actually been decreasing there.

According to the evidence available, European countries that have enacted and enforced legislation against racist and discriminatory speech post-1945 have not ended up sacrificing liberal values in the process (see Bleich 2011b for this). In Oslo, Dworkin went on to argue that the so-called 'racism paragraph', §135(a) of the Norwegian General Penal Code, introduced in 1970, and last amended in 2005, was 'unconstitutional' in light of the Norwegian Constitution's new §100, introduced in 2004. If anything, this is a histrionic claim, inasmuch as neither the Government Commission on Freedom of Expression (1996–99) in its proposals for a new §100 of the Constitution, nor the parliamentarians who in 2004/05 deliberated on the new constitutional paragraph, nor the Norwegian Supreme Court has ever subscribed to this view (see Bangstad 2012b for details).

It has become commonplace in Norway to argue that the strong presence of right-wing populists in democratic arenas both locally and nationally has functioned as a 'safety valve' that has prevented greater levels of extreme right-wing violence in Norwegian society.[10] Academic proponents of this hypothesis (and it has never been proved more than such) often refer to the work of the Dutch political scientist Ruud Koopmans, who, basing his conclusions on findings from Austria and Germany in the 1990s, argued that the presence of radical right-wing parties actually reduced the potential for extreme right-wing and racist violence in these countries (Koopmans 1996). Yet the available research on this subject is by no means conclusive with regard to the existing quality of the findings (Jupskås 2012: 213). In Norway, it is also a fact that the number of reported racist incidents rose from 140 per annum in 1987 (when the Progress Party made its electoral breakthrough) to 200 per annum in the following ten years (ibid.: 214), arguably lending more credence to the view that populist right-wingers may act more as 'voice amplifiers' rather than constituting a 'safety valve'.

Freedom of expression is seen in contemporary Norway as occupying a privileged place in a hierarchy of ranked human rights. In an interview with a Norwegian newspaper a mere week after 22/7, the chairman of the influential Norwegian Freedom of Expression Foundation Fritt Ord, Georg Fredrik Rieber Mohn (1945–), a former Norwegian attorney general (1986–97) and magistrate at the Norwegian

Supreme Court (1997–2007), stated that 'freedom of expression was, in a certain sense, supra-ordinate to other human rights' (Hustad 2011). A similar view has been articulated by a former op-ed editor at *Aftenposten*, Knut Olav Åmås (see Åmås 2007).

When Norwegian elites with great powers of definition in Norwegian society and politics are to a greater or lesser extent wedded to such a view of the international human rights conventions and treaties that Norway is a signatory to, it often becomes a moot point to note that such a hierarchy of human rights does not in fact exist in these same conventions and treaties. The United Nations Declaration of Human Rights (UDHR) 1948, the European Convention on Human Rights (ECHR) 1950 and the International Covenant on Civil and Political Rights (ICCPR) 1966 all provide great leeway for individual states to define their own legal and social parameters for freedom of expression and its limits. Furthermore, academics who have in recent years studied and analysed the practice of the European Court of Human Rights (ECtHR) in Strasbourg have concluded that in cases concerning hate speech and freedom of expression the court often invokes the principle of individual states' 'margin of appreciation' (Vance 2004: 209). This principle provides states bound by the ECHR and the findings of the ECtHR space to define for themselves which kinds of hate speech they want to define as liable to criminal punishment, with reference to the state's own historical and societal context (Barendt 2011). Furthermore, as philosopher Kwame Anthony Appiah has argued, 'the promulgation of human rights, by international institutions, hardly guarantees assent – and even assent hardly guarantees anything in particular' (Appiah 2005: 264). This means that to the extent that individual states may want a hierarchy of human rights in which freedom of expression is seen as an overriding right, they may have considerable leeway to achieve this.

The media elites are integral in defining the parameters and terms of mediated public debates in Norway. Yet dominant conceptions of freedom of expression and its limits in liberal elite circles in Norway should in no way be confused with those of the population at large. From their privileged positions, Norwegian liberal media editors more often than not appear to hold absolutist positions on freedom of expression. A quantitative survey from 2013 points to the disconnect between such elites and the population at large on this issue.[11] To the great consternation of Norwegian liberal media editors and some newspaper reporters (Wang-Naveen 2013), who in this report commissioned by the Fritt Ord Foundation must have seen evidence of their own failures in spite of decades of concerted effort in 'civilizing' the Norwegian general public into holding the same absolutist conceptions of freedom of expression that they themselves held, the survey found that a mere 21 per cent of the national representative sample considered freedom of expression to be the primary aim that Norway ought to pursue in the next ten years. Fifty-seven per cent of those surveyed considered the upholding of law and order to be the overriding aim that Norway ought to pursue for these years (see TNS Gallup 2013: 20). Eighty-nine and 90 per cent respectively considered that incitement to violence or threats against individuals and groups should be punishable under law, and 73 per cent considered surveillance of individuals holding extreme views to be acceptable (ibid.: 42). Thirty-six and 32 per cent respectively of those surveyed considered it acceptable to limit the rights of religious extremists and racists to hold open public meetings and demonstrations (ibid.: 6). The survey also revealed that political left–right divides did not provide much of a clue to the views of respondents. It was, in other words, simply not a simple case of right-wingers valuing freedom of expression more than left-wingers. The fact that declared supporters of the Conservative and the Progress parties among the survey respondents were reserved about the virtues of liberal free speech absolutism may be seen as somewhat paradoxical, given that the two parties in question were the only parties who had adopted political programmes pledging to abolish §135(a) ahead of the Norwegian parliamentary elections of September 2013. While various forms of racist and/or discriminatory speech directed at Muslims and other minorities in Norway appear to have continued unabated after 22/7, and, according to some accounts, have actually become worse (Nordby 2011), and threats against politicians and public intellectuals on the internet have increased, mainstream Norwegian media's attention to and moderation of hate speech on newspaper discussion forums on the internet, as well as attention to and regulation of racist and/or discriminatory speech expressed in its paper editions, have in fact seen some modest improvement. *Aftenposten*'s former op-ed editor, Knut Olav Åmås, had argued in an August 2011 interview that the limit of freedom of expression was 'racism, hatred directed against individuals and groups, as well as incitement to criminal acts and violence' (Åmås in Øvrebø 2011). Åmås here seems to endorse the view that as long as contributors of op-ed pieces to *Aftenposten* do not explicitly advocate racist views and incitement to violence in the present, then their past and consistent record of doing so matters little. It is therefore unsurprising that *Aftenposten* would facilitate the debut of Anders Behring Breivik's main ideological inspiration, Peder Are 'Fjordman' Nøstvold Jensen, as an opinion essay contributor to Norway's largest and most in-fluential newspaper in April 2013, in a piece in which 'Fjordman' interestingly enough loudly proclaimed that 'the media attempts to scare people [like me] to silence by stigmatizing [*brennmerke*] certain opinions which the ruling elites disapprove of' (Jensen 2013a).

The verdict in the 22/7 trial against Anders Behring Breivik made it clear that the terror attacks in which he murdered seventy-seven people, most of them defenceless teenagers, were *political* in nature. The victims were – as we have seen in this book – targeted by Behring Breivik owing to ideological conviction to the effect that Norwegian social democrats (or 'cultural Marxists', according to his rather pe-culiar political understanding) had opened the 'floodgates' of an impending 'Islamization' of Norway by permitting Muslims to settle in the country over the course of the past forty years. That ideologi-cal conviction was one which had been reinforced by timeless hours spent in the echo chambers of 'Eurabia' propagandists on the inter-net. Anders Behring Breivik may have been a 'lone wolf terrorist' but he was acting upon rhetoric embedded in larger social movements (see Berntzen and Sandberg 2014 for this). The relationship between his words and actions is neither direct nor unmediated. There is reason to believe that thousands of Norwegians share some of his ideas about Islam and Islamization as an 'existential threat' (see Berntzen 2011 for this). In light of the historical evidence on mass murder and genocide in modern history, it can be argued that there is a relationship between words and actions.

From Austin (1962) to Searle (1969), modern philosophers of language have demonstrated that to speak is to act upon the material world – often in ways intended to affect the material world in specific ways. To characterize a group of young Norwegian Muslims as 'quislings' as Norwegian civil society activist Hege Storhaug did in an *Aftenposten* op-ed in early 2011 (Storhaug 2011a), or indeed to characterize leftists as 'quislings' as her former adviser Bruce Bawer does in his latest book (Bawer 2012b), is not to make a neutral statement devoid of implications for those so characterized; rather, for those acquainted with the basics of Norwegian modern history, this is to engage in speech acts that incite one's interlocutors against particular groups of people in Norway.

In recent years, extreme and populist right-wingers in Norway and Europe have more often than not found common interests with Islamists in turning aside from social tolerance and advancing more absolutist conceptions of freedom of expression. They are not necessarily consistent in their support for more absolutist conceptions of freedom of expression, though. For whereas Islamists want to prohibit forms of speech deemed offensive to Muslims through law or a resort to violence and intimidation, extreme and/or populist right-wingers have made the case for banning the Qur'an (Geert Wilders in the Netherlands), prohibiting Lutheran Christian bishops from criticizing Norwegian asylum policies or withdrawing state support from anti-racist civil society organizations.[12] It is in this polarized social and discursive climate that both trends reap support and legitimacy. The aim of racist and/or discriminatory speech, whether it be directed against Muslims, Jews, Romas, gays or women, is to undermine the assurance that individuals of any such 'minority' background are entitled to enjoy a degree of equality in a liberal and democratic society (see Waldron 2012: 94). Such absolutist conceptions also serve to provide a focal point for the proliferation and the coordination of social attitudes and behaviour expressed in and through such speech. They invite others to join forces with them, and thereby demonstrate to such persons that they are not alone in their bigotry (ibid.: 95). According to Waldron, what a liberal and democratic state seeks to protect by having and enforcing laws against racist and/or discriminatory speech is a liberal good; namely, formally equal rights to citizenship and dignity[13] for all citizens, regardless of colour, creed, sexual orientation or gender. Of course, absolute liberalism in this as in many other fields may in fact lead to absolute illiberalism, as pointed out long ago by the Norwegian philosopher Hans Skjervheim (Skjervheim 1968).

It has become something of a liberal platitude to cite the great US Supreme Court judge Brandeis to the effect that the answer to 'hate speech' is 'more speech'.[14] This raises the question of whether one expects those targeted, threatened or vilified by such speech to engage in 'counter-speech' regardless of the circumstances for exercising such verbal or textual expression and the repercussions thereof (see West 2012: 234). For racist and/or discriminatory speech is not per se motivated by any attempt to further the cause of democratic deliberation: 'Racist speech does not function as an invitation to conversation. It does not offer reasons or arguments with which its audience can engage; and the visceral hostility it expresses effectively forecloses, rather than opens, the opportunity for further discussion' (ibid.: 235).

In actual practice, 'hate speech acts of hate speakers are acts which are capable of inhibiting the ability of their targets to speak back' (Gelber 2012: 53). Empirical research on the responses to 'hate speech' by the targets of such speech in the public sphere suggests that individuals so targeted are unlikely to respond with 'counter-speech' since they often fear that, if they respond, the consequence may be violence (Nielsen 2012: 149). Proponents of the 'more speech' position also fail to address the question of what the 'appropriate' and 'reasonable' 'response' to racial epithets would be (ibid.: 158). Let me provide a recent example of racist and discriminatory speech directed against a Norwegian Muslim in order to illustrate the problems that the remedy of 'more speech' or 'counter-speech' simply fails to address.

In November 2012, a young Norwegian convert to Islam, Per Yousef Bartho Assidiq, who for some years had been active in the Norwegian computer-mediated public spheres, reported the various Facebook postings that he had received from 'white' Norwegian right-wingers. In the posts, Muslims like himself were referred to as 'vermin' ('*skadedyr*'), 'rats' ('*rotter*'), and the Norwegian government as 'quislings'. As for himself, he was warned that he would one day be 'fucked in the arse [*rævpult*] well and thoroughly before we throw you to the pigs'. After the Oslo police failed to even open an investigation into these threats, Assidiq posted a selection of these Facebook posts on his personal blog[15] and also recounted his story in a newspaper, where he reiterated the threats, abuse and intimidation he had been exposed to.

Brettschneider (2012: 3) argues that hateful viewpoints expressed in and through hate speech threaten the ideal of 'free and equal citizenship' which underlies public equality in a liberal democracy. Gelber (2011: 84) contends that the very purpose of hate speech is 'to exclude its targets from participating in the broader deliberative process'. In effect, some forms of speech are designed to and do silence the speech of others (see also Maitra and McGowan 2012: 8).

My own research into young Norwegian Muslims who are active in the computer-mediated public spheres in recent years suggests that Assidiq's experiences are far from unique (see Bangstad forthcoming). Unlike Assidiq, however, many young Norwegian Muslims refrain from active engagement in and with the Norwegian mediated public sphere, precisely to avoid the prospect of similar harassment, and, intimidated by threats received on these sites, a number of active participants in the mediated public sphere have in fact withdrawn into relative silence.

If 'more speech' or 'counter-speech' is in fact the great solvent that free speech absolutists think it is, what, then, is the 'reasonable' and 'appropriate' 'response' to being called a 'rat', 'vermin' or to being threatened with anal rape? Is the appropriate 'freedom of speech' response simply to assert that one is perchance neither a 'rat' nor 'vermin', and to suggest, 'No, thanks, I don't like to be fucked in the arse'? To date there has been no 'great liberal debate' in which racists, fascists, neo-Nazis and their targets have engaged one another in 'democratic deliberation' aimed at 'working out their differences'. This has yet to take place, and chances seem few that such a debate will ever materialize in the real world with its considerable social and political differentiations. The most absolutist conceptions of free speech in this context provide us with few concrete guidelines concerning instances of speech that are neither meant to be nor can conceivably form part of any form of democratic deliberation.

Many academic discussions about freedom of expression and its limitations proceed without any concrete references to actual instances of racist and/or discriminatory speech. They proceed without empirical bases for the effect of such freedom of expression on 'world-making' and on concrete human individuals. In this book, I have spent much time providing concrete examples of such speech, whether it be in the form of Anders Behring Breivik's tract *2083* (Chapter 3), or the Norwegian far right's discourse on Islam and Muslims (Chapter 3) or the 'Eurabia' literature (Chapter 4).

My findings show that regardless of the various views on what constitutes appropriate means and methods for blocking the purported 'Islamization' of Norway and Europe, there is a discursive continuum between various far-right formations in Norway and Europe at present. Unfortunately this continuum makes it more likely than not that we will also in the future see more extreme right-wing violence and possibly terror in Norway and Europe, motivated by similar hatreds of Muslims, Islam and 'multiculturalist elites' such as those motivating Anders Behring Breivik.

The aim of the 'world-making' of many of the far-right political formations in Norway and Europe is to attempt to saturate the public sphere with racist and/or discriminatory speech and thereby serve both to dull the senses and confuse the social morals of most people and inure them to such hatreds and intolerance. Such ideological campaigns, then, have material effects, namely to create a world in which infringements of the dignity and equal citizenship of immigrants and/or people of minority background may become routine and acceptable. This is also the reason why we should be less sanguine about free speech absolutists and their recited truths.

In his classic work *How to Do Things with Words* (Austin 1962), Oxford professor of moral philosophy and philosopher of language J. L. Austin (1911–60) writes that to perform a perlocutionary speech act is to say something which 'will often, or even normally, produce certain consequential effects upon the feelings, thoughts, or actions of the audience, or of the speaker, or of other persons'. This may, for Austin, 'be done with the design, intention and purpose of producing them' (ibid.: 101). We also know from the modern history of mass murder and genocide, from the Shoah/Holocaust to Cambodia to

Rwanda and on to Bosnia, that not only are 'words weapons' (Poole 2006), but a 'war of words' usually precedes acts of mass murder and genocide (Vetlesen 2005: 169).[16] However, this is not to assert that these 'wars of words' *cause* mass murder and genocide, nor do 'wars of words' uttered in advanced liberal and secular societies necessarily pose the same risks as in fragile and crisis-ridden developing societies. Such a conclusion would be naive and reductionist. In his testimony to the court in the 22/7 trial, Anders Behring Breivik in fact pointed directly to this linkage when he asserted that he had found it 'difficult' to massacre his defenceless, witlessly frightened and sometimes pleading teenage victims at Utøya, and that he could do so only by dehumanizing them. Behring Breivik's first psychiatric assessors appear to have completely disregarded the *words* of war with which he prepared for his actual *acts* of war against Norwegian social democrats, who, according to his war of words, bore the main responsibility for allowing the presence of Muslims in Norway in the first place and hence the purported 'Islamization of Norway'.

But Behring Breivik's defence lawyer, Geir Lippestad, made it clear in early December 2011 that he regarded those who had been part of generating the 'war of words' which reverberated through Behring Breivik's twisted mind in the months and years preceding 22/7 as bearing a moral if not a criminal responsibility. Lippestad and his team called Islamophobic blogger 'Fjordman' (Peder Are Nøstvold Jensen) and Hans Rustad of Document.no as witnesses in the trial. 'Someone creates fertile soil for these opinions. They do not emerge in and of themselves,' said Lippestad in an interview with the tabloid *VG* on 6 December 2011 (Brenna et al. 2011b). Lippestad is, by virtue of his task as Behring Breivik's legal representative probably the person who since 22/7 has had the most extensive contact with the mass murderer. And it was Lippestad who was to repeat this message after the conclusion of the 22/7 trial in Oslo on 24 August 2012. In a newspaper interview in November 2012, he reiterated that 'it was the internet that radicalized Behring Breivik'. Anders Behring Breivik, Lippestad claimed, 'did perhaps have a slightly difficult childhood, but not worse than anyone else'. Letting it be known that he still received many phone calls and e-mails from supporters of Behring Breivik, who even spoke and wrote under their full personal names,

Lippestad concluded that 'those who think that Breivik is alone, are regretfully wrong. There are enormous numbers of people who share parts of his universe' (Sletholm 2012b).

Predictably, Lippestad's assignment of moral responsibility to the ideological actions of Jensen and Rustad has been roundly condemned by editors in the Norwegian media. In an editorial in *Aftenposten* on 7 December 2011, it was argued that this 'could contribute to clouding the sharp distinction between extreme opinions and criminal acts' (Aftenposten 2011b). *Bergens Tidende*'s editorial the following day characterized Lippestad's statement as implying the attribution of a 'derailed responsibility' to his 'political leading stars' (Bergens Tidende 2011). *Aftenposten*'s editor took issue with Lippestad's attributing of responsibility to the 'Eurabia' authors who had inspired Behring Breivik, and first and foremost Peder Are 'Fjordman' Nøstvold Jensen. At stake here is not only the question of how the relationship between words and actions is to be understood in the specific case of Anders Behring Breivik and 22/7, but also, ultimately, the conceptualization of freedom of expression and its limits. Understanding the complexity of this relationship requires an understanding of the rapidly shifting conceptualizations of freedom of expression in Norway since the 1990s.

In this chapter, I analyse how the shift towards more absolutist conceptions of freedom of expression emerged as a result of rethinking and restructuring attributed to this theme by the Norwegian media, as well as by the political, legal and intellectual elites in the 1990s and 2000s. I do not want to suggest a mono-causality wherein these processes are understood as having been caused by a singular factor; a number of factors were central to the growth of this rethinking and restructuring, including the increasing commercialization of the Norwegian media in the 1980s and 1990s, the development of a largely unregulated blogosphere in the 1990s and 2000s, the saturation media coverage of the high-profile Rushdie affair in Norway from 1989 to 1994, which was followed up by a media event of equal proportions, namely the cartoon crisis of 2005/06. That these developments were not only local or national but were of a global nature indicates that they are not to be understood in isolation, particularly from developments in Scandinavia and Europe.

There is a strong argument for exploring the concrete manifestations of these developments in their localized contexts. A number of western European countries actually penalize racist and/or discriminatory speech (see Bleich 2011b for an overview) in a tacit admission that such speech is ultimately directed at undermining the rights to equal citizenship and dignity of individuals of minority background in liberal and democratic societies (Waldron 2010: 1647).

The Norwegian Supreme Court has been somewhat inconsistent in its application of the relevant legal paragraphs in recent years. In a verdict, dated 30 March 2012, the Norwegian Supreme Court found an unnamed person guilty of violating §135(a), and upheld the verdict of the lower courts.[17] The individual in question had, while in an intoxicated state, been refused entry to a bar by a doorman in the city of Stavanger (on Norway's west coast) and reacted offensively. The doorman was of African origin, and on the date in question (in July 2010), in the presence of a significant number of people, the individual referred to the doorman as a 'fucking Negro' (*'jævla neger'*) and a 'fucking darkie' (*'jævla svarting'*). A work colleague of the African doorman called to the scene was referred to as a 'nigger lover', and asked why 'Negroes are permitted to work in Norway'. The verdict in this case may indicate a lowering of the bar for prosecution as well as convictions for racist and/or discriminatory speech under §135(a) of the Norwegian General Penal Code.

Until the Norwegian Supreme Court's verdict in this case, the last Supreme Court conviction for breaches of the Norwegian racism paragraph occurred in 2007, when it convicted neo-Nazi leader Tore Tvedt of the organization Vigrid of racism under §135(a) for anti-Semitic statements made in a 2003 newspaper interview.[18]

A more important verdict, in light of the precedent it would set, appears to have been the Norwegian Supreme Court's acquittal in 2002 of Norwegian neo-Nazi leader Terje Sjølie of Boot Boys for anti-Semitic and anti-immigrant statements. In the Sjølie case, a divided Norwegian Supreme Court concluded that freedom of expression overrode guarantees of protection against hate speech for minorities. At that time, the attorney general, Tor-Aksel Busch, who prosecuted the case for the Norwegian state at the Supreme Court, warned that the Sjølie verdict would set precedents with regard to minorities' protection against racist and discriminatory speech. The precedent it would set is not so much a matter of the actual application of the law in terms of §135(a) by Norwegian courts (here, the 2007 Tvedt case reflects prevailing legal sentiment), but rather a matter of the number of reports to police and prosecutions under §135(a) that would be likely to occur following the Sjølie decision. Hate crimes in Norway are – as elsewhere – under-reported, and victims of such crimes are known to sometimes be reluctant to report such crimes to the police. This was the case for those Muslims and/or individuals of immigrant background who experienced harassment on the streets of Oslo in the hours after Anders Behring Breivik's terror attack at Government Headquarters on 22/7, as had been the case in the preceding years, and as it continues to be up to the present (Harr and Partapouli 2012).

The Sjølie verdict came under strong criticism from both the UN-CERD Committee[19] and ECRI.[20] This, in combination with the recommendations of a Government Commission on Legal Protection Against Ethnic Discrimination in 2002 (Holgersen et al. 2002),[21] led to a number of changes to Norway's anti-discrimination and anti-racism laws designed to prevent a recurrence of one of the internationally more shameful episodes in its legal history.

Based on the proposals of the 2002 Government Commission, in 2005 Norwegian authorities raised the maximum penalty for crimes under §135(a) from two to three years' imprisonment; gross negligence (rather than actual intent) became sufficient in order to penalize racist and/or discriminatory speech; it would no longer be necessary for statements which infringe upon §135(a) to be made in public; and not only hateful speech but also actions may be penalized. The legal threshold for prosecuting racist and discriminatory speech was in other words significantly lowered. In the revision of the Norwegian General Penal Code in general adopted by parliament in 2009, it was decided that §135(a) should become §185(a), and that racist and/or discriminatory speech based on targeted individuals' 'reduced functional ability' (i.e. potentially covering both reduced physical and/or mental capacities) be included in the remit of the law. This revision has at the time of writing in 2013 yet to take effect.

The paradox is that in actual practice since then Norway appears to have had fewer prosecutions under §135(a). There is little reason to think this has to do with lower levels of actually occurring racist and discriminatory speech in Norwegian society. As late as 2009, Norwegian authorities alleged that the laws against racism and discrimination had been strengthened to the extent that the Supreme Court verdict in the Sjølie case would now be inconceivable (see ECRI 2009: 13 for this claim). Norwegian authorities alleged to the same monitoring bodies that in amending the laws on racism and discrimination in Norway, including §135(a) of the Norwegian General Penal Code, they had signalled to the Norwegian public that racist and/or discriminatory expressions would be punished to a greater extent than hitherto (ibid.: 12). Yet since then, the protection against racist and discriminatory speech for Norwegian citizens has in practice seemed weaker than ever, and this in an era in which these same monitoring bodies have warned Norwegian authorities to take appropriate measures against Islamophobia and other forms of racist and discriminatory speech, particularly on the internet (ibid.). Laws that are merely symbolic, that are seldom if ever applied, soon lose both their effectiveness and their legitimacy (Barendt 2011). The political programmes of both the Conservative Party and the Progress Party ahead of the parliamentary elections of September 2013 committed the parties to the abolition of §135(a) of the Norwegian General Penal Code. Yet when the parties presented their common platform for a coalition government in October 2013, no reference whatsoever was made to this electoral pledge.[22] The Conservative Party, in which there is a significant presence of lawyers, appears divided on this issue, and so far it seems that those who caution against a course of action with potential ramifications for Norway's commitments under international conventions have won the argument over §135(a).

Freedom of speech in the era of the internet

There is, in the words of Stanley Fish, 'no such thing as free speech' (Fish 1994). Freedom of speech is in other words not an absolute, and never has been, even in liberal democracies (Levmore and Nussbaum 2010: 6), let alone in the USA, which arguably has fewer restrictions on free speech than any other country in the world (Jacobsen and Schlink 2012). Free speech absolutism arguably does not exist in a pure and unadultered form either, for even the most ardent supporters of free speech would probably baulk at the suggestion that it should be permitted to lie in a court of law, or that citizens should be freely permitted to issue all kinds of threats against their fellow citizens. So we must therefore conceive of actual positions regarding freedom of expression inherent in free speech absolutism as ranging from more to less absolutist conceptions. Nor does universal recognition of freedom of speech require uniform legal solutions or interpretations (see Grimm 2009: 22). That there is a balance to be struck between valuable and offensive speech is hardly a novel insight or one peculiar to the age of the internet (Levmore and Nussbaum 2010: 5). Yet Norway's 22/7 brought a growing realization in Norwegian media, political and legal elites that an absence of regulation and moderation presents particular new challenges.

'The digital reality presents us with new challenges. Things are said on the internet that we would be hard pressed to accept in an ordinary conversation, or in a print newspaper. But nevertheless, we do not confront this as forcefully as we do in regular debates,' said Norwegian Labour prime minister Jens Stoltenberg in an interview in December 2011, in which he pledged a continued struggle against right-wing extremism and 'hatred of Islam' (Kristjánsson and Vegstein 2011).

John Stuart Mill's 1859 treatise *On Liberty* (Mill 1989 [1859]) is often regarded as a foundational text for modern champions of freedom of speech. Here, Mill argues that a 'collision of opinions' is a prerequisite for arriving at 'truth' in liberal and democratic societies, which is itself a prerequisite for 'the mental well-being of mankind' (ibid.: 53). Mill was certainly no absolutist: freedom of speech is limited by his general 'harm principle', which implies that using a freedom of speech that implies an incitement to violence against individuals or groups is not permissible. And Mill holds that speech that is not 'part of an argument aimed at truth' deserves no particular protection (Levmore and Nussbaum 2010: 8). He is certainly aware that freedom of speech may be misused to suppress facts or arguments, to misstate a case or to misrepresent an opponent's opinions (Mill 1989 [1859]: 54). Yet as long as this is done 'in good faith' the law has no reason to interfere with it.

It is important to note that, for Mill, freedom of speech is primarily an instrument of the weak ('the comparatively defenceless') and, as such, is an instrument in the defence of individual liberty against the state or powerful elites (ibid.). This conception is in fact a salutary reminder to the many Norwegian elites who – in arguing for the value of freedom of speech – consider it an Enlightenment 'cultural patrimony' that defines *us* (the proponents of 'secular reason') as against *them* (the forces of 'religious unreason') and in doing so leaves *us* 'with the ideological comfort of fighting on the side of the powerful while presenting oneself as a member of a beleaguered and courageous minority' (Toscano 2010: 100). While readily admitting that 'men are not more zealous for truth than they are for error' (Mill 1989 [1859]: 31), Mill still contends that man is 'capable of rectifying his mistakes, by discussion or experience' (ibid.: 23). The problems of the Millsian conception of freedom of speech and its limits in the digital age thus relate to the appropriateness of its rationalistic bias.

In the halcyon days of the development of the internet, technological optimists often argued that it would lead to a democratic pluralization of ideas and opinions in which more people would be able to have a voice and to be heard. Now, having a voice is in itself no guarantee of being heard, as millions of bloggers, tweeters and Facebook users have long since discovered. In light of the available evidence from recent years, it seems difficult to avoid the conclusion that these platforms have provided avenues for the creation of new counter-publics and sub-publics with their own peculiar dynamics. These new publics are to a large extent unedited, unmediated and uncensored; they often represent a subculture in which the Rawlsian 'duty of civility' is virtually absent and invective, harassment and personal attacks predominate. And more often than not, people of minority backgrounds – whose voices are at the outset disadvantaged – are targeted by the lack of civility (Nussbaum 2011).

But perhaps more serious in challenging us all, these new publics combined with the internet's manifold potentials for anonymity and the creation of fictive identities often contribute to a selective reinforcement of groupthink (Sunstein 2009), extremism and polarization (Adams 2011). 'Group influences create ideological amplification,' writes legal scholar Cass Sunstein (Sunstein 2003: 4). Writing about this in the context of debates on multiculturalism, immigration and Islam in Europe, Dilip Gaonkar and Charles Taylor in 2006 warned that 'block [group] thinking' concerning Islam and Muslims appears to have an 'explosive potential': block thinkers are 'prime recruits for Samuel Huntington's "clash of civilizations" and its attendant scenarios' (Gaonkar and Taylor 2006: 454). Block thinking is found at all times and among all parties, but in the present debates on Islam and Muslims it 'fuses a varied reality into a single indissoluble unity, and … does so on two dimensions: first, the different manifestations of Islamic piety or culture are seen as alternative ways of expressing the same core meanings; and second, all the members of this religion or culture are seen as expressing these core meanings' (ibid.).

This underlying logic is expressed in Behring Breivik's tract as well as in the internet musings of the Norwegian blogger 'Fjordman' from which he drew inspiration ahead of 22/7 (see Chapter 4). Central to their Islamophobic world view is the assumption that Muslims are essentially one and the same, bound to and overdetermined by Islam, with aspirations marked by a will to power over Europeans. Thus conceived, Muslims are to be feared by Europeans by virtue of their sheer existence and their potential numbers in Europe, and the 'fact' that Islam is 'inherently violent' and 'conflictive'. In Chapter 4, we saw how this underlying logic plays out in Norwegian versions of the Eurabia genre: everything from the hijab to children is said to be an instrument in a conspiracy directed by the Muslim Brothers in Egypt to establish Islamic control and rule over Norway and Europe. From this point of view, the Muslims' use of their right to freedom of expression becomes a sinister instrument. Throughout this depiction, the lines between Islamists and ordinary Muslims are deliberately blurred.

The social-psychological insight that we are as humans predisposed to seek confirmation of the convictions, thoughts and ideas we already happen to hold, the so-called 'confirmation bias' (Nickerson 1998), is not particularly novel. Freedom of speech in the context of democracy is, as a modern conception, intended to counteract this human proclivity. 'Democracy requires citizens to see things from one another's point of view, but instead we are more and more enclosed in our own bubbles. Democracy requires a reliance on shared facts, instead we are being offered parallel but separate universes,' writes Eli Pariser in *The Filter Bubble: What the internet is hiding from you* (Pariser 2011: 5). Pariser investigates how prominent internet search engines and popular networking sites have increasingly become able (and willing) to customize information based on personal preferences, thus ensuring that our access to information on the internet contributes to reinforcing and maintaining whatever 'filter bubble' we live with. So much so that, armed with a rationalistic view à la Mill on freedom of speech and its limits, we are apparently led into a dead end in the face of an altered terrain: if you sincerely believe in the prospect of an impending 'Islamization of Europe', trawling certain websites will confirm this view down to the most minute details and offer remedies – from democratic to undemocratic, peaceful to violent. That is, in fact, what Anders Behring Breivik did in the months and years preceding 22/7. His modus operandi had much to do with confirming prejudices and little or nothing to do with determining the truth of a question through any process of criticizing, filtering and sharing of 'facts' which is central to scientific and scholarly pursuits.

Norwegian conceptions of the public sphere

No other theorist has had a greater impact on Norwegian late-modern elite conceptions of the public spheres than German philosopher Jürgen Habermas. In 1996 the Norwegian government appointed a sixteen-member Commission on Freedom of Expression (*Ytringsfrihetskommisjonen*) as a direct result of the Rushdie affair in Norway. After the failed (and as yet unresolved) assassination attempt on Salman Rushdie's Norwegian publisher, William Nygaard, at his home in Oslo west in October 1993, the Norwegian minister of culture, Åse Kleveland of the Labour Party, resolved to appoint a commission tasked with investigating the conditions of freedom of expression in Norway and the Nordic countries (Austenå 2011: 116).

Norway's support of Salman Rushdie between 1988 and 1994 revealed an emerging consensus in a coalition of Norwegian writers, publishers and publicists, newspaper editors, politicians and academics. Indeed, Norwegians were central in the international mobilization of support for Rushdie: the Norwegian translation of *The Satanic Verses* was its very first translation anywhere in the world (ibid.: 70);

Norway was, at the initiative of the Norwegian Writers' Union and the Norwegian PEN Association, the first country to establish a national Rushdie Committee; and Norwegian publishing director Sigmund Strømme was on the board of London-based Article 19, which organized the international mobilization in support of Rushdie.

Four days after Iranian leader Ruhollah Ayatollah Khomeini's so-called fatwa[23] against Rushdie, on 18 February 1989, a body of Norwegian Muslim leaders established the Islamic Defence Council (Det Islamske Forsvarsrådet) in Oslo. The council, which consisted of an ad hoc coalition of Norwegian-Pakistani Sunni Muslims and a sprinkling of Shia Islamists supportive of the Iranian regime, made it clear that they wanted to use Norway's blasphemy laws to prevent the publication of a Norwegian translation of Rushdie's novel and the import and distribution of copies of the English original.[24] In Oslo on 26 February 1989, about three thousand Norwegian Muslims protested against the publication of Rushdie's novel in Norway (Austenå 2011: 78).

The Rushdie affair not only helped cement a shift in public and media discourses whereby Norwegians of Muslim background would no longer be identified by national origin but by their religious affiliation (Muslim), it also led to specifically Muslim 'identity politics' in Norway. The Islamic Defence Council may in fact be seen as the precursor of the umbrella organization for Norwegian Muslims, the Islamic Council of Norway, which was established in 1993.

What is of interest here, however, is that the Rushdie affair in Norway and its legal and political ramifications led to a particular 'framing' of the question of freedom of expression and its limits in the Norwegian context. And that framing, developed between 1988 and 1994, was reinforced by the cartoon crisis of 2005/06. This framing – rightly or wrongly – places Muslims in the position of constituting the main threat to freedom of expression – whether this be artistic or political – in Norway.

The first Commission on Freedom of Expression and *The Dangerous Freedom of Expression*, 1993

The commission established at the instigation of Minister Kleveland in 1993 after the assassination attempt on William Nygaard consisted of three members: Toril Brekke and Peter Norman Waage had been central in the Norway campaign in support of Rushdie; the third, political scientist Bernt Hagtvet, appeared to share their presuppositions. The commission's mandate and funding were quite limited: according to their own account, they developed their report during some weeks of meetings and discussions (Brekke et al. 1994: 5). On the initiative of another prominent Norwegian editor and PEN Association member, Anders Heger, the commission's report was published in 1994 as a sixty-three-page pamphlet entitled *The Dangerous Freedom of Expression* (*Den farlige ytringsfriheten*).

The pamphlet frames the problematic in question and its recommendations in ways that were relatively novel in Norway. The report advances the view that the principles of freedom of expression constitute one of 'our' (i.e. Norwegians') 'fundamental rules for ordered co-existence' (*'våre grunnleggende regler for ordnet samliv'*). One notes here an early hint of what has arguably become a ubiquitous phenomenon across western European states in recent years: the 'nationalization of liberal values' (Laegaard 2007: 39), whereby 'our' dehistoricized and decontextualized 'values' are seen to be under threat from an extra- or sub-national 'them'. The report is unsurprisingly (in light of the national repercussions of the Rushdie affair being its impetus) blunt about precisely which groups in Norway pose contemporary threats against freedom of expression.

The authors refer to the case of an 'Iraqi refugee in Norway' who had recently published what it described as 'a series of very critical articles about Islam in the local press'. This Iraqi refugee, the report argues, had become 'a mistaken victim of Norwegian "political correctness", which places concerns for the group over the concern for the individual' (Brekke et al. 1994: 10). On the basis of this example, the authors go on to argue that freedom of expression is properly conceived of as linked to the individual (ibid.: 11). The authors contend that from 'a liberal and democratic point of view' Norwegian society has every right to insist on 'their own rules of freedom of expression being respected within the ranks of ethnic groups who lack this tradition of rights' (ibid.: 14). In ever so few words, the authors imply that Muslims in Norway – by virtue of their real or purported identification with Islam – lack a religious and historical tradition in which freedom of expression is valued[25] and that Norwegian society (as represented by the state) will, therefore, have to teach them to value such freedom.

Throughout the report, the authors cite J. S. Mill's 1838 work *On Liberty* extensively and approvingly. They are especially interested in Mill's concept of the 'yoke of public opinion' but invoke this concept for a particular purpose: to provide a rationale for advancing and legitimizing a Millsian 'free marketplace of ideas' within minority groups in Norway in particular. It is the mavericks and the dissenters – as exemplified by the unnamed Iraqi refugee – who have a particular need for freedom of expression (ibid.).

One might argue that the authors here have read the Millsian invocation of the 'yoke of public opinion' quite selectively: the Iraqi refugee in question is the previously mentioned Walid al-Kubaisi, a central 'Eurabia' theorist (see also Bangstad 2013). Selectivity is revealed by the commission when it notes in passing that Jürgen Habermas's normative ideal of a 'dominance-free' dialogue entails the participants' commitment to intellectual reasonableness, but that this proves difficult when the Norwegian media did not at the time account for the critical views of 'many Norwegians' towards the present official refugee and asylum policy (Brekke et al. 1994: 30). Here again, it seems that the underlying assumption is that it is not the minorities which should be empowered by freedom of expression, but rather those among the majority who are sceptical or antagonistic towards these very same minorities and who are not well served by the limits on freedom of expression entailed in the prevailing understandings of 'the media'. The commission does not account for the repeated references to the 'Iraqi refugee' critical of Islam (i.e. al-Kubaisi), who had at the time close personal relationships with two of the commission members (Hagtvet and Waage). Their choice of example can therefore hardly be seen as coincidental.

'Where its task is cultural liberation, liberal reason requires the use of force whenever persuasion (the use of reason) does not work,' writes Talal Asad (1990: 464). Among the commission's recommendations were the following: the Norwegian state should develop compulsory courses concerning laws, rights and duties for those granted citizenship or leave to stay in Norway for longer periods of time (in other words, to teach immigrants values, such as freedom of expression) (Brekke et al. 1994: 14); that the blasphemy paragraph in the Norwegian penal code be abolished (ibid.: 52); and central to the Commission on Freedom of Expression, that Paragraph 100 of the Norwegian Constitution be amended to guarantee the explicit protection of freedom of expression (ibid.: 46).

The Commission on Freedom of Expression, 1996–99

In August 1996, a commission tasked with 'a fundamental reflection upon the place of freedom of expression in our society' was appointed by the Ministry of Justice and Police in Norway. The eighteen-member-strong commission was chaired by Francis Sejersted, a professor at the University of Oslo. Sejersted, a well-known and respected historian of Norwegian social democracy (see Sejersted 2011), was an intellectual affiliated to the Norwegian Conservative Party (Høyre), chairman of the Norwegian Nobel Peace Prize Committee from 1991 to 1999, and chairman of the Norwegian Fritt Ord Foundation from 2000 to 2011. As is often the case in a society in which state institutions can plausibly be described as technocratic, the commission would be dominated by academics based at higher academic institutions in close proximity to the government bureaucracies in Oslo or with political networks in government bureaucracies. Ten of the eighteen members were male. Only two had what could be described as an ethnic minority background (Ole Henrik Magga, an associate professor of Saami origins, and Nazneen Khan – later Khan-Østrem – a lecturer of Afghan-Norwegian origins). In terms of its composition, the small proportion of ethnic and/or other minorities among members of the commission is hardly unique for a government-appointed inquiry, yet, given the commission's mandate and the potential ramifications of its report for minorities, one might have expected a higher level of minority representation.

According to its mandate, the commission's essential task was to revise the constitutional protection of freedom of expression based on a discussion of the legal and political grounds for this protection (Sejersted et al. 1999: 96). The commission held open consultative meetings in various Norwegian cities for three years, from 1996 until it presented its report and recommendations in 1999. It also invited

US Supreme Court Justice Antonin Scalia to be a guest lecturer on the constitutional protection of freedom of expression under the First Amendment of the US Constitution.

The commission's 1999 report *Ytringsfrihed bør finde sted* (*Freedom of Expression Must Take Place*) is, if anything, a thorough and extensive discussion of the available academic literature on freedom of expression, both internationally and nationally. One can detect a series of rationalistic presuppositions from the manner in which the authors of the commission report conceptualize both freedom of expression and its limitations: in keeping with arguments made by a long line of Western philosophers from Karl Popper to Ronald Dworkin, the commission contends that freedom of expression is 'a constitutive element of democracy' (ibid.: 24). Not only that, but the commission seems to imply – *pace* the unranked nature of freedom of speech in relation to *other* human rights under international human rights conventions and treaties – that '... freedom of expression in its essence is not a concern which may give way to other concerns. It is constitutive of society, [something] which implies that if one infringes on it, the very order of society is threatened' (ibid.: 136). The report sketches a teleological historical development whereby the institutionalization of the modern public sphere, the simultaneous delineation of both a public and a private sphere, democracy, and the differentiation of political power are all factors leading to greater freedom of expression for individuals as a protection against encroachment by the state.

However, the reader is cautioned not to understand this trajectory as a simple linear progression. Negative examples in this respect are in the eyes of the report's authors provided by the eighteenth-century Norwegian state, where state leaders conceptualized the limitations placed on free expression as being related to the state authorities' need to be protected against certain forms of speech, rather than being motivated by a concern for individuals and their freedom (ibid.: 48). And this was evident again, not least in the Quisling regime installed by the German Nazi occupiers of Norway from 1940 to 1945, which 'abolished' (*opphevet*) freedom of expression and introduced censorship (ibid.: 59). The argumentative thrust of the 1999 report undoubtedly favours expanding freedom of expression as both a societal and a legal virtue. The report enlists court decisions by the European Court of Human Rights (ECHtR) in Strasbourg in arguing for a more liberal approach (ibid.: 80).[26]

But more important and in line with the often grandiose procliv-ities of both state and civil-society actors in post-Second World War Norway, the report invokes 'ambitions to lead the way in the defence of human rights and democracy' as an argument for enshrining greater protections for freedom of expression through a constitu-tional clause. For in this manner, the authors contend, 'it will provide us with an opportunity to refer to our own constitution as a potential standard for freedom of expression in other countries' (ibid.: 111).

Without ever explicitly articulating this position, the report espouses an idea of freedom which the liberal philosopher Isaiah Berlin in his seminal *Four Essays on Liberty* (Berlin 1969) referred to as 'negative freedom': the absence of formal (social, legal or politi-cal) restrictions on an individual's ability to think and to act upon the world. Individual reason and self-restraint, the report seems to contend, will ultimately mean that freedom of expression is an unmitigated good for both individuals and society, and that those few who set out to do harm with 'fighting words' (denigrating or derogatory utterances about their fellow human beings) will be con-tested and exposed.

However, as Talal Asad (1993: 295) has pointed out, it is not an uncontested truth to say that being unregulated is being really free. In an influential and nuanced critique of liberal notions, Charles Taylor advanced the view of negative freedom as an 'opportunity concept' and positive freedom as an 'exercise concept'. That is to say, in light of 'negative freedom', being free is 'a matter of what we can do ... whether or not we do anything to exercise these options'. In light of 'positive freedom', however, being free relates to 'the exercising of control over one's life' ... or that 'one is free only to the extent that one has effectively determined oneself and the shape of one's life' (Taylor 1985 [1979]: 213).

Notwithstanding the report's stated concerns with the increasing commercialization of the Norwegian media (Sejersted et al. 1999: 81) and the increased use of media and market strategists among corporate actors, it nonetheless by and large confirms the celebratory self-understandings of the Norwegian media with the function of forming a system of checks and balances on various forms of power in Norwegian society (ibid.: 77). The report's blindness to power extends to the very powers of the commission to define future parameters of the legal and societal regulations of freedom of expression: 'The political process should take place before an open stage' – the report proclaims – for 'power should have a face' (ibid.: 124).

But those expecting some meta-textual reflections on the social, political and legal power wielded by academics and intellectuals aligned to technocratic power in late-modern social democratic Norway (such as the very praxis of the commission's own members) will search in vain for it here. To those willing to be sufficiently subversive as to argue that the media are suffused by and expressive of certain forms of power, the report makes little in the way of response, except for repeated assertions such as: 'The press is arguably better than what its many trenchant critics would contend' (ibid.: 78).

The report is clear about freedom of expression being first and foremost an individual right. It states that freedom of expression is primarily a freedom for unpopular expressions and that special protections for political expressions are central to the very idea of freedom of expression (ibid.: 101, 32). To the extent that freedom of expression has stronger limitations in Norway than in other societies, it reflects Norwegian egalitarianism and consensus-seeking (ibid.: 84). Societal pressures to conform (*konformitetspresset*), whereby individual actors in the public sphere who fear social sanctions censor themselves, is conceptualized in the report as a pre-eminent threat to freedom of expression (ibid.: 84).

The report engages in a particular construction of the subject of Norwegian public spheres. This construct reflects some of the authors' rationalistic presuppositions: a 'democratic principle' (*demokratiprinsippet*), whereby publicity is the basis for checks on both public and private powers, presupposes that publication or the threat thereof occasions decency (*anstendighet*) and reasonableness (*rimelighet*) (ibid.: 77, 78). It is for the media to ensure such decency and reasonableness. 'Demands for limitations to freedom of speech (including freedom of information) are surprisingly often reflective of [an] almost irrational fear' (ibid.: 77).

Having thus declared those who advocate limitations on the freedom of expression both irrational and pathological, the report contends that 'our democratic system, including the right to vote and freedom of expression, is based [on] the conception [*forestilling*] that the public sphere is by and large populated by mature, adult and decent human beings' (ibid.: 78). One need in other words not doubt the controlling and self-disciplining function of the media and the discerning consumer-subject.

More than ten years after this report was issued, there are those whose actions challenge this conclusion. These include certain Norwegian followers of op-ed articles in mainstream print media, as well as participants in various social media where racist and/or Islamophobic statements have become ubiquitous. A preliminary study of the online 'free comments' sections of mainstream Norwegian newspapers from 2010 undertaken by the Norwegian Centre Against Racism in the same year indicated that very little editorial control over these sections was exercised and that racist utterances from presumably 'mature, adult and decent human beings' were widespread (Karlsen 2010).

It would perhaps be somewhat presumptuous to expect the commission's 1999 report to be capable of predicting future developments in this field, but the report is, in fact, full of praise for 'the anarchy' which the internet brings (Sejersted et al. 1999: 90). In light of what we now know about the impact of the internet on the radicalization of a number of terrorists (whether they be radical Islamist or extreme right-wing) this assertion seems if anything sanguine. From the report we furthermore learn that it is 'a defining question ... how the plural public spheres (*offentligheter*) interact' (ibid.: 87).

Even if the heightened profile of freedom of expression and its increased public interest had a lot to do with the Rushdie affair, the report itself has surprisingly little to say about that actual issue. The affair remains a largely unarticulated presence throughout the report. To the extent that the report does refer to that event, it is in the context of blasphemy legislation, which the commission recommends abolishing (ibid.: 181). The report notes that the Rushdie affair 'manifests the problem of blasphemy in multicultural societies' and 'reflects tendencies which require critical vigilance on behalf of freedom of expression' (ibid.: 77). Pressure for the reactivation of the blasphemy paragraph, the report asserts, originates from the expansion of 'originally foreign [*fremmede*] religions' as well as 'the new identity politics' (ibid.: 179). The coded language of these paragraphs is, in and of itself, interesting: for 'foreign' religions, read Islam; for 'identity politics', read public assertions of Islam by practising Muslims.

The report contends that the preconditions and possibilities for minorities in Norway to partake in 'open and enlightened' conversation provide a 'test case' for the conditions of freedom of expression (ibid.: 85, 135). Though the report mentions that an infrastructure of both law and support is needed to ensure the possibilities of expression for minorities, the commission concluded that it had 'no specific recommendations' on this point (ibid.: 135).

Not even when the report refers to the various 'others' of Norwegian state and/or society do we get anything reminiscent of a philosophical reflection on the limits of reason in combating various forms of racism and xenophobia when they are expressed in and through the public sphere – nor do we hear of the societal power differentials which at any time define what are considered permissible and non-permissible forms of speech. In 1997, under §135(a) of the penal code, Jack Erick Kjuus (1927–2009), a lawyer and politician aligned with the Norwegian extreme right, was convicted of racism. This conviction is mentioned in the commission's report since, at the time the report was being written, it constituted the central verdict concerning §135(a) (ibid.: 205). Thus the case was used as a backdrop as the report extensively discussed freedom of expression in relation to racist expressions.

The Norwegian Supreme Court Case upheld the lower court's conviction of Kjuus. In 1995, ahead of the 1997 parliamentary elections, Kjuus had distributed pamphlets in Oslo for his party the White Electoral Alliance (Hvit Valgallianse). His leaflets called for the forced sterilization of children who, although resident in Norway, were actually adopted from non-Western countries, as well as the forced sterilization of sexual partners of white Norwegians – partners whose origins were considered to be 'non-Western' – together with their offspring. Kjuus was sentenced to sixty days' imprisonment and a fine of 20,000 Norwegian kroner (NOK) by a divided Supreme Court. Kjuus later appealed the verdict to the European Court of Human Rights (ECHtR) in Strasbourg, but the appeal was found inadmissible. Though the Commission on Freedom of Expression's report never mentions this, legal opinion about the case was divided, and it led to a mobilization of support for Kjuus' human right to freedom of expression, especially from a number of Norwegian newspaper editors and academics.

Among those who testified in defence of the rights of Kjuus was Sigurd Skirbekk (1934–), a professor of sociology at the University of Oslo and an elder brother of commission member Professor Gunnar Skirbekk. Sigurd Skirbekk, politically aligned with the Norwegian Centre Party (Senterpartiet) had by then been known for years for his xenophobic and anti-immigration booklets. His younger brother, Gunnar Skirbekk (1937–), would later supervise a doctoral dissertation in philosophy at the University of Oslo which basically contended that the Norwegian Supreme Court's verdict in the Kjuus case represented a violation of freedom of expression (Lundeby 2000). The report's discussion of the Kjuus verdict implies that its authors – although possibly not every member of the commission – were sympathetic to the views of the minority of the Norwegian Supreme Court justices in the Kjuus case: they argued that he would have to be acquitted because as a politician (even if his party never attracted more than a few hundred voters) his utterances about adopted children formed part of his political speech, particularly protected under Norwegian conceptualizations of freedom of expression as expressed in the Norwegian Constitution's §100.

What, then, does the commission suggest about racist expressions in the context of free speech? Its suggestions fall into line with the general tenor of its arguments concerning freedom of expression. Without any reference to secondary literature or empirical data what-soever, the report contends that 'publicity has provided the best form of control, and the best protection for underprivileged groups regardless of who was in power' (Sejersted et al. 1999: 94). This is, to say the least, contestable, inasmuch as it seems to be an argument of a *universalistic* nature. And the historical record does suggest that publicity, in many instances, has not necessarily had such salutary effects for the underprivileged. See, for instance, Nazi Germany, the civil war in Rwanda, and the civil war in Bosnia. These examples demonstrate that publication of the 'fighting words' – which in each case preceded 'fighting actions' – offered limited protection indeed for those who would become victims of 'crimes against humanity'.

A more recent reminder of the perils of limiting oneself to platitudes about freedom of expression comes from Greece, where the fascist party Golden Dawn has emerged as one of the most popular parties during the present conditions of severe financial austerity, by targeting people of immigrant background with racist speech, and inciting and coordinating violence against immigrants. These facts are well known and reported, yet the Greek police, whose members appear to have within their ranks many supporters of Golden Dawn, rarely ever investigate, let alone prosecute, Greek fascists for these racist attacks (Margaronis 2012).

There was, in fact, one member of the commission who dissented from the majority's view during internal meetings and hearings. That sole dissenting voice belonged to documentary film-maker Maria Fuglevaag Warsinski (later Warsinski-Warsi),[27] who opposed the position of 'no state interference with the freedom of expression' on the basis of her experience while reporting the atrocities of the Balkan wars of the 1990s. According to the written report, freedom of expression is basically a form of protection from discrimination; when discriminatory attitudes are expressed in public, rather than being subject to prosecution, they may be contested through public criticism (Sejersted et al. 1999: 203). The commission does raise the possibility that 'the public correction [of discriminatory attitudes] may in all areas function according to the ideals referred to' (ibid.: 204) and that this situation may in fact lead to such attitudes becoming more 'widespread [*alment utbredt*]' (ibid.: 204). Except for noting that there may be 'valid reasons' (*gode grunner*) for a law that may counter attempts from agitators in the form of repeated expressions of discriminatory attitudes, the report does not offer any further reflections on this problematic.

The report stopped short of advocating the abolition of §135(a) of the Norwegian penal code; it did, however, advocate the abolition of protection against racist and/or discriminatory speech based on religious faith (ibid.: 207). This is something that seems to reflect the secular and non-religious presuppositions of many of the most central members of the commission. Criteria relating to religious faith – we learn – stand in opposition to other criteria in that there is an element of personal choice or will (of having a religious faith in the first place). This will of course strike most religious believers as odd, for even though one may actively 'choose' one's religious affiliation as an adult living in a liberal and secular society, one certainly does not 'choose' to be born a child of Christian, Muslim or Jewish parents. Furthermore, the report's authors argue that the inclusion of these criteria in the racism paragraph is detrimental to the right of free and open critique of religion and culture (ibid.: 207).

The Freedom of Expression Commission's 1999 views on the 'racism' paragraph were, however, contested by the 2002 Commission on Legal Protections Against Ethnic Discrimination (Holgersen 2002: 207–8). The latter commission argued that the Freedom of Expression Commission had offered little in the way of concrete guidance and recommendations to Norwegian courts on how to balance freedom of expression and protections against racist and discriminatory speech, and it indicated that the former commission had an unbalanced view of the value of contrary expressions in the public sphere. Where Sejersted's commission recommended a strengthening of legal protections for freedom of expression, the Holgersen commission recommended a strengthening of legal protections against racist and discriminatory speech. In terms of legal statutes, it would seem from what transpired in the following years that the views of the Holgersen commission had prevailed, but actual legal practice with regard to the racism paragraph suggests that the Sejersted commission's views prevailed.

Habermas, rationality and modern public spheres

The philosophical basis for the Sejersted commission's view of freedom of expression is found in Habermas's early work, particularly in his seminal *The Structural Transformation of the Public Sphere* (Habermas 1991 [1962]). Central to the appropriation of Habermas in this context was the professor of philosophy, Gunnar Skirbekk, from the University of Bergen[28] (see Holst and Molander 2009 for Skirbekk's role), whose own work in Norwegian provided the foundation for the commission's work. It is important to note here that what the commission appropriates in arguing for an extension of freedom of expression in Norway and a weakening of legal protections against racist and discriminatory speech[29] is Habermas's work from the 1960s – a 'classical Habermas' apparently tailored to the commission's particular needs, and, as such, a construct adopted by the commission's members.

In the preface to the first edition of *The Structural Transformation of the Public Sphere*, Habermas had already categorically noted that his conception of the bourgeois public sphere was one peculiar to the eighteenth and nineteenth centuries in Europe, and not transferable or generalizable to other times, past or future (Habermas 1991 [1962]: xvii). The two last chapters of Habermas's original work also make it clear that he conceived of the bourgeois public sphere as having disintegrated with the emergence of modern mass media and manufactured public opinion. Yet for those who have championed Habermas's notion of the modern public sphere in the Norwegian context, including the Norwegian Commission on Freedom of Expression, such reservations and Habermas's own restatements of his classical work (see Habermas 1992, but also Habermas 2008 [2005], chs 1 and 5) have barely registered in the face of academic critiques (see Calhoun 1992; Fraser 2007). Not that Norwegian philosophers of Gunnar Skirbekk's mould and age are not aware of these restatements, nor of Habermas's post-2001 'post-secular' turn, as expressed in his view that so-called 'secular' and 'religious' citizens must always be prepared to engage in a mutual learning process in liberal and secular societies (Habermas 2008 [2005]: 143).[30] It is rather that Norwegian philosophers of Skirbekk's age and mould are generally not convinced by it, and disapprove of the idea that the Habermasian burden implies that secularists must 'reflect on their limits' (ibid.: 310) – in much the same manner as is incumbent upon the religious minded.[31]

In *Publics and Counterpublics* (2002), Michael Warner refers to the 'endlessly repeated discovery that public politics does not in fact conform to the idealized self-understanding which makes it work' (ibid.: 146). Habermas's *The Structural Transformation of the Public Sphere* (Habermas 1991 [1962]), which has been central to the literature on public spheres ever since, was a Gibbonesque narrative of the rise and decline of the bourgeois and liberal public sphere[32] in Europe. The book's thesis concerns the structural transformation of the public sphere from 'critical participation to consumerist manipulation' (Peters 1993: 543). As Eley (1992: 292) pointed out, Habermas was 'less interested in the realized political dimension of the public sphere' than in 'abstracting a strong ideal against which later forms of the public sphere can be set'.

We now know that Habermas made numerous omissions in tracing the emergence of the public sphere in eighteenth- and nineteenth-century Europe, and in imposing on his analysis his own normative ideals of universal access, rational discourse and dominance-free communication. He 'missed the extent to which the public sphere was always constituted by conflict' (ibid.: 306); he ignored the fact that 'the very inception of the public sphere was itself shaped by a new exclusionary ideology directed at women' (ibid.: 311); he neglected any reflection on the fact that 'the claim to rational discourse' was 'simultaneously a claim to power in Foucault's sense' (ibid.: 331); he failed to examine other, non-liberal, non-bourgeois, competing publics (Fraser 1992: 115) inasmuch as his conception is a bourgeois, masculinist conception (ibid.: 117); and he consigned women's exclusion from the bourgeois public sphere by virtue of 'their ideological consignment to a separate realm called the private' to historical oblivion (Ryan 1992: 260).[33] Furthermore, Habermas has often been accused of developing a unitary conception of the public sphere (cf. Calhoun 1992; Fraser 1992);[34] of locating identity formation entirely in the realm of private life, and therefore outside of politics and public discourse (Calhoun 1993: 275) to such an extent that it 'represses difference' and 'undermines the capacity of a public sphere to carry forward a rational-critical discourse' (ibid.: 279); of providing a definition of public spheres which limit them to rational-critical discourse (Calhoun 1992: 162) and is henceforth inadequate for conceptualizing the role of public spheres in creating social solidarity (ibid.: 159).

Fraser (1992) proposed the concept of *subaltern counter-publics* to describe 'parallel discursive arenas where members of subordinated social groups invent and circulate counterdiscourses [to] formulate oppositional interpretations of their identities, needs and interests' in the case of 'stratified societies ... whose basic institutional framework generates unequal social groups in structural relations of dominance and subordination' (ibid.: 123, 122). Warner takes the view that Fraser's notion of counter-publics comes all too close to obscuring the fact that counter-publics are publics too, and therefore, much like other publics, operate with similar limitations, exclusions and contradictions (Warner 2002: 113), a view echoed by Salvatore and LeVine (2005: 6) in their critique of the conceptualization of counter-publics as 'mere resistance movements'.

As Fraser (2007) has pointed out, the Habermasian concept of the public sphere was linked to a particular *social imaginary*, namely that of deliberative democracy for a territorially bounded polity, or in other words to the democratization of the modern Westphalian territorial nation-state (ibid.: 10–11). The theory of the public sphere, in historian Harold Mah's apt phrase, 'is inscribed in a discourse of modernity' (Mah 2000: 180). Charles Taylor refers to the public sphere as a *metatopical space* or a non-local common space 'in which people who never meet understand themselves to be engaged in discussion and capable of reaching a common mind' (Taylor 1992: 228–9). In a similar argument, Calhoun (1993: 269) notes that 'an effective rational-critical discourse aimed at the resolution of political disputes' is central to the concept of the public sphere.

Two caveats may be entered here: it is of course entirely possible that the notion of reaching 'a common mind' was central to the ideal of the classical bourgeois and liberal public sphere (although Eley 1992 is among the Habermasian critics who give us reason to doubt this), but to whatever extent this was ever so, this proposition is no longer tenable in a media and mediated age in which polarized and polarizing opinions are central to the functioning and legitimacy of the various modern media. And even if the public sphere is a 'placeless place' in which those who express their views never actually meet, it does not follow that they won't ever meet in real life. This is particularly the case in relatively small and homogeneous societies like Norway.

Central to Habermas's notion of the public sphere was its potential for functioning as the arena where critique could be articulated as a corrective to the power of the state. The modern public sphere is, in Taylor's words, 'a space of discussion which is self-consciously seen as being outside power' (Taylor 1992: 232). It is *extrapolitical* 'as a discourse *on* and *to* power, rather than *by* power'.

But here, one runs into another difficulty, because 'there has never been a state without some influence upon the character of its citizens' (Appiah 2005: 154) and because the ability of the modern state to shape the character of its citizens and to enable, regulate and delimit the public sphere has vastly expanded in the modern era. While it might be the case that 'the sovereign state cannot (never could) contain all the practices, relations and loyalties of its citizens' (Asad 2003: 179), nevertheless to think of modern public spheres as separate and distinct from state power, rather than in various ways suffused by it, risks idealizing and essentializing them. As Calhoun points out, the latter sections of Habermas's *Structural Transformation* foreshadow his later work by describing the (late) modern public sphere as 'a setting for states and corporate interests to develop legitimacy not by responding appropriately to an independent and critical public but by seeking to instill in social actors motivations that conform to the needs of the overall system dominated by ... states and corporate actors' (Calhoun 1992).

Concluding credo

A confluence of interests and forces among Norwegian political, media and legal elites since the Rushdie affair of 1988–94 created conditions in which minority protections against racist and discriminatory speech as guaranteed by Norwegian law and Norwegian obligations under international law have been rendered all but in-effective and symbolic – in the name of stronger protections for freedom of expression.

I have argued that the rationalistic framework within which this problematic has been rethought and reconceptualized is anchored in a construal of classical Habermasian ideas about the functioning of modern public spheres. Yet these constructions fail to take into account the extent to which the classical Habermasian framework is itself based on a thoroughly historicizing and contextualizing perspective. Furthermore, it seems as if this construal, with its neglect of the asymmetrical nature and ordering of mediated public spheres in late-modern liberal and secular societies such as Norway's and its relative ignorance of the functioning of internet hate speech, is ill suited to the analysis of the present challenges concerning racist and/ or discriminatory speech. 'It is sometimes said that the free market in ideas, of which free speech is an instance, will weed out at least the grosser forms of hate speech. There is no guarantee of this ... The notion that it will do so of its own accord is a fantasy entertained, sometimes sincerely, by the powerful,' argues Newey (2013).

It is not entirely coincidental that some of the strongest defenders of absolutist conceptions of freedom of expression in Norway (as elsewhere in Europe) are found in Islamophobic circles and networks. A recent case in point is that Hans Rustad, editor of Document.no, travelled to Malmö in Sweden with the Danish director of *the* International Free Press Society, Lars Hedegaard, to establish a Swedish Free Press Society.[35] For the struggle in which far-right Islamophobes across the political-discursive continuum – but most significantly Europe's right-wing extremists – are engaged is centrally a struggle of mediated representation. It is a struggle over the very definition of the terms in which debates on Islam, Muslims and integration in western European societies are set: in other words, over the 'framing of Muslims' (Morey and Yaqin 2011) through which the notion of an invariable *Homo islamicus* who intrinsically 'hates the West' (Lyon 2012) may be generated and maintained. But it is also more than that: what is at stake is a struggle that ultimately entails 'world-making' and 'world-unmaking', and as such a struggle for very fundamental liberal values relating to formally equal rights to citizenship, individual dignity, tolerance for others and freedom of religion and conscience for minorities in post-Second World War Europe. The radical right's 'ideas, master frames, diagnoses and radical (negative) prognoses have succeeded in shaping a new, broader and social "common sense" that is accepted by wider political and social constituencies', argues Kallis (2013: 60), and it could in Norway and in western Europe hardly have succeeded in this without invoking freedom of expression in order to advance its ideas and arguments in public. Extreme and/or populist right-wing defences of freedom of expression should not be taken at face value by anyone: it is not by coincidence that Geert Wilders in virtually the same breath that he calls upon Europeans to defend freedom of expression against the purported threats to it emanating from Muslim minorities in Europe and the 'totalitarian political ideology' of Islam (Wilders 2011) calls for the banning of the Qur'an as a 'fascist book' (Weaver 2010). Nor is it coincidental that one of the concerns of Peder Are 'Fjordman' Nøstvold Jensen upon having learned that the Norwegian Fritt Ord Foundation had decided to support a book manuscript of his took the very same foundation to task for having supported people who had publicly criticized him in the past (Jensen 2013b). What this tells us is that the invocations of freedom of expression by contemporary European Islamophobes of the counter-jihadist variety are more than anything strategic: the freedom of expression that they call upon liberal elites to support is the proverbial 'freedom for thought that they like', not the freedom of expression of all minorities alike. In one of the most absurd statements on what led to Anders Behring Breivik's terror on 22/7, Geert Wilders' erstwhile political associate Ayaan Hirsi Ali, upon receiving the Axel Springer Award in Germany in May 2012, alleged that Behring Breivik had engaged in terror owing to 'all outlets to express his views' having been 'censored' in Norway (see Citizen Times 2012). There is after all no public record of Behring Breivik having been censored anywhere before 22/7; he did in fact publish extensive commentaries on various right-wing blogs across Norway, Scandinavia and Europe in the preceding years, and the staggering number of counter-jihadist blogs and websites available online attest to his views being expressed in a number of places. In Norway, a footnote in a report to parliament from the Norwegian Centre Against Racism in late 2012 in which it was alleged that the Progress Party's precursor, the Anders Langes Parti (ALP), had received financial support from the apartheid regime in South Africa in the 1970s led to the PP leadership issuing threats through the media than any NGOs which to their mind did not 'act neutrally in the public sphere' would have their state support cut in the event that the party should come to power after the parliamentary elections of September 2013. In the PP's alternative budget for 2013, the party pledges to cut all state support to immigrant organizations in Norway, an efficient means of stifling minorities' freedom of expression in Norway (Hanssen and Therkelsen 2013).

In the Scandinavian context, popular support for populist or extreme right-wing views on Islam and Muslims has little do with economics, and much more to do with language and representation (see also Goodwin 2011 and Mudde 2007). It also follows from this that though adherents of extreme or populist right-wing views generally have lower levels of education than others, the notion that knowledge in and of itself is a sufficient antidote against contemporary Islamophobia in Norway and western Europe is flawed. The promoters of Islamophobia that we have encountered in this book are often highly educated. By means of the internet blogosphere and by publishing a number of books that are aimed at a popular market that is often relatively illiterate with regard to Islam and Muslims, they have managed to create a parallel universe in which any opposing or contradictory views, opinions or empirical fact are systematically filtered out. Though they often regard and cast themselves as heroic defenders of both 'Reason' and 'The Enlightenment', they are seldom open to reasonable arguments.

Their tunnel visions of the world, much like those of radical Islamists, present us with a potential for violence in our society among those who assimilate such ideas uncritically. In light of Norway's 22/7, such tunnel visions, whether they emanate from far-right milieus or radical Islamists, can no longer be ignored. Adherents of 'Eurabia' literature are more than prepared to use any number of fabrications and distortions of empirical data and facts in order to alter the terms of this debate. As a result, virtually any number of issues and concrete challenges pertaining to this debate are, by means of simple reductionism, presented as revolving around Islam and Muslims. In volume I of his *The Open Society and Its Enemies*, the liberal philosopher Karl R. Popper noted that 'unlimited tolerance must lead to the disappearance of tolerance. If we extend unlimited tolerance even to those who are intolerant, if we are not prepared to defend a tolerant society against the onslaught of the intolerant, then the tolerant will be destroyed, and tolerance with them' (Popper 2003 [1945]: 602–3). Though there are certainly problems with this formulation, inasmuch as it may lend itself to an absolutization of tolerance, it points to the necessity of liberal and secular society defending itself against the intolerant and the illiberal who seek to tear asunder the fabric of trust and reciprocal obligations between citizens formally equal in rights and dignity to which such societies aspire.

'Freedom of opinion is a farce, unless factual information is guaranteed, and the facts themselves are not in dispute,' wrote Hannah Arendt in the essay 'Truth and politics' from 1966 (Arendt 2003 [1966]: 554). There is of course no novelty in the fact that today's politicians of either left- or right-wing persuasion sometimes tell lies in order to promote specific political agendas or aims.[36] Yet for Arendt, there was a basic distinction to be made between errors made in good faith, and deliberate falsehoods or lies (ibid.: 562). The former are defensible in a politics that wishes to remain within the bounds of moral action, the latter are not defensible. 'The liar,' Arendt writes, 'lacking the power to make his falsehood stick, does not insist on the gospel truth of his statement but pretends that this is his "opinion", to which he claims his constitutional right' (ibid.: 563). One notes here why it is that freedom of expression matters so much to those who (either from personal conviction or strategic political interest) resort to the production and dissemination of deliberate falsehoods in politics. 'The blurring of the dividing line between factual truth and opinion belongs among the many forms that lying can assume, all of which are forms of action,' concludes Arendt (ibid.). John Stuart Mill once observed that 'an article in a newspaper is to the public mind no more than a drop of water on a stone; and like that it produces its effect by repetition' (as cited in Collini 2012: 118). Lies and fabrications being put forward for political reasons in and through the media therefore require repetition in order to take effect on the public mind. The Norwegian mainstream media, which according to their self-conception are the pre-eminent defenders of freedom of expression, for obvious reasons do not see it as their role to ascertain the veracity of the arguments put forward in mediated public debates. In a recent case before the Press Complaints Commission (Pressens Faglige Utvalg, PFU or PCC), an organ designed to monitor the ethical standards of the Norwegian press, and to all practical extent and purposes controlled by the Norwegian media itself,[37] the PCC maintained the principle that Norwegian editors had no independent responsibility with regard to ensuring that what reaches print is either factually correct or respectful of a person's integrity or reputation. The case related to *Aftenposten*'s op-ed editors printing a letter to the editor in which it was – with specific reference to a Norwegian professor of social anthropology – insinuated that Norwegian anti-racists were in fact 'responsible' for 22/7.[38]

As Norway approached the two-year commemoration of those who lost their lives on 22/7, on 14 June 2013 the Fritt Ord Foundation announced that it had awarded Anders Behring Breivik's main ideological inspiration, the extreme right-wing blogger Peder Are 'Fjordman' Nøstvold Jensen, the substantial amount of 75,000 Norwegian kroner for a planned book on 22/7. The ground for this rewarding and legitimization of 'Fjordman' had been well and thoroughly prepared by the prominent media editor, popular author and Fritt Ord board member Frank Rossavik, who, in defending Fritt Ord's decision in a regular column for the weekly *Morgenbladet*, analogized his own 'critique of Islam' after 2001 with that of 'Fjordman' and called for 'understanding' of him (Rossavik 2013). Casting 'Fjordman' and by implication his fellow ideological travellers as mere 'critics of Islam', the foundation in its public statements implied that it would mean infringing freedom of expression not to support Nøstvold Jensen's writings, which, to the consternation of Nøstvold Jensen himself, it cast as a purported 'defence' (ibid.). And this in spite of the fact that Nøstvold Jensen appears to have a substantial readership on the counter-jihadist websites that he regularly publishes on, and since 22/7 has counted on financial support from Daniel Pipes' Middle East Forum through the Legal Project (Korsvold 2013), which is also known to have funded Geert Wilders. As the maverick Norwegian communication adviser and publishing editor Elin Ørjasæter tweeted her personal congratulations to Nøstvold Jensen and offered to publish a Norwegian version of his book without actually having seen anything of it (Fidjestøl 2013), Nøstvold Jensen's biographer Simen Sætre declared himself to be 'proud', and the respected editor and Norwegian PEN chairman William Nygaard opined that he supported the Fritt Ord Foundation's funding of Nøstvold Jensen by arguing that 'Fjordman himself does not incite violence' (Therkelsen and Prestegård 2013), liberal elite denials and obfuscation of the ideology which inspired Behring Breivik appeared to have come full circle. For though 'Fjordman's' Islamophobic rants prior to 22/7 would fail to meet the so-called 'Brandenburger' test of incitement to violence,[39] there can be little doubt that an individual who has advocated the physical removal of Muslims from Europe, and called upon Europeans to 'arm themselves' in defence against the purported Islamic invasion and colonization of Europe, does *ipso facto* advocate violent means of ethnic cleansing. Interestingly enough, 'Fjordman's' biographer Simen Sætre had by 2013 changed his mind about the purported innocence of 'Fjordman's' calls for ethnic cleansing of Muslims in Norway and Europe, and Norwegian liberal media editors' contributions to whitewashing his record and making him a part of legitimate controversies over Islam, Muslims and immigration in Norway after 22/7 (Sætre 2013b). 'Would the Fritt Ord Foundation also fund actors calling for the physical removal of Jews from the West?' Sætre asked rhetorically (Sætre 2013c). And he was – predictably enough – roundly condemned by the very same liberal media editors he had dared to criticize openly (Tornes 2013). Sætre's latest intervention in fact pointed us to a challenge which stands at the heart of debates on freedom of expression and its limits in Norway after 22/7: liberal intellectual and media elite's invocations of free speech absolutist ideas by virtue of their own inevitable and inexorable logic leave us more or less unable to draw any lines between acceptable and unacceptable speech in the public sphere. The fact of the matter is that certain mainstream media in Norway after 22/7 accorded great prominence to far-right speech on Islam, Muslims and immigration, and to the apologists for such speech. And so it should surprise no one that *Aftenposten*, a mere two and a half years after 22/7, printed a eulogy for Anders Behring Breivik's favourite website Document. no, which has continued to regularly print essays that are both racist and Islamophobic in content, penned by the newspaper's regular columnist, the PP-sympathizing IT specialist, popular author and blogger Bjørn Stærk (Stærk 2013).

There are academics and media editors aplenty in Norway and elsewhere who will argue that the populist right wing has only acted as a channel for sections of the population legitimately concerned with immigration and integration, and particularly Muslim immigration and Muslim integration, in recent years, rather than as an amplifier of those concerns. In this scenario, adherents of the populist right wing's anti-immigration and anti-Muslim agendas are only reflections of the rational self-interest of sections of the population who are not part of the social, economic, academic and political elites of the country, and who fear that they are in the process of being required to carry an excessive social, economic and cultural burden owing to the integration of immigrants, and particularly those of Muslim background (see Raknes 2012 for one exponent of this view). In line with this argument, those who subscribe to this hypothesis often contend that the Norwegian populist right wing has channelled these concerns and fears in democratic ways, and thereby impeded the growth of extreme right-wing movements in Norway (see, for example, Strømmen in Høiland 2012). If the most recent reports from the Norwegian Police Security Services (PST) are anything to go by, liberal media editors' providing more column space for Norwegian extreme right-wingers to express their opinions after 22/7 has not dented their presence online. The past two years have seen not only an increased awareness of the phenomenon on the part of Norwegian intelligence agencies but also an increase in online threats and harassment from Norwegian right-wing extremists (Bakke and Stabell 2013).

The basic problem with both hypotheses, which are often based on rational choice theory and post hoc theorizing, however, is that they are virtually untestable. However, it is my contention that to the extent that populist right-wing rhetoric on Islam and Muslims in Norway has borrowed extensively from the 'Eurabia' genre, it has functioned as an amplifier, rather than merely a channel for anti-immigration and anti-Muslim views and sentiments. There are certainly no reasons to suggest that the Progress Party significantly impeded or delayed Anders Behring Breivik's radicalization. The pseudo-academic netherworld of the 'Eurabia' genre is one inhabited by Islamophobes who believe they are at 'war' with Muslims in present-day Europe and that the presence of Muslims in Europe must be fought, primarily but not necessarily exclusively, by democratic means. To think that extreme and populist right-wing rhetoric on Islam and Muslims may be neatly delineated and compartmentalized is to blind oneself to the discursive realities of the past ten years in Norway, as well as in a number of other western European countries.

Anders Behring Breivik was, until he took their message into hitherto unchartered waters, one person swept up in this discursive reality. Given the ongoing development of a multicultural Europe, we ignore Behring Breivik, his ideological motivations and his fellow travellers at our peril. But let us not be fooled. The greatest threats to equality of citizenship and liberal democracy in Norway, Scandinavia and western Europe in our time stem neither from the extreme right wing nor from radical Islamists. For both the former and the latter are fortunately too organizationally weak, incoherent and discredited to pose a significant threat to society in general. That is not to suggest, however, that we ought simply to extend our toleration towards them. For the risk that we then incur is to act as enablers of the very process of societal schismogenesis (Bateson 1935) that both extreme right-wing and radical Islamists seek to further.

'Massacring children is an inefficient way of launching a book,' noted the acknowledged Norwegian terrorism expert Brynjar Lia in his testimony in the 22/7 trial (cited in Hverven and Malling 2013). In that sense, Anders Behring Breivik had already lost the battle he wanted to wage by slaughtering men and women, as well as dozens of innocent youth, in an orgy of extreme violence on 22/7. He had lost long before that fateful day. The 'cordon sanitaire' which once surrounded the exclusionary discourses emanating from far-right milieus had in Norway already fallen in the 1990s, and those who thought the mainstreaming of these discourses would be stopped in its tracks after 22/7 have been proved wrong. The greatest material threats to equal rights to citizenship, inclusion and participation in contemporary liberal democracies in western Europe remain those emanating from the exclusionary discourses and from the mainstreaming and sanitizing of extreme right-wing discourses and rhetorical tropes by the populist right wing in Norway and other Scandinavian and western European countries. As the horror of 22/7 slowly, painfully but surely fades into the historical past, that challenge remains with us for the foreseeable future.

NOTES

1 Human terror

1 Norway has a population of 5.0 million; its capital and largest city, Oslo, 690,000.

2 For Norwegian as well as many Scandinavian social democrats, Utøya holds pride of place. It was a commemorative gift to the AUF from the Labour Party-aligned Oslo and Akershus Trade Union Confederation (Oslo og Akershus Faglige Samorganisasjon) in 1950. By many accounts, the years after the Second World War were the golden years of Norwegian social democracy in which the platform for the extensive Norwegian welfare state was laid (Sejersted 2011) and large-scale social engineering ensured reasonable and decent accommodation for most Norwegians. It was here, at Utøya, that generations of future Norwegian Labour Party politicians would get their introduction to social democratic politics, meet friends and peers, and experience their first romantic encounters. For an account of Utøya's history by Labour Party-aligned authors, see Moen and Giske (2012).

3 See Hegghammer and Tierney (2010) for a typical contribution to this genre, referred to by international news media in the immediate aftermath of the bomb at Government Headquarters after it was reposted by the US magazine *Atlantic Monthly* on their website shortly after the first bomb. It is noteworthy in this connection that among the terrorism experts at the TERRA Research Programme at FFI prior to 22/7 there was not a single expert linked to, or focused upon, anything other than radical Islamist terror and that these terrorism experts have in the past decade been the experts most regularly consulted by the Norwegian Police and Defence Intelligence Services.

4 Norway forms part of the NATO-controlled International Security Assistance Force (ISAF) in Afghanistan and has had a military presence in Afghanistan since the ousting of the Taliban in 2001. Norway currently has an estimated five hundred soldiers stationed in Afghanistan.

5 Norway got involved in the 'cartoon crisis' over a Danish newspaper's commissioning of cartoons widely seen as offensive by Muslims worldwide, when the editor of a small Christian-evangelical newspaper, *Magazinet* (circulation 5,000), decided to reprint the cartoons on 10 January 2006 (Klausen 2009). According to Klausen, this was 'an important milestone in the escalation of the conflict' because it was at this point that the fifty-seven-nation-strong Organization of the Islamic Conference (OIC) decided that it was faced with a campaign against Muslims (ibid.: 47). Unlike their Danish counterparts whose media spin suggested that this was exclusively a matter concerning freedom of speech (Hervik 2011: 176), the Norwegian government, via its Ministry of Foreign Affairs (Utenriksdepartmentet, UD), instructed its embassies in the Middle East to apologize for the offence caused by the cartoons (Klausen 2009: 77). This pragmatic approach did not prevent

the Norwegian embassy in Damascus, Syria, from being burned to the ground by demonstrators encouraged by the absence of Syrian diplomatic protection of the embassy grounds (ibid.: 191). Nor did it spare the Norwegian government from acerbic comments from leading Norwegian media editors who declared that the Ministry of Foreign Affairs' response was illustrative of 'liberals failing liberals' (Åmås 2007).

6 Technically, this would be proved correct, inasmuch as police investigations of Anders Behring Breivik have so far failed to provide any evidence of his being part of any extreme right-wing terrorist group.

7 Mohammed Shoaib Sultan, former secretary-general of the Islamic Council of Norway, researcher at the Norwegian Centre Against Racism, personal communication, 2011.

8 Anders Behring Breivik was a paid-up member of the Progress Party from 1999 to 2004, and a member of the party's youth organization from 1997 to 2006 (Vikås 2011).

9 It is interesting to note that both Borchgrevink and Seierstad in their books on 22/7 ascribe Wenche Behring Breivik's strident views on Islam, Muslims and immigration to the influence of her son. Yet the fact that Wenche Behring Breivik 'all her life' voted for the Progress Party suggests that the influence may not have been entirely unidirectional. From Marit Christensen's book on Wenche Behring (Christensen 2013) we learn that she was an avid newspaper reader, and so she could not have been entirely unaware of the fact that the founder of the PP's precursor, the Anders Langes Parti (ALP), Mr Anders Lange, a prominent Norwegian supporter of apartheid in South Africa, was by any reasonable standards a man who held racist convictions. We

also learn from Christensen's book that Wenche Behring Breivik as a young diplomatic housewife in Kensington, London, during her short-lived marriage to Jens David Breivik pulled her son out of an elite kindergarten for the children of diplomats when she discovered that it was 'full of Negro children' (ibid.: 87). This would rather suggest a person who throughout her life was uncomfortable with the idea of a Norway which was not entirely white.

10 I thank Professor Thomas Hylland Eriksen for this information.

11 Vikernes, born in Bergen in Norway in 1973, and known as 'Count Grishnack' in Norwegian black metal music circles, was sentenced to twenty-one years' imprisonment in 1994 for a string of arson attacks on Norwegian churches and the brutal knife murder of his fellow black metal band member Øyvind Aarseth (Løkeland-Stai et al. 2013). Court psychiatrists at the time declared him to be lacking in mental capabilities. While in prison he became a self-declared neo-Nazi, continued his career as a black metal musician, releasing record albums under the band name Burzum, and married a young French sympathizer with whom he would eventually have three children. Burzum records received glowing reviews in Norwegian mainstream media, and these reviews detached Vikernes' music from the ideological messages contained in their lyrics. Vikernes was released from prison after sixteen years in 2009, and eventually moved to the small village of Salon La Tour in the Corrèze region of south-western France. The French police's charges relating to the plotting of terrorism, which were the result of his French wife's legal purchase of four firearms purportedly for 'self-defence', would eventually be dropped in favour of charges relating to the infringement of French hate speech

laws for racist speech against Jews and Muslims (Sætren et al. 2013). Vikernes has in blog posts expressed considerable sympathy for Behring Breivik's ideas, even if he criticized him for the use of terror against 'ethnic' (i.e. white) Norwegians (which he thought more appropriately ought to have been directed against Jews). He has lauded Hitler and Quisling for representing 'divine goodness' (Sletholm 2013), and recommended that his French sympathizers vote for the French National Front of Marine Le Pen on various websites.

12 Demokratene was established by a splinter group from the Progress Party led by the former PP MP Vidar Kleppe (1963–) in Oslo in 2002. Kleppe had been suspended from the PP in 2002 for allegedly undermining the PP chairman Carl I. Hagen. Demokratene hold strong anti-immigration and anti-Muslim views, and are staunch supporters of Israel and a strengthening of Christian identity politics in Norway. They have, however, failed to garner much electoral support. In several provinces of Norway, memberships in SIAN and Demokratene appear to be overlapping. In August 2011, Norwegian private channel TV2 aired a video clip filmed in secret in which Håvard Krane and Kaspar Birkeland, mayoral candidates for Demokratene in Kristiansund and Ålesund respectively, during a gathering of SIAN members at a hotel, openly discussed killing Norwegian government ministers (Leirvåg and Skjærstad 2011).

13 The term 'mother of the nation' for Brundtland in Norwegian is also an intertextual inscription of her in the panoply of grandees of social democratic politicians after the Second World War: Norway's prime minister during post-Second World War reconstruction, Einar Gerhardsen (1897–1987, prime minister for three periods between 1945 and 1965), was also known as '*landsfaderen*' or 'the father of the nation'.

14 For academic studies of the commemorations of 22/7, see the contributions to the edited volume of Aagedal et al. (2013).

15 In the following months, this statement would repeatedly be cited by the civil society activist Hege Storhaug of the state-subsidized Human Rights Service (HRS) in Oslo in support of her agendas. However, it is noteworthy that in the speech that Prime Minister Stoltenberg gave in Oslo Cathedral (*domkirken*) the preceding day, he used a similar line, but added that 'our answer is more democracy, more openness, and more humanity. *But never naiveté*' (my emphasis).

16 According to the Oxford English Dictionary (OED), a quisling is 'a traitor who collaborates with an enemy force occupying their country'. The term has its origins in the Second World War, when the Norwegian army officer and Nazi Vidkun Quisling (1887–1945) governed Norway as prime minister on behalf of the German occupying forces. As one of very few Nazi collaborators during the Second World War in Norway, Quisling was executed at the Akershus Fortress in central Oslo after the war. However, use of the term 'quisling' applied to groups of Norwegian Muslims had its precursors before 22/7. In an op-ed in Norway's leading newspaper, *Aftenposten*, in early 2011, the lesbian secular feminist Hege Storhaug of the state-supported Human Rights Service (HRS) likened a group of Norwegian Muslims who had demonstrated against the publication of a new 'Mohammed' cartoon in 2010 to 'quislings' (Storhaug 2011a).

17 Norwegian police districts have not, however, received any formal complaints from Muslim individuals

harassed or threatened in the aftermath of the first attack on 22/7. As not all hate crimes are reported by their victims, this does not necessarily imply that such crimes did not take place.

18 The acting director of the National Police Directorate, Mr Øystein Mæland, a political appointee of the then minister of justice Knut Storberget (Labour Party), who had no police background whatsoever, was forced to resign in the aftermath of the commission's report over factually incorrect statements he made to Norwegian media. On 22 July 2011 he had only been in the position for two weeks, and stated to the commission that he was unaware of the existence of the plans in the event of a terror attack (22/7 Commission 2012: 155).

19 This tip was received by Oslo police at 15.35 p.m. local time, and written down on a yellow Post-it note, which was then left lying around untouched for twenty minutes. Police tracking cars going out of Oslo were never informed about the vehicle registration number (22/7 Commission 2012: 102).

20 A police helicopter on stand-by for use in critical incidents has been available to Oslo police since 2003. Mobilizing the helicopter on 22 July 2011 may not have made much difference, as most of the helicopter staff were in any event on summer holidays at the time (22/7 Commission 2012: 294).

21 In their first attempt to cross over the small strait to Utøya, the elite police forces from Oslo overloaded the police's inflated rubber boat to such an extent that the boat capsized (22/7 Commission 2012: 138). The elite police forces were eventually assisted by private boat owners in the area, who ferried them across to Utøya (ibid.: 138).

22 See the following link in Norwegian for the conclusions of the parliamentary committee: www.stortinget.no/no/Saker-og-publikasjoner/Publikasjoner/Innstillinger/Stortinget/2012-2013/inns-201213-210/3/8/#a4.

23 See Olsen (2012) for one prominent Norwegian terrorism researcher, Thomas Hegghammer of FFI in Norway, doing so.

24 I thank Henrik Arnstad for providing references on this topic in personal correspondence in December 2013.

25 See, for example, Borchgrevink (2012), who, on the basis of documents relating to Behring Breivik's family's contact with psychiatric services, argues that Behring Breivik was emotionally maltreated by a mentally disturbed single mother and may as a result have suffered from reactive disturbances of attachment.

26 See Sønstelie and Sønstelie (2011), Pracon (2012), Fatland (2012) for survivors' testimonies; the 22/7 Commission (2012) and Stormark (2011) for the attacks.

27 See Schau (2012) and Østli (2013) for books about the trial.

28 It should be noted here that as far as contested analytical concepts go, the term Islamophobia is in no sense unique in these respects: terms such as 'homophobia' and 'anti-Semitism' are also not ideal for analytical purposes, and may also be misused and instrumentalized. Yet in the Norwegian context at least, these terms are much more readily accepted, and far less contested, than the term Islamophobia.

29 The late Fred Halliday's proposed alternative, 'anti-Muslimism' (see Halliday 1999), seems particularly ill suited in this respect.

30 Author's field notes, 2010.

31 Author's interview with Hamzah Ahmed Nordahl-Rajpoot, a young

Norwegian Ahmadi of Norwegian-Pakistani background, 2011.

32 Author's interview with Hadia Tajik, MP for the Labour Party and from September 2012 to October 2013 minister of culture in Norway, 2011.

33 I thank Dr Gavan Titley for making this point in an article on the ideoscape of Behring Breivik (Titley 2013), from which I have drawn here.

34 See Bangstad (2012a) for a reflection on the limits of public engagement of academics in Norway on these issues.

35 I thank Professor Richard Ashby Wilson for this point.

2 Muslims in Norway

1 Hamzah Ahmed Rajpoot, interview with author, Oslo, 24 February 2010.

2 Julian Y. Kramer, interview with author, Oslo, 4 December 2010.

3 Norway has twice (1973, 1992) turned down EEC/EU memberships in popular referendums – yet has formal relationships with the EU at various levels, and somewhat paradoxically implements more EU directives than any member state of the EU.

4 For these statistics, see the official web pages of Statistics Norway at: www.ssb.no/innvgrunn/tab-2012-08-30-01.html.

5 The discrepancy between the two estimates stems from the fact that in official Norwegian statistics, a Norwegian born to two immigrant parents is counted as an immigrant, regardless of whether s/he is born in the country.

6 See Roald (2004) for a study of Scandinavian converts to Islam.

7 Mrs Lena Larsen, personal correspondence with author, 2010.

8 Larsen is affiliated with the Arab-dominated Islamic Society of Norway or Al-Rabita al-Islamiyya fi Nurwij, established in 1987 in Oslo (Vogt 2008: 70), and was acting chairperson for the

Islamic Council of Norway from 1998 to 2003. When the chairman of the Islamic Council of Norway, Mr Kebba Secka, an imam of Gambian origin, formally resigned in 2000 after a TV programme concerning the attitude of male Norwegian imams towards female circumcision, Larsen was selected as the new chairperson (Jacobsen 2009: 34, fn. 23). Involved in the European Muslim Network, she has undertaken extensive research on the European Council for Fatwa and Research (ECFR) (see Larsen 2011).

9 Lindstad, a medical doctor by education, was an adherent of the radical left organization AKP-ML, a Maoist-Leninist organization promulgating armed revolution in Norway in the 1970s. Having served as a volunteer medical doctor for long periods during the civil war in Lebanon (1976–89), Lindstad converted to Islam after the Iranian Revolution in 1979. Founder of the Muslim kindergarten Urtehagen in Oslo, and a regular contributor to the op-ed and letters-to-the-editor pages of various Norwegian newspapers, Lindstad has a limited following among Shias in Norway, owing to his regularly professed sympathies for the Iranian Islamist regime, and his close contacts with the Iranian embassy in Oslo. The Norwegian reporter Odd Karsten Tvedt revealed in a book published in 2005 that Lindstad's wife once doubled as an agent for the Israeli intelligence services Mossad during the civil war in Lebanon (Tvedt 2005).

10 See Naguib (2001) for a detailed study of Norwegian mosques.

11 Author's e-mail correspondence with Mrs Gunnlaug Daugstad, social anthropologist and senior researcher at Statistics Norway, 2009.

12 For the most up-to-date and extensive empirical study of living

conditions and discrimination experienced by Norwegian-Somalis living in Oslo to date, see Open Society Foundation (2013).

13 Charles Taylor defines a social imaginary as 'the ways people imagine their social existence, how they fit together with others, how things go on between them and their fellows, the expectations that are normally met, and the deeper normative notions and images that underlie these expectations' (Taylor 2004: 23).

14 Secularity may here usefully be described with reference to Charles Taylor's definition in *A Secular Age* as 'a move from a society where belief in God is unchallenged, and indeed, unproblematic, to one in which it is understood to be one option among others, and frequently not the easiest to embrace' (Taylor 2007: 3).

15 Established in 2008 at Oslo University College (OUC), the largest university college in Norway, and the higher education institution in Norway with the highest percentage of students of minority background, IslamNet has between 500 to 1,000 paid-up members. It regularly organizes Islamic conferences with Salafi scholars affiliated with Mumbai-based Islamic televangelist Zakir Naik's Islamic Research Foundation (IRF). In 2010 IslamNet was barred from further use of the OUC's facilities, owing to concerns over its practice of gender segregation. In 2013, the University of Oslo and the Oslo and Akershus University College (OAUC, formerly OUC) both turned down applications for registration as student organizations submitted by groups linked to IslamNet.

16 Issued by the so-called Contact Group for the Church of Norway and the Islamic Council of Norway (a group established in 1992/93), the statement on conversion was dated 2007, and

the statement on violence in the family and close relationships was dated 2009. See www.kirken.no/english/news.cfm?artid=149142 (accessed 10 June 2011) for the former and www.kirken.no/english/doc/engelsk/Joint_declaration _violence_relations_0911.pdf (accessed 10 June 2011) for the latter. The statement condemning anti-Semitism was issued by the Council for Religious and Life Stance Communities in Norway (established 1996) during the Israeli war on Gaza in 2009. See kyrkja.no/?event=dolink&FamID=67638 (accessed 10 June 2011).

17 Author's interview with Bushra Ishaq of MSS, 2009.

18 I borrow the term 'Islamic contextualism' from Tayob (1995: 161–83), who uses the term with reference to discursive and ideological developments within the Muslim Youth Movement (MYM) in South Africa.

19 This congregation is aligned with the global Minhaj ul-Quran International (MQI), established by Sheikh Muhammad Tahir ul-Qadri (1951–) in Lahore, Pakistan, in 1981.

20 Sources regarding Sagene skole are Storvik (2011) and Bergsli (2011). I would like to thank Chief Editor Kaia Storvik at Dagsavisen in Oslo and Joron Pihl at Oslo University College for information provided in this section.

21 In an incisive critique of Norwegian state feminism, which emerged out of the Norwegian feminist struggles in the 1970s and 1980s, Holst (2010) has pointed to its anchoring in an educated middle-class elite, and its discursive and practical marginalization of both working-class and immigrant women whose lifestyle and life-choices may differ from the hegemonic models being promoted by state feminists.

22 A nascent body of work in political science and related social sciences

explores the governance of Islam and of Muslims in various European contexts. See Laurence (2012) and Bader et al. (2012) for two prominent titles in this field. It is noteworthy that none of these titles makes reference to Norway and that no academic studies of governance of Islam in Norway have so far been undertaken.

23 See www.eos-utvalget.no/file store/SM2013.pdf for the full report.

24 For the first academic account of the background and ideology of Islam-Net, see Bangstad and Linge (2013).

25 In this section on IslamNet, I draw extensively on findings from an MA study by Marius Linge on IslamNet, which I supervised throughout 2012. See Linge (2013a). Personal permission to draw from these findings is gratefully acknowledged.

26 For studies of the background to the TJ in British India, see Sikand (2002) and Masud (2000).

27 See NRK's interview with Toverud Jensen on 20 December 2012.

28 See www.islamnet.no/om-oss/om-oss/2061.

29 For the first full academic account of the background and religious ideology of IslamNet in Norwegian, see Bangstad and Linge (2013).

30 Author's personal correspondence with Mohammad Shoaib Sultan, adviser on right-wing extremism at the Norwegian Centre Against Racism and former secretary-general of the Islamic Council of Norway, 2012.

31 FATA is a tribal administrative area where the laws of the Pakistani state do not apply. The Frontier Crimes Regulation was first introduced in 1901 and hence dates from British colonial times. Section 40 entitles the Deputy Commissioner to sentence and imprison individuals for up to three years on suspicion of planning homicides or sedition.

Under FRC, the accused have no right to appeal, no right to legal representation and no right to present reasoned evidence, and the code has therefore been condemned by a number of human rights organizations.

3 The fear of small numbers

1 In his testimony to the 22/7 trial, and despite protestations from the defendant, Ulrik Malt, professor of psychiatry at the University of Oslo, offered the suggestion that Behring Breivik might be suffering from Tourette's and Asperger's syndromes, and that his hypergraphia was a symptom of this. It is important to note in this context, however, that hypergraphia need not be a symptom of mental or physical illness. On the other hand, if we consider that Behring Breivik in the same period in which he produced his tract *2083* also wrote thousands of e-mails (see Stormark 2012), then the suggestion of hypergraphia seems more than plausible.

2 Please note that for the purposes of consistency, I have opted to alter the citations from the tract in this chapter from UK to US English.

3 See Section 3.40, entitled 'Applying deceptive means in urban guerilla warfare', for this.

4 The Phalange had been set up by Bashir Gemayel's father Pierre Gemayel, after a visit to Nazi Germany in 1936. The Phalangist massacre of twenty-seven unarmed Palestinians at Ayn al-Rumaneh in Beirut on 'Black Saturday', 13 April 1975, which Bashir Gemayel, a lawyer by education, appears to have ordered (Fisk 2001: 79), unleashed the civil war in Lebanon (1975–90). When Israel invaded Lebanon on 6 June 1982, the Phalangists under Gemayel became their closest allies. Bashir Gemayel was elected president of Lebanon on 23 Aug-

ust 1982, and was killed in a bomb attack on the Phalangist headquarters on 14 September 1982 (ibid.: 329, 353). The perpetrator of the attack, Habib Tanious Shartouni (1958–), was a Maronite Christian militant with the Syrian Social Nationalist Party in Lebanon, and spent eight years in a Lebanese prison before escaping to Syria in 1990. In 'retaliation' for the assassination of Bashir Gemayel, the Phalangists massacred an estimated 3,500 Palestinian and Lebanese Shia civilians in the refugee camps of Sabra and Shatila in Beirut with the assistance of the Israeli Defence Forces (IDF), between 16 and 18 September 1982.

5 Police investigations into Behring Breivik's alleged Knights Templar network has, according to newspaper reports, failed to turn up any evidence that such a pan-European network actually exists or that there was a secret re-founding session with twelve European 'delegates' in London in 2002.

6 In September 2011, Norwegian police made a formal request to interrogate Milorad Ulemek in connection with its investigations into 22/7, but Serbian authorities have not responded to this request (Johansen and Foss 2012). According to police investigators' testimonies in court in the course of the 22/7 trial, Norwegian police have not found any indications suggesting that Behring Breivik met Ulemek either in Liberia or anywhere else.

7 In the counter-jihadist genre, a central figure is the US-based political analyst Serge (Srjda) Trifković, a one-time adviser to the interim president of Republika Srpska Biljana Plavsić in the 1990s (Poohl 2011). The author of books such as The Sword of the Prophet and Defeating Jihad, Trifković has argued in web posts that if Europe is to survive, European political, media and academic elites must be exposed as 'traitors to

their nations and their culture' (cited in Strømmen 2011b: 71). Trifković appears as a central source in Behring Breivik's tract, mainly via the inserted excerpts from essays by Fjordman (ibid.).

8 Personal information given to Bangstad in September 2011 by a senior publishing editor who wishes to remain anonymous. The academic publishing house in question deleted the e-mails and the attached tract some time before 22/7 and has not been able to recover them.

9 After a long and unbroken series of public relations disasters after 22/7, Janne Kristiansen, who was head of the PST on 22/7, was forced to leave office on 12 January 2012, after she inadvertently disclosed that Norwegian military intelligence had a presence in Pakistan in open parliamentary hearings on 22/7 in Parliament (Weiby 2012).

10 Ayn Rand's Atlas Shrugged is also named as the favourite book of Behring Breivik in the tract. In Norway, Rand's books have for a number of years appeared on the reading lists of aspiring and established PP politicians.

11 For an analysis of the tract in light of criminological theories about self-narratives, see Sandberg (2013).

12 For a seminal title on publics and counterpublics, see Warner (2002).

13 On 23 June 2011, Document.no editor Hans Rustad published the entire record of Anders Behring Breivik's postings on the website (Document.no 2011). The excerpts used in this chapter have been translated from Norwegian by the present author.

14 For an apologetic and psychologizing account of 'Fjordman's' life and background, see Sætre (2013a).

15 After 22/7 Storhaug claimed that though she and her partner Rita Karlsen of HRS had met 'Fjordman' at a restaurant in Oslo in 2003, she could not

recall his name or what he looked like. She also declared that she had found his views abhorrent (an 'unpleasant, bloody doomsday prophecy'), so she did not want to meet him again. She also stated that she and the HRS took exception to the 'Eurabia' genre (Storhaug 2011a). As Øyvind Strømmen remarked in a pointed response, this raised the question of why she introduced on the HRS website in February 2007 'another fantastic essay by Fjordman', why her website repeatedly promoted Bat Ye'or's work, and why her close associate, Bruce Bawer of HRS, has also consistently promoted Ye'or's work (Strømmen 2011c, 2011d) – and also why, in a portrait interview with *Dagbladet* in 2006, she declared that 'Islamists have a worldwide caliphate as their goal' and that she was prepared to take up arms against these Islamists and head for the woods if need be (Gjerstad 2006).

16 The author has been in contact with a number of academics who happened to be in Cairo on 9/11 or who followed Arab media at the time. None of these recalls having witnessed such celebrations in public in Cairo on the day in question or recalls having seen any media reports that this happened. However, Cairo is a city of an estimated twenty million inhabitants, so it is virtually impossible to rule out such an event.

17 For detailed documentation of this record of incitement to violence on 'Fjordman's' part, see Enebakk (2012).

18 In Norse mythology, as compiled by Snorri Sturlason in the *Edda* in the thirteenth century, Ragnarök is the cataclysmic end of the world as we know it through an epic battle and the occurrence of various natural disasters, from the ashes of which a new world will arise.

19 After all, Behring Breivik also repeatedly insists on his 'not being racist',

'against Muslims', etc., in the tract. But actions, in this case, speak louder than words.

20 Here, Strømmen also endorsed the highly tendentious political neologism 'Islamofascism' (Strømmen 2011b: 13). It is unclear who first coined the term 'Islamofascism', but an early usage can be found in a UK newspaper item by the Scottish author and columnist Malise Ruthven (Fekete 2011: 9), and it was popularized by neoconservative intellectuals such as Norman Podhoretz in the USA and Douglas Murray in the UK during the so-called 'war on terror'.

21 For studies of the neoconservative movement, a movement that reached the apotheosis of its political and social influence in the USA in the course of President George W. Bush's (2000–08) 'war on terror', see Vaïsse (2010) and Drolet (2011).

22 For a short introduction to the 'counter-jihadist' genre, see Strømmen (2011a).

23 See Brown (2006: 19–24) for a discussion of the term in its contemporary Western liberal usages, and Žižek (2008) for a critique.

24 In a comparison of various welfare states, Banting et al. (2006) list Norway among the states in western Europe with the least multiculturalist policies. To the extent that the Norwegian state can be said to have espoused such policies, it has mainly been in the context of granting extensive jurisdiction over land and language policies to the indigenous Saamis of northern Norway after 1980. This policy has in fact been a qualified success, as the extensive conflicts brought about by the Norwegian state's historical pursuit of assimilation policies with regard to the Saami have subsequently abated.

25 The parties in question are the Labour Party (AP), the Conservative

Party (H), the Socialist Left Party (SV), the Christian Democratic Party (KrF), the Centre Party (Sp) and the Liberal Party (V). The Norwegian Labour Party was briefly a member of the Comintern from 1919 to 1923, but cannot be said to have ever been communist (Sejersted 2011: 146–7). The Socialist Left Party (SV) was founded by a socialist-oriented faction opposed to Norwegian involvement with the NATO military alliance and its endorsement of nuclear deterrence in the Labour Party under the name of the Socialist People's Party (SF) in 1961 (ibid.: 193).

26 After all, in some of the more disturbing and disturbed passages of the tract, he writes about his own mother, sister and ex-stepfather's sexual and intimate histories by way of a warning against the supposed effects of 'feminism' and 'multiculturalism', and his own father's alleged breaking off contact with him and between him and all his half-siblings from his father's later marriages. In other passages, he contemplates the possible execution of his stepmother as a 'category B traitor' for being a social democrat and having worked for the Norwegian Directorate of Immigration (UDI) for a number of years before her retirement. According to Norwegian journalist Marit Christensen, who recorded a number of interviews with Behring Breivik's mother, Wenche Behring Breivik, after 22/7, she was by no means part of the feminist struggle in Norway (Christensen 2013: 160). The mother had been scandalized by learning of her mass-murdering son's description of her and his sister as sexually promiscuous in 2083 (ibid.: 153–4). Christensen describes Behring Breivik's late mother as being as timid in her rather troubled relationships with men as most Norwegian women of her age, born before the sexual revolution of the

1960s. Anders Behring Breivik's defence attorney, Geir Lippestad, claims that his negative description of his mother and sister in 2083 was designed to prevent them from being associated with him in the aftermath (Lippestad 2013: 111–12).

27 During the past decade, the canard that Norwegian social-democratic governments have pursued multiculturalist policies in the past has been frequently advanced by populist right-wing politicians and academics in Norway. For one example provided by the PP-aligned political scientist Asle Toje, see Melgård (2011).

28 See Dubow (1995) for 'scientific racism' as a precursor to apartheid; see Schafft (2004) for an exploration of 'scientific racism' in Nazism.

29 Quisling, an erstwhile close associate of the Norwegian polar hero and humanitarian Fridtjof Nansen during the latter's relief efforts during the hunger induced by Stalinist collectivization in the Ukraine in the 1930s, assumed power in a *coup d'état* when German Nazi forces invaded Norway on 9 April 1940. Quisling was an anti-Semite, and his government oversaw the deportation of Norwegian Jews to the Nazi concentration camps in eastern Europe during the Second World War. Quisling was charged and sentenced for treason after the war, and executed at Akershus Fortress in Oslo in October 1945. For Quisling, see Høidal (1989).

30 For a classic text about denials of racism among elites in Europe, see Van Dijk (1992).

31 For cases in point, see Eriksen (1986) and Hagtvet (1993).

32 For cases in point one can look to Professor of Social Anthropology Fredrik Barth's claim in 2007 that 'when Norwegians talk about racism, they mean to refer to prejudices and stereotypes ... Racist views are hardly found among

Norwegians' (see Barth in Gjerdåker 2007) and Professor of the History of Ideas Trond Berg Eriksen's assertion in various Norwegian media after 22/7 that 'anti-racists are the only ones who maintain the concept of race' and that 'harassment of Muslims in Norway is not racism' (Simenstad 2011). Even when members of Norwegian elites do engage in open expressions of biological racism, it is hardly ever marked as such in public discourse: in September 2012, the Norwegian Professor of History at the University of Stavanger, Nils-Rune Langeland, at the time a visiting professor at Oslo and Akershus University College (HiOA), posted a Facebook post that referred to Punjabis (i.e. Muslims from Punjab in Pakistan) as 'genetically weak illiterates' (Ashraf 2012). Langeland has to date not faced any kind of rebuke or sanction by his employer for his statements, which are indisputably racist. He was later relieved of his post at HiOA owing to conflicts with a senior colleague.

33 For a standard work on the Lebanese civil war and the Israeli invasion of 1982, see Fisk (2001).

34 A standard reference work on Shia Islam argues that the doctrine of *taqiyya* or religious dissimulation was developed during the imamate of the sixth imam, Ja'far as-Sadiq (699 or 705–765 CE), in Medina, in order to protect the followers of as-Sadiq from the 'brutally repressive campaign' against the descendants of Imam 'Ali by the 'Abbaside Caliph al-Mansur (Momen 1985: 38–9).

35 From Norway, for instance, we have survey data suggesting that the level of religious faith is highest among Norwegian-Somalis of Muslim background, and lowest among Norwegian-Iranians of Muslim background (Daugstad et al. 2008: 156–7). Further-

more, findings show that younger people of immigrant background (including Muslims) born in Norway are less likely to be religious than their parents born abroad (Løwe 2008: 68).

36 In this section, which would be hilarious were it not for what we know of the terrible results of Behring Breivik's acts on 22/7, he contemplates approaching a 'representative from a jihadi-salafi group' in order to attempt to acquire WMD. Here, he emphasizes the importance of asking such a representative for a 'temporary truce' (*hudna*) before formal negotiations commence.

37 For a sober assessment of the often fictive and wildly inaccurate demographic statistics of the 'Eurabia' genre, see Larsson (2012).

38 In recent years in Norway, several initiatives involving Norwegian secondary schools, and directed by the Directorate of Integration and Diversity (IMDI), have been designed to put a stop to this practice.

39 Nationalsozialistische Deutsche Arbeiterpartei, the German National-Socialist Workers' Party (Hitler's party), which ruled Germany 1933–45.

4 Convergences

1 I adopt the term 'framing' from Morey and Yaqin (2011). For these authors, framing entails 'repeated acts of representation by politicians, the press and media' and 'amounts to a refraction, not a reflection, of reality' (ibid.: 2–4).

2 Sigurd Jorsalfar or Sigurd the Crusader (c. 1090–1130) was King of Norway from 1103 to 1130. He was the first European king to go with his army on a crusade in support of the Kingdom of Jerusalem from 1107 to 1110, travelling through Iberia, Rome and Constantinople. Sigurd cast himself as a 'Knight Templar' out to rescue Europe from an impending Islamization which was but

the culmination of an omni-temporal battle between European Christendom and Oriental Islam; it is easy to see the attraction of this pseudonym for the perpetrator of Norway's 22/7.

3 Hegnar Online is the internet edition of *Finansavisen*, a daily newspaper focused on financial news established in 1992 by Norwegian business tycoon and multimillionaire Trygve Hegnar (1943–). In 2010 it had a daily print run of 25,000 copies. The Hegnar Online forum has been known for some time to have moderators with a liberal approach to racist and Islamophobic speech. Berg (2011) compared debates on three Norwegian newspaper-aligned internet forums and found that Hegnar Online had the most liberal and least moderated approach and the lowest standards. In connection with its coverage of the forced resignation in 2008 of Norway's first minister of an immigrant background, Minister for Children and Equality Manuela Ramin-Osmundsen (1963–) of the Labour Party, Hegnar Online was reported to the Norwegian police for breaches of the Norwegian General Penal Code, paragraph §135(a).

4 Document.no is a populist and right-wing website established in 2003 by Hans Rustad, a former member of the Norwegian Maoist-Leninist Party AKP-ML and reporter with the Norwegian press bureau Norsk Telegrambyrå (NTB). In the 1990s, Rustad covered the Balkan wars for NTB. The website received a lot of international and national media attention following 22/7 after it was reported that Behring Breivik had been very active on its internet forum, especially in 2009, when he contacted Rustad with suggestions for improving the site. Document.no has a regular readership running into tens of thousands. In 2012, Rustad started to refer to himself as a 'cultural conservative'

on the webpages he edits. See Berntzen (2011) for an introduction.

5 The leader of the Bamble branch of the PP in Telemark, Knut Røe-Berntsen, was forced to resign as local party chairman after posting a note on his Facebook page in December 2011 in which he alleged that AUF leader Eskil Pedersen 'ran away [from Utøya] without attempting to rescue anyone [on 22/7]'. A PP politician from Hamar, Johnny Wæhler, was expelled from the party in February 2012 after he posted twin images of Labour Party Prime Minister Jens Stoltenberg and Anders Behring Breivik behind prison bars on his Facebook page with the caption 'A traitor to the nation and a genocidaire!' (Hagen and Dahl 2012). In November 2011, Odd Beston from the PP in Hurum outside of Oslo got into trouble for having characterized African males as 'monkeys from Africa' on his Facebook page (Gilbrant 2011b). And in February 2012, a PP politician from Time in Rogaland, Edvard Auestad, posted a message on his Facebook page suggesting that 'we must perhaps locate our guns, all of us, and go to war against the foreigners' (Nygård 2012). The latter two have at the time of writing in February 2012 not faced any formal reactions from the PP.

6 The Anders Langes Parti (ALP) was merged with the so-called Reform Party in 1977. Carl I. Hagen, who had been elected as a substitute MP for the ALP in 1973, became the new party chairman.

7 Dr Rhoodie would become central to the 'Muldergate' or 'Information Scandal' in apartheid South Africa in 1978, when it became known that the Information Department had used secret funds to buy sections of the liberal English press in South Africa for the ruling National Party (NP) and had set up an English-language newspaper, *The Citizen*, in order to garner support for the apartheid government from English-

speaking South Africans. Rhoodie was charged, but later acquitted; the scandal eventually led to the resignation of B. J. Voerster as State President in 1979 (see Davenport and Saunders 2000: 454–60).

8 See Runciman (2013) for an insightful account of the repeated crises of legitimization of modern Western liberal democracies.

9 Most notably Stein Erik Hagen, Christen Sveaas, Ola Mæhle and Øystein Stray Spetalen. The PP's declared support for the removal of inheritance taxes and other taxes for top income earners in Norway is seen by some of the wealthiest Norwegians as in their interest.

10 I would like to thank Axel West Pedersen at the Institute for Social Research (ISF) for sharing the data with me in personal correspondence, 4 November 2013.

11 The White Electoral Alliance was established in Oslo in 1995 by Jack Erik Kjuus (1927–2009). As head of the party, Kjuus called for the forced sterilization of non-white 'foreign partners' in marriage unless said party was willing to leave the country. He also called for the forced sterilization of adopted children from 'non-Western' regions. In 1997, Kjuus was sentenced under the Norwegian General Penal Code's racism paragraph §135(a) for these statements. His party collapsed soon thereafter.

12 The congregation that Hagen addressed is part of the 'New Christian Right' in Norway (Leirvik 2006: 151), a Christian evangelical right which strongly identifies with similar political and religious movements in the USA, is staunchly and one-sidedly pro-Israel and regards the state of Israel as a manifestation of biblical prophecies; furthermore it sees itself as being involved in a worldwide struggle with Islam.

13 It would of course be news to most serious historians that Hitler had

ever planned to 'Islamize the world' (sic), but this rhetorical flourish suggests that there was a confused conflation of 'colonization' and 'Islamization' at work in Hagen's speech.

14 Among Gabriel's contentious and contestable claims in this book is that the indiscriminate killing of civilians of al-Qaeda-style terrorism since the late 1990s is really in line with Islamic teachings. Similar claims are made by the Somali-born polemicist Ayaan Hirsi Ali in her book *Nomad* (2010): 'After 9/11 I found it impossible to ignore his [Osama bin Laden's] claims that the murderous destruction of innocent (if infidel) lives is consistent with the Quran. I looked in the Quran, and I found it to be so' (ibid.: xiv). A Norwegian translation of Gabriel's book *Islam and Terrorism* was published in 2002 by Prokla-Media. According to the publisher, it had been distributed to Norwegian members of parliament as early as 2003.

15 The author thanks Professor Oddbjørn Leirvik for information about Prokla-Media.

16 For Bawer's statements to this effect, see Bawer (2006: 68).

17 When the first ever coalition government between the Conservative Party and the Progress Party in Norway came into power after the parliamentary elections of September 2013, Hege Storhaug's HRS was rewarded for its long-standing support for the PP with an entirely unsolicited budgetary increase of some 80 per cent from the Department of Children, Equality in Inclusion, to which the PP's Solveig Horne had been appointed as minister (Johansen 2013).

18 For Spencer's central role in US Islamophobic networks since 2001, see Ali et al. (2011).

19 Thanks are due to Senior Researcher Cora Alexa Døving for the reference.

20 Somewhat puzzlingly, Mudde, in his book on radical right-wing parties in Europe, does not include the Progress Party on his list of such parties in Norway. In the aftermath of 22/7, Mudde would call for 'careful assessment' of the attacks, yet went on to identify the PP as a 'moderate conservative protest party' (Mudde 2011). Mudde's characterization, later taken up by the Norwegian newspaper reporter and popular author Øyvind Strømmen, goes against the grain of the consensus of the overwhelming majority of Norwegian and Scandinavian political scientists who have studied the PP during the last twenty years and who characterize the party as belonging to a populist right-wing family. Unlike these political scientists, however, Mudde appears not to have undertaken any research on the PP, and to be unfamiliar with the Norwegian language.

21 See Ot. prop. no. 75 (2006–2007) presented to the Norwegian Ministry of Work and Inclusion in 2007 for the Progress Party's proposals.

22 Input from HRS was in fact acknowledged in Tybring-Gjedde's interview after the speech. HRS, established in 2001 (Fekete 2009: 93), had initially been secured state support through a special state budgetary allocation initiated by the Progress Party under the Bondevik II Government (2001–05). HRS also contributed to the Progress Party's Parliamentary Caucus' Commission on Immigration and Integration's Report in 2007 (see Fremskrittspartiet 2007: 1).

23 In October 2010, Tybring-Gjedde presented a lecture to a gathering of 'Friends of Document' ['*Dokuments venner*'] in Oslo. He had been invited by the editor of Document.no, Hans Rustad. In a speech later made available on Document.no, Tybring-Gjedde alleged that '90 percent of all immigration to

Europe after 1990 had been from Muslim countries' and that there would be 'an estimated 52 million Muslims in Europe by 2025'. For a summary and critique, see Klev (2011). Both claims are wildly incorrect, and based on the demographic scenarios found in 'Eurabia' literature.

24 Anders Behring Breivik's tract states that 'Islam is less a personal faith than a *political ideology* [my emphasis] that exists in a fundamental and permanent state of war with non-Islamic civilizations, cultures and individuals'. (ABB 1.5).

25 Anders Behring Breivik's tract describes *taqiyya* as 'religious or political deception', a 'systematic lying to the infidel' which 'must be considered part and parcel of Islamic tactics'. Citing a 'Hugh Fitzgerald' in Robert Spencer's *Jihad Watch*, who is believed to be a pen name for Spencer himself (see spencer watch.com/who-is-hugh-fitzgerald/), the tract goes on to argue that while it has its origins in Shia Islam, it is now practised by non-Shia (i.e. Sunnis) as well, and that it is as such 'a central part of the Islamization of Europe'. In a twist of historical logic, Sunni Muslims here become its main agent, since they are held to be 'actively using it in [their] relations with the Western world' and to practise it 'whether they acknowledge the fact or not' (ABB 1.5).

26 Amundsen, known as one of the most extreme among PP politicians on these issues, was removed from his post as the party's spokesperson on immigration and integration shortly after 22/7. In spring 2011, Amundsen wondered aloud on Facebook about the need for a new 'crusade' (*korstog*). Amundsen's FB page was closed down on 23 July, after one of his FB friends had posted a comment on it expressing glee over the massacring of social democrats.

27 Groruddalen is a mainly lower-

income and working-class residential area in eastern Oslo developed in the 1960s and 1970s. It is home to 130,000 people, or close to one in every five residents in Oslo. From the very onset of residential development and expansion in Groruddalen, its residents have lived with widespread media and political stigmatization characterizing it as a 'problem area'. As part of a process of upward social mobility among people of immigrant background in Oslo, many have moved from inner-city areas in Oslo to Groruddalen, which now has the highest proportion of residents with an immigrant background of any residential area in Oslo.

28 Note here how boys of immigrant background, even if born and raised in Norway and with Norwegian citizenship, are collectively marked as foreigners or non-Norwegians in this section of Tybring-Gjedde's speech.

29 The leader of the Labour Party Youth Movement, AUF, Eskil Pedersen (twenty-six), pressed charges for violation of the so-called 'racism' paragraph §135(a) of the Norwegian General Penal Code against Tybring-Gjedde in the aftermath of these statements. One month later, the Norwegian police decided not to press charges against Tybring-Gjedde.

30 Norway recognized civil partnerships for gays and lesbians in 1993. In 2009, a new law on marriage provided Norwegian gays and lesbians with the same rights to marriage and adoption of children as Norwegian heterosexuals.

31 Berg has in recent years been a regional chairman of the right-wing and strongly pro-Zionist *Med Israel for Fred* (With Israel for Peace), which supports Israeli settlement expansion in occupied Palestinian territories in the West Bank, and has in this capacity in public lec-

tures in Norway advanced the view that Muslim countries have gained control over the UN.

32 After the Norwegian parliamentary elections of September 2013, Åmås, who was *Aftenposten*'s op-ed and cultural affairs editor from 2006 to 2013, was appointed as secretary to the new minister for culture, Mrs Torhild Widvey of the Conservative Party.

33 In the aftermath of 22/7, the most senior demographer at Statistics Norway, Lars Østby, published an op-ed in the liberal weekly newspaper *Morgenbladet* in which he concluded that on the basis of his own research into demographic trends in the Norwegian population of immigrant background, 7 per cent of the population would be Muslim by 2060 (Østby 2011).

34 Given the serious human rights violations of the Iranian Islamist regime, with which this author professes no sympathies whatsoever, one could argue that this hardly takes much doing at all, but this is of course not the point here.

35 In the context of the liberal defence of murder among prominent US intellectuals during the 'war on terror', Tony Judt wrote that 'long nostalgic for the comforting verities of a simpler time, today's liberal intellectuals have at last discovered a sense of purpose: They are at war with "Islamo-fascism"' (Judt 2008: 386). Though the latter term has never been popular among Norwegian newspaper reporters and editors, the comment is certainly apposite in the Norwegian context too.

36 My interpretation of this is inspired by Gardell (2011).

5 Dusklands

1 Vaïsse (2010) provides a short and precise rebuttal of the main claims of the 'Eurabia' genre.

2 To her close friend and associate

Spencer, Bat Ye'or is 'the great historian of dhimmitude' (Spencer 2005: 31); to Manji she is 'an Egyptian-born European scholar' (Manji 2004: 61); and to Bruce Bawer, who has also been in close contact with her over the years, she is 'an historian' (Bawer 2006: 32). Academic laurels come easily in the mutual admiration society of 'Eurabia' authors. Hence to Bawer, Robert Spencer, who has no academic qualifications whatsoever in Islamic studies or related fields, is also an 'Islam expert' (ibid.: 218).

3 Littman's own curriculum vitae at a website she and her husband maintained, www.dhimmitude.org/d_bycv. html, makes much of these appearances, yet as Duin (2002) reported, at Georgetown University in 2002 a number of students, including students of a Jewish background, walked out of her lecture in protest. Littman's testimony to the Senate Foreign Relations Committee was in fact a testimony to the Near East and South Asia Subcommittee in a hearing on 'religious persecution in the Middle East', whereas her testimony to the Congressional Human Rights Caucus in 2002 was on 'human rights and the concept of jihad'.

4 See David G. Littman's contributions to the edited volume *The Myth of Islamic Tolerance: How Islamic Law Treats Non-Muslims* by Robert Spencer (Spencer 2005) for details on this.

5 From the list of contributors in Spencer (2005: 592) one learns that he, together with close associate René Wadlow, represented the Association for World Education at the UCHR in Geneva (www.awe-international.com/), as well as the World Union for Progressive Judaism (www.wupj.org/index. asp). What is less well known is that in 1961 David G. Littman, representing a cover organization, the Oeuvre Suisse de Secours aux Enfants de l'Afrique du Nord (OSSEAN), and his wife Gisèle were involved in a Mossad-led operation to evacuate some 530 Jewish children from Morocco to Israel via Switzerland. Littman and his wife, who were based in Casablanca, posed as Christians during this operation. In 2009, David G. Littman was awarded the 'Hero of Silence' Order by the Israeli president Shimon Peres for his part in Operation Mural; www.newenglishreview. org/David_G._Littman/Conferring_ the_%22Hero_of_Silence%22_Order_on_ David_G._Littman_(July_1,_2009)/.

6 For two reviews of her work by a historian, see Betts (1997) and Griffith (1998). See Sells (2003) for a critical exploration of her work.

7 Ferguson's commitment to Bat Ye'or's work in particular and the Eurabia genre in general is long standing. 'Eurabia', an op-ed by Ferguson, was published in 2004 (Ferguson 2004). In company with Martin Gilbert, Daniel Pipes and Bruce Bawer, Ferguson provided a blurb for Bat Ye'or's 2005 book *Eurabia: The Euro-Arab Axis* (Ye'or 2005a); Ferguson writes that 'no writer has done more than Bat Ye'or to draw attention to the menacing character of Islamic extremism. Future historians will one day regard her coinage of the term "Eurabia" as prophetic. Those who wish to live in a free society must be eternally vigilant. Bat Ye'or's vigilance is unrivalled.' For incisive critiques of Ferguson's recent work, see Mishra (2011) and Bromwich (2011).

8 In an unpublished paper, Hetland (2011) notes that among right-wing intellectuals and writers who often appear in 'Fjordman's' texts are Alain Finkelkraut, Roger Scruton, William S. Lind, Ibn Warraq (a pseudonym), Robert Spencer, Andrew Bostom, Sigurd Skirbekk, Lars Hedegaard, Serge Trifković, Theodore Dalrymple, Ali Sina, Hugh Fitzgerald,

Bernard Lewis and Daniel Pipes. In communication with Sætre (2013a: 106–7), Jensen asserted that he had started reading Ibn Warraq's texts at the university library at the American University of Cairo after 9/11, and discovered Ali Sina's texts through him.

9 The notion of a Judaeo-Christian civilization is, as Mark Silk has demonstrated, a quintessentially modern one, invented by liberal Protestant theologians in the USA since the 1930s (Silk 1984: 70–1). Though aimed at a laudable unity and reconciliation between Christians and Jews under and after the horrors unleashed by European Nazis against Jews in that period, the very notion of a Judaeo-Christian civilization risks underplaying the extent to which European Jews were construed as 'the other' of European nationalism until our own age, and persecuted and stigmatized in far wider circles.

10 That is, the precursor to the European Union (EU).

11 The OIC, established in 1969, is an interstate organization of mostly Muslim countries, headquartered in Riyadh in Saudi Arabia.

12 I thank Pål Norheim for this point, made in a critical review of Ye'or's work published in a Norwegian journal in 2011 (Norheim 2011).

13 The only reference to the speech that the author has been able to find through online searches is to a republication in *Lebanon News*, 8(1), 14 September 1985, pp. 1–2.

14 See Trifković's comments on Sherman's 'legacy' at www.balkanstudies. org/sites/default/files/newsletter/ Sherman%20Legacy.pdf.

15 See www.dhimmi.org/LectureE1. html for the original text.

16 For a more extensive exploration of conspiracy theories, see Sunstein and Vermeule (2009).

17 Other key writers in the Eurabia genre are: the late Italian Oriana Fallaci (*The Rage and the Pride*, *The Force of Reason*), the Briton Melanie Phillips (*Londonistan*), the American Robert Spencer (*Stealth Jihad: How Radical Islam is Subverting America without Guns or Bombs*), the Canadian Mark Steyn (*America Alone: The End of the World as We Know It*) and the American-Norwegian Bruce Bawer (*While Europe Slept: How Radical Islam is Destroying the West from Within*, *Surrender: Appeasing Islam, Sacrificing Freedom*). (See Carr 2006.) Less well known is French author Sylvain Besson (*La Conquête de l'Occident: Le projet secret des Islamistes*). Strong echoes of the Eurabia thesis are also found in the work of Somali-born atheist Ayaan Hirsi Ali's works (see Ali 2010), the work of her husband, Professor Niall Ferguson (see Ferguson 2011), and the work of Christopher Caldwell (see Caldwell 2009).

18 Røe Isaksen's comments at the launch are available at konservativ. no/2013/02/demokrati-eller-islamisme/.

19 In recent years, and since his retirement from Norwegian politics, Berg has combined writing for folkloristic publications with chairmanship of a local branch of the strongly pro-Israeli and evangelical Christian organization With Israel for Peace (*Med Israel for Fred*, MIFF).

20 It would, of course, be an understatement to say that Berg's caricatures have little to do with any discernible reality in Norway or elsewhere: multiculturalism can hardly be said to be about recognizing all particularities as equally valid or a normative cultural relativism; the majority of Norwegians who on two occasions (1974 and 1994) voted down membership of the EEC or EU were hardly described as xenophobes, and the 90 per cent of Norwegians surveyed

who favour curbs on immigration have only rarely been described as racist.

21 Berg's reference here is to the blog HonestThinking, a Norwegian blog run by the most well-known biological racist in Norway, Ole Jørgen Anfindsen.

22 On page 102, Berg even alleges that the state of Bangladesh practises Islamic *hudud* punishments such as stoning and cutting off limbs. It appears that Berg may here be confusing Bangladesh with Pakistan under the military dictatorship of Zia ul-Haq from 1980 to 1988.

23 Compare Bawer (2012b) and Storhaug (2012) for this.

24 See the link at internationalfreepresssociety.wordpress.com/board-of-advisors/.

25 In Denmark, Krarup, an MP for the DPP since 2001, is known for having compared the opposition to the presence of Muslims in Denmark to opposition to the German Nazi occupation of Denmark in the years 1940 to 1945, and for having compared the Muslim hijab to the Nazi swastika (Hervik 2011: 1). He self-identifies as a 'national conservative', whereas his daughter Winkel Holm self-identifies as a 'cultural conservative'.

26 In an interview after the assassination attempt on Hedegaard broadcast on the programme *Deadline* on Danish television on 17 March 2013, the distinguished Danish reporter Martin Krasnik did what few Norwegian media editors and reporters have bothered to do, namely to confront the 'Islam critic' Hedegaard with some of his most extreme statements on Islam and Muslims, and those of his fellow travellers among counter-jihadists. See: www.youtube.com/watch?v=YsfNyYQ81yM.

27 The nomination of Bawer's 2006 book for this award generated a heated public debate among the twenty-four board members of the National Book Critics Circle, with Eliot Weinberger

charging that Bawer had engaged in 'racism as criticism' and the president of the board, John Freeman, asserting that he had 'never been more embarrassed by a choice [of nominees]', on the grounds that this book is 'hyperventilated rhetoric [which] tips from actual critique into Islamophobia' (Cohen 2007). For his part, Robert Spencer, named by Bawer as an 'Islam expert' (Bawer 2009: 218) in his book, declared in a laudatory review in Daniel Pipes' *Middle East Quarterly* that 'the suicide of Europe that Bawer so ably recounts is yet in the process of playing itself out' (Spencer 2007).

28 True to the low standards of documentation and referencing which characterize the 'Eurabia' genre, Bawer of course never provides references to the 'polls' he refers to.

29 Here, too, Bawer does not provide any references whatsoever, so it is well nigh impossible for the reader to ascertain which 'estimates' he refers to.

30 Note here the structural resemblances between the claims of 'Fjordman' and his Danish friends about the 9/11 'celebrations' in Cairo, Egypt.

31 Allegations of assaults by homophobic Muslim male youth, whether in Oslo or Amsterdam, form part of the standard repertoire in Bawer's books. In *While Europe Slept*, there are two such allegations recorded from Oslo alone. But as far as can be ascertained, Bawer and his Norwegian partner have never reported any of these instances to local police, nor has anyone been charged with hate crimes against Bawer or his partner. This is not to suggest that Muslim homophobia in Norway does not exist and is not a potential threat to gays.

32 Bawer, for his part, is of course also 'vigorous' in his misrepresentations of Norway and its people. Zahir Mukhtar

is not of 'Norway's Muslim Council' (Bawer 2009: 197); the *Klassekampen* newspaper is not a 'Communist newspaper' (ibid.: 196). Former Norwegian prime minister Kåre Willoch, from the Conservative Party, has never 'explicitly rejected the right of Israel to exist' (ibid.: 152); the Norwegian Press Complaints Commission is not an arm of the Norwegian government, but is controlled by the Norwegian media (ibid.: 49); and Lena Larsen, a Norwegian convert to Islam, has never been on record as saying that her ideal is a 'sharia state' (ibid.: 96).

33 Bawer had evidently discovered in the three years since 2006 that 'Islamization', and not 'Islamicization', was the correct term for what he describes.

34 The term 'quisling' has by chance also been a standard and favourite term of Bawer's friend and associate Hege Storhaug of the HRS. See Storhaug (2011a) for an example.

35 In the passages on his relationship with 'Fjordman' (a 'polite, friendly, smart, serious' man 'who knew what he was talking about when he talked about Arabic culture and Islam'), Bawer also admits that he was the one who introduced 'Fjordman' to Bat Ye'or and Robert Spencer at a conference in The Hague in the Netherlands in 2006.

36 Personal information from Ammar Hamdan at al-Jazeera's office in Oslo, Norway, September 2011.

37 See Bangstad and Bunzl (2010).

38 At Godlia Cinema in eastern Oslo, PP Member of Parliament Øystein Hedstrøm addressed a secret meeting of the Norwegian Society (Den Norske Forening) on 2 September 1995. *Dagbladet*, which had undercover reporters at the meeting, published a news item on the meeting on its front page on 3 September 1995. Among the members of the nationalist right-wing scene present at Godlia was Bastian Heide, convicted of racism and for making bomb threats against the multicultural Sagene School in Oslo in 1984; Erik Gjems Onstad, a former PP member who supported the apartheid regime in South Africa, and was active in FMI in the 1980s and 1990s; and Jack Erik Kjuus, later to be convicted for racism in 1997.

39 A copy of the letter, obtained from the Norwegian Ministry of Culture under a Freedom of Information Act in 2010, is in the author's possession.

40 In a pointed response, the Norwegian editor of the anti-fascist magazine *Monitor*, Tor Bach, argued that al-Kubaisi was part of a 'whitewashing of extremists' (Bach 2005).

41 One might legitimately ask here, with French philosopher Jacques Derrida (2001): what gives anyone the right to forgive on behalf of the perpetrator in the absence of the victim?

42 Al-Kubaisi was raised in Baghdad, Iraq, then under secular Baathist rule. In light of the severe repression of all opposition forces under Saddam Hussein's regime, not least among them Sunni or Shia Islamist forces, it is of course more than fanciful to believe that al-Kubaisi had any personal insight into Islamism by virtue of his upbringing. For detailed accounts of this repression, see Tripp (2000); Fisk (2005); Cockburn (2008).

43 Another theme developed by neoliberal ideologue Paul Berman in his 2003 bestseller, but unlike al-Kubaisi, Berman also lumps together the secular and socialist Iraqi Baathism of Saddam Hussein and Islamism. After Norway's 22/7, al-Kubaisi took this one step farther, by declaring in a debate at the student society at NTNU in Trondheim that 'Islamism' was akin to 'Nazism'. I thank Professor Ulrika Mårtensson at NTNU for this information.

44 The idea of Islamism as the

equivalent of fascism features prominently in US neoconservative discourses, represented by Norman Podhoretz's call to arms for a 'World War IV' against an alleged 'Islamo-fascism' (Podhoretz 2007), which was picked up by Republican president George W. Bush. The analogy between Islamism and fascism has also been appropriated by neoliberal Paul Berman (Berman 2010). Al-Kubaisi's denunciations of a supposed appeasement of Islamism on the part of the left has been a staple of US neoconservative discourse for years (Vaïsse 2010) and is echoed by Bawer (Bawer 2009) as well as Berman (Berman 2010).

45 Akef, who was selected as the 'Supreme Guide' (*murshid al-amm*) of the Muslim Brothers in 2004, and served in that position until his voluntary retirement as the first Supreme Guide to leave office before his death, was a one-time member of the Muslim Brother's military 'secret apparatus' (*al-jihaz al-sirri*), founded in 1942 or 1943, and served twenty years in prison from 1954 to 1974 (Wickham 2013: 26, 102, 129). According to Wickham, Akef's reign as Supreme Guide saw a strengthening of the conservative old guard's powers within the highest body of the Muslim Brothers, the Guidance Bureau, and the marginalizing of younger reformists.

46 MEMRI (Middle East Media Research Institute) was founded in Washington, DC, in 1998, by Yigal Carmon, formerly a high-ranking officer in the Israeli army's Intelligence Services. It was launched with the aim of 'informing the debate over US policy in the Middle East and selects and translates news items from Arab and Iranian media into various languages'. As several commentators have noted, it is not unreasonable to see MEMRI as a propaganda arm of the Israeli state, notwithstanding the fact that MEMRI

has established an important inventory of modern and contemporary Arab anti-Semitism and anti-Westernism. See Achcar (2010: 181–2).

47 The public intellectuals in question were Abid Raja (1975–), a prominent lawyer and politician for the social liberal left (Venstre) party, and Mohammed Usman Rana (1985–), a medical doctor of a liberal-conservative persuasion, who have both been prominent in public debates on Muslims and integration in Norway in recent years.

48 For a study of the *wasatiyya* trend, see Browers (2009). The claim that Ramadan 'represents' the MB is also hard to square with the criticisms of MB in Ramadan (2012).

49 Notes by Sindre Bangstad: from the launch of *Gender Me*, a documentary on gay Muslims by Norwegian-Turkish film-maker Nefise Özkal Lorentzen (1964–) at Vika Cinema in Oslo in 2008. Al-Kubaisi introduced the film at this launch, which was funded by Fritt Ord.

50 Statistical data suggest that women originating in countries where Islam is the main religion who settled in Norway have a slower process of approximation to average Norwegian fertility patterns (Østby 2004: 127). Women from Somalia (3.7 children per woman in 2002), Pakistan (3.5 children per woman in 2002) and Iraq (3.1 children per woman in 2002) have significantly higher fertility patterns than average Norwegians (2.1 children per woman in 2002) (ibid.: 127–9). However, there is a clear tendency towards convergence with average Norwegian fertility patterns with increased time of residence, from first to second generation, and with higher levels of female education and labour market participation among Muslim women in Norway. Østby's nuanced accounts of Muslim fertility patterns and demographics in

Norway have led to him receiving death threats.

51 Zainab al-Ghazali (1917–2005) was an Egyptian Islamic activist and proselytizer (*dai'iya*) imprisoned for her MB activities for six years under Gamal 'Abd al-Nasir. The daughter of a prominent Egyptian cotton merchant educated at al-Azhar University, in 1935 she was briefly a member of the Egyptian Feminist Union established by Huda Sha'rawi in 1923. Al-Ghazali left the EFU over the organization's secular orientation, and established the Muslim Women's Society (Jama'at al-Sayyidat al-Muslimat, MWS) the same year. In 1948, al-Ghazali brought the MWS under the umbrella of Hassan al-Banna's MB. I have found no evidence to the effect that al-Ghazali had anything to do with the invention of the modern hijab, which unlike the hijab traditionally worn by Egyptian women leaves the woman's face uncovered. For al-Ghazali, see Ahmed (1992); Badran (1995, 2009); Mahmood (2005: 67–70).

52 The modern hijab in Egypt was officially introduced by the secular-oriented and feminist Huda Sha'rawi (1879–1947), who very publicly and to great scandal dropped her facial veil (niqab) upon her return from an international feminist congress in Paris in 1925 (see Badran 1995, 2009). Egyptian anthropologist Fadwa al-Guindi has documented that the so-called *al-ziyy al-Islami* emerged among young Islamic female activists (*al-mitdayyin*, later *al-islamiyyin*) at Egyptian colleges in the 1970s (El-Guindi 1999). This modern variety consists of an *al-jilbab*, an unfitted, long-sleeved, ankle-length gown in austere and solid colours and thick opaque fabric, and an *al-khimar*, a headcover that covers the hair and extends to the forehead, comes under the chin to conceal the neck, and falls down over the chest and back (ibid.: 133–4, 143). This modern variety of the hijab is by no means the most common among Norwegian hijab-wearers at present. It is factually correct, however, that the popularity of its usage increased dramatically on the back of the peaceful re-Islamization of Egyptian society from the Arab Crisis of 1967 and onwards, and that MB activists played an important part in its popularization (see Ahmed 2011 for this).

6 The weight of words

1 For some examples of this spurious line of argumentation, which conflates protections against racist and/or discriminatory speech with protections against 'blasphemy' in the Norwegian context in recent years, see Rønning and Wessel-Aas (2011), Rossavik (2012) and Larsen (2012).

2 See Appiah (2012) for a good and nuanced legal-philosophical critique of the concept of 'defamation of religion', which the Organization of Islamic Co-operation (formerly the Organization of the Islamic Conference, OIC) has since the Durban Conference in 2001 sought to criminalize through initiatives in various UN bodies.

3 The term 'racism paragraph' is in fact a bit of a misnomer, inasmuch as the paragraph in question also covers public expressions of discriminatory attitudes that cannot *strictu sensu* be qualified as 'racist'. Paragraph §135(a) covers expressions which threaten or harass another person, or which advocate hatred, persecution or contempt against persons on account of their (a) skin colour, ethnic or national origin; (b) religion or view of life; or (c) homosexual inclination, lifestyle or orientation. In an amendment to §135(a) adopted by the Norwegian parliament in 2009, but which at the

time of writing in 2013 is still to take legal effect, expressions targeting a person's 'reduced functional ability' were included in the paragraph's remit under (d). Such expressions have to be 'public' in order to be criminal, or in other words to 'reach a greater number of people'; moreover, symbols are also included in its remit. Contributions to such expressions are also liable to criminalization under the paragraph, and the maximum penalty under the paragraph is three years of imprisonment. When the 2009 amendments enter into effect alongside the new Norwegian General Penal Code, §135(a) will become §185(a).

4 See Høyesterett Rt. 1981-1305 (the Vivi Krogh Case).

5 See, for instance, Dworkin (2006).

6 Cass Sunstein (1993) argues that there are five defining claims that are central to what he refers to as 'free speech absolutism' in the US context. These can be summarized as (1) Any effort to regulate speech, by the nation or the states, threatens the principle of free expression; (2) All speech stands on the same footing (i.e. 'viewpoint absolutism'); (3) Free expression is not limited to 'political speech'; (4) Any restrictions on speech, once permitted, have a sinister and nearly inevitable tendency to expand; and (5) 'Balancing of competing interests ought so far as possible not to play any role in free speech law' (ibid.: 5–6).

7 For the purposes of this book, I prefer the term 'racist and/or discriminatory speech' to 'hate speech', since the latter is arguably 'too broad a designation to be usefully analysed as a single category' (see Young 2011: 385).

8 See Ronald Dworkin, 'Speech at the "Challenges to multiculturalism. A conference on migration, citizenship and free speech"', 25/26 June 2012, Oslo, www.youtube.com/watch?v=6wJQ658e-4

U&list=PL686F0E2B94DC818D&index=5 &feature=plpp_video.

9 www.politi.no/vedlegg/lokale_ vedlegg/politidirektoratet/Vedlegg_1022. pdf.

10 See Øyvind Strømmen in Lepperød (2011) for one recognized and much-used Norwegian expert on right-wing extremism who advances this view with no reference to any empirical research whatsoever.

11 See: www.fritt-ord.no/images/ uploads/ytringsfrihetsbarometeret_ presentasjon).pdf for the full report.

12 In January 2013, two central MPs of the Progress Party in Norway made it clear to the Norwegian media that they would make sure that the Norwegian Centre Against Racism would no longer receive any state funding owing to their alleged 'lack of neutrality' should the party come to power after the parliamentary elections of September 2013. This threat was issued after a report from the Norwegian Centre Against Racism published in 2012 had noted in a footnote that the precursor to the PP, the Anders Langes Party (ALP), may have received funding from the Ministry of Information in apartheid South Africa (see Steen et al. 2013). The PP's two MPs backed down from the threat only when spokespersons for its would-be partners in government, the Conservative Party, made it clear that they opposed such measures.

13 For a good account of dignity discourses in the contemporary era, see Rosen (2012).

14 The 'more speech' argument in legal circles often refers back to Louis D. Brandeis' (1856–1941) concurring opinion in *Whitney* v. *California* (1927), in which Brandeis argued that: '[i]f there be time to expose through discussion the falsehood and fallacies, to avert the evil by process of education, the remedy to

be applied is more speech, not enforced silence'. See, for example, Obama (2012) and Cole (2012) for contemporary lines of argumentation which can be traced back to Brandeis.

15 See assidiq.com/?p=855.

16 This has been amply documented by writers from Viktor Klemperer (2006 [1957]) to Philip Gourevitch (1998) to Alexander L. Hinton (Hinton 2002).

17 See Høyesterett HR-2012-00689-A (Saks nr. 2012/143), 30 March 2012, www.lovdata.no/hr/hr-2012-00689-a.html.

18 On the website of his neo-Nazi organization and on mainstream newspaper discussion forums, Tvedt, a middle-aged neo-Nazi with a long record of racist and discriminatory speech, asserted in a 2003 interview with *VG* that Jews are 'parasites whom we must cleanse'.

19 In its sixty-fifth session in 2005, the UN-CERD Committee found that the verdict of the Norwegian Supreme Court in the Sjølie case violated Articles 4 and 6 of the 1966 International Convention on the Elimination of All Forms of Racial Discrimination (ICERD); it called upon Norwegian authorities to 'take measures to ensure that statements such as those made by Sjølie in the course of his speech [in 2000] are not protected by freedom of speech under Norwegian law'. These UN-CERD Committee findings are not necessarily binding for signatory states.

20 ECRI (The European Commission Against Racism and Intolerance), a monitoring body working under the auspices of the Council of Europe and established in 1993, issues regular reports on situations concerning racism and discrimination in the Council of Europe's member countries.

21 The Holgersen Commission, which had been appointed by the Nor-

wegian Ministry for Municipalities and Provinces in 2000 and led by Professor of Law and Norwegian ECRI rapporteur Gudrun Holgersen from the University of Bergen, presented its report in 2002.

22 See: www.oslohoyre.no/wp-content/uploads/2013/10/plattform.pdf.

23 As several of Salman Rushdie's supporters in the Arab and Muslim world noted at the time, Khomeini's fatwa (legal edict) did not qualify as such: it failed to adhere to procedural rules and conventions for issuing fatwas; it implied that it was binding also on Muslims who did not follow Khomeini as a *faqih* (Islamic jurisconsult); and it was non-rescindable – see al-Azm (1994) and Mozaffari (1997). It has been argued that the 'fatwa' against Rushdie was in reality an expression of *firmans* in Persian tradition (Mozaffari 1997), whereby a secular ruler has the right to condemn to death anyone who insults him personally. According to established academic convention, however, it has become known as the 'fatwa against Rushdie', and I have therefore opted to retain this usage.

24 The two most prominent members of the Islamic Defence Council were Pakistani-born Alama Mushtaq Ahmed Chisti (d. 2002) of the Central Jamaat-e-Ahl-e-Sunnat in Oslo, a Sufi-oriented mosque congregation, and former Norwegian-born Maoist-Leninist turned convert to Islam and Khomeinist Trond Ali Lindstad, a medical doctor by profession. Divisions within the council soon became apparent when Lindstad maintained his unequivocal support for Ayatollah Khomeini's call for Rushdie's murder (Austenå 2011: 77, 81) and Chisti asserted that it would be impermissible to do so in a country in which this was in clear violation of the law (ibid.: 75). Following divisions over the appropriateness of the legal route, the

Islamic Defence Council had decided by 1991 not to pursue a blasphemy charge against Rushdie's Norwegian publishers (ibid.: 85).

25 The fact that this reflects at best a superficial or at worst a non-existent knowledge of traditions of debate and dissent in Islamic history on the part of the authors need not concern us here. Internal normative pluralism (*ikhtilaf* in Arabic) is an accepted principle in Islamic jurisprudence (see El Fadl 2001), and dissent or heresy (*zandaqa* in Arabic) existed in the Arab Muslim world when it was virtually non-existent in Europe (Majid 2007: 13–14).

26 Bleich (2011b: 22–3) argues that the opposite is in fact the case when it comes to racist and/or discriminatory speech in ECHtR jurisprudence.

27 I thank the husband of commission member Nazneen Khan-Østrem, Olav Østrem, for providing crucial information on this during an interview in 2011.

28 Skirbekk, who is now professor emeritus at the University of Bergen, has been a member of a number of government-appointed commissions through his career. Politically, he is aligned with the right wing of the governing Labour Party. Skirbekk has on a number of occasions expressed concern over the presence of Muslims in Norway in particular, many of whom in his view have not undergone sufficient 'modernization of consciousness' (see Skirbekk 2009). His son, Tarjei Skirbekk, was for a number of years a personal adviser to Norway's foreign minister, Jonas Gahr Støre. See also Bangstad (2013) for Skirbekk's role in relation to the promotion of a prominent Norwegian contributor to the 'Eurabia' genre, Walid al-Kubaisi.

29 The commission did not call for the abolition of Norway's so-called 'racism' paragraph (§ 135 [a] in the Norwegian General Penal Code) in its recommendations, but argued that legal protections targeting individuals' religious beliefs should be exempt from criminal liability. This recommendation was never adopted by the Norwegian government, but is, in an era in which all xenophobic and Islamophobic movements in Norway claim to be engaged in a 'critique of religion', an indication that the commission aimed to weaken minorities' legal protection against racist and discriminatory speech.

30 For updated academic discussions of the concept of the modern public sphere and religion, see Butler et al. (2011).

31 Yates (2007) argues, however, that the burden Habermas imposes is still assymetrical and heavily weighted in favour of secularists, even in Habermas's post-secular phase.

32 I am leaving aside here the question of whether the very translation of Habermas's original term *Öffentlichkeit* (i.e. publicness) into the English term 'the public sphere' causes part of the misapprehension of Habermas's work on the theme by an academic audience basing their work on the English version of Habermas's 1962 book (cf. Peters 1993 and Mah 2000).

33 This standard feminist critique may not be completely fair to Habermas's original account. After all, he does refer to the very exclusion of women in several paragraphs in his 1962 work (see Habermas 1991 [1962]: 56, 73 for two examples).

34 Though it should be noted that Habermas's original account refers to 'the fiction of the *one* public' (Habermas's own emphasis) (Habermas 1991 [1962]: 56), thus suggesting that he was perfectly aware of the problematic.

35 See www.internationalfree presssociety.org/2012/02/the-free-

press-comes-to-sweden-by-the-editors-of-sappho-dk/.

36 See Runciman (2008) for an excellent study of the history of political hypocrisy.

37 Media representatives are in a majority on the PCC in Norway, and the representatives of civil society and other sectors on the PCC are person-ally nominated by the chairman of the Norwegian Press Association. The PCC means of sanctioning media outlets that violate basic ethical standards are limited to a public rebuke. Norwegian media editors often keen to criticize politicians and bureaucrats for a lack of adherence to principles of basic divi-sions of power have vigorously defended this system, which is very obviously geared to protect their own interests, and not those of the public they purport to serve.

38 For the case in question in a Norwegian summary from the PCC, see: www.pfu.no/case.php?id=2707.

39 With reference to the US Supreme Court verdict in *Brandenburg* v. *Ohio* (1969), in which the court held that in order for a person to be convicted for incitement to a violation of the law under the US First Amendment, the un-lawful action must be both 'immanent' and 'likely'. These terms are of course anything but unambiguous, and in *Hess* v. *Indiana* (1973), the court furthermore held that incitement to an illegal action in some indefinite future time was legally permissible.

REFERENCES

N.B.: Æ, Ø, Å are (in that order) the last letters of the Norwegian alphabet

Aagedal, O., P. K. Botvar and I. M. Høeg (eds) (2013) *Den offentlige sorgen: Markeringer, ritualer og religion etter 22. juli* [Public mourning: commemorations, rituals and religion after 22 July], Oslo: Universitetsforlaget.

Aardal, B. (1999) *Velgere i 90-årene* [Voters in the 1990s], Oslo: NKS-Forlaget.

— (2011) 'Folkeopinionen – demokratiets grunnvoll' [Public opinion – the foundation of democracy], in B. Aardal (ed.), *Det politiske landskapet. En studie av stortingsvalget 2009* [The political landscape. A study of the parliamentary election of 2009], Oslo: Cappelen Damm.

Aardal, B. et al. (2007) 'Valgundersøkelsen' [The electoral survey], Report no. 31/2007, Oslo and Kongsvinger: SSB/Statistics Norway.

Aase, T. H. (1992) *Punjabi Practices of Migration: Punjabi Life Projects in Pakistan and Norway*, Unpublished Dr Polit dissertation in Social Anthropology, University of Bergen, Norway.

Abu-Lughod, L. (2013) *Do Muslim Women Need Saving?*, Cambridge, MA, and London: Harvard University Press.

Achcar, G. (2010) *The Arabs and the Holocaust: The Arab–Israeli War of Narratives*, trans. G. M. Goshgarian, New York: Metropolitan Books.

Adams, T. (2011) 'Why anger is all the rage', *Guardian Weekly*, 2 September.

Adamson, F. B. (2011) 'Engaging or contesting the liberal state? "Muslim" as a politicised identity category in Europe', *Journal of Ethnic and Migration Studies*, 37(6): 899–915.

Aftenposten (2011a) 'Overlevende raser mot NRK' [Survivors rage against the NRK], *Aftenposten.no*, 7 August.

— (2011b) 'Uakseptabel sjikane mot Tybring-Gjedde' [Unacceptable harassment of Tybring-Gjedde], *Aftenposten.no*, 7 December.

Agderposten (1993) 'Dette har skjedd' [This has happened], *Agderposten*, 12 July.

Ahmed, L. (1992) *Women and Gender in Islam: Historical Roots of a Modern Debate*, New Haven, CT, and London: Yale University Press.

— (2011) *A Quiet Revolution: The Veil's Resurgence, from the Middle East to America*, New Haven, CT, and London: Yale University Press.

Akkerman, T. and A. Hagelund (2007) 'Women and children first! Anti-immigration parties and gender in Norway and the Netherlands', *Patterns of Prejudice*, 41(2): 197–214.

Al-Azm, S. J. (1994) 'Is the *fatwa* a *fatwa*?', in A. Abdallah (ed.), *For Rushdie: A collection of essays by 100 Arabic and Muslim writers*, New York: George Braziller Inc., pp. 21–4.

Ali, A. H. (2010) *Nomad: A Personal Journey through the Clash of Civilizations*, London and New York: Simon and Schuster.

Ali, W. et al. (2011) *Fear Inc. The Roots of the Islamophobia Network in America*, Washington, DC: Center for American Progress.

Al-Jazeera (2012) 'US blacklists Syrian rebel group al-Nusra', *Al-Jazeera.com*, 11 December.

Al-Kubaisi, W. (1996) *Min Tro, din Myte. Islam møter norsk hverdag* [My faith, your myth. Islam meets Norwegian daily life], Oslo: Aventura.

— (2004) 'Den sanne historien om skaut og slør i islam' [The true story of the scarf and the veil in Islam], Op-ed, *Aftenposten*, 3 February.

— (2005) 'Norge for nordmenn' [Norway for Norwegians], *Klassekampen*, 5 February.

— (2009) 'Hijab er islamismens uniform' [The hijab is the uniform of Islamists], *Fritanke.no*, 11 February.

— (2010a) 'Djevelens verksted?' [The devil's own workshop], Op-ed, *Klassekampen*, 27 November.

— (2010b) 'Vår religiøse skjebne' [Our religious destiny], Op-ed, *Dagbladet*, 24 November.

— (2011) 'Myten om islamofobi' [The Islamophobia myth], *Opplystemuslimer.no*, 26 October.

Allen, C. (2010) *Islamophobia*, London: Ashgate.

Allevi, S. (2005) 'How the immigrant has become Muslim: public debates on Islam in Europe', *Revue européene des migrations internationales*, 21(2): 1–21.

Al-Rasheed, M. (2002) *A History of Saudi Arabia*, Cambridge: Cambridge University Press.

— (2007) *Contesting the Saudi State: Islamic Voices from a New Generation*, Cambridge: Cambridge University Press.

— (2013) *A Most Masculine State: Gender, Politics and Religion in Saudi Arabia*, Cambridge and New York: Cambridge University Press.

Alstadsæter, R. (2004) 'Hagen angrep islam' [Hagen attacked Islam], *Nrk.no*, 13 July.

Amundsen, P. W. (2010) 'Til kamp for friheten' [Onwards in the struggle for freedom], *Dagsavisen*, 6 December.

— (2011) 'Hvorfor jeg er kritisk til islam' [Why I am critical of Islam], *Aftenposten*, 16 December.

Andersen, B. (2012) 'Oslo is being ghettoized', in S. Indregard (ed.), *Motgift: Akademisk respons på den nye høyreekstremismen* [Counterpoison: academic responses to the new right-wing extremism], Oslo: Manifest/Flamme Forlag, pp. 172–86.

Andersen, I. et al. (2012) 'Breivik spanet på NRK-ansatte' [Breivik surveilled NRK-employees], *NRK.no*, 4 February.

Anderson, B. (1983) *Imagined Communities: Reflections on the Origin and Spread of Nationalism*, London and New York: Verso.

Appadurai, A. (2006) *Fear of Small Numbers: An Essay on the Geography of Anger*, Durham, NC, and London: Duke University Press.

Appiah, K. A. (2005) *The Ethics of Identity*, Princeton, NJ: Princeton University Press.

— (2012) 'What's wrong with defamation of Religion?', in M. Herz and P. Molnar (eds), *The Content and Context of Hate Speech*, New York: Cambridge University Press, pp. 164–83.

Arendt, H. (2003 [1966]) 'Truth and politics', in H. Arendt (2003), *The Portable Hannah Arendt*, ed. and introduced by P. Baehr, New York and London: Penguin Press, pp. 545–76.

Art, D. (2011) *Inside the Radical Right: The Development of Anti-Immigrant Parties in Western Europe*, New York: Cambridge University Press.

Asad, T. (1990) 'Multiculturalism and British identity in the wake of the Rushdie Affair', *Politics and Society*, 18(4): 455–80.

— (1993) *Genealogies of Religion: Discipline and Reasons of Power in Christianity and Islam*, Baltimore, MD, and London: Johns Hopkins University Press.

— (2003) *Formations of the Secular. Christianity, Islam, Modernity*, Stanford, CA: Stanford University Press.

Asad, T. et al. (2009) 'Is critique secular? Blasphemy, injury and free speech', The Townsend Papers in Humanities no. 2, Berkeley: The Townsend Center for Humanities at the University of California – Berkeley.

Ash, T. G. (2011) 'The Internet nourished Norway's killer, but censorship would be folly', Op-ed, *Guardian*, 29 July.

Ashraf, F. A. (2012) 'Framtida fra Punjab' [The future from Punjab], Op-ed, *Dagbladet*, 16 November.

Assidiq, Y. B. (2013) 'Da jeg ble rekruttert av PST' [When I was recruited by the PST], *Aftenposten.no*, 20 February.

Austenå, A.-M. (2011) *Arven etter Sataniske Vers: den politiske kampen om ytringsfrihet og religion* [The legacy of *The Satanic Verses*: the political conflict over freedom of expression and religion], Oslo: Cappelen Damm.

Austin, J. L. (1962) *How to Do Things with Words*, The 1955 William James Lectures, 2nd edn, Oxford and New York: Oxford University Press.

Avelin, A. L. (2012) 'Buffermyten' [The buffer myth], *Dagsavisen*, 10 April.

Bach, T. (2005) 'Kubaisi hvitvasker ekstremister' [Kubaisi whitewashes extremists], *Klassekampen*, 29 April.

Bader, V., M. Maussen and A. Moors (eds) (2012) *Colonial and Post-Colonial Governance of Islam: Continuities and Ruptures*, Amsterdam: Amsterdam University Press.

Badran, M. (1995) *Feminists, Islam and Nation: Gender and the Making of Modern Egypt*, Princeton, NJ: Princeton University Press.

— (2009) *Feminism in Islam: Secular and Religious Convergences*, Oxford: Oneworld Publications.

Bail, C. A. (2012) 'The fringe effect: civil society organizations and the evolution of media discourse about Islam since the September 11th attacks', *American Sociological Review*, 77(6): 855–79.

Bakke, T. and E. Stabell (2013) 'Politikerne mest utsatt for hat fra høyreekstremister' [Politicians most exposed to hatred from right-wing extremists], *Nrk.no*, 17 July.

Bakkefoss, A. (2013) 'Bruker sosiale medier til å radikalisere unge muslimer og spre propaganda' [Uses social media in order to radicalize young Muslims and spread propaganda], *Aftenposten.no*, 12 January.

Balibar, É (1991) 'Is there a "neo-racism?"', in E. Balibar and I. Wallerstein, *Race, Nation Class: Ambiguous Identities*, London and New York: Verso.

Bangstad, S. (2009) 'Contesting secularism/s: Islam and secularism in the work of Talal Asad', *Anthropological Theory*, 9(2): 188–208.

— (2011) 'The morality police are coming! Muslims in Norway's media discourses', *Anthropology Today*, 27(5): 3–7.

— (2012a) 'Review of Chris Allen's *Islamophobia*', *Contemporary Islam Online First*.

— (2012b) 'Failing to protect minorities against racist and/or discriminatory speech? The case of Norway and §135(a) of the Norwegian General Penal Code', *Nordic Journal of Human Rights*, 30(4): 483–514.

— (2012c) 'Terror in Norway', *American Anthropologist*, 114(2): 351–2.

— (2013) 'Eurabia comes to Norway', *Islam and Christian–Muslim Relations*, 24(3): 1–23.

— (forthcoming) *The Politics of Mediated Presence: New Muslim Voices in Norwegian Mediated Public Spheres*, Scandinavian Academic Press.

Bangstad, S. and M. Bunzl (2010) '"Anthropologists are talking" about Islamophobia and anti-Semitism in the new Europe', *Ethnos*, 75(2): 213–28.

Bangstad, S. and M. Linge (2013) 'IslamNet-puritansk salafisme i Norge' [IslamNet – puritan Salafism in Norway], *Kirke og kultur*, 116(4): 254–71.

Banting, K. and W. Kymlicka (2006) 'Introduction: Multiculturalism and the welfare state: setting the context', in K. Banting and W. Kymlicka (eds), *Multiculturalism and the Welfare State: Recognition and Redistribution in Contemporary Democracies*, Oxford and New York: Oxford University Press, pp. 1–45.

Banting, K., S. Soroka and R. Johnston (2006) 'Do multiculturalism policies erode the welfare state? An empirical analysis', in K. Banting and W. Kymlicka (eds), *Multiculturalism and the Welfare State: Recognition and Redistribution in Contemporary Democracies*, Oxford and New York: Oxford University Press, pp. 49–91.

Barendt, E. (2011) 'Religious hatred laws: protecting groups or beliefs?', *Res Publica*, 17(1): 41–53.

Bar-On, T. (2011) 'Transnationalism and the French Nouvelle Droite', *Patterns of Prejudice*, 45(3): 199–203.

Barrett, R. J. (1996) *The Psychiatric Team and the Social Definition of Schizophrenia. An anthropological study of reason and illness*, Cambridge and New York: Cambridge University Press.

Barth, F. (1969) 'Introduction', in F. Barth (ed.), *Ethnic Groups and Boundaries: The Social Organization of Cultural Difference*, Boston, MA: Little, Brown & Co.

Bateson, G. (1935) 'Culture contact and schismogenesis', *Man*, 35(1): 178–83.

Bawer, B. (2006) *While Europe Slept: How Radical Islam is Destroying the West from Within*, New York and London: Doubleday.

— (2009) *Surrender: Appeasing Islam, Sacrificing Freedom*, New York: Doubleday.

— (2011) 'Inside the mind of the Oslo murderer', *Wall Street Journal*, 25 July.

— (2012a) *The New Quislings: How the International Left Used the Oslo Massacre to Silence Debate about Islam*, London and New York: HarperCollins.

— (2012b) 'Norwegian schools preach the wonders of niqab', *Front Page Magazine*, 10 January.

Bayat, A. (2007) *Making Islam Democratic: Social Movements and the Post-Islamist Turn*. Stanford, CA: Stanford University Press.

BBC (2010) 'Indian preacher Zakir Naik is banned from UK', www.bbc.co.uk, 18 June.

— (2013) '"Neo-Nazi" musician Vikernes in French terror arrest', www.bbc.co.uk, 16 July.

Beim, J. (2011) 'Pia Kjærsgaard angriber norsk søsterparti' [Pia Kjærsgaard attacks Norwegian sister party], *Politiken*, 2 August.

Berg, H. (2007) *Letter to Lady Liberty: Europe in Danger*, Oslo: Koloritt Forlag.

— (2011) 'Lite presist' [Not very precise], Letter to the editor, *Klassekampen*, 24 November.

— (2013) *Demokrati eller islamisme: Europa under islam?* [Democracy or Islamism: Europe under Islam?], Geilo: Hermon Forlag.

Berg, I. (2011) *Nettdebatt og demokrati: Styring eller anarki?* [Internet debate and democracy: governance or anarchy?], Unpublished MA dissertation in Political Science, University of Oslo, Norway.

Berg, J. and G. Ødegård (2012) 'Utøya-effekten som ikke forsvant' [The Utøya-effect which did not disappear], Op-ed, *Dagbladet*, 27 January.

Bergens Tidende (2011) 'Ansvar på ville

veier' [Responsibility derailed], Editorial, 7 December.

Berger, P. L., G. Davie and E. Fokas (2008) *Religious America, Secular Europe? A Theme and Its Variations*, Aldershot: Ashgate.

Berggren, H. (2010) *Underbara dagar framför oss: En biografi över Olof Palme* [Wondrous days ahead of us: a biography of Olof Palme], Stockholm: Norstedts.

Berglund, F., I. S. Reynert and B. Aardal (2011) 'Valgundersøkelsen 2009' [The electoral survey 2009], Oslo and Kongsvinger: SSB/Statistics Norway.

Bergsli, A. T. (2011) 'Gikk fra bombetrusler til parademarsj' [From bomb threats to parade march], *Dagsavisen*, 18 May.

Berlin, I. (1969) *Four Essays on Liberty*, Oxford: Oxford University Press.

Berman, P. (2003) *Terror and Liberalism*, New York: Norton.

— (2010) *The Flight of the Intellectuals*, New York: Mellville House.

Bernstein, R. (1990) 'The rising hegemony of the politically correct', *New York Times*, 28 October.

Berntzen, L. E. (2011) *Den eksistensielle trusselen. En sosiologisk studie av motstand mot islam, muslimsk kultur og innvandring til Norge* [The existential threat. A sociological study of opposition to Islam, Muslim culture and immigration in Norway], Unpublished MA thesis in Sociology, University of Bergen, Norway.

Berntzen, L. E. and S. Sandberg (2014) 'The collective nature of lone wolf terrorism: Anders Behring Breivik and the anti-Islamic social movement', *Terrorism and Political Violence*, www.tandfonline.com/doi/pdf/10.1080/09546553.2013.767245

Betts, R. B. (1997) 'Review of Bat Ye'or and Theodore Hall Patrick', *Middle East Policy*, 5(3): 200–3.

Betz, H.-G. (2013) 'Mosques, minarets, burqas and other essential threats: the populist right's campaign against Islam in western Europe', in R. Wodak, M. Khosravinik and B. Mral (eds), *Right-wing Populism in Europe: Politics and Discourse*, London and New York: Bloomsbury, pp. 71–89.

Bilgrami, A. (1992) 'What is a Muslim? Fundamental commitment and cultural identity', *Critical Inquiry*, 18(4): 821–42.

Bisgaard, A. B. (2010) 'Vil spre sunn frykt' [Wants to spread healthy fear], *Morgenbladet*, 3 December.

Bjurwald, L. (2011) *Europas skam: Rasister på fremmarsj* [Europe's shame: racists on the march], trans. from the Swedish by I. U. Gundersen, Oslo: Cappelen Damm.

Bjørklund, T. (1999) *Et lokalvalg i perspektiv* [A local election in perspective], Oslo: Tano Aschehoug.

Bleich, E. (2011a) 'What Is Islamophobia and how much is there? Theorizing and measuring an emerging comparative concept', *American Behavioral Scientist*, 55(12): 1581–1600.

— (2011b) *The Freedom to be Racist: How the United States and Europe Struggle to Preserve Freedom and Combat Racism*, New York and Oxford: Oxford University Press.

Blindheim, A. M. (2013) 'Her ligger FrPs dypeste hemmeligheter' [This is where the PP's deepest secrets are buried], *Dagbladet.no*, 25 May.

Blom, S. (2011) 'Holdninger til innvandrere og innvandring 2011' [Attitudes towards immigrants and immigration 2011], Oslo: SSB/Statistics Norway.

— (2012) 'Innvandreres bostedspreferanser – årsak til innvandrertett bosetning? Rapport 44/2012' [The residential preferences of immigrants – the cause of high residential density of immigrants?], Oslo and Kongsvinger: SSB/Statistics Norway.

Blom, S. and K. Henriksen (eds) (2008) *Levekår blant innvandrere i Norge 2005/2006* [Standards of living among immigrants in Norway 2005/06], Oslo and Kongsvinger: SSB/Statistics Norway, www.ssb.no/a/publikasjoner/pdf/rapp_200805/rapp_200805.pdf.

Borchgrevink, A. S. (2012) *En norsk tragedie. Anders Behring Breivik og veiene til Utøya*, Oslo: Gyldendal. English edn: *A Norwegian Tragedy: Anders Behring Breivik and the Massacre on Utøya*, Cambridge and Malden, MA: Polity Press.

Botvar, P. K. (2010) 'Endringer i nordmenns religiøse liv' [Changes in the religious lives of Norwegians], in P. K. Botvar and U. Schmidt (eds), *Religion i dagens Norge: Mellom sekularisering og sakralisering* [Religion in contemporary Norway: between secularization and sacralization], Oslo: Universitetsforlaget, pp. 11–24.

— (2012) 'Frivillighetens nye ansikt' [The new face of voluntary work], *Dagsavisen*, 20 January.

Bourdieu, P. (1978) *Outline of a Theory of Practice*, trans. R. Nice, Cambridge and New York: Cambridge University Press.

Bowen, J. R. (2005) 'Commentary on Bunzl', *American Ethnologist*, 32(4): 524–5.

— (2007) *Why the French Don't Like Headscarves: Islam, the State and Public Space*, Princeton, NJ: Princeton University Press.

— (2011) 'Europeans against multiculturalism', *Boston Review*, 36(4).

— (2012a) *Blaming Islam*, Cambridge, MA, and London: MIT Press.

— (2012b) *A New Anthropology of Islam*, Cambridge: Cambridge University Press.

Brandvold, Å. (2010b) 'Kulturell marxisme' [Cultural Marxism], *Klassekampen*, 16 September.

— (2011) 'Var det ord som drepte 22.juli?' [Did words kill on 22 July?], *Klassekampen*, 11 November.

— (2012) 'Ruvende løvemor' [Towering lioness], *Klassekampen*, 14 January.

Brandvold, Å. and L. M. Simenstad (2012) 'Quislings arvtakere i Norge' [The legatees of Quisling in Norway], *Klassekampen*, 1 February.

Brandvold, Å. and L. Torvaldsen (2013) '– Jeg støtter Breivik' [– I support Breivik], *Klassekampen*, 28 June.

Breivik, A. B. (2012) '22/7: Flere enn 200 løgner er identifisert i den rettspsykiatriskerapporten' [22/7: more than 200 lies identified in the psychiatric assessment to the court], *VG.no*, 4 April.

Brekke, T. (2005) 'Sinister nexus: USA, Norge og Krekar-saken' [Sinister nexus: USA, Norway and the Krekar case], *Internasjonal Politikk*, 63(2): 279–96.

— (2012) *Fundamentalism: Prophecy and Protest in an Age of Globalization*, Cambridge and New York: Cambridge University Press.

Brekke, T., B. Hagtvet and P. N. Waage (1994) *Den farlige ytringsfriheten* [The dangerous freedom of expression], Oslo: Cappelen.

Brenna, J. (2011) 'Forsvarer Lippestad mener at Fjordman og hans likesinnede må ta ansvar for at en gal mann gikk til angrep på 22.juli' [Defence lawyer Lippestad argues that Fjordman and his sympathizers must accept responsibility for the attack of a mad man on 22 July], *VG.no*, 6 December.

Brenna, J. and M. Hopperstad (2013) '16-åring reiste med storesøster for å hjelpe muslimer i Syria' [Sixteen-year-old travelled with her adult sister in order to assist Muslims in Syria], *VG.no*, 20 October.

Brenna, J. et al. (2011a) 'Breiviks mor

oppdaget våpen i 2010' [Breivik's mother discovered guns in 2010], *VG.no*, 23 December.

— (2011b) 'Lippestad: Du har et ansvar når du uttrykker deg på ekstrem måte' [Lippestad: You have a responsibility when you express yourself in an extreme manner], *VG.no*, 6 December.

Brettschneider, C. (2012) *When the State Speaks, What Should It Say? How Democracies Can Protect Expression and Promote Equality*, Princeton, NJ: Princeton University Press.

Brochmann, G. and K. Kjelstadli (2008) *A History of Immigration: The Case of Norway 900–2000*, Oslo: Universitetsforlaget.

Bromark, S. (2012) *Selv om sola ikke skinner. Et portrett av 22.juli* [Even if the sun doesn't shine. A portrait of 22 July], Oslo: Cappelen Damm.

Bromwich, D. (2011) 'The disappointed lover of the West', *New York Review of Books*, 58(19): 20–2.

Browers, M. L. (2009) *Political Ideology in the Arab World: Accommodation and Transformation*, Cambridge: Cambridge University Press.

Brown, A. (2011a) 'Anders Breivik's manifesto mapped', *Guardian*, 7 September.

— (2011b) 'Anders Breivik's spider web of hate', *Guardian*, 7 September.

Brown, W. (2006) *Regulating Aversion: Tolerance in the Age of Identity and Empire*, Princeton, NJ, and Oxford: Princeton University Press.

Brox, J. (2011) 'Fjordman jobba i Hebron' [Fjordman worked in Hebron], *Klassekampen*, 8 August.

Bruce, S. (2004) *God is Dead: Secularization in the West*, London: Blackwell.

Bruknapp, G. (2009) *Hatkriminalitet* [Hate criminality], Unpublished MA dissertation in Sociology, University of Oslo.

Brunborg, H. and I. Texmon (2010) 'Befolkningsframskrivninger 2010–2060' [Population projections 2010–2060], Økonomiske analyser [Economic analyses], 4/2010.

Buan, V. (2011) 'PST: Flere trusler på nettet etter 22.juli' [PST: More threats on the internet after 22 July], *Aftenposten*, 7 December.

Bunzl, M. (2007) *Anti-Semitism and Islamophobia: Hatreds Old and New in Europe*, Chicago, IL: Prickly Paradigm Press.

Buruma, I. (2006) *Murder in Amsterdam: The Death of Theo van Gogh and the Limits of Tolerance*, New York: Penguin Press.

Butler, Jon (2010) 'Disquieted history in *A Secular Age*', in M. Warner, J. van Antwerpen and C. Calhoun (eds), *Varieties of Secularism in* A Secular Age, Cambridge, MA, and London: Belknap Press, pp. 193–216.

Butler, Judith (2009) *Frames of War: When is Life Grievable?*, London: Verso.

Butler, Judith, J. Habermas, C. Taylor, C. West, E. Mendieta, J. van Antwerpen and C. Calhoun (eds) (2011) *The Power of Religion in the Public Sphere*, New York: Columbia University Press.

Caldwell, C. (2009) *Reflections on the Revolution in Europe: Immigration, Islam and the West*, New York and London: Doubleday.

Calhoun, C. (1992) 'Introduction: Habermas and the public sphere', in C. Calhoun (ed.), *Habermas and the Public Sphere*, Cambridge, MA: MIT Press, pp. 1–51.

— (1993) 'Civil society and the public sphere', *Public Culture*, 5(1): 267–80.

Carr, M. (2006) 'You are now entering Eurabia', *Race & Class*, 48(1): 1–22.

Ceobanu, A. M. and X. Escandell (2010) 'Anti-immigrant parties in Europe: ideological or protest vote?', *Annual Review of Sociology*, 36: 309–28.

Cesari, J. (2005) 'Ethnicity, Islam, and les banlieues: confusing the issues', in Social Sciences Research Council (SSRC), *Special Forum on Riots in France*, riotsfrance.ssrc.org/Cesari/, accessed 22 February 2012.

Christensen, M. (2013) *Moren: Historien om Wenche Behring Breivik* [The mother: the story of Wenche Behring Breivik], Oslo: Aschehoug.

Cigar, N. (2003) 'The nationalist Serbian intellectuals and Islam: defining and eliminating a Muslim community', in E. Qureshi and M. A. Sell (eds), *The New Crusades: Constructing the Muslim Enemy*, New York: Columbia University Press, pp. 314–52.

Citizen Times (2012) 'The advocates of silence', 11 May.

Cockburn, P. (2008) *Muqtada al-Sadr and the Fall of Iraq*, London: Faber & Faber.

Cohen, P. (2007) 'In books, a clash of Europe and Islam', *New York Times*, 8 February.

Cohn, N. (1957) *The Pursuit of the Millennium: Revolutionary Millenarians and Mystical Anarchists of the Middle Ages*, London: Secker & Warburg.

Cole, D. (2012) 'More speech is better', *NYR Blog*, 16 October.

Collini, S. (2012) *What are Universities For?*, London: Penguin Books.

Connor, P. (2010) 'Contexts of immigrant receptivity and immigrant religious outcomes: the case of Muslims in western Europe', *Ethnic and Racial Studies*, 33(3): 376–403.

Dabashi, H. (2011) *Brown Skin, White Masks*, London and New York: Pluto Press.

Dagbladet (2010) 'FrP-politiker sammenlikner hijab med Ku Klux Klan' [FrP politician compares the hijab to Ku Klux Klan], *Dagbladet.no*, 3 March.

Daugstad, G. et al. (2008) 'Innvandring og innvandrere 2008' [Immigration and immigrants 2008], Oslo and Kongsvinger: SSB/Statistics Norway.

Davenport, R. and C. Saunders (2000) *South Africa: A Modern History*, 5th edn, London: Macmillan Press.

D'Eramo, M. (2013) 'Populism and the new oligarchy', *New Left Review*, 82(3): 5–28.

Derrida, J. (2001) *On Cosmoplitanism and Forgiveness*, London: Routledge.

Dickey, C. (2012) 'Can't someone tell Geert Wilders to stop his anti-Muslim diatribes before somebody gets hurt?', *Newsweek*, 23 January.

Document.no (2011) 'Anders Behring Breiviks kommentarer hos Document.no' [Anders Behring Breivik's comments at Document.no], *Document.no*, 23 July, www.document.no/anders-behring-breivik/, accessed 15 February 2012.

Donham, D. (2011) *Violence in a Time of Liberation. Murder and Ethnicity at a South African Gold Mine, 1994*, Durham, NC, and London: Duke University Press.

Drolet, J.-F. (2011) *American Neoconservatism: The Politics and Culture of a Reactionary Idealism*, New York: Columbia University Press.

Dubow, S. (1995) *Scientific Racism in Modern South Africa*, Cambridge and New York: Cambridge University Press.

Duin, J. (2002) 'State of "dhimmitude" seen as threat to Christians, Jews', *Washington Times*, 30 October.

Dworkin, R. (2006) 'The right to ridicule', *New York Review of Books*, 23 March.

Dzamarija, M. T. (ed.) (2010) 'Barn og unge med innvandrerforeldre- Demografi, utdanning, inntekt og arbeidsmarked' [Children and young people with immigrant parents – demography, education, income and labour market], Oslo and Kongsvinger: SSB/Statistics Norway.

Døving, C. A. (2012) 'Norge snikislam-
iseres' [Norway undergoing stealth
Islamization], in S. Indregaard (ed.),
*Motgift: Akademisk respons på den
nye høyreekstremismen* [Counter-
poison: academic responses on the
new right-wing extremism], Oslo:
Manifest/Flamme Forlag, pp. 87–97.

Eagleton, T. (1991) *Ideology: An Introduction*, London: Verso.

ECRI (2009) *ECRI Report on Norway –
Fourth Monitoring Cycle*, Brussels:
Council of Europe.

Eide, E. and T. H. Eriksen (2012) 'Innledn-
ing: Den flerstemte drabantbyen'
[Introduction: The multivocal
suburb], in S. Alghasi, E. Eide and
T. H. Eriksen (eds), *Den globale
drabantbyen: Groruddalen og det nye
Norge* [The global suburb: Groruddalen and the new Norway], Oslo:
Cappelen Damm, pp. 7–14.

Eley, G. (1992) 'Nations, publics and
political cultures: placing Habermas
in the nineteenth century', in C. Calhoun (ed.), *Habermas and the Public
Sphere*, Cambridge, MA: MIT Press,
pp. 289–340.

El Fadl, K. A. (2001) *Speaking in God's
Name: Islamic Law, Authority and
Women*, Oxford: Oneworld Publish-
ers.

— (2005) *The Great Theft: Wrestling
Islam from the Extremists*, San Fran-
cisco, CA: Harper Perennial.

El-Guindi, F. (1999) *Veil: Modesty, Privacy,
Resistance*, Oxford and New York:
Berg Publishers.

Elgvin, O. and K. R. Tronstad (2013) 'Nytt
land, ny religiøsitet? Religiøsitet og
sekularisering blant ikke-vestlige
innvandrere i Norge' [New country,
new religiosity? Religiosity and
secularization among non-Western
immigrants in Norway], *Tidsskrift for
Samfunnsforskning*, 53(1): 63–91.

Ellinas, A. E. (2011) *The Media and the
Far Right in Western Europe: Playing
the Nationalist Card*, Cambridge:
Cambridge University Press.

Enebakk, V. (2012) 'Fjordmans Radikali-
sering' [The radicalization of Fjord-
man], in Ø. Sørensen, B. Hagtvet
and B. A. Steine (eds), *Høyrekestreme
ideer og bevegelser i Europa* [Extreme
right-wing ideas and movements in
Europe], Oslo: Dreyer, pp. 45–101.

Engset, S. and S. Sandvik (2012) 'Janne
Kristiansen: – Breivik er ikkje direkte
høgreekstremist' [Janne Kristiansen:
– Breivik not directly a right-wing
extremist], *NRK.no*, 12 November.

Enstad, J. D. (2013) 'Hitlers russiske gjen-
ferd' [Hitler's Russian ghost], Op-ed,
Morgenbladet, 12 June.

Eriksen, T. B. (1986) 'Hva er rasisme?'
[What is racism?], *Kirke og kultur*,
91(5): 257–66.

Eriksen, T. H. (2011a) 'Anders Behring
Breivik: tunnel vision in an online
world', *Guardian*, 25 July.

— (2011b) 'A darker shade of pale: cultural intimacy in an age of terrorism',
Guest editorial, *Anthropology Today*,
27(5): 1–2.

Eriksen, T. H. and A. Høgmoen (2011) 'Et
lite stykke anti-Norge' [A small piece
of anti-Norway], *Samtiden*, 121(1):
29–39.

Esposito, J. L. and I. Kalin (2011) *Islamophobia: The Challenge of Pluralism
in the 21st Century*, New York and
London: Oxford University Press.

Esposito, J. L. and D. Mogahed (2007)
*Who Speaks for Islam? What a Billion
Muslims Really Think*, New York:
Gallup Press.

Eyerman, R. (2008) *The Assassination of
Theo van Gogh: From Social Drama to
Cultural Trauma*, Durham, NC, and
London: Duke University Press.

Fallaci, O. (2006) *The Force of Reason*,
trans. the author, Rome: Rizzoli
International.

Fangen, K. (2008) *Identitet og praksis: Etnisitet, klasse og kjønn blant soma-liere i Norge* [Identity and practice: ethnicity, class and gender among Somalians in Norway], Oslo: Gylden-dal Akademisk.

— (2012) 'Mellom konspirasjonsteori og galskap' [Between conspiracy theory and madness], in S. Østerud (ed.), *22.juli: Forstå – forklare – forebygge* [22 July: understanding – explaining – preventing], Oslo: Abstrakt Forlag, pp. 178–99.

Fassin, D. (2006) 'Riots in France and silent anthropologists', *Anthropology Today*, 22(1): 1–3.

Fatland, E. (2012) *Året Uten Sommer* [The year without summer], Oslo: Kagge Forlag.

Fekete, L. (2007) *A Suitable Enemy: Racism, Migration and Islamophobia in Europe*, London and New York: Pluto Press.

— (2009) *A Suitable Enemy: Racism, Migration and Islamophobia in Europe*, London and New York: Pluto Press.

— (2011) 'Breivik, the conspiracy theory and the Oslo massacre', European Race Audit Briefing Paper no. 5, London: Institute of Race Relations, September.

Ferguson, N. (2004) 'Eurabia?', *New York Times*, 4 April.

— (2011) *Civilization: The West and the Rest*, London and New York: Allen Lane.

Fidjestøl, A. (2013) 'Forlag til Fjordman' [Publisher for Fjordman], *Morgen-bladet*, 21 June.

Fish, S. (1994) *There's No Such Thing as Free Speech ... and It's a Good Thing Too*, New York and Oxford: Oxford University Press.

Fisk, R. (2001) *Pity the Nation: Lebanon at War*, 3rd edn, Oxford and New York: Oxford University Press.

— (2005) *The Great War for Civilization: The Conquest of the Middle East*, New York: Random House.

Flood, K. (2004a) 'Fallaci skaper ny debatt: Skriver om Islams inntog i Eurabia' [Fallaci generates new de-bate: writes about Islam's incursion in Eurabia], *Aftenposten*, 7 April.

— (2004b) 'Norsk helt i provoserende Fallaci-bok' [Norwegian hero in provocative book from Fallaci], *Aftenposten*, 28 April.

Fløgstad, K. (2012) 'Offentleg marxo-fobi' [Public Marxophobia], Op-ed, *Klassekampen*, 2 June.

Flåthe, P. (2012) 'Frp-leder i Bamble må gå etter Utøya-kommentarer' [PP leader in Bamble forced to resign after Utøya comments], *Dagbladet*, 7 January.

Fraser, N. (1992) 'Rethinking the public sphere: a contribution to the critique of actually existing democracy', in C. Calhoun (ed.), *Habermas and the Public Sphere*, Cambridge, MA: MIT Press, pp. 109–43.

— (2007) 'Transnationalizing the public sphere: on the legitimacy and efficacy of public opinion in a post-Westphalian world', *Theory, Culture and Society*, 24(4): 7–30.

Fredriksen, K. (2012) 'Rekordmange nye AP-medlemmer' [Record number of new Labour Party members], *Dagsavisen*, 12 January.

Freeden, M. (2003) *Ideology: A Very Short Introduction*, Oxford and New York: Oxford University Press.

Fremskrittspartiet (The Progress Party) (2007) *Stortingsgruppens innvan-drings- og integreringsutvalg. Rapport – Juni 2007* [The Parliamentary Cau-cus's Immigration and Integration Commission. Report – June 2007], Oslo: FrP.

Fritt Ord (2010) 'Blogg: juryresultatet av Fritt Ords utlysning' [Blog: the result of Fritt Ord's call], www.

fritt-ord.no/no/hjem/mer/blogg_jury resultatet_av_fritt_ords_utlysning/.

Fuglehaug, W. (2012) 'Spesialenheten undersøker omfattende 22.juli lekkasjer' [The Special Police Unit to investigate extensive leaks from 22 July investigations], *Aftenposten. no*, 5 February.

Gabriel, M. A. (2002) *Islam and Terrorism*, Lake Mary, FL: FrontLine.

Gaonkar, D. and C. Taylor (2006) 'Block thinking', *Public Culture*, 18(3): 453–5.

Gardell, M. (2011) *Islamofobi* [Islamophobia], trans. into Norwegian by A. Leborg, Oslo: Spartacus.

Gelber, K. (2011) *Speech Matters: Getting Free Speech Right*, St Lucia: University of Queensland Press.

— (2012) '"Speaking back": the likely fate of hate speech policy in the United States and Australia', in I. Maitra and M. K. McGowan (eds), *Speech and Harm: Controversies over Free Speech*, Oxford: Oxford University Press, pp. 50–72.

Gellner, E. (1983) *Nations and Nationalism*, Oxford and Cambridge, MA: Blackwell.

Gilbrant, J. M. (2011a) 'Mette Hanekamhaug fikk terrormanifest' [Mette Hanekamhaug received terror manifesto], *Dagbladet*, 27 July.

— (2011b) 'Det verste er at det finnes kvinner i Norge som synes apekatter fra Afrika er sååå fine' [The worst thing is that there are women in Norway who think monkeys from Africa are sooo cute], *Dagbladet*, 8 November.

Gilroy, P. (2002 [1987]) *There ain't No Black in the Union Jack: The Cultural Politics of Race and Nation*, With new introduction, Abingdon: Routledge.

Gitmark, H. and E. Løkeland-Stai (2013) 'Har overvåket muslimer ulovlig' [Have illegally surveilled Muslims], *Dagsavisen*, 25 April.

Gjerdåker, S. (2007) 'Slutt å kalla fordommar for rasisme' [Stop referring to prejudices as racism], *Dag og Tid*, 21 September.

Gjerstad, T. (2006) 'Krigsklar' [Ready for war], *Dagbladet*, 30 October.

— (2011) 'Frp for trygdede flest' [The PP for people on social welfare], *Dagens Næringsliv*, 7 July.

Gjestvang, A. (2012) *En Dag i Historien* [One day in history], Oslo: Pax Forlag.

Goldberg, D. T. (2006) 'Racial Europeanization', *Ethnic and Racial Studies*, 29(2): 331–64.

Goodwin, M. (2011) *Right Response: Understanding and Countering Right-wing Extremism in Europe*, London: Royal Institute of International Affairs (Chatham House).

Gordon, J. (2011) 'An Egyptian Jew in exile: an interview with Bat Ye'or', *New English Review*, October.

Gourevitch, P. (1998) *We wish to inform you that tomorrow we will be killed with our families: Stories from Rwanda*, New York: Farrar, Straus & Giroux.

Gray, J. (2007) *Black Mass: Apocalyptic Religion and the Death of Utopia*, London: Allen Lane.

Gressgård, R. and C. Jacobsen (2008) 'Krevende toleranse: Islam og homoseksualitet' [A demanding tolerance: Islam and homosexuality], *Tidsskrift for Kjønnsforskning*, 32(2): 22–40.

Griffin, R. (2012) *Terrorist's Creed: Fanatical Violence and the Human Need for Meaning*, London: Palgrave Macmillan.

Griffith, S. H. (1998) 'Review of Bat Ye'or', *International Journal of Middle East Studies*, 30(4): 619–21.

Grimm, D. (2009) 'Freedom of speech in a globalized world', in I. Hare and J. Weinstein (eds), *Extreme Speech and*

Democracy, New York and Oxford: Oxford University Press, pp. 11–22.

Gualteri, A. (2004) *The Ahmadis: Community, Gender, and Politics in a Muslim Society*, Montreal and Kingston: McGill-Queen's University Press.

Gullestad, M. (2006) *Plausible Prejudice: Everyday experiences and social images of nation, culture and race*, Oslo: Universitetsforlaget.

Gullestad, S. E. (2012) '22.juli i et psykologisk perspektiv' [22 July in a psychological perspective], *Nytt Norsk Tidsskrift*, 29(1): 5–15.

Haakaas, E. and K. Sæter (2010) *Svindel uten grenser: En reise i svart drosjeøkonomi* [Swindle without borders: Travels in the black market taxi economy], Oslo: Aschehoug.

Habermas, J. (1991 [1962]) *The Structural Transformation of the Public Sphere: An Inquiry into a Category of Bourgeois Society*, trans. T. Burger and F. Lawrence, Cambridge, MA: MIT Press.

— (1992) 'Further reflections on the public sphere', in C. Calhoun (ed.), *Habermas and the Public Sphere*, Cambridge, MA: MIT Press, pp. 421–2.

— (2008 [2005]) *Between Naturalism and Religion. Philosophical Essays*, trans. C. Cronin, Cambridge/Oxford: Polity Press.

Hagelund, A. (2003) 'A matter of decency? The Progress Party in Norwegian immigration politics', *Journal of Ethnic and Migration Studies*, 29(1): 47–65.

Hagen, R. and K. B. Dahl (2012) 'En landssviker og en folkemorder' [A traitor to the nation and a genocidaire], *Østlendingen.no*, 13 February.

Hagtvet, B. (1993) 'I politikk og tanke' [In politics and thought], *Samora*, 2: 18–19.

Halliday, F. (1999) 'Islamophobia reconsidered', *Ethnic and Racial Studies*, 22(4): 892–902.

Halvorsen, K. and S. Stjernø (2008) *Work, Oil and Welfare: The Welfare State in Norway*, Oslo: Universitetsforlaget.

Hamid, S. (2009) 'Abdur-Raheem Green, the life of a British convert to Salafism', in R. Meijer (ed.), *Global Salafism: Islam's New Religious Movement*, New York: Columbia University Press, pp. 445–7.

Hanssen, S. S. and H. Therkelsen (2013) 'Vil saumfare frivillighets-Norge' [Wants shake-up of voluntary Norway], *Dagsavisen*, 22 January.

Harr, A. G. G. and K. H. Partapouli (2012) *Om trakassering av muslimer og innvandrere etter eksplosjonen i Regjeringskvartalet 22.07.2011* [Concerning the harassment of immigrants and Muslims after the explosion at Government Headquarters on 22/7 2011], Report to the 22/7 Commission, Oslo: Antirasistisk Senter/Antiracist Centre.

Hattestein, H. (2013) 'Per Sandbergs bok: Fri diktning om Svelgen' [Per Sandberg's book: free imagination about Svelgen], *Firdaposten.no*, 12 December.

Haukali, I. (2011) 'Siv Jensen – Vil fremdeles snake om snikislamisering' [Siv Jensen – will continue to talk about stealth Islamization], *TV2.no*, 18 August.

Hawkes, D. (2003) *Ideology*, London: Routledge.

Haykel, B. (2009) 'On the nature of Salafi thought and action', in R. Meijer (ed.), *Global Salafism: Islam's New Religious Movement*, New York: Columbia University Press, pp. 33–57.

Haakaas, E. and K. Sæter (2010) *Svindel uten grenser: En reise i svart drosjeøkonomi* [Swindle without borders: a journey into the black taxi economy], Oslo: Aschehoug.

Hegghammer, T. (2009) 'Jihadi-Salafis

or revolutionaries? On religion and politics in the study of militant Islamism', in R. Meijer (ed.), *Global Salafism: Islam's New Religious Movement*, New York: Columbia University Press, pp. 244–67.

— (2011) 'The rise of the macro-nationalists', Op-ed, *New York Times*, 30 July, www.nytimes.com/2011/07/31/opinion/sunday/the-rise-of-the-macro-nationalists.html?_r=0.

Hegghammer, T. and D. Tierney (2010) 'Why does al-Qaeda have a problem with Norway?', *Atlantic Monthly*, 13 July.

Heinze, E. (2006) 'Viewpoint absolutism and hate speech', *Modern Law Review*, 69(4): 543–82.

Hernes, H. (1987) *Welfare State and Women Power. Essays in State Feminism*, Oslo: Scandinavian University Press.

Hervik, P. (2011) *The Annoying Difference: The Emergence of Danish Neonationalism, Neoracism, and Populism in the Post-1989 World*, New York and Oxford: Berghahn Books.

Hetland, Ø. (2011) *Fjordmans Verden* [The world of Fjordman], Unpublished manuscript, Oslo: HL-Centre.

Hinton, A. L. (2002) *Annihilating Difference: The Anthropology of Genocide*, Berkeley: University of California Press.

HL Centre (2012) *Antisemittisme i Norge? Den norske befolkningens holdninger til jøder og andre minoriteter* [Anti-Semitism in Norway? The attitudes of the Norwegian population towards Jews and other minorities], Oslo: HL Centre. Available in Norwegian at: www.hlsenteret.no/aktuelt/2012/HL_Rapport_2012_web.pdf.

Hoffman, B. (2006) *Inside Terrorism*, Revised and expanded edn, New York: Columbia University Press.

Holgersen, G. et al. (2002) *Rettslig vern mot etnisk diskriminering* [Legal protections against ethnic discrimination], Report to the Ministry for Municipalities and Provinces NOU 2002: 12, Oslo: Kommune og regionaldepartementet.

Holm, K. W. (2012) 'Historien om en heksejakt' [The history of a witch-hunt], *Document.no*, 7 February.

Holmes, S. (2012) 'Waldron, Machiavelli and hate speech', in M. Hertz and P. Molnar (eds), *The Content and Context of Hate Speech: Rethinking Regulation and Responses*, Cambridge and New York: Cambridge University Press, pp. 345–52.

Holst, C. (2010) *Feminism, Epistemology and Morality*, Münster: VDM Verlag.

Holst, C. and A. Molander (2009) 'Freedom of expression and freedom of discourse. Examining a justificatory strategy', in H. Rønning and A. Kierulf (eds), *Freedom of Speech Abridged? Cultural, legal and philosophical challenges*, Gothenburg: Nordicom, pp. 35–53.

Hopperstad, M., M. Vikås, R. J. Widerøe, H. H. Torgersen, B. J. G. Brenna, D. Ravndal and G. Andersen (2011) 'Peder Jensen er drapsmannens forbilde: Fjordman' [Peder Jensen is the hero of the murderer: Fjordman], *VG.no*, 5 August.

Huntington, S. P. (1996) *The Clash of Civilizations and the Remaking of World Order*, New York: Simon & Schuster.

Hustad, J. (2010) 'Til kamp mot brorskapen' [Fighting the Brotherhood], *Dag og Tid*, 26 November.

— (2011) 'Ope rettsak og eit ope samfunn' [An open trial and an open society], *Dag og Tid*, 12 August.

Hverven, T. E. (2012) 'Megalomani og selvutslettelse' [Megalomania and self-destruction], in S. Østerud (ed.), *22.Juli: Forstå – forklare – forebygge*

[22 July: understanding – explaining – preventing], Oslo: Abstrakt Forlag, pp. 33–51.

Hverven, T. E. and S. Malling (2013) *Terrorens ansikt: Skisser fra 22.juli rettssaken* [The face of terror: sketches from the 22 July trial], Oslo: Flamme Forlag.

Høidal, O. K. (1989) *Quisling: A Study in Treason*, New York: Oxford University Press.

Høiland, K. (2012) 'Viktig å kartlegge høyreekstremisme' [Important to chart right-wing extremism], *Aftenposten*, 25 March.

Høstmælingen, N. (2005) 'The permissible scope of legal limitations on the freedom of religion or belief in Norway', *Emory International Law Review*, 19: 989–1032.

Høyesterett (Norwegian Supreme Court) (2002) Rt-2002-1618 (361-2002) (The Sjølie verdict), www.guardian.co.uk/news/datablog/interactive/2011/sep/07/norway-breivik-manifesto-mapped, accessed 10 February 2012.

Ihlebæk, J. (2011) 'Varetektsfengsel i åtte uker' [In custody for eight weeks], *Aftenposten.no*, 25 August.

IMDI (2010) *Integreringsbarometeret* [The integration barometer], Oslo: IMDI/Directorate of Integration and Diversity, www.imdi.no/Documents/Rapporter/Integreringsbarometeret_2010.pdf.

— (2012) *Integreringsbarometeret* [The integration barometer], Oslo: IMDI/Directorate of Integration and Diversity, www.imdi.no/Documents/Rapporter/Integreringsbarometeret_2012.pdf.

Isungset, O. (2010) *Hvem skjøt William Nygaard?* [Who shot William Nygaard?], Oslo: Tiden Norsk Forlag.

Ivarsflaten, E. (2008) 'What unites right-wing populists in western Europe?', *Comparative Political Studies*, 41: 3–23.

Jacobsen, A. and B. Schlink (2012) 'Hate speech and self-restraint', in M. Herz and P. Molnar (eds), *The Content and Context of Hate Speech: Rethinking Regulation and Responses*, New York: Cambridge University Press, pp. 217–41.

Jacobsen, C. M. (2002) *Tilhørighetens mange former: Unge Muslimer i Norge* [The many forms of belonging: young Muslims in Norway], Oslo: Pax Forlag.

— (2005) 'Religiosity of young Muslims in Norway: the quest for authenticity', in J. Cesari and S. McLoughlin (eds), *European Muslims and the Secular State*, Aldershot: Ashgate.

— (2009) 'Norway', in G. Larsson (ed.), *Islam in the Nordic and Baltic Countries*, London and New York: Routledge, pp. 18–39.

— (2011) *Islamic Traditions and Muslim Youth in Norway*, Leiden and Boston, MA: Brill.

Jacobsen, C. M. and O. Leirvik (2010) 'Norway', in J. S. Nielsen et al. (eds), *Yearbook of Muslims in Europe*, vol. 2, Leiden: Brill, pp. 387–99.

Jensen, P. A. N. (2003) 'Islam og det åpne samfunn' [Islam and the open society], *VG*, 21 August.

— (2004) *Blogging Iran – A Case Study of Iranian English Language Weblogs*, Unpublished MA thesis, TIK, University of Oslo.

— (2013a) 'Medienes myter' [The myths of the media], Op-ed, *Aftenposten*, 25 April.

— (2013b) 'Feil av Fritt Ord?' [An error on the part of Fritt Ord?], Letter to the editor, *Aftenposten*, 24 June.

Jensen, S. (2011) 'Norwegian politics after Breivik', Op-ed, *Wall Street Journal*, 3 August.

Johansen, P. A. (2013) 'Kritisk til hvordan midlene fordeles' [Critical to how the funds are allocated], *Aftenposten.no*, 8 November.

Johansen, P. A. and A. B. Foss (2012) 'Serbisk sommel i terrorjakten' [Serbian delays in terror hunt], *Aftenposten. no*, 18 February.

Johnsen, N. (2010) 'Rekrutterer etniske nordmenn til omstridt islam' [Recruits ethnic Norwegians to controversial Islam], *VG.no*, 10 June.

Johnsrud, I. (2011) 'FrP-topp: Innvandrergutter er hissigere enn norske' [FrP head: Immigrant boys more resentful than Norwegians', *VG.no*, 13 May.

Jones, T. (2005) 'Short cuts', *London Review of Books*, 20 October.

Jorde, S. (2008) 'Apartheidregimet ga penger til FrP-forløper' [The apartheid regime provided funding for precursor to the PP], *Verdensmagasinet X*, 22 April, www.xmag.no/id/784.

Judt, T. (2005) *Postwar: A History of Europe since 1945*, New York and London: Penguin Press.

— (2008) *Reapprisals: Reflections on the Forgotten Twentieth Century*, London and New York: Heinemann.

Jupskås, A. R. (2009) 'Høyrepopulisme på norsk. Historien om Anders Langes Parti og Fremskrittspartiet' [Right-wing populism in Norwegian. The story of Anders Lange's Party and the Progress Party], in T. E. Simonsen, A. G. Kjøstvedt and K. Randin (eds), *Høyrepopulisme i Europa* [Right-wing populism in Europe], Oslo: Unipub, pp. 27–79.

— (2011) 'Høyrepopulisme er langt fra høyreekstremisme' [Right-wing populism far from right-wing extremism], Op-ed, *Dagbladet.no*, 29 September.

— (2012) *Ekstreme Europa* [Extreme Europe], Oslo: Cappelen Damm.

Kallis, A. (2013) 'Breaking taboos and "mainstreaming the extreme": the debates on restricting Islamic symbols in contemporary Europe', in R. Wodak, M. Khosravinik and B. Mral (eds), *Right-wing Populism in Europe: Politics and Discourse*, London and New York: Bloomsbury, pp. 55–71.

Kaplan, E. (2004) *With God on Their Side: George W. Bush and the Christian Right*, New York: New Press.

Karlsen, K. (2011) 'Velgernes dom' [The verdict of the voters], *Dagbladet*, 1 September.

Karlsen, T. (2010) 'Derfor øker netthetsen' [The reason why hatred on the net grows], *Ny Tid*, 27 August.

Keeley, B. L. (1999) 'Of conspiracy theories', *Journal of Philosophy*, 96(3): 109–26.

Keshvari, M. (2010) 'Islamistenes farlige grep' [The dangerous grip of the Islamists], *Aftenposten*, 30 November.

Khalidi, R. (2005) *Resurrecting Empire: Western Footprints and America's Perilous Path in the Middle East*, London and New York: I. B. Tauris.

Khan, M. (2009) *Tilbakeblikk: Da pakistanerne kom til Norge* [Looking back: when the Pakistanis came to Norway], Oslo: Pax.

Klausen, J. (2009) *The Cartoons that Shook the World*, New Haven, CT, and London: Yale University Press.

Klemperer, V. (2006 [1957]) *The Language of the Third Reich: LTI: Lingua Tertii Imperii*, trans. from the German by M. Brady, London and New York: Continuum.

Klev, R. (2011) 'Tybring-Gjeddes frykt og fakta' [Tybring-Gjedde's fear and facts], *VG*, 1 September.

Klug, B. (2012) 'Islamophobia – a concept comes of age', *Ethnicities*, 12(5): 665–81.

Knausgård, K.-O. (2012) 'Breivik slaktade unga människor av same rädsla för gränslöshet som drev fram fascismen' [Breivik slaughtered young people out of the same fear of boundlessness which generated fascism], Op-ed, *Dagens Nyheter*, 22 July.

Koopmans, R. (1996) 'Explaining the rise of racist and extreme right violence in western Europe: grievances or opportunities?', *European Journal of Political Research*, 30: 185–216.

Korbøl, A. (1972) *Pakistansk innvandring til Norge: Dannelse av et minoritetssamfunn?* [Pakistani immigration to Norway: the making of a minority society?], Oslo: Institutt for Samfunnsforskning/Institute of Social Research.

Korsvold, K. (2013) 'Fjordman støttes økonomisk fra USA' [Fjordman financially supported from the USA], *Aftenposten*, 17 April.

Kramer, J. Y. (1978) 'Ethnicity and community: Indian migrants in a Norwegian town', *Colloques Internationaux du Centre National de la Recherche Scientifique*, 582: 661–7.

Kristiansen, A. A., T. P. Krokfjord and S. G. Meldalen (2012) 'Breivik planla å arrangere fest for muslimer i Oslo Spektrum' [Brevik planned to organize party for Muslims at Oslo Spektrum], *Dagbladet.no*, 5 February.

Kristiansen, B. S. (2013) 'Anklager Sandberg for løgn i skandaleboka' [Accuses Sandberg of lies in scandalous book], *Dagbladet.no*, 12 December.

Kristjánsson, M. and L. U. S. Vegstein (2011) 'Kjemper videre mot hatet' [Struggles on against hate], *Klassekampen*, 1 December.

Krokfjord, T. P. and S. G. Meldalen (2012) 'Breivik var inspirert av hemmelig antiislamnettverk' [Breivik was inspired by secretive anti-Islam network], *Dagbladet.no*, 26 March.

Krokfjord, T. P., S. G. Meldalen and A. H. Johansen (2012) 'Breivik roser Vidkun Quisling i avhør' [Breivik praises Vidkun Quisling in interrogations], *Dagbladet.no*, 6 February.

Kvilesjø, S. E. (2011) 'Terrorsiktet erkjenner massedrap' [Man charged with terror confesses to mass killings], *Aftenposten.no*, 23 July.

Lacroix, S. (2011) *Awakening Islam: The Politics of Religious Dissent in Contemporary Saudi Arabia*, trans. G. Holoch, Cambridge, MA, and London: Harvard University Press.

Laegaard, S. (2007) 'Liberal nationalism and the nationalisation of liberal values', *Nations and Nationalism*, 13(1): 37–55.

Lankford, A. (2013) *The Myth of Martyrdom: What Really Drives Suicide Bombers, Rampage Shooters, and Other Self-Destructive Killers*, London and New York: Palgrave Macmillan.

Larsen, A. I. (2012) 'Muhammedstriden: Ytringsfrihet under press' [The Muhammad cartoon conflict: freedom of expression under pressure], *Samtiden*, 4.

Larsen, L. (2011) *Islamsk rettstenkning i møte med dagliglivets utfordringer*. [Islamic jurisprudence in the encounter with everyday challenges], Unpublished PhD dissertation in Humanities, University of Oslo.

Larsson, G. (2012) 'The fear of small numbers: Eurabia literature and censuses on religious belonging', *Journal of Muslims in Europe*, 1: 142–65.

Latour, B. (1986) *Laboratory Life: The Construction of Scientific Facts*, Princeton, NJ: Princeton University Press.

Laurence, J. (2012) *The Emancipation of Europe's Muslims: The State's Role in Minority Integration*, Princeton, NJ, and London: Princeton University Press.

Lauzière, H. (2010) 'The construction of *Salafiyya*: reconsidering Salafism from the perspective of conceptual history', *International Journal of Middle Eastern Studies*, 42(3): 369–89.

Lawrence, B. (2005) *Messages to the*

World: The Statements of Osama Bin Laden, trans. J. Howarth, London and New York: Verso.

Lehman, J. (2011) 'De sprider hatet' [They spread the hatred], *Expo*, 16(3): 33.

Leirvik, O. (2006) 'Kva var karikatursaka eit døme på?' [What was the cartoon issue all about?], *Kirke og kultur*, 2: 147–60.

Leirvåg, A. and B. Skjærstad (2011) 'Ordførerkandidat i hemmelig lydopptak: Ville henrette regjeringsmedlem' [Mayoral candidate in secret sound recording: wanted to execute member of government], *TV2.no*, 4 August.

Lentin, A. and G. Titley (2011) *The Crises of Multiculturalism: Racism in a Neo-Liberal Age*, London and New York: Zed Books.

Lepperød, T. (2011) 'Kunstig å koble FrP til høyreekstremisme' [Tendentious to link the PP to right-wing extremism], *Nettavisen.no*, 25 November.

Levmore, S. and M. C. Nussbaum (2010) 'Introduction', in S. Levmore and M. C. Nussbaum (eds), *The Offensive Internet: Speech, Privacy and Reputation*, Cambridge, MA, and London: Harvard University Press, pp. 1–15.

Lewis, B. (1984) *The Jews of Islam*, Princeton, NJ: Princeton University Press.

— (1990) 'The roots of Muslim rage', *Atlantic Monthly*, 266(3): 47–60.

— (2002) *What Went Wrong? Western Impact and Middle Eastern Response*, Oxford and New York: Oxford University Press.

— (2006) 'The new anti-Semitism', *The American Scholar*, 75(1): 25–36.

— (2007) *Europe and Islam. The 2007 Irving Kristol Lecture*, Washington, DC: AEI Press.

Lia, B. (1998) *The Society of the Muslim Brothers in Egypt: The Rise of an Islamic Mass Movement 1928–1942*, Reading: Ithaca Press.

Liestøl, A. K. and C. Wernersen (2011) 'Nordlendinger positive til islam og muslimer' [Northern Norwegians more positive towards Islam and Muslims], *Nrk.no*, 27 October.

Lincoln, B. (2006) *Holy Terrors: Thinking about Religion after September 11*, 2nd edn, Chicago, IL, and London: University of Chicago Press.

Lind, W. (2000) 'The origins of political correctness', Blog post on Accuracy in Academia, 5 February, www.academia.org/the-origins-of-political-correctness/, accessed 8 February 2012.

Linge, M. (2013a) *The Islamic Network: A Case Study of How Salafi Da'wa Emerges, Mobilizes and Transforms in a Norwegian Context*, Unpublished MA in International Relations, Department of History, Université Saint-Joseph, Beirut.

— (2013b) 'Den konservative muslimske vekkelsen: Om IslamNet, Profetens Ummah og salafismens fremvekst i Norge' [The conservative Muslim awakening: on IslamNet, the Prophet's umma and the rise of Salafism in Norway', *Samtiden*, 4: 38–52.

Linton, M. (2012) *De hatade. Om radikal-högerns måltavlor* [The hated ones. On the targets of the radical right], Stockholm: Atlas.

Lippestad, G. M. (2013) *Det vi kan stå for* [What we stand for], Oslo: Aschehoug.

Lockman, Z. (2007) *Contending Visions of the Middle East: The History and Politics of Orientalism*, Cambridge and New York: Cambridge University Press.

Lode, V. (2013) '– Jeg er stolt av å lede et populistisk parti' [– I'm proud to be leading a populist party], *Dagbladet. no*, 13 September.

Lodge, T. (2011) *Sharpeville: An Apartheid Massacre and Its Consequences*,

London and New York: Oxford University Press.

López, F. B. (2011) 'Towards a definition of Islamophobia: approximations of the early twentieth century', *Ethnic and Racial Studies*, 34(4): 556–73.

Lunde, S. (1979) 'Erik Gjems-Onstad innrømmer: E-agent for Rhodesia' [Erik Gjems-Onstad admits: E-agent for Rhodesia], *VG*, 19 April.

Lundeby, E. (2000) *Free Speech and Political Exclusion*, Unpublished Dr Art. dissertation in Philosophy, University of Oslo.

Lyon, J. (2012) *Islam through Western Eyes: From the Crusades to the War on Terrorism*, New York: Columbia University Press.

Løkeland-Stai, E., S. Prestegård and T. Sandberg (2013) 'Mistenkes for plan om terroraksjon' [Suspected of terror plotting], *Dagsavisen*, 17 July.

Løwe, T. (2008) 'Levekår blant unge med innvandrerbakgrunn: Unge oppvokst i Norge med foreldre fra Pakistan, Tyrkia og Vietnam' [Living conditions among young people with immigrant backgrounds: youth born in Norway with parents from Pakistan, Turkey and Vietnam], Report no. 14/2008, Oslo and Kongsvinger: SSB/Statistics Norway.

Magnus, P. C. (2010) 'Brorskapets ansikt' [The face of the Muslim Brotherhood], *Klassekampen*, 18 December.

Mah, H. (2000) 'Phantasies of the public sphere: rethinking the Habermas of historians', *Journal of Modern History*, 72(1): 153–82.

Mahmood, S. (2005) *The Politics of Piety: The Islamic Revival and the Feminist Subject*, Princeton, NJ: Princeton University Press.

— (2011) 'Religion, feminism and empire: the new ambassadors of Islamophobia', in L. M. Alcoff and J. D. Caputo (eds), *Feminism,*

Sexuality and the Return of Religion, Bloomington and Indianapolis: Indiana University Press, pp. 77–102.

Maitra, I. and M. K. McGowan (2012) 'Introduction and overview', in I. Maitra and M. K. McGowan (eds), *Speech and Harm: Controversies over Free Speech*, Oxford: Oxford University Press, pp. 1–23.

Majid, A. (2007) *A Call for Heresy: Why Dissent is Vital to Islam and America*, Minneapolis: University of Minnesota Press.

Mala, E. and J. D. Goodman (2011) 'At least 80 dead in Norway shooting', *New York Times*, 22 July.

Malacinski, L. (2012) 'Lars Hedegaard frifundet for racisme' [Lars Hedegaard acquitted on racism charges], *Jyllands-Posten*, 20 April.

Maliepaard, M., M. Lubbers and M. Gijsberts (2010) 'Generational differences in ethnic and religious attachment and their interrelation: a study among Muslims in the Netherlands', *Ethnic and Racial Studies*, 33(3): 451–72.

Malkenes, S. (2012) *Apokalypse Oslo* [Apocalypse Oslo], Oslo: Samlaget.

Malm, A. (2009) *Hatet mot muslimer* [The hatred against Muslims], Stockholm: Atlas.

— (2012) 'Phantom Islam: scapegoat fetishism in Europe before and after Utøya', in V. A. Bachmann, L. Bialasiewicz and J. D. Sidaway (eds), 'Bloodlands: critical geographical responses to the 22 July 2011 events in Norway', *Environment and Planning: Society and Space*, 30: 197–9.

Mamdani, M. (2004) *Good Muslim, Bad Muslim: America, the Cold War, and The Roots of Terror*, New York: Pantheon Books.

Manji, I. (2004) *The Trouble with Islam: A Muslim's Call for Reform in Her Faith*, New York: St Martin's Press.

Mannheim, K. (1936) *Ideology and Utopia*, London: Routledge.

Margaronis, M. (2012) 'Fear and loathing in Athens: the Rise of Golden Dawn and the far right', *Guardian*, 26 October.

Masud, M. K. (2000) *Travellers in Faith: A Study of the Tablighi Jama'at as a Transnational Movement for Faith Renewal*, Leiden: Brill.

Mauno, H. (2011) 'To menn og en moské' [Two men and a mosque], *Dagsavisen*, 14 May.

Meijer, R. (2009) 'Introduction', in R. Meijer (ed.), *Global Salafism: Islam's New Religious Movement*, New York: Columbia University Press, pp. 1–33.

Meland, A. (2009) 'Kan bli 860 000 innbyggere i Oslo i 2030' [Could be 860,000 inhabitants in Oslo by 2030], *Dagbladet.no*, 11 June.

— (2010) 'Dette er det islamske nettverket' [This is the Islamic network], *Dagbladet.no*, 23 February.

Meland, A. and M. Melgård (2011) 'Fjordman foreslo nazi-løsning' [Fjordman suggested Nazi solution], *Dagbladet. no*, 6 August.

Melgård, M. (2011) 'Har vi multikulturalisme i Norge?' [Do we have multiculturalism in Norway?], *Fri Tanke*, 3/4: 26–31.

Meyer, A. H. (2011) 'Det er tid for ettertanke' [It's time for reflection], *Klassekampen*, 28 July.

Midtbøen, A. H. and J. Rogstad (2012) *Diskrimineringens omfang og årsaker: Etniske minoriteters tilgang til norsk arbeidsliv* [The extent of and reasons for discrimination: the access of ethnic minorities to the Norwegian labour market], Report no. 1: 2012, Oslo: Institute for Social Research, www.samfunnsforskning.no/Publik asjoner/Rapporter/2012/2012-001.

Mill, J. S. (1989 [1859]) *On Liberty*, ed.

Stefan Collini, Cambridge and New York: Cambridge University Press.

Mishra, P. (2011) 'Watch this man', *London Review of Books*, 33(21): 10–12.

Mjelde, I. (2007) *Sakseierskap, dagsorden og medierammer. Tabloide mediers fremstilling av FrPs og SVs valgkampsaker under Stortingsvalgkampen 2005* [Issue ownership, agendas and media frames. The tabloid media's portrayal of the PPs and the Socialist Left Party's election issues during the parliamentary election campaign of 2005], Unpublished MA dissertation, Department of Media and Communication, University of Oslo.

Moen, J. S. and T. Giske (2012) *Utøya: En biografi* [Utøya: a biography], Oslo: Gyldendal.

Momen, M. (1985) *An Introduction to Shi'i Islam*, New Haven, CT, and London: Yale University Press.

Moore, S. F. (2001) 'Certainties undone: fifty turbulent years of legal anthropology', *Journal of the Royal Anthropological Institute*, 7(1): 95–116.

Morey, P. and A. Yaqin (2011) *Framing Muslims: Stereotyping and Representation after 9/11*, Cambridge, MA, and London: Harvard University Press.

Morgenbladet (2009) 'Er Huntingtons antagelser om sivilisasjonenes sammenstøt bekreftet?' [Have the hypotheses of Huntington concerning the clash of civilizations been confirmed?], *Morgenbladet*, 9 January.

Mosveen, E., H. Ertzeid and A. Pedersen (2005) 'Ble tipset om muslimsk nettverk' [Tipped off about Muslim network], *VG*, 23 May.

Mozaffari, M. (1997) *Fatwa: Violence and Discourtesy*, Aarhus: Aarhus University Press.

Mubashir, N. (2007) *Mitt navn er Ola Noman* [My name is Ola Noman], Oslo: Kagge Forlag.

Muchielli, L. (2009) 'Autumn 2005: A

review of the most important riot in the history of French contemporary society', *Journal of Ethnic and Migration Studies*, 35(5): 731–51.

Mudde, C. (1999) 'The single-issue party thesis: extreme right parties and the immigration issue', *Western European Politics*, 22(3): 182–97.

— (2007) *Populist Radical Right Parties in Europe*, Cambridge and New York: Cambridge University Press.

— (2011) 'Norway's catastrophe: democracy beyond fear', *OpenDemocracy*, 27 June.

Murtnes, S. (2011a) 'Kadra: Muslimer ble jaget nedover gatene' [Kadra: Muslims were chased through the streets], *VG.no*, 31 July.

— (2011b) 'Kokkvold: Direkte uanstendig å koble politikere til terrorhandlinger' [Kokkvold: Indecent to link politicians with acts of terror], *VG.no*, 25 November.

Naguib, S. A. (2001) *Mosques in Norway: The Creation and Iconography of Sacred Space*, Oslo: Novus Forlag.

Netavisen P77 (2010) 'Lars Hedegaard i krig med islam og the New World Order' [Lars Hedegaard at war with Islam and the New World Order], *Netavisen P77*, 7 October.

Newey, G. (2013) 'Unlike a Scotch egg', *London Review of Books*, 5 December.

Nickerson, R. S. (1998) 'Confirmation bias: an ubiquitous phenomenon in many guises', *Review of General Psychology*, 2(2): 175–220.

Nielsen, L. B. (2012) 'Power in public: reactions, responses, and resistance to offensive public speech', in I. Maitra and M. K. McGowan (eds), *Speech and Harm: Controversies over Free Speech*, Oxford: Oxford University Press, pp. 148–74.

Nordby, C. M. (2011) 'Rosetoget er gått' [The rose procession has passed], *Aftenposten.no*, 10 October.

Norheim, P. (2011) 'Hvem stjal arvesølvet?' [Who stole the hereditary silver?], *Vagant*, 23(4): 53–69.

Norris, P. and R. Inglehart (2004) *Sacred and Secular: Religion and Politics Worldwide*, Cambridge and New York: Cambridge University Press.

NTB (2012a) 'Domstol: Ingen krigsforbrytertiltalte serbere var i Liberia' [Court says: no Serbs charged with war crimes in Liberia], NTB, 10 January.

— (2012b) 'Behring Breivik hevder han villedet rettspsykiaterne' [Behring Breivik claims to have misled court psychiatrists], NTB, 19 February.

— (2012c) 'Profetens Ummah knytter bånd til britisk islamistgruppe' [The Prophet's Ummah establishes links with British Islamist group], *NTB.no*, 2 December.

Nussbaum, M. C. (2011) 'American Civil War: Review of Stefan Collini's "That's offensive! Criticism, identity, respect"', *New Statesman*, 17 March.

— (2012) *The New Religious Intolerance: Overcoming the Politics of Fear in an Anxious Age*, Cambridge, MA, and London: Belknap Press.

Nygård, J. P. (2012) 'Du spøker ikke med vold mot minoriteter' [You don't joke about violence against minorities], Letter to the editor, *Dagsavisen*, 10 February.

Obama, B. (2012) 'President Obama's speech to the UN General Assembly – full transcript', *Guardian.co.uk*, 25 September.

ODE (2003) *Oxford Dictionary of English*, 2nd edn, Oxford and New York: Oxford University Press.

OECD (Organisation for Economic Co-operation and Development) (2012) *Settling In: OECD Indicators of Immigrant Integration 2012*, www.oecd-ilibrary.org/docserver/download/8112051e.pdf?expires=1357 998859&id=id&accname=ocid195785

&checksum=6109617B2B301FF1F8C5 415A5F96B4AF, accessed 12 January 2013.

Olsen, M. N. (2012) 'Terror og tårer' [Terror and tears], *Morgenbladet*, 17 August.

Olsen, M. N. and A. B. Bisgaard (2011) 'Eurabiske vers' [Eurabian verses], *Morgenbladet*, 19 August.

Olsen, S. V. and R. Leite (2011) 'Breivik skilte seg ikke ut' [Breivik was not noteworthy], *Dagbladet.no*, 5 September.

Open Society Foundation (2013) 'Somalis in Oslo', Report commissioned by the Open Society Foundation's 'At Home in Europe' project, New York and London: Open Society Foundation, www.opensocietyfoundations. org/sites/default/files/somalis-oslo-20131210_0.pdf.

Oslo Magistrate's Court (2012) 'Dom – 22.juli-saken' [Verdict in the 22 July trial], www.lovdata.no/nyhet/dok/toslo-2011-188627-24.html.

Parekh, B. (2000) *Rethinking Multiculturalism: Cultural Diversity and Political Theory*, London: Macmillan Press.

Pariser, E. (2011) *The Filter Bubble: What the internet is hiding from you*, London and New York: Viking.

Passmore, K. (2002) *Fascism – a Very Short Introduction*, Oxford and New York: Oxford University Press.

Pelinka, A. (2013) Right-wing populism: concept and typology', in R. Wodak, Ruth, M. Khosravinik and B. Mral (eds), *Right-wing Populism in Europe*, London and New York: Bloomsbury, pp. 3–23.

Peters, J. D. (1993) 'Distrust of representation: Habermas on the public sphere', *Media, Culture and Society*, 15(4): 541–71.

Pew Reports (2011) *The Future of the Global Muslim Population*, Washington, DC: Pew Research.

PFU (2011) 'PFU-sak 007/11' [PFU-case 007/11], www.pfu.no/case. php?id=2431, accessed 14 February 2011.

Phillips, A. W. (2007) *Multiculturalism without Culture*, Princeton, NJ: Princeton University Press.

Pick, D. (2012) *The Pursuit of the Nazi Mind: Hitler, Hess and the Analysts*, Oxford and New York: Oxford University Press.

Pilbeam, B. (2011) 'Eurabian nightmares: American conservative discourses and the Islamisation of Europe', *Journal of Transatlantic Studies*, 9(2): 151–71.

Podhoretz, N. (2007) *World War IV: The Long Struggle against Islamofascism*, New York: Vintage Books.

Politidirektoratet (National Directorate of Police) (2012) *22.juli 2011: Evaluering av politiets innsats* [22 July 2011: an evaluation of police efforts], Oslo: Politidirektoratet, www.politi.no/vedlegg/rapport/Vedlegg_1648.pdf.

Politiet (2012) *Trendrapport 2012* [Report on trends 2012], Oslo: Oslo Police, www.politi.no/vedlegg/lokale_vedlegg/oslo/Vedlegg_1549.pdf.

Poohl, D. (2011) 'Breviks värld' [Breivik's world], *Expo*, 3: 28–32.

Poole, S. (2006) *Unspeak: Words are Weapons*, London and New York: Abacus.

Popper, K. R. (2003 [1945]) *The Open Society and Its Enemies*, vol. I: *The Spell of Plato*, London and New York: Routledge Classics.

Pracon, A. (2012) *Hjertet mot steinen* [The heart against the stone], Oslo: Cappelen Damm.

PST (Police Security Services) (2010) Åpen trusselvurdering [Open threat assessment], Oslo: PST.

— (2011) Åpen trusselvurdering [Open threat assessment], Oslo: PST.

— (2012) *Evalueringsrapport* [Evaluation

report], Oslo: PST, www.pst.no/media/43446/evaluering22072011_PST.pdf.

Puar, J. K. (2007) *Terrorist Assemblages: Homonationalism in Queer Times*, Durham, NC, and London: Duke University Press.

Raja, A. (2010) *Dialog: Om Vold, Undertrykkelse og Ekstremisme* [Dialogue: about violence, repression and extremism], Oslo: Cappelen Damm.

Raknes, K. (2012) *Høyrepopulismens hemmeligheter* [The secrets of right-wing populism], Oslo: Spartacus.

Ramadan, T. (2012) *Islam and the Arab Awakening*, New York and Oxford: Oxford University Press.

Rasch, J. S. and A. A. Kristiansen (2011) '1003 personer fikk Breiviks manifest kort tid før det smalt' [1,003 persons received the manifesto of Breivik before the blast], *Dagbladet.no*, 27 July.

Rattansi, A. (2007) *Racism: A Very Short Introduction*, Oxford: Oxford University Press.

Razack, S. (2004) 'Imperilled Muslim women, dangerous men and civilised Europeans: legal and social responses to forced marriages', *Feminist Legal Studies*, 12: 129–74.

— (2008) *Casting Out: The Eviction of Muslims from Western Law and Politics*, Toronto and London: University of Toronto Press.

Remnick, D. (2013) 'The party faithful', *New Yorker*, 21 January.

Respons (2012) 'Medievaner og holdninger' [Media habits and attitudes], Survey presented at the Nordic Media Days 2012, Bergen: Respons.

Reyes, A. (2011) 'Strategies of legitimization in political discourse: from words to actions', *Discourse and Society*, 22(6): 781–807.

Roald, A. S. (2004) *New Muslims in the European Context. The Experience of Scandinavian Converts*, Leiden: Brill.

Robins, R. S. and J. Post (1997) *Political Paranoia: The Psychopolitics of Hatred*, New Haven, CT, and London: Yale University Press.

Rogstad, J. (2001) *Sist blant likemenn? Synlige minoriteter på arbeidsmarkedet* [Last among equals? Visible minorities on the labour market], Oslo: Institutt for Samfunnsforskning/Institute for Social Research.

Rosen, M. (2012) *Dignity: Its History and Meaning*, Cambridge, MA, and London: Harvard University Press.

Rosenqvist, R. (2012) 'Er det utilregnelighetsregelen det er noe galt ved?' [Is there something wrong with the rule on criminal insanity?], *Nytt Norsk Tidsskrift*, 29(4): 349–61.

Rossavik, F. (2012) 'Ett steg videre' [One step further], Editorial commentary, *Bergens Tidende*, 22 September.

— (2013) 'Overjeg og underjeg' [Id and ego], *Morgenbladet*, 11 June.

Roy, O. (2010) *Holy Ignorance: When Religion and Culture Part Ways*, trans. Ros Schwartz, New York: Columbia University Press.

Runciman, D. (2008) *Political Hypocrisy: The Mask of Power, from Hobbes to Orwell and Beyond*, Princeton, NJ, and Oxford: Princeton University Press.

— (2013) *The Confidence Trap: A History of Democracy in Crisis from World War I to the Present*, Princeton, NJ, and Oxford: Princeton University Press.

Ruthven, M. (2011) 'The new European far-right', NYR blog, 11 August, www.nybooks.com/blogs/nyrblog/2011/aug/09/new-european-far-right/.

Ryan, M. P. (1992) 'Gender and public access: women's politics in nineteenth-century America', in C. Calhoun (ed.), *Habermas and the Public Sphere*, Cambridge, MA: MIT Press, pp. 259–89.

Rydgren, J. (2007) 'The sociology of the

radical right', *Annual Review of Sociology*, 33: 241–62.

Rønning, H. and J. Wessel-Aas (2011) 'Meninger, ytringer, handlinger' [Opinions, expressions, acts], *Nytt Norsk Tidsskrift*, 27(1): 113–15.

Said, E. W. (2000 [1985]) 'Orientalism reconsidered', in A. M. Lyon (ed.), *Orientalism: A Reader*, New York: New York University Press, pp. 345–61.

Salvatore, A. and M. LeVine (2005) 'Introduction: Reconstructing the public sphere in Muslim majority societies', in A. Salvatore and M. LeVine (eds), *Religion, Social Practice and Contested Hegemonies: Reconstructing the Public Sphere in Muslim Majority Societies*, New York and Basingstoke: Palgrave Macmillan, pp. 1–27.

Sandberg, P. (2013) *Mot min vilje. Opklaring av et politisk liv* [Against my will. Explanations for a political life], Oslo: Juritzen.

Sandberg, S. (2013) 'Are self-narratives strategic or determined, unified or fragmented? Reading Breivik's manifesto in light of narrative criminology', *Acta Sociologica*, 56(1): 65–79.

Sandli, E. (2011) 'Breivik gjemte seg bak 30 ulike kallenavn' [Breivik hid behind thirty different aliases], *Dagbladet*, 21 November.

Sandli, E. and E. Røst (2012) 'Her er tiltalen mot Breivik' [Here are the charges against Breivik], *Dagbladet*, 7 March.

Sandvik, H. (2010) 'Alt du har ofret, Europa' [All you have sacrificed, Europe], *Bergens Tidende*, 25 November.

— (2013) 'For dei grå blant oss' [For the grey among us], *Bergens Tidende*, 13 September.

Saunders, D. (2012) *The Myth of the Muslim Tide: Do Immigrants Threaten the West?*, New York: Vintage Books.

Sayyid, B. S. and A. Vakil (eds) (2011) *Thinking through Islamophobia: Global Perspectives*, New York and London: Columbia University Press.

Schafft, G. E. (2004) *From Racism to Genocide: Anthropology in the Third Reich*, Urbana and Chicago: University of Illinois Press.

Schau, K. (2012) *Rettsnotater: 22.Julirettssaken, Oslo Tinghus, 2012* [Notes from the court: the 22 July trial, Oslo's Magistrate's Court, 2012], Oslo: No Comprendo Press.

Schmidt, U. (2010) 'Norge: et religiøst pluralistisk samfunn?' [Norway: a religiously plural society?], in P. K. Botvarand and U. Schmidt (eds), *Religion i dagens Norge: Mellom sekularisering og sakralisering* [Religion in contemporary Norway: between secularization and sacralization], Oslo: Universitetsforlaget, pp. 25–42.

Schwartz, A. (2006) 'The protocols of the elders of Brussels', *Haaretz.com*, 20 June.

Scott, J. W. (2007) *The Politics of the Veil*, Princeton, NJ, and Oxford: Princeton University Press.

Searle, J. R. (1969) *Speech Acts: Essays in the Philosophy of Language*, Cambridge and New York: Cambridge University Press.

Seierstad, Å. (2013) *En av oss: En Fortelling om Norge* [One of us: a tale of Norway], Oslo: Kagge Forlag.

Sejersted, F. (2011) *The Age of Social Democracy. Norway and Sweden in the Twentieth Century*, trans. R. Daly, ed. M. B. Adams, Princeton, NJ, and Oxford: Princeton University Press.

Sejersted, F. et al. (1999) 'Ytringsfrihet bør finde sted: Forslag til ny Grunnlov paragraph 100' [Freedom of expression should take place: proposals for a new Constitutional Paragraph 100], NOU, 27, Oslo: Department of Justice and Police.

Sells, M. A. (2003) 'Christ killer, Kremlin, contagion', in E. Qureshi and M. A. Sells (eds), *The New Crusades: Constructing the Muslim Enemy*, New York: Columbia University Press.

Seymour, R. (2011) '2083: Breivik's 21st century fascist manifesto', in T. Tietze, E. Humphrys and G. Rundle (eds), *On Utøya*, Sydney: Elguta Press.

Shryock, A. (ed.) (2010) *Islamophobia/ Islamophilia: Beyond the Politics of Enemy and Friend*, Bloomington: Indiana University Press.

Sikand, Y. (2002) *The Origins and Development of the Tabligh Jama'at (1920–2000): A Cross-Country Comparative Study*, New Delhi: Orient Longman.

Silk, M. (1984) 'Notes on the Judeo-Christian tradition in America', *American Quarterly*, 36(1): 65–85.

Simenstad, L. M. (2011) 'Antirasistene er de eneste som opprettholder rasebegrepet' [Anti-racists the only ones who maintain the concept of race], *Klassekampen*, 25 August.

Simenstad, L. M. and Å. Brandvold (2011) 'Psykiaterstrid om Breivik' [Conflict among psychiatrists over Breivik], *Klassekampen*, 6 December.

Simenstad, L. M., Å. Brandvold and S. Tallaksen (2012) 'Holder fast på diagnosen' [Sticks to the diagnosis], *Klassekampen*, 14 January.

Simonnes, K. (2013) 'I stjålne klær? En analyse av endringer i Høyres, Arbeiderpartiets og Fremskrittspartiets innvandrings- og integreringspolitikk' [Wearing stolen attire? An analysis of changes in the Conservative Party, the Labour Party and the Progress Party's immigration and integration policy], *Norsk Statsvitenskapelig Tidsskrift*, 29(2): 144–58.

Skanðhamar, T., L. R. Thorsen and K. Henriksen (2011) 'Kriminalitet og straff blant innvandrere og øvrig befolkning' [Crime and punishment among immigrants and the other population], Rapport 21, Oslo and Kongsvinger: SSB/Statistics Norway.

Skarmøy, L. S. and S. H. Svendsen (2011) 'Dansk partileder refser Siv Jensen: – Hun mangler ryggrad' [Danish party leader chastises Siv Jensen: – She lacks spine], *VG.no*, 2 August.

Skarvøy, L. J., M. A. Andersen and M. Vikås (2011) 'Per Sandberg i Stortinget: Ap har til de grader spilt et offer etter 22.juli' [Per Sandberg in parliament: the Labour Party has to an incredible extent played the role of a victim after 22 July], *VG.no*, 23 November.

Skevik, E. and Ø. D. Johansen (2010) 'Høyreekstreme hyller utspill fra Frp-topp' [Right-wing extremists laud statement from PP leader], *VG.no*, 16 August.

Skirbekk, G. (2009) 'Behovet for en modernisering av medvitet og dermed for sjølvkritisk rasjonalitetskritikk og religionskritikk' [The need for a modernization of consciousness and thereby a self-critical critique of rationality and religion], in A. Brunvoll, H. Bringeland, N. Gilje and G. Skirbekk (eds), *Religion og kultur: Ein fleirfagleg samtale*, Oslo: Universitetsforlaget, pp. 87–105.

Skjervheim, H. (1968) *Det Liberale Dilemma og Andre Essays* [The liberal dilemma and other essays], Oslo: Dreyer.

Slaatta, T. (2012) 'Øyeblikk i skriftens historie' [Moments in the history of writing], in S. Østerud (ed.), *22.Juli: Forstå – forklare – forebygge* [22 July: understanding – explaining – preventing], Oslo: Abstrakt Forlag, pp. 51–69.

Sletholm, A. (2012a) 'Nå er det flere katolikker enn muslimer i Norge'

[Now there are more Catholics than Muslims in Norway], *Aftenposten.no*, 3 December.

— (2012b) 'Det var nettet alene som radikaliserte Breivik' [It was exclusively the internet which radicalized Breivik], *Aftenposten.no*, 20 November.

— (2013) 'Vikernes: – Hitler og Qusling representerer "guddommelig godhet"' [Vikernes: – Hitler and Qusling represent 'divine goodness'], *Aftenposten.no*, 16 July.

Solhjell, B. V. (2011) 'Lærdommer av sviket' [Learning from the betrayal], Op-ed, *Dagbladet.no*, 25 January.

Solli, B. (2012) 'Bait-un-Nasr og "følelse av sted"' [Bai tun-Nasr and the 'sense of place'], in S. Alghasi, E. Eide and T. H. Eriksen (eds), *Den globale drabantbyen: Groruddalen og det nye Norge* [The global suburb: Groruddalen and the new Norway], Oslo: Cappelen Damm, pp. 198–212.

Spaans, R. (2010) 'Venstresida tek feil' [The left is wrong], *Klassekampen*, 25 November.

Spaijj, R. (2010) 'The enigma of lone-wolf terrorism: an assessment', *Studies in Conflict and Terrorism*, 33(9): 854–70.

Spencer, R. (2005) 'The myth of Islamic tolerance', in R. Spencer (ed.), *The Myth of Islamic Tolerance: How Islamic Law Treats Non-Muslims*, Amherst, MA: Prometheus Books.

— (2007) 'Review of Bruce Bawer's While Europe Slept', *Middle East Quarterly*, 15(4).

— (2008) *Stealth Jihad: How Radical Islam is Subverting America without Guns or Bombs*, Washington, DC: Regency Publishing.

Spielhaus, R. (2012) 'Measuring the Muslim: about statistical obsessions, categorisations and the quantification of religion', in J. S. Nielsen, S. Akgönül, A. Alibašić, H. Goddard and B. Maréchal (eds), *Yearbook of Muslims in Europe*, vol. 3, Leiden: Brill, pp. 437–55.

Spivak, G. C. (1993) 'Can the subaltern speak?', in P. Williams and L. Chrisman (eds), *Colonial Discourse and Postcolonial Theory*, Hertfordshire: Harvester Wheatsheaf.

SSB (Statistics Norway) (2009) *Befolkningsframskrivninger 2009–2060* [Demographic projections 2009–2060], Oslo and Kongsvinger: SSB/Statistics Norway, www.ssb.no/befolkning/statistikker/folkfram/aar/2009-06-11.

— (2012) 'Fortsatt lavere ledighet blant innvandrermenn' [Unemployment continues to decrease among immigrant males], *SSB.no*, 22 November, www.ssb.no/emner/06/03/innvarbl/, accessed 12 January 2013.

Stampnitzky, L. (2013) *Disciplining Terror: How Experts Invented Terrorism*, New York and Cambridge: Cambridge University Press.

Steen, R. B. (2012) *Svartebok over norsk asylpolitikk* [The black book of Norwegian asylum policies], Oslo: Manifest Forlag.

Steen, R. B. et al. (2013) 'Kampen mot en fotnote' [The struggle against a footnote], Op-ed, *Dagsavisen*, 21 January.

Steinkeller, A. (2012) 'Norges innvandrere – både høyt og lavt utdannet' [Norway's immigrants – both highly and lowly educated], *Samfunnsspeilet*, 26(5): 27–33.

Stolcke, V. (1995) 'Talking culture: new boundaries, new rhetorics of inclusion in Europe', *Current Anthropology*, 36(1): 1–24.

Storhaug, H. (2009) *Rundlurt: Om innvandring og islam i Norge* [Completely fooled: about immigration and Islam in Norway], Oslo: Kagge Forlag.

— (2010) 'Islamofobi-begrepet begraves'

[The concept of Islamophobia is buried], *rights.no*, 12 August, www.rights.no/publisher/publisher.asp?id=36&tekstid=4431.

— (2011a) 'En stigende uro' [A growing disquiet], Op-ed, *Aftenposten*, 6 January.

— (2011b) 'Uenighet strekker tankene' [Disagreement stretches the mind], Letter to the editor, *Dagbladet*, 10 August.

— (2012) 'Oss med fobier' [Those of us with phobias], *www.rights.no*, 4 January.

Stormark, K. (2011) *Da terroren rammet Norge. 189 minutter som rystet verden* [When the terror struck Norway. 189 minutes that shook the world], Oslo: Kagge Forlag.

— (2012) *Massemorderens private e-poster* [The private e-mails of the mass murderer], Oslo: Spartacus.

Storvik, K. (2011) '17.mai for alle!' [17 May for everyone!], Editorial comment, *Dagsavisen*, 18 May.

Storvoll, S. (2007) *Kristenfiendtlighet i pressen? Norske avisers dekning av kristendom og islam* [Hostility towards Christianity in the press? Norwegian newspaper's coverage of Christianity and Islam], Unpublished MA dissertation, Department of Media and Communications, University of Oslo.

Strømmen, Ø. (2007) *Eurofascism*, Own imprint.

— (2011a) 'Violent "counter-jihadism": what – and who – inspired Anders Behring Breivik's violence?', *Foreign Affairs.com*, 27 July.

— (2011b) *Det mørke nettet. Om høyreekstremisme, kontrajihadisme og terror i Europa* [The dark net. On right-wing extremism, contra-jihadism and terror in Europe], Oslo: Cappelen Damm.

— (2011c) 'Storhaugs bibliotek' [Storhaug's library], *Dagbladet*, 12 August.

— (2011d) 'Storhaugs dårlige hukommelse' [Storhaug's feeble memory], *Dagbladet*, 9 August.

— (2012) 'Utviklingstrekk i norsk høgreekstremisme' [Developments in Norwegian right-wing extremism], Note 4/12 to the Norwegian 22 July Commission dated 17 January, www.22julikommisjonen.no, accessed 22 February 2012.

Strømmen, Ø. and S. Indregard (2012) 'Den nye høyreekstremismen' [The new right-wing extremism], in S. Indregard (ed.), *Motgift: Akademiske Responser på den nye høyreekstremismen* [Counter-poison: academic responses on the new right-wing extremism], Oslo: Manifest, pp. 20–42.

Stærk, B. (2012) 'Han representerer ingen' [He doesn't represent anyone], Op-ed, *Aftenposten.no*, 3 May.

— (2013) 'På sitt beste er det obligatorisk lesning' [At its best, it makes for compulsory reading], *Aftenposten.no*, 17 December.

Sultan, S. (2012) 'Medlemskap i norske moskeer' [Membership in Norwegian mosques], in I. Breistein, F. Ingunn and I. M. Høeg (eds), *Religionsstatistikk og medlemsforståelse* [Statistics on religion and the understanding of membership], Trondheim: Akademika, pp. 165–80.

Sundsbø, S. (2011) 'Sluttet i SV' [Left SV], *Nordstrand Blad*, 17 January.

Sunstein, C. R. (1993) *Democracy and the Problem of Free Speech*, New York: Free Press.

— (2003) *Why Societies Need Dissent*, Cambridge, MA, and London: Harvard University Press.

— (2009) *Going to Extremes: How Like Minds Unite and Divide*, Oxford and New York: Oxford University Press.

Sunstein, C. R. and A. Vermeule (2009)

'Conspiracy theories: causes and cures', *Journal of Political Philosophy*, 17(2): 202–27.

Svendsen, C. et al. (2013) 'Dette er de norske Syria-jihadistene' [These are the Norwegian Syria-jihadists], *Nrk. no*, 29 November.

Sæbø, M. (2013) 'Ordkrigen om apartheid' [The war of words over apartheid], *Verdensmagasinet X*, 11 December, www.xmag.no/id/1712.

Sætre, J. (2013) 'Fjordman får Fritt Ord-støtte' [Fjordman given Fritt Ord support], *Nrk.no*, 14 June.

Sætre, S. (2013a) *Fjordman: Portrett av en anti-islamist* [Fjordman: portrait of an anti-Islamist], Oslo: Cappelen Damm.

— (2013b) 'Renvaskelsen av Fjordman' [The whitewashing of Fjordman], *Samtiden*, 4: 54–73.

— (2013c) 'Renvaskelsen av Fjordman' [The whitewashing of Fjordman], Op-ed, *Klassekampen*, 26 November.

Sætren, L. et al. (2013) 'Varg Vikernes er løslatt' [Varg Vikernes has been released], *Nrk.no*, 18 July.

Søndberg, A. and F. Abdolhosseini (2011) 'Lars Hedegaard er dømt for rasisme' [Lars Hedegaard convicted of racism], *Politiken.dk*, 3 May.

Sønstelie, R. (2003) 'Vil gi Bush freds-prisen' [Wants to award the Peace Prize to Bush], *VG.no*, 8 May.

Sønstelie, S. M. and E. Sønstelie (2011) *Jeg lever, pappa! 22.juli- dagen som forandret oss* [Dad, I'm alive! 22 July – the day that changed us], Oslo: Schibsted.

Taylor, C. (1985 [1979]) 'What's wrong with negative liberty?', in C. Taylor, *Philosophy and the Human Sciences. Philosophical Papers II*, Cambridge and New York: Cambridge University Press.

— (1992) 'Modernity and the rise of the public sphere', The Tanner Lectures on Human Values, delivered at Stanford University, 15 February.

— (1994 [1992]) 'The politics of recognition', in A. Guttmann (ed.), *Multiculturalism: Examining the Politics of Recognition*, Princeton, NJ: Princeton University Press, pp. 25–75.

— (2004) *Modern Social Imaginaries*, Durham, NC, and London: Duke University Press.

— (2007) *A Secular Age*, Cambridge, MA, and London: Belknap Press.

Taylor, M. (2011a) 'Breivik sent "manifesto" to 250 UK contacts hours before Norway killings', *Guardian*, 26 July.

— (2011b) 'Anders Behring Breivik had links to far-right EDL, says anti-racism group', *Guardian*, 26 July.

Tayob, A. (1995) *Islamic Resurgence in South Africa: The Muslim Youth Movement*, Cape Town: University of Cape Town Press.

Therkelsen, H. (2011) 'Likestiller islam og nazisme' [Analogizes Islam and Nazism], *Dagsavisen*, 1 February.

Therkelsen, H. and S. Prestegård (2013) 'Fritt Ord får kritikk for Fjordman-støtte' [Fritt Ord criticized for support of Fjordman], *Dagsavisen*, 15 June.

Thorenfeldt, G. and A. Meland (2009) 'Hvis muslimene blir i flertall' [If the Muslims become the majority], *Dagbladet.no*, 15 June.

— (2011) 'Frykter for Fjordmans sikkerhet' [Fears over Fjordman's safety], *Dagbladet.no*, 3 August.

Titley, G. (2013) 'They called a war, and someone came: the communicative politics of Breivik's ideoscape', *Nordic Journal of Migration Research*, 3(4) (unpaginated).

Tjønn, H. et al. (2004) 'Jubel for Hagens utfall mot islam' [Cheers for Hagen's attacks on Islam], *Aftenposten*, 14 July.

TNS Gallup (2013) *Ytringsfrihetsbarometeret 2013* [The freedom of expression barometer 2013], Oslo: TNS Gallup/Fritt Ord.

Todorov, T. (2009) *In Defence of the Enlightenment*, trans. G. Walker, London: Atlantic Books.

— (2010) *The Fear of Barbarians: Beyond the Clash of Civilizations*, trans. A. Brown, Cambridge and Malden, MA: Polity Press.

Toje, A. (2012) *Rødt, hvitt og blatt: Om Demokratiet i Europa* [Red, white and blue: about democracy in Europe], Oslo: Dreyer Forlag.

Torgersen, H. H. (2011) 'Fjordman er fascist' [Fjordman is a fascist], *VG.no*, 17 November.

Torgersen, H. H. et al. (2011) 'Frp-topp sammenliknet islam med nazismen' [PP leader compared Islam to Nazism], *VG.no*, 11 August.

Tornes, E. (2013) 'Å ville lese vrangt' [To want to read erratically], Editorial commentary, *Aftenposten.no*, 28 November.

Toscano, A. (2010) *Fanaticism: On the Uses of an Idea*, London and New York: Verso.

Townsend, C. (2002) *Terrorism – a Very Short Introduction*, Oxford and New York: Oxford University Press.

Trilling, D. (2012) *Bloody Nasty People: The Rise of Britain's Far Right*, London and New York: Verso.

Tripp, C. (2000) *A History of Iraq*, Cambridge and New York: Cambridge University Press.

— (2009) 'All (Muslim) politics is local', Review essay, *Foreign Affairs*, 88(5): 124–30.

Tronstad, K. R. (2008a) 'Religion', in S. Blom and K. Henriksen (eds), *Levekår blant innvandrere i Norge 2005/2006* [Quality of life among immigrants in Norway 2005/2006], Oslo: SSB/Statistics Norway.

— (2008b) 'Diskriminering' [Discrimination], in S. Blom and K. Henriksen (eds), *Levekår blant innvandrere i Norge 2005/2006* [Quality of life

among immigrants in Norway 2005/2006], Oslo: SSB/Statistics Norway.

Tvedt, O. K. (2005) *Krig og diplomati. Oslo–Jerusalem 1978–1996* [War and diplomacy. Oslo–Jerusalem 1978–1996], Oslo: Aschehoug.

22/7 Commission (2012) *Rapport fra 22. juli-kommisjonen* [Report of the 22/7 Commission], NOU 2012: 14, Oslo: Departmentenes Servicesenter, www.regjeringen. no/pages/37994796/PDFS/NOU 201220120014000DDDPDFS.pdf.

Tybring-Gjedde, C. (2011) 'Veien videre' [The road onwards], Letter to the editor, *Aftenposten*, 11 August.

— (2012) 'Ytringens pris' [The price of speech], *Aftenposten*, 17 January.

Tybring-Gjedde, C. and K. Andersen (2010) 'Drøm fra Disneyland' [Dream from Disneyland], *Aftenposten*, 25 August.

Utvik, B. O. (2006) *Islamist Economics in Egypt: The Pious Road to Development*, Boulder, CO: Lynne Rienner.

Vaïsse, J. (2010) *Neoconservatism: The Biography of a Movement*, trans. A. Goldhammer, Cambridge, MA, and London: Belknap Press.

Valentine, S. R. (2008) *Islam and the Ahmadiyya Jama'at: History, Belief, Practice*, New York: Columbia University Press.

Vance, S. (2004) 'The permissibility of incitement to religious hatred offenses under European convention principles', *Transnational Law & Contemporary Problems*, 14: 201–54.

Van Dijk, T. A. (1992) 'Discourse and the denial of racism', *Discourse & Society*, 3(1): 87–118.

Van Vuuren, J. (2013) 'Spur to violence? Anders Behring Breivik and the Eurabia conspiracy', *Nordic Journal of Migration Research*, 3(4) (unpaginated).

Vassenden, A. (2007) *Flerkulturelle forståelsesformer* [Multicultural forms of understanding], Unpublished Dr Polit. dissertation in Sociology, University of Oslo.

Vepsen.org (2011) 'Ville kvitte seg med motstandere' [Wanted to get rid of opponents], *Vepsen.org*, 5 December.

— (2012) *Hatgrupper 2011. Årsrapport fra Vepsen.org* [Hate groups 2011. Annual report from Vepsen.org], vepsen. org/2012/01/hatgrupper-2011/.

Vetlesen, A. J. (2005) *Evil and Human Agency: Understanding Collective Evildoing*, Cambridge and New York: Cambridge University Press.

— (2011) 'Narratives of entitlement', Draft ms presented at the University of Oxford.

Vidino, L. (2010) *The New Muslim Brotherhood in the West*, New York: Columbia University Press.

Vikås, M. (2011) 'Anders Behring Breivik – fra fødsel til 22.juli' [Anders Behring Breivik – from birth to 22 July], *VG.no*, n.d.

Vikås, M. et al. (2011a) 'Avhørene' [The interrogations], *VG*, 18 November.

— (2011b) 'Vendepunktet kom da naboer feiret på 11/9' [The turning point came when Egyptian neighbours celebrated on 9/11], *VG.no*, 5 August.

— (2012) 'Fjordman var nummer en for Anders' [Fjordman was number one for Anders], *VG.no*, 20 April.

Vogt, K. (2008) *Islam på norsk: Moskeer og islamske organisasjoner i Norge* [Islam in Norwegian: mosques and Islamic organizations in Norway], Oslo: Cappelen Damm.

Vogt-Kielland, C. (2002) 'Ensom venn på Stortinget' [Lonely friend in parliament], *Dagbladet*, 4 April.

Wahab, A. A. (2010) 'Føler seg misbrukt i TV2-film' [Feels misrepresented in TV2 documentary], *Klassekampen*, 4 December.

Waldron, J. (2010) 'Dignity and defamation: the visibility of hate. The 2009 Oliver Wendell Holmes Lectures', *Harvard Law Review*, 123: 1597–657.

— (2012) *The Harm in Hate Speech*, Cambridge, MA, and London: Harvard University Press.

Wang-Naveen, M. (2013) 'Vår egen talende frykt' [Our own telling fear], *Aftenposten*, 3 May.

Warburton, N. (2009) *Free Speech – a Very Short Introduction*, Oxford: Oxford University Press.

Warner, M. (2002) *Publics and Counterpublics*, New York: Zone Books.

Weaver, M. (2010) 'Geert Wilder's trial for inciting racial hatred opens in the Netherlands', *Guardian*, 4 October.

Weaver, S. (2010) 'Liquid racism and the Danish Prophet Muhammad cartoons', *Current Sociology*, 58(5): 675–92.

Weiby, H. E. (2012) 'Janne Kristiansen går av som PST-sjef' [Janne Kristiansen leaves office as PST chief], *Nrk.no*, 19 January.

West, C. (2012) 'Words that silence? Freedom of expression and racist hate speech', in I. Maitra and M. K. McGowan (eds), *Speech and Harm: Controversies over Free Speech*, Oxford: Oxford University Press, pp. 222–48.

Westlie, B. (2008) *Min Fars Krig* [My father's war], Oslo: Aschehoug.

Wickham, C. R. (2013) *The Muslim Brotherhood: Evolution of an Islamist Movement*, Princeton, NJ, and Oxford: Princeton University Press.

Wiktorowicz, Q. (2006) 'Anatomy of the Salafi movement', *Studies in Conflict and Terrorism*, 29(3): 207–39.

Wilders, G. (2011) 'European free speech under attack', *Wall Street Journal*, 22 aFebruary.

Wilson, R. A. (2011) *Writing History in International Criminal Trials*, New

York and Cambridge: Cambridge University Press.

Winkel Holm, K. (2012) 'Historien om en heksejakt' [History of a witch hunt], *Document.no*, 7 February.

Wollebæk, D., B. Enjolras, K. Steen-Johnsen and G. Ødegård (2012) 'After Utøya: how a high-trust society reacts to terror: trust and civic engagement in the aftermath of July 22', *Politics and Society*, January.

Yates, M. (2007) 'Rawls and Habermas on religion in the public sphere', *Philosophy and Social Criticism*, 33(7): 880–91.

Ye'or, B. (1983) 'Terres Arabes: terres de "dhimmitude"', *La Rassegna Mensile di Israel*, 44(1–4): 94–102.

— (1996) *The Decline of Eastern Christianity under Islam: From Jihad to Dhimmitude, Seventh–Twentieth Century*, trans. M. Kochan and D. G. Littman, Madison and Teaneck: Fairleigh Dickinson University Press.

— (2002) 'Le Dialogue Euro-Arabe et la naissance d'Eurabia', *Observatoire du monde juif*, Bulletin no. 4/5, December, pp. 44–55.

— (2005a) *Eurabia: The Euro-Arab Axis*, Madison and Teaneck: Farleigh Dickinson University Press.

— (2005b) 'Dhimmitude: Jews and Christians under Islam', in R. Spencer (ed.), *The Myth of Islamic Tolerance: Jews and Christians under Islam*, Amherst, MA: Prometheus Books, pp. 147–9.

— (2011) *Europe, Globalization and the Coming Universal Caliphate*, Madison and Teaneck: Farleigh Dickinson University Press.

Young, C. (2011) 'Does freedom of speech include hate speech?', *Res Publica*, 17.

Zaheer, R. et al. (2011) 'Mediene og de ekstreme' [The media and the extremists], *Ny Tid.no*, 19 November.

Zaman, K. (2012) 'Her er de mest ekstreme islamistene i Norge' [These are the most extreme Islamists in Norway], *TV2.no*, 3 November.

— (2013) 'Her fant TV2 Arfan Bhatti' [This is where TV2 found Arfan Bhatti], *TV2.no*, 6 October.

Žižek, S. (ed.) (1994) *Mapping Ideology*, London: Verso.

— (2008) 'Tolerance as an ideological category', *Critical Inquiry*, 34(2): 660–82.

— (2011) 'A vile logic to Anders Breivik's choice of target', Op-ed, *Guardian*, 8 August.

Zuckerman, P. (2008) *Society without God: What the Least Religious Nations Can Tell Us about Contentment*, New York and London: New York University Press.

Zúquete, J. P. (2008) 'The European extreme-right and Islam: new directions?', *Journal of Political Ideologies*, 13(3): 321–44.

Øia, T. (1998) *Generasjonskløften som ble borte: Ungdom, innvandrere og kultur* [The generational gap which disappeared: youth, immigrants and culture], Oslo: Cappelen Akademisk Forlag.

Østberg, S. (2003) *Muslim i Norge. Religion og hverdagsliv blant unge norsk-pakistanere* [Muslim in Norway. Religion and everyday life among young Norwegian Pakistanis], Oslo: Universitetsforlaget.

Østby, L. (2004) 'Innvandrere i Norge – Hvem er de, og hvordan går det med dem?' [Immigrants in Norway – who are they, and how are they doing?], Oslo: SSB/Statistics Norway.

— (2008) 'Levekårsundersøkelse blant innvandrere – hvordan og hvorfor' [Quality of life study among immigrants – the how and why], in S. Blom and K. Henriksen (eds), *Levekår blant innvandrere i Norge*

2005/2006 [Quality of life among immigrants to Norway 2005/2006], Oslo: SSB/Statistics Norway.

— (2011) 'Muslimsk flertall i Norge?' [Muslim majority in Norway?], *Morgenbladet*, 26 August.

Østli, K. S. (2011a) 'Eskil Pedersen må gå med voldsalarm' [Eskil Pedersen has to carry an alarm], *Aftenposten.no*, 5 November.

— (2011b) 'Ser bort i fra tiltaltes politiske budskap og ståsted' [Disregards the political message and views of the accused], *Aftenposten. no*, 30 November.

— (2013) *Rettferdighet er bare et ord: 22.juli og rettssaken mot Anders Behring Breivik* [Justice is but a word: 22 July and the trial against Anders Behring Breivik], Oslo: Cappelen Damm.

Østli, K. S. and T. A. Andreassen (2011) 'Behring Breiviks to ansikter' [The two faces of Behring Breivik], *Aftenposten.no*, 26 November.

Øvrebø, O. (2011) 'Alle ideer må diskuteres i det åpne rom' [All ideas must be discussed in open public spaces], Interview with Knut Olav Åmås of *Aftenposten*, *Vox Publica*, 18 August.

Åmås, K. O. (2006) 'Mens Europa sover' [While Europe sleeps], *Aftenposten*, 3 May.

— (2007) *Verdien av uenighet: Dissens og debatt i Norge* [The value of disagreement: dissent and debate in Norway], Oslo: Kagge Forlag.

— (2009) 'En frihet under press' [A freedom under pressure], *Aftenposten*, 27 May.

— (2010) 'Islams helt – og skurk' [Islam's hero and villain], *Aftenposten*, 1 September.

— (2011a) 'Norway attacks: when a nation lost its innocence at the crack of gunfire', *Observer*, 24 July.

— (2011b) 'Mer debatt, ikke mindre' [More debate, not less], *Aftenposten*, 28 July.

INDEX